Stealing from America

Stealing

FROM

America

A HISTORY OF CORRUPTION

FROM JAMESTOWN TO REAGAN

6/6

Nathan Miller

PARAGON HOUSE

New York

First Paragon House edition, 1992

Published in the United States by

Paragon House
90 Fifth Avenue
New York, N.Y. 10011

Library of Congress Cataloging-in-Publication Data

Miller, Nathan, 1927–
Stealing from America : a history of corruption from
Jamestown to Reagan / Nathan Miller.
p.   cm.
Rev. ed. of: The Founding Finaglers. 1st ed. New York, N.Y.:
David McKay Company, Inc., 1976.
Includes bibliographical references and index.
ISBN 1-55778-344-6
1. Political corruption—United States—History.   I. Title.
JK2249.M55   1992
320.973—dc20   91-40703
                                CIP

Manufactured in the United States of America

To
the Memory
of
My
Mother and Father

9-18-95 gift Wayne Davis

Contents

Preface

CORRUPTION IS AS American as cherry pie. From Jamestown to Iran-Contra it runs through our history like a scarlet thread. The grafting politician, corrupt business tycoon, crooked labor baron, and hypocritical preacher are prominent features of American folklore. Graft and corruption played a vital role in the development of modern American society and the creation of the complex, interlocking machinery of government and business that determines the course of our affairs. Large-scale chiseling has always been a left-handed form of endeavor in this country, operating parallel with—and often more efficiently than—legitimate enterprise.

Nevertheless, the importance of corruption in shaping the United States has largely gone unrecognized. Every time there is a new scandal, analysts strain to put the events into some sort of perspective, yet they reveal almost total ignorance of the successive waves of corruption that have swept over America. If they were to be believed, the public pocket had never been picked until the hapless Ulysses S. Grant entered the White House.

The purpose of this book is to flip over the flat rock of our history and see what crawls out. I expect there will be howls of protest that this is a cynical, biased, and unfair work. Yet, since long before the reign of George Bush, Americans have been alternatively angered and entertained by the unbridled venality of their elected leaders without doing much about it. We demand upright government but have a sneaking contempt for the priggishness of reformers and a relish for scalawags. As Benjamin Franklin once put it, "There is no kind of dishonesty into which otherwise good people more easily fall, than that of defrauding the government."

In recent years, it seems that almost every morning newspaper and nightly news show tells of some leader in government or business or the church violating his trust and then lying about it. Nevertheless, there are those who claim that Washington is probably cleaner than ever before. They say that the amount of disclosure forced by the post-Watergate reforms is the reason for the appearance of increased corruption. There are sharper tools in the hands of prosecutors, and the urge of journalists to win the fame and fortune accorded to Bob Woodward and Carl Bernstein make it more difficult to be a crook. Perhaps. But there seems no end to those who follow the trail of the bouncing buck.

Usually the Gilded Age is acknowledged as the front-runner in the corruption sweepstakes. The Harding administration, with Teapot Dome and its other outrages, is the runner-up, with everyone else but the Nixon operation back in the pack. Recently, however, the Reagan regime gave all three a run for the most corrupt administration in American history. All have certain common characteristics. They are Republican (although the GOP has no lock on corruption) and the top ranks are staffed with people drawn from business. Business is not necessarily more corrupt than any other area, but businessmen usually view Washington with disdain. Such attitudes translate into a lack of respect for the intricate rules and regulations that have been established to steer government employees away from conflicts of interest and other breaches of ethics. Most of them don't understand the fine print.

In each of these cases, the president was far removed from day-to-day operations. Each adopted a chairman-of-the board management style that, for one reason or another, gave loyal subordinates with their own agendas—sometimes to get rich quick in Washington—too free a rein. Nixon was different from Grant, Harding, and Reagan, however. He was the only president to arouse suspicions that the Chief Executive himself might be a crook.

Two questions were usually put to me while this book was underway: (1) How many volumes are you going to write? (2) What do you mean by corruption?

To track the spoor of corruption through every byway of American history would indeed require a book two or three times as long as this one. Therefore I have restricted the story primarily to larceny on the national level. Now, what exactly do I mean by corruption? I do not mean sexual escapades or personal morality. But I have proceeded beyond ordinary bribery, conflict of interest, and till-tapping to include improper and/or illegal use of government authority for financial gain or political advantage. Thus my net is spread quite wide.

For the most part, this book has been excavated from standard historical sources, and I have placed my own "spin" on what I have found. In some cases this may represent an ex post facto judgment, but that's an author's privilege. "Historical facts are like a child's box of letters," J. A. Froude, the English historian, once said. "You have only to pick out such letters as you want, to spell any word you want."

One thing more. I would like to thank Don Fehr for visualizing the possibilities in this book and placing it under contract and Chris O'Connell, who edited it. And once again, I am indebted to my wife Jeanette.

Miller's Law
of Corruption

The rate of corruption in a government is an inverse ratio to the state of development of the nation itself.

Simply stated, this means that when a country is under-developed, usually the only way to make a fast buck is to rip off the government, so there will be a high incidence of corruption. But as a nation grows, and new ways of getting rich are created, the rate of governmental corruption should decrease, all things being equal.

Sometimes, however, all things are not equal. For proof, one need to look no further than the history of the United States.

Ruled by shady men, a nation itself becomes shady.

H.L. MENCKEN

I

Brave New World

FROM THE VERY beginning, America was a beacon to Europe's restless and dispossessed. Some men came to the New World in search of gold. Some men came in search of land; and some came in search of religious freedom or political liberty. Captain Samuel Argall came in search of graft.

The ship that brought Argall to take up his duties as "Deputy Governor and Admiral General" of Jamestown, the first permanent English settlement in the New World, loomed out of the early morning mist of May 15, 1617. Languid puffs of smoke blossomed along her sides as she exchanged salutes with a crude fort on the low-lying Virginia shore. These formalities out of the way, Argall, polished sword and burnished breastplate glistening in the sun, hastened ashore to inspect his new dominion with a cool, appraising eye.

Argall was something unexpected in the experience of the struggling Virginia colony. The governors who had preceded him were rough fellows, often cruel and dictatorial, yet for the most part they had been men of some integrity. Whatever their other shortcomings, they had worked disinterestedly for the colony and for England. Argall, however, appeared determined to make his fortune from the administration of this lonely outpost of empire. He was the first to bring to the New World the principles of graft and corruption that had long been basic to almost every form of public endeavor in England and throughout Europe.

A less discerning—or perhaps less greedy—man might have been disappointed by what Argall found in Virginia. Ten years after the arrival of the first settlers, the colony still trembled on the brink of disaster. The dead outnumbered the living, and the survivors had "scarce ragges to cover their naked bodyes." Emaciated, haunted faces bore silent witness to the horrors they had endured in what poets who had never set foot in Virginia rhapsodized into "Earth's onely Paradise."

Life in the colony was bitter and brutal. Romantic legends of swashbuckling cavaliers and baronial splendors that were to become staples of the Virginia tradition still lay in the future. In reality, the First Families of Virginia were a mixed bag of dissolute younger sons; hardbitten, unemployed soldiers; and a few ambitious gentlemen—all dropped down amid simple artisans and laborers, who were, no doubt, surprised to be in such company. The dream of a pot of gold at the end of the rainbow was the only thing shared by this band. They had no intention of making permanent homes in America, but had braved the wilderness only in hopes of getting rich quick and returning to England. It was devil take the hindmost—and he did, all too often, through disease, starvation, and Indian attack.

Jamestown itself was in hardly better shape than its inhabitants. The village was "in ruinous condition," Argall discovered. It consisted of a cluster of crude wattle-and-daub huts with a few clapboard buildings scattered among them. The settlement huddled behind a ragged wooden palisade "not sufficient to keepe out Hogs." There were also several straggling outposts where desultory efforts were made at farming, but the settlers, despite periods of near famine, regarded the planting of food crops as an unprofitable bore. The work was too hard and too dull. Tobacco had a ready market in England, so they spent almost all their efforts cultivating the weed, even planting it in the streets. To add to the misery of the colonists, the long swelter of the Chesapeake summer had already begun, and unhealthy vapors were rising from the surrounding mud flats and marshes. Nevertheless, the ambitious Argall saw only the beckoning of golden opportunity in his unpromising fiefdom.[1]

Seventeenth-century Englishmen believed there was nothing immoral or illegal in an official accepting—or even soliciting—graft and bribes. Corruption, in fact, was the lubricant that greased the wheels of the nation's administrative machinery. England, like most European nations, had no tradition of an uncorrupted, professional civil service. The modest administrative establishment of the medieval kings had been staffed almost entirely by churchmen, who were paid for their services with ecclesiastical preferment. Under the onslaught of the Reformation and Counter-Reformation this system had crumbled. Yet the concentration of power in the hands of the monarchy, and the increasing complexity of government, required an ever greater number of officials. The laymen who succeeded the clerics expected salaries, but tax rates were notoriously low and provided little money for this purpose. As a result, rulers turned a blind eye as government officials, drawing inadequate salaries and often burdened with debts incurred in buying their jobs, fattened their purses by extorting fees, soliciting bribes, and pocketing revenues. The prevailing philosophy was that the public, which demanded services from the government, should pay the officials who provided them.

Officeholders were allowed to use their posts for maximum personal advantage. Notions of service and duty to the public—supposedly a basic underpinning of the modern state—were almost unknown. Peerages and offices were hawked about to the highest bidder. In fact, the title of baronet was created solely for the purpose of sale. Lord Burghley, Queen Elizabeth's great counselor, grew fat on what he carefully referred to as "gratuities." His son, Sir Robert Cecil, later the Earl of Salisbury, and as Lord Treasurer the most powerful man in England, was on the payroll of the king of Spain—and vigorously complained when his quarterly payments were late. "If I were to imitate the conduct of your republic and begin to punish those who take bribes," King James I told the Venetian ambassador, "I should soon not have a single subject left." Nearly a century later, Samuel Pepys, then Secretary of the Admiralty, observed: "It was not the salary of any place that did make a man rich, but the opportunity of getting money while he is in the place."

It was possible, however, to overstep the bounds of permissible corruption. The Earl of Suffolk, one of Cecil's successors as Lord Treasurer, was ousted when his demands for bribes became too insistent. And Francis Bacon was impeached as Lord Chancellor and fined the substantial sum of forty thousand pounds for accepting gifts from litigants who had business in his court. Bacon's defense was that the bribes had not influenced his judgments. In the words of the old English proverb: "He refuseth the bribe but putteth forth his hand."[2]

Kings and ministers regularly used their powers of patronage to reward their friends, clients, and supporters with lucrative jobs overseas. These were often granted to men who had no intention of leaving the comforts of England. Stay-at-homes farmed out their duties to deputies who shared the emoluments of office or paid a flat rate for them. Fees intended for one man had to provide income for two—which meant that the necessity for graft was multiplied. When John Stuart Mill described imperialism as "a vast system of outdoor relief for the upper classes," he was referring to India, but he could just as well have been speaking of the earliest English colonies in the New World.

Fittingly enough, Virginia began as a speculation. The colony was founded not by the Crown but by a joint-stock company with the aim of turning a profit for its shareholders. Everything else— to render England a public service by increasing trade, to reduce her dependence on other nations for basic commodities, to provide a safety valve for her excess population—was secondary to the profit motive.

England was a late starter in the race for the riches of the New World, which had been monopolized by Spain for more than a century. Lacking colonies or the resources to establish them, the Elizabethans turned to piracy with considerable zest. Legalized hijacking—or privateering—was good business. Treasure-laden Spanish galleons lumbering homeward with the loot of the Indies were easy targets for English freebooters. One of Sir Francis

Drake's raiding voyages resulted in dividends of 4,700 percent for his lucky backers. Captain Thomas Cavendish bagged the fattest prize of all, taking the Manila Galleon in 1587. Men gazed with wonder as his ships moved up the Thames under damask sails, with sailors decked out in silk finery and heavy gold chains. Thus, Englishmen were conditioned to think of the New World in terms of gold and silver and pearls and silks, rather than as a place where they would experience the drudgery and hardship of colonization.[3]

The accession of James I to the throne in 1603, and peace with Spain, created a propitious moment for establishing an English foothold in America. Investors who had made fortunes in privateering sought new outlets for their money and energies, and daring souls willing to gamble their lives in hopes of getting rich were ready for any scheme. The old legends of golden cities that had lured the Spanish conquistadores into the heartland of America now enticed Englishmen across the Atlantic. For example, *Eastward Ho!*, a popular play of the day, thought to have been at least partially written by Ben Jonson, said of Virginia:

I tell thee golde is more plentiful there than copper is with us. . . . Why, man all their dripping pans and chamber pottes are pure golde. . . . And for rubies and diamonds, they goe forth on holy-days and gather 'em by the seashore. . . .

Investors were wary, however, as previous attempts to plant colonies in America had proved disastrous. Mystery and catastrophe swallowed up Sir Walter Raleigh's ill-fated attempt to plant a colony at Roanoke Island in 1587. The Crown, perennially short of cash, could offer only enthusiastic encouragement. Individual entrepreneurs were too undercapitalized to shoulder the expense, risk, and responsibility of establishing overseas colonies. The remedy for these difficulties lay readily at hand. During the reign of Queen Elizabeth, foreign trade had been greatly stimulated by the use of joint-stock companies, a rudimentary form of the modern corporation. Risks were spread among loose associations of investors who hazarded their capital rather than their skins. The Muscovy Company and the Levant Company had opened profitable commerce with Russia and the Near East, and the newly founded East India Company already showed promise of providing spectacular dividends to its shareholders. America seemed the next logical place for the trading companies to extend their operations.

The Virginia Company was chartered in 1606 with a patent that included the great sweep of the Atlantic Coast from what is now North Carolina to Maine.[4] The company had the blessings of King James—and empty coffers. The principal promoter, Sir Thomas Smith, a merchant prince with a guiding hand in the affairs of the Muscovy and East India companies, moved immediately to use the resources of the former to fill the latter. Smith, who became treasurer and general manager of the company, had a cool, logical head, a superb speculative sense, and the business ethics of a gypsy horse trader. He also had a marvelous ability to give the appearance of promoting the national interest while lining his own pockets.

In addition to this financial buccaneer, the insiders included a real pirate king—Sir Robert Rich, later Earl of Warwick and England's largest owner of privateers. Although James I was outspoken in his opposition to piracy, Rich envisioned Virginia as a base from which his private fleet, flying flags of convenience now that there was peace between Spain and England, could raid Spanish commerce. The presence of such powerful men with contacts among the biggest financial powers and at Court was sufficient to arouse the interest of smaller investors, who quickly convinced themselves that any venture in which Smith and Rich held an interest could not help but be a rousing success.

To strengthen this touching faith, Smith mounted a razzle-dazzle public relations campaign. A torrent of speeches, sermons, and tracts—"divine, human, historical, political"—poured from the presses under Smith's sponsorship. Eminent churchmen, poets, and philosophers were put on the payroll to make extravagant claims about the riches that lay waiting in Virginia. "There are valleys and plaines streaming with sweet Springs . . . there are hills and mountains making a sensible proffer of hidden treasure," proclaimed one tract.[5] There was no mention of malaria, dysentery, or hostile Indians. Smith's prestige was instrumental in persuading the officials of some of England's smaller cities and towns to invest public funds—and their own savings—in the company's stock.

For those who were willing to hazard their lives in the new colony, one body equaled one share of stock—so that persons unable to buy shares agreed to work on the company's plantation in Virginia for a specific period of time. When this term was completed, they were to be given plots of land of their own. The last farewells were said, and shortly before the end of 1606 the emigrants, about one hundred forty men and boys, were off to the New World in three frail vessels. Few would survive the hardships to come.

Like so many Englishmen who achieved fame—or notoriety—in the colonization of America, Samuel Argall resembles a jack-in-the-box that suddenly pops into view for a moment and then disappears, only to reappear later.[6] His antecedents are shadowy, and little is known of him before he came to Virginia to assume control of the colony's affairs. He was said to have been a member of an old Kentish family, and possibly a relative of Sir Thomas Smith. Argall had never before held a civil post, but an apprenticeship as an explorer and fighting seaman had taken him to all parts of the world. Perhaps he had observed that colonial administrators in the most obscure places seemed able to enrich themselves with little effort from the bribes and other opportunities for graft available; and he probably resolved that if such a ripe plum should ever fall into his lap, he would take the fullest advantage of it.

Argall made his first appearance in Virginia in 1609, when he was assigned to find a short, safe route across the Atlantic to the colony. The usual course was by way of the Canary Islands to Puerto Rico, and then to the Chesapeake—a voyage that was circuitous, unhealthy, and open to Spanish attack. Argall sailed straight across the Atlantic from the Canaries, cutting weeks off the trip. On one occasion he was credited with a nick-of-time arrival with supplies that saved the settlers from starvation. Such actions quickly earned him a reputation as "an ingenious, active and forward young Gentleman" who bore watching for the future.

Already, Argall had exhibited the daring and deviousness that were to mark his subsequent career. In the summer of 1613, he sailed for the coast of Maine, saying he planned to supply the hard-pressed colonists with salted fish. Observers noted that Argall's ship, the *Treasurer*, was armed with fourteen guns and carried sixty musketeers—a strange crew and cargo for a peaceful fishing vessel. In reality, he was going north not to fish but to hunt Frenchmen.

Argall had a secret commission to destroy a colony established by the French in 1611 on Mount Desert Island off the coast of Maine in defiance of what the Virginia Company considered to be its exclusive patent. Without warning, and with the *Treasurer's* guns firing, Argall sailed into the French harbor and easily captured the town and the few ships at anchor there. The English filled their vessel with loot, set fire to the cluster of houses, and sailed away to plunder the rest of the French settlements on the Maine coast. On the way back to Jamestown with his spoils— "much wheat, clothing, horses and working tools"—Argall stopped at the Dutch settlement at the mouth of the Hudson River long enough to force the governor to swear allegiance to the king of England. This declaration was to be of use to the English when they laid claim to New Netherland a half-century later.

Also important was Argall's kidnapping of Pocahontas, the daughter of the powerful Indian chief Powhatan, in 1612. He took her from a village along the Potomac where she had lived since inspiring one of the great American legends. Four years earlier, according to the famous story told by Captain John Smith, a leader of Jamestown's first group of settlers, Pocahontas had saved his life after he had been captured by her father's tribe. As Smith related the tale, Powhatan ordered two great stones to be brought before him. At a signal, Smith was seized and dragged to this makeshift altar, where several braves stood ready with huge clubs to beat out his brains. Suddenly, the young Pocahontas dashed from the crowd of onlookers, threw her arms about the hapless Englishman, and pleaded for his life—or so

Smith said. Powhatan acceded to the wishes of his favorite daughter.

This is indeed a pretty story—the stuff of which myths are made—but historians have cast considerable doubt on the veracity of Smith's account. Nevertheless, Pocahontas was well known in Jamestown, where she often amused herself by gathering the boys of the village about her in the marketplace and leading them in cartwheels through the streets "naked as she was."

Now a sedate young lady of eighteen, Pocahontas was a valuable prize in Argall's eyes. He planned "to possesse myself of her by any strategem that I could use" with the idea of exchanging the girl for some English prisoners and stolen arms and tools held by her father. Taking his vessel around to the Potomac, Argall, alternating persuasion with bribes and threats, induced the local chief to aid him in enticing Pocahontas aboard ship. And so Argall committed what may have been the first kidnapping in the history of the New World.

Anxious for the safety of his daughter, Powhatan offered to free the prisoners and make restitution of the stolen goods. But Argall now sought bigger game. If Powhatan was so eager to come to terms, he reasoned, perhaps he could be shaken down for even more. With all speed, the English captain made for Jamestown with his captive. Although the chief was furious over Argall's latest bit of double-dealing, he sent a sizable supply of corn to the settlement to ransom his daughter. The settlers kept the corn—and Pocahontas, too. Treated with kindness, she became reconciled to her situation, was converted to Christianity under the name of Rebecca, and was married to John Rolfe, a widowed English planter. In the spring of 1616 she accompanied her husband to England, where she was received like royalty by King James and his consort.

In the meantime, Argall's freebooting methods had brought him to the attention of the Earl of Warwick. With the backing of this influential "King of Privateers," Argall was appointed deputy governor of Virginia the following year. Warwick had great plans for the use of Virginia, and Argall seemed just the fellow to carry them out. Argall was to serve in place of Lord de La Warr, who held the governorship but had not visited the colony in five years because of ill health—or so he said. Pocahontas and her husband planned to return with Argall, Rolfe having been named secretary of the colony, or the governor's chief aide and advisor. Between them, they constituted the nucleus of America's first political machine. Unhappily, as their ship lay at anchor off Gravesend awaiting a fair wind, Pocahontas succumbed to the rigors of the English winter. She was laid to rest in the chancel of the local church overlooking the Thames, far from her wilderness home. Not long afterward, Argall and Rolfe were off to Virginia.

Upon his arrival in the colony, after "a speedy and prosperous voyage," Argall seems at first to have adopted the governing principle of Tiberius, that a good shepherd should shear his sheep rather than flay them.[7] Acting with customary zeal, Argall's earliest steps were to improve the defenses of the colony and to provide a sufficient food supply. Under the regime of Captain George Yeardley, who had been serving as acting governor, the Indians were allowed to come and go about Jamestown as they pleased, and some even learned to use firearms and kept them in their possession. In fact, Yeardley employed several braves to hunt for him and had given them weapons. Argall put an immediate stop to this dangerous practice. Orders were issued making it a crime to teach an Indian to shoot—with a penalty of death for both trainee and instructor.

To make certain that the colonists did not starve as a result of their own carelessness and greed, the governor decreed that they should immediately plant two acres of corn for each acre of tobacco. Violators would be punished by the confiscation of all their tobacco and with a year's slavery in the service of the colony. Experiments were also launched in the production of wheat, and laws requiring strict church attendance were rigidly enforced.

Having set this high moral tone for his administration, Argall now turned his attention to the business that had brought him to Jamestown—lining his own pockets with swag.[8] The settlers were somewhat mystified when he issued orders forbidding all contact with the ships and crews trading with the colony. Not until later did the logic behind this edict dawn upon them. It kept any complaints that they might have had about Argall's systematic plundering of the colony's assets from reaching England.

Decree followed decree as Argall, working with a small group of insiders that included John Rolfe, seized every opportunity to enrich himself. Trade with the Indians was forbidden to individual settlers and was monopolized by Argall. The tobacco trade was concentrated in his hands and he bought cheap and sold dear. Settlers who had completed their terms of service and were entitled to grants of land were kept in bondage unless they were able to pay bribes to Argall. Some of the indentured workers were rented out to private planters, and Argall pocketed their wages. The rest were transferred from the company's lands to Argall's own aptly named estate, "Argall's Gift," a few miles upriver from Jamestown. While Argall's plantation prospered, the company's estate fell into ruin. The governor also sold the company's cattle and other livestock, as well as its stores of corn to the highest bidder. Even the services of the soldiers in the color guard provided for the governor were disposed of at a profit.

Despite Argall's efforts to prevent news of his operations from reaching London, rumors of his peculations finally reached the ears of the stockholders. These unsettling reports arrived at a momentous time in the Virginia Company's history. Growing dissatisfaction with the continued failure of Sir Thomas Smith to produce profits had resulted in factionalism and demands for his ouster. Small investors, fed up with the domination of the company's affairs by Smith and the large merchants, found their champion in Sir Edwin Sandys, the assistant treasurer and the leader of the Parliamentary opposition to the Stuarts. At first, Warwick allied himself with the Sandys faction in the maneuvering to replace Smith. But when Sandys launched an attack on Argall's stewardship of the colony—an appointment due largely to Warwick's influence—the earl again switched sides and supported Smith.

Denouncing Argall's excesses, Sandys angrily charged that when the governor had arrived in Virginia, the "Company's Garden" had yielded an annual profit of three hundred pounds. Fifty-four men were employed on this land and at a salt works established for the colony's use. Eighty-one tenants paid rents in corn, which, along with the tribute from the Indians, amounted to about twelve hundred bushels, Sandys said. In addition, there were eighty head of cattle and eighty-eight goats. But after two years of Argall's administration, the "whole estate of the public was gone and consumed, there being not left to the Company either the land aforesaid or any tenant, servant, rent or tribute corn, cow or salt-work, and but six goats only, without one penny yielded to the Company for their so great a loss.[9]

To put a halt to Argall's plundering, the authorities prevailed upon Lord de La Warr, the ailing ex-governor, to return to Jamestown after an absence of seven years in England. De La Warr was ordered to remove Argall before he stole everything of value in the colony and to ship him home for trial. All his land and goods which "it is reported he hath gotten together . . . to the Colonie's prejudice" were to be confiscated. De La Warr, however, died at sea long before his ship arrived in Virginia, and the plan calling for Argall's arrest was foiled. Now fully aware that his days in power were numbered, Argall stepped up his looting of the colony's resources.

Expecting a replacement from London at any moment, Argall swept up as much of the remaining movable property as he could get his hands on and shipped the spoils home. To prevent seizure of his loot in case of a mishap, he consigned the plunder to the Earl of Warwick's care. The noble lord said he had accepted control of these goods only to ensure the safety of the company's property. Naturally, everything would be returned to the rightful owners in due course. Somehow, though, he never found the proper moment to fulfill that promise.

In a final orgy of corruption, Argall boldly grabbed property belonging to the estate of Lord de La Warr, the late governor. When Captain Edward Brewster, de La Warr's steward, protested, Argall, operating under martial law, ordered him condemned to death on charges of mutiny. So outrageous was this sentence that the colony's clergymen persuaded the governor— "after much Intreaty and after many Repulses"—to spare the unfortunate Brewster's life. Instead of being hung for trying to prevent his late master's property from being stolen by the rapacious Argall, Brewster was banished to England after being forced to swear he would say nothing disparaging about the conditions in Virginia.

Argall might as well have saved himself the bother, for there was no need of Brewster's accusations to stir trouble. After learning of the death of Lord de La Warr, the company dispatched George Yeardley, who had preceded Argall as deputy governor, to lay him by the heels. Warwick tried to block the appointment, but when this failed he still had one last card to play. The earl succeeded in holding up the departure of the ship that was to carry Yeardley to Virginia and hastily pushed off his own swift-sailing vessel, the *Eleanor*, to rescue his imperiled henchman. She arrived at Jamestown early in April 1619—allowing Argall just enough time to stow the last of his booty aboard. Little more than a week later, Yeardley arrived to find that Argall had made a clean getaway. So well had Argall done his work that the only property still remaining on the company's estate was of "no great value," the chagrined Yeardley reported. A century later, William Stith, one of Virginia's first historians, estimated Argall's total loot at eighty thousand pounds—a tremendous fortune by the standards of the day.[10]

Aloof and contemptuous, Argall returned to England and cavalierly challenged the Virginia Company to take legal action against him. Desultory efforts were made by Sandys and his allies to bring Argall to book, but nothing came of them. Obviously, any steps against Argall would have implicated Warwick—and he was far too important a personage to be offended. Besides, the bitter strife and shifting alliances among the Smith, Sandys, and Warwick factions as they maneuvered for control of the company left little time or energy for dealing with Argall's sins.

Smith was finally ousted from the company's management when Warwick, angry at the old man's failure to support him in the Argall affair, again united with Sandys. Pleading illness, age, and responsibilities with the East India Company, Smith was allowed to save face by resigning. Sandys, who was chosen as treasurer to succeed him, found his accounts in a complete muddle. Even after years of audits and investigations, it was never completely determined where thousands of pounds in capital had disappeared. Under the vaunted business management of Smith, the Virginia Company's assets had vanished in a miasma of incompetence and corruption.[11]

And what became of Argall? Two years after his hasty flight from Jamestown, he was knighted. In 1625, Sir Samuel Argall, as he was newly styled, became commander of a sizable force of king's ships that captured a fleet of French merchantmen in the English Channel said to be worth a hundred thousand pounds in prize money. Argall had become so successful that when King James finally became exasperated by the constant bickering among the Virginia Company's directors and ordered the corporation dissolved, he named Argall, along with Sir Thomas Smith, to the commission to devise a royal government for the colony.

While these titans were locked in combat for control of the Virginia Company, other colonies—and other methods of corruption—were being established on the barren shores of New England.[12] In the two decades that followed the landing of the first band of colonists at Plymouth in 1620, an estimated twenty thousand settlers flocked to the Massachusetts Bay area, usually under the leadership of their pastors. A great deal was expected of this Puritan commonwealth. Virginia was shackled with the chains of political, economic, and human venality, but the New Englanders brought to America a vision of God's kingdom on earth. After all, these "Unspotted Lambs of the Lord," as they unabashedly called themselves, flaunted a fine Calvinistic sense of right and wrong. They were, in fact, the first Americans to elect their own leaders, the first to use secret ballots—and the first to steal an election.

Unlike the settlers of Virginia, who regarded their sojourn in America as only a temporary exile, the Puritans had come to stay. Their colony was not to be a mere plantation, operated by the settlers for the profit of absentee shareholders in England. To ensure local control, the Puritans had transferred the entire administrative apparatus of the Massachusetts Bay Company with its General Court and charter to America. The effect of this decision was to transform an ordinary mercantilist colony into a self-governing commonwealth. Under the terms of the charter, control of the colony was in the hands of officials elected by the freemen at meetings of the General Court, the colony's governing body.

This was no guarantee of popular government, however. Although the Puritans had fled an England ruled by Stuart monarchs who believed in the divine right of kings, most of their leaders—especially John Winthrop, who, as governor, dominated the early history of the Massachusetts Bay Colony—believed in the divine right of spiritually inspired leaders to rule the multitude. Winthrop's suspicion of the political sagacity of the people was as great as that of Alexander Hamilton's a century and a half later. He had carefully searched his Bible and he could find no mention of "democracy" or "liberty."

Yet there was the colony's charter, with its proclamation of popular government, for all to read. Thus, a pressing problem for the Puritan leadership was how to hold elections without actually allowing the people to have a free choice. The solution was to limit the right to vote to the spiritually elect. Only church members, a group carefully restricted in size by the rigidity of the rules governing membership, were given the franchise. They could be counted upon to cast their ballots the way their leaders expected—or so it was thought. As a result, New England was ruled by a self-perpetuating elite of men of wealth and good family who regarded themselves as God's stewards on earth.

Even so, conformity was difficult to enforce in a colony settled by determined men and women whose independence and individuality had brought them to America in the first place. Besides, there was an abundance of free land that beckoned any settler who found the yoke of conformity pressing down too heavily upon his neck. As a result, there were occasions when the commonfolk resisted solutions imposed upon them by their betters.

For example, in December 1634, the spiritually elect of Boston went to the polls to choose seven men who were to oversee the distribution of town land that had been held in common. Voting by secret ballot, these freemen flatly rejected Winthrop and several of the "chief men" who had confidently expected to be chosen as usual. Instead, according to Winthrop's *Journal*, the electors chose men of "the inferior sort" out of fear that the rich might grab the best land for themselves and leave little for the ordinary folk.[13]

This was nonsense, snorted Winthrop. He contended that a large part of the unassigned land should be held in common for distribution among newcomers as they arrived in the colony. Sound doctrine, no doubt. It would have had a more telling effect among the discontented if Winthrop had not already accumulated 1,800 acres, and his fellow land barons, Sir Richard Saltonstall and Thomas Dudley, did not hold nearly equal amounts. In contrast, the average family possessed only about a hundred acres of land. Alarmed at having lost their uncontested grip upon the colony for the first time, the oligarchs appealed to the clergy for aid and comfort.

The Reverend John Cotton, the colony's reigning divine, was not found wanting in this emergency. Just a few months before, he had preached a sermon holding that the province's leaders were entitled to perpetual re-election to ensure stability. Cotton contended that they held the same rights to high office as they did to their estates and other property. Moving quickly to deal with the new crisis, he summoned his flock to a sermon on the necessity of respect for their betters. From his pulpit, Cotton thundered that "it was the Lord's orders among the Israelites to have all such business committed to the elders"—and this ought to be good enough for the simple folk of Massachusetts Bay. Hellfire and damnation awaited any people so lacking in religious spirit as to ignore this Biblical precedent. The offending election was set aside, and with Cotton's admonitions ringing in their ears, the freeholders again went to the polls. This time they chose Winthrop and the slate preferred by the large propertyholders to distribute the land.

Corruption and petty tyranny were not confined to the English colonies. Between New England and Virginia, the Dutch, ignoring England's claims to sovereignty just as the English had ignored the papal bulls dividing the New World between Spain and Portugal, planted a colony in the Hudson River valley in 1624.[14] This colony was christened New Netherland. Two years later, Governor Peter Minuit bought title to Manhattan Island from the Indians for sixty guilders ($24) worth of beads and other trinkets. New Amsterdam is usually thought of as the quaint and tidy village of Washington Irving's fictitious Father Knickerbocker, where red-faced burghers and their broad-beamed fraus made merry. The reality, however, was far grimmer. The history of the colony was marked by corruption, disorderly behavior, and ceaseless bickering.

Founded neither as an economic outpost of empire nor as a haven for religious refugees, New Netherland's origins were even more narrowly commercial than those of Virginia. The Dutch West India Company, which ruled the colony, regarded it solely as a springboard for gaining control of the valuable fur trade of the Hudson Valley. Every consideration was subordinated to the scramble for pelts and profits. Farmers were regarded as little more than necessary evils, and it was a long time before individuals were allowed to hold title to a single acre of land.

When the West India Company finally realized that its vast acreage must be populated if the colony was to withstand the pressures from the English to the north and south, a semi-feudal system of patroonships was established. Anyone who brought out fifty families at his own expense was offered extensive tracts of land with full baronial privileges—such as establishing their own magistrates' courts, the issuance of hunting and fishing permits, and a monopoly of trade with the Indians. The directors of the company—among them Kiliaen Van Rensselaer, a wealthy Amsterdam jeweler—gobbled up all the best land, particularly on Staten Island and along the Hudson, for the foundation of their empires in the wilderness. Van Rensselaer, alone, secured a tract estimated at 700,000 acres.

The old statement that a corporation has no soul was never truer than in New Amsterdam. Treated little better than indentured servants by the West India Company, the frustrated populace resorted to smuggling and other forms of illict trade to make their fortunes. Although the inhabitants thought they were justified in cheating the company, they complained rather impatiently about the corrupt character of the governors sent from Holland to rule them. A prominent churchman, in writing of Peter Minuit, declared: "We have a governor, who is most unworthy of his office; a slippery man, who under the treacherous mask of honesty is a compound of all iniquity and wickedness."

Wouter Van Twiller, old Van Rensselaer's nephew, followed Minuit as governor. While he was said to be drunk most of the time, this did not prevent him from amassing a sizable fortune while in office. He appropriated from ten thousand to fifteen thousand acres of land on Long Island without even bothering to inform the West India Company; had a *bouwery*, or farm, on the present site of Greenwich Village; and before being removed from office grabbed Nut Island in the harbor, which was renamed Governor's Island in his honor. Unlike Samuel Argall, Van Twiller remained in the colony after his dismissal. Although his former subjects grumbled and gossiped about how he had amassed his rich lands and fine herds, Van Twiller exhibited a cynical indifference and divided his time between improving his farms and cattle and visiting the local taverns.[15]

But if Van Twiller's open indulgence in graft raised eyebrows among the citizenry, his successor, William Kieft, was really a shock to them.[16] The new governor turned out to be Manhattan's first reformer. Kieft began by trying to put an end to the smuggling that had become a staple of the colony's economy. And as if this were not enough, he attempted to uplift the moral standards of the turbulent town. "Fighting, lewdness, rebellion, theft, perjury, calumny, and all other immoralities" were forbidden. Strict curbs were placed on the taverns, and visiting sailors were restricted to their ships during the night in an attempt to put an end to drunken carousing. This led to the opening of the first speakeasys, with fully a third of the local taverns operating illegally. Not unexpectedly, Kieft's reforms were unpopular. One town character denounced the governor as "a villain and a traitor" and offered to shoot him on sight if no one else would do it.

Kieft's downfall resulted not from his reforms but from his

greed. Unlike most of the Dutch settlers, who adopted an easygoing attitude toward their Indian neighbors, Kieft regarded dead Indians as the only good Indians and hoped to grab off their land without the usual trinkets and palaver. The Indians, however, refused to be exterminated and avenged themselves on isolated settlements and lonely farmers. In little more than two years, an estimated sixteen hundred Indians were killed, while countless Dutchmen fell to the tomahawk and the scalping knife. The colony's survivors took refuge behind a wooden palisade that marked the outer limits of New Amsterdam—and gave Wall Street its name. With their fields lying fallow and their homes burned, they finally persuaded the West India Company that Kieft had outlived his usefulness.

Peter Stuyvesant, the peg-legged governor of Curaçao, was appointed to replace Kieft. Irascible, dictatorial, and known as "Hardheaded Pete," he ruled with a rod of iron, but was probably the most competent governor New Netherland ever had. Early on, Stuyvesant was faced with demands from some of the citizens for a legislative probe of Kieft's administration. The new governor would have none of that. He realized full well that if he permitted an investigation of his predecessor's affairs—no matter how warranted it might be—a precedent would be established that could haunt him if his successor decided to investigate his conduct. Noting that Kieft had been brought down by appeals to Holland, Stuyvesant warned the dissenters: "If anyone during my administration, shall appeal, I will make him one foot shorter, and send the pieces to Holland, and let him appeal that way."

Yet for all of Stuyvesant's bluster and bustle, New Netherland did not prosper. The settlers were convinced that greed was the underlying policy of the government; that taxes were levied without any consideration to ability to pay; that the company siphoned money out of the colony which it never returned; and that trade restrictions encouraged monopolies and smuggling, making it difficult for honest men to earn a living. So, in 1664, when a small English fleet appeared off the town and commanded the Dutch to surrender, Stuyvesant stomped his wooden leg in vain. New Amsterdam became New York without a shot and

almost without a tear. The good burghers seemed to have decided that nothing could be worse than the incompetent rule of
the Dutch West India Company.

But that was before they had made the acquaintance of Benjamin Fletcher.

II

Of Pirates and Profits

"THE CHIEF END of many Governours coming to the Plantations [has] been to get Estates for themselves," a disgruntled Virginian bitterly complained at the dawn of the eighteenth century. "Very unwarrantable Methods have sometimes been made use of to compass these Ends." No colony suffered as much from royal governors who matched this description as did New York—and no governor fitted it better than Colonel Benjamin Fletcher. He arrived in New York on August 29, 1692, a tall, florid, and rather pompous fellow with the stamp of long years of military service upon him. Little was known about the new governor except that he had served in the Low Countries and Ireland, and as "a necessitous man" had received the governorship of New York, with its annual salary of six hundred pounds as his reward. Fletcher's subjects were duly impressed by his martial aspect, but it was not long before some wryly noted that the frigate which brought him was aptly named. She was the *Wolf*.[1]

New York was then a bubbling caldron of revolutionary unrest. The Glorious Revolution of 1688 which swept the Catholic King James II from the throne and replaced him with his Protestant daughter, Mary, and her husband, William of Orange, had been comparatively peaceful in England. But events had taken a tragic and violent turn in New York. Francis Nicholson, the lieutenant governor, and his chief advisors, among them Nicholas Bayard, a nephew of Peter Stuyvesant; Stephanus Van Cortlandt; and Frederick Philipse, all grandees who had grown wealthy under James's rule, stood fast for the king—at least until they could determine which way the wind was blowing in England. The mass of New Yorkers favored William and Mary, however, and a drunken threat by Nicholson to burn the town touched off a revolt.

Jacob Leisler, a militia captain and merchant, seized power with the announced intention of preserving the province for the Protestant sovereigns.[2] Leisler, originally a penurious soldier in the employ of the Dutch West India Company who had married a well-to-do widow, had long been dissatisfied with the graft and corruption that pervaded every aspect of life in New York. In the nearly three decades since Stuyvesant had hauled down the Dutch flag, the land barons and large merchants had tightened their stranglehold on the province's economic and political life.

The English had not only recognized the patroonships granted by the Dutch, but had expanded them. Power and privilege were completely monopolized by a new aristocracy based upon enormous grants of land, or manors, as they were now called. Wealth and status were transformed into office and political influence, which in turn was converted into privileged access to the land. Philipse, for one, had concentrated his huge holdings into the manor of Philipsburgh. Robert Livingston, the shrewd son of a Scottish clergyman with a keen eye for good land, controlled 160,000 acres in what is now Dutchess and Columbia counties. Van Cortlandt obtained a patent for Van Cortlandt Manor consisting of 85,000 choice acres in the Hudson highlands.

The harbor was filled with a forest of masts—so many that an acute observer would have noticed more ships crowding the wharves than needed to carry the province's exports of furs and naval stores to England. Many of them were too rakish and well-armed to be mere innocent trading vessels. A few hours in the waterfront taverns or the mercantile coffeehouses would have provided a solution to the mystery. New York had become a thieves' market where pirates disposed of loot taken on the high seas. Merchants broadminded enough to overlook the momentary awkwardness of a few bloodstains on goods offered for sale at bargain prices were turning handsome profits.

Yet, this was only a surface prosperity in which the farmers, freemen, and tradesmen had little share. Increasingly restless, they muttered about the way the magnates arrogantly manipulated the government to add to their own opulence. There was a smoldering demand for an end to monopolies and for wider opportunities for the little fellow. The common folk found their champion in Jacob Leisler. Although he was pigheaded, and an anti-Catholic bigot who railed against "the Scarlet Whore of Rome," Leisler's twenty-one months at the head of the government had overtones of a social revolution. He tried to put an end to the worst aspects of corruption and to break the grip of the great landlords and wealthy traders on the affairs of the province. Leisler's legislature enacted laws abolishing the special privileges enjoyed by the merchants of New York City. Some of the more suspect large land grants were annulled, and Nicholas Bayard, among others, was jailed. Daily wages paid tradesmen and laborers were increased, and the requirements for becoming a freeman were liberalized. As a result, the yeoman farmers and the small businessmen flocked to Leisler's standard.

But the magnates, fearful of being despoiled of their wealth and influence, regarded him as a dangerous rabble-rouser. Emissaries were sent to England to circulate horror stories about the excesses of Leisler's administration and to influence opinion against him. For a long time, William and Mary were too busy putting down Jacobite rebellions in Scotland and Ireland to pay much attention to what was going on in America, giving Leisler the mistaken idea that royal recognition had been given to his regime.

The new governor finally dispatched by William and Mary in 1690 was an Irish soldier bearing the ominous name of Henry Sloughter. With him went a small squadron of warships and two companies of regular troops under the command of Major Richard Ingoldesby. Sloughter was delayed at sea and Ingoldesby arrived ahead of him. At once he made an alliance with the aristocratic faction and demanded that Leisler surrender. Leisler obstinately refused, declared that he would give up authority only to the new governor, and barricaded himself in Fort William Henry at the tip of Manhattan. Hotheads on both sides prevailed. During an exchange of gunfire on March 17, 1691, one of the redcoats was killed, sealing Leisler's fate. Two days later, Sloughter arrived and ordered Leisler and several members of his council arrested on charges of treason and murder.

The court that tried Leisler and his associates was packed with their enemies and quickly brought in a verdict of guilty. Sloughter's signature on the death warrant was reportedly obtained while he was drunk, a common condition of the new governor. On May 16, 1691, Leisler suffered the penalty meted out to traitors on the present site of City Hall Park, a fitting place for the execution of a man opposed to graft and corruption. He was hanged, cut down while still alive, and disembowled. "The shrieks of the people were dreadful," wrote an observer.[3]

With the judicial murder of Leisler accomplished, the magnates set about removing every trace of his reforms. One of the first acts of Sloughter's council was to reaffirm the legality of all existing land grants. Edicts were also issued reducing wage levels and tightening the requirements for becoming a freeman. To discourage anyone else from following Leisler's example—as if the horror of his execution had not been deterrent enough—it was decreed that any persons who might "disturbe the peace and quiet of this, their Majestyes Government as it is now established, shall be Deemed and Esteemed as Rebells and Traitors." This was an even broader and harsher definition of treason than that prevailing in England.

Bayard and Van Cortlandt got themselves named to the commissions that were to examine claims for compensation for alleged losses suffered under Leisler's regime—and then, to no one's surprise, entered vast claims for damages themselves. As for Sloughter, he received his reward in the form of a special grant of funds, voted to cover unexpected expenses incurred in restoring law and order to New York. In reality, charged the Leislerites, this was an open payoff for his support of the aristocratic faction. Sloughter now spent most of his time in an alcoholic haze, no doubt contemplating the riches that would soon be his, but he never reaped this harvest for he died in July 1691, probably from the effects of drink.

Before Colonel Fletcher left London to govern New York, the Lords of Trade had impressed upon him the need for a policy of pacification there to end the campaign of violence and vengeance against Leisler's followers. The aristocratic faction was alarmed to hear their new governor talk of "burying all heats and animosities." This sounded like pro-Leisler talk to them. Did it mean that their privileges were again endangered? Would Leislerian mobs seeking revenge snatch them from their beds in the dark of night? Fletcher, however, was merely toying with them. Not only had the governor taken note of the suspiciously large numbers of ships in the harbor but he was determined to obtain a piece of the action for himself. Apparently he reasoned that any proposition designed to buy a seemingly honest official would be far more liberal than one begrudged to a grubby grafter with an outstretched palm. He was right. The merchant-traders rapidly saw the light and the governor was made a partner in good standing in their commercial and speculative enterprises.

Although Fletcher extended the most enthusiastic welcome to the pirates granted by any governor, New York was not the first colony to throw open its doors to the buccaneers. There were few places untainted by cooperation with the pirates. Charleston, South Carolina, had long been a hospitable haven for the Brethren of the Coast. Newport, Rhode Island, where there was "a greater plenty of European goods than in any place on the Main tho' they have not so much as a vessel that goes from thence to England," offered excellent facilities for ship repair and resupply. Philadelphia was full of honest Quaker merchants who brought pirate merchandise with no questions asked. An exasperated William Penn noted that it was being said in London that the citizens of his colony "not only wink att but Imbrace pirats, Shipps and men." In New England, the thrifty Puritans put aside their moral scruples when it came to making a profit. Free-spending pirates were so welcome in Boston that when a public-spirited citizen tried to alert the authorities to the presence of one notorious brigand, his neighbors almost lynched him. The mob need not have been concerned about the safety of their hero, for he was under the protection of the governor, with whom he was sharing his booty.[4]

Most of the pirates operating along the American coast and in the West Indies had served as privateers during the various wars of the late seventeenth century. They merely stepped over the thin line separating piracy from privateering. Such men had always been welcome in the colonies, because they attacked traditional enemies and paid for their supplies in gold and silver. The passage of the Acts of Trade and Navigation, a sheaf of restrictive laws aimed at ensuring a monopoly of the lucrative colonial trade for England, also helped brighten the welcome offered the pirates in American seaports. Barred from legally trading with any other nation, the colonists were forced to buy and sell at prices fixed by the merchants of London and Bristol, who were notorious for buying cheap and selling dear. On top of this, they were subject to any customs duties the covetous mother country might levy.

Smuggling was the most obvious means of evading the full force of the Navigation Acts, so the colonists quickly became adept at this form of enterprise. For example, the planters of Maryland and Virginia surreptitiously exported large quantities of tobacco to the West Indies and to Europe. The Dutch island of Curaçao became the center of an illicit trade in which American produce was exchanged for the goods of Europe and the East. But as a general rule, the colonists preferred to deal with the pirates rather than the smugglers when it came to imports. They charged lower prices.

At about the same time that the American colonists sought to evade English restrictions on their trade, there was a significant shift in the hunting grounds of the pirates. Treaties and stricter controls had tightened the noose about buccaneering in the West Indies—and about the necks of some of its leading practitioners— so they searched for a safer place to conduct their operations. The Red Sea and Indian Ocean became the new centers of piratical endeavors. For almost a century, the ships of the English, Dutch, and French East India companies, laden with the riches of India, had plowed these waters without fear or interference. In the beginning, the Red Sea pirates, as they became known, limited their attacks to Moorish and Indian vessels. After all, observed one pirate chieftain, it was "no sin for Christians to rob heathens." The lure of plunder overcame this commendable restraint, and soon all ships were considered fair game.

For all its possibilities, however, piracy in the Eastern seas had a serious drawback. Buccaneering was a business and there was a need for a convenient base of operations where loot could be "fenced," supplies obtained, and ships manned. The eye of some of the more perceptive pirates fell upon the island of Madagascar, lying off the east coast of Africa. It was an ideal spot, offering fresh water, abundant food, and secure harbors. Best of all, it was unclaimed by any of the major European nations. News of the bargains to be obtained at Madagascar quickly reached New York, and the rapacity of the merchants was aroused.[5]

The redoubtable Frederick Philipse financed an ex-pirate named Adam Baldridge in setting up a trading post on the island and reaped a rich harvest. Philipse was said to have cleared ten thousand pounds on one shipload of merchandise sent to Madagascar and to have netted at least a hundred thousand pounds from the "Red Sea trade." Operating with licenses purchased from Governor Fletcher, the New York merchants enjoyed a brisk trade with Madagascar. Goods sent to the island were pedestrian stuff—primarily clothes, tools, naval stores, rum, powder and arms—which was sold at huge markups. In return, cargoes of spices and tea, gold and precious stones, silks and satins flowed into New York. One ship alone brought back merchandise that was disposed of for more than thirty thousand pounds. The narrow streets of lower Manhattan took on the sights and smells of an Eastern bazaar. The loot of the Indies piled up on the wharves and passed over the counters of the merchants. Piracy had turned out to be good business for them—and for Benjamin Fletcher.

Soon it was noticed that this once "necessitous man" was living well above his modest salary. Fletcher traveled about in viceregal style in a glittering coach and six, the first sported by any colonial governor in America. He wore delicate lace and showered his wife and daughter with silks and jewels. The governor's mansion was hung with elaborate tapestries upon which no duty had been paid. His guests dined off expensive china and were invited to admire a fine collection of gold and silver snuffboxes. Having met his temporal needs, Fletcher turned to matters of the spirit. As thunderous a Bible-thumper as any Puritan divine—he took time out twice a day for prayer—the governor was one of the organizers of Trinity Church and donated a prayer book and pew to the congregation. Considering the source of the benefaction, the church's location was apt—at Wall Street on Broadway.

Still more opportunities awaited Fletcher. Madagascar offered little in the way of recreational opportunities for visiting pirates. Life was so dull that for excitement on one occasion fourteen crewmen chose up sides, pooled their prize money, and fought to the death for it. Twelve men were killed, leaving the surviving pair of gladiators to split their winnings. It was little wonder that some of the more successful corsairs sought to return to America to enjoy their plunder in style.

Fletcher was ready, as always, to oblige as long as the returning pirates paid a good price to insure a peaceful homecoming. As soon as their ships anchored in New York, Daniel Honan, Fletcher's clerk, was on hand to exact a toll of one hundred pounds from each in exchange for a pardon. By 1695, some sixty mariners from the Red Sea had drifted into New York to seek a snug harbor. One of Fletcher's more lucrative deals was with Captain Edward Coates, who had been flying the black flag in the Red Sea aboard the *Jacob*. Having amassed a fortune estimated at 160,000 pounds, Coates was ready to retire to a life of ease ashore. He judiciously purchased Fletcher's goodwill with a gift of the *Jacob*—after all, he wouldn't need her anymore—which the governor sold the next day for eight hundred pounds. Fletcher also picked up his usual fee from each of the crew eager for a spree in the fleshpots of New York. Captain Coates later swore that in addition to his ship, it cost him thirteen hundred pounds to secure Fletcher's benevolent protection. No detail was too small to catch the governor's eye. When Captain George Rayner complained that the local sheriff had seized his sea chest, which was presumably packed with plunder, Fletcher issued an order that it be returned forthwith—the price was fifty pounds.

The streets of New York teemed with "reformed" pirates who swaggered about with their rolling gait, adding a racy touch to life in the town. The pirates were boon companions—as long as one met them in the dram shops and not aboard a richly laden merchantman on the high seas. They were generous with their money and good storytellers. Captain Thomas Tew, son of a well-respected Rhode Island family and one of the most notorious of the Red Sea rovers, was a frequent guest at the home of Governor Fletcher. Tew was a gentleman, reasoned Fletcher, and besides, he was said to have amassed a fortune of at least a hundred thousand pounds from his adventures. Fletcher and the pirate captain were often seen, heads together, in the governor's famous coach, laughing at Tew's rollicking stories and jokes. Later, when complaints about Fletcher's relationship with Tew reached London, he piously contended that he had been trying to persuade the dashing buccaneer to turn over a new leaf. "I wish'd in my mind to reclaime him from a vile habit of swearing," alleged the governor. "I gave him a booke to that purpose."[6]

That was not all that Fletcher gave him. There was an exchange of gifts—jewels for the governor and his family and a gold watch for Tew, "supposedly to seal his promise to discharge his next cargo of pirated goods in New York" rather than Boston or Newport, it was later charged. Tew was also given a commission authorizing him to go on a privateering voyage against French commerce in the Gulf of St. Lawrence. Several other skippers with shady reputations were also granted similar commissions with no questions asked, except whether they could post the bond demanded by Fletcher.

The trade routes to Canada offered little opportunity for taking prizes worth a sizable investment, and it was obvious these commissions simply licensed the holders to commit piracy on the high seas. The pirates lost no time in sailing to their old haunts in the Red Sea. Tew captured several prizes before being killed in action, and the others committed the usual bloody atrocities. In one case, a captured merchantman was set afire, leaving the hapless crew to either burn to death or drown. Fletcher met the charges of negligence—and worse—with a shrug. "I never knew or so much as heard that any of [them] intended for the Red Sea or the Indies," he declared. "And if [they] did abuse the commission they had and turned pirates afterwards, tis an event of which like instances does some times happen."[7]

Although the foundation of Fletcher's newfound wealth was the Red Sea trade, he neglected none of the opportunities for graft traditionally available to a colonial governor. As an old campaigner, his eye first fell upon the small garrison recruited to defend the province against the threat of French invasion and Indian attack. Following time-honored procedures, the governor began to "pinch the bellies" of his soldiers by pocketing funds intended for supplies. He also appropriated for his own use money voted by the assembly for defense by padding the payroll and keeping the extra money. The amounts realized from these mean-spirited practices, however, were chicken feed compared to Fletcher's profits in real estate.[8]

In return for bribes, and with a stroke of his quill pen, Fletcher created powerful new landed families and added to the vast holdings of the grandees. To Captain John Evans, skipper of the Royal Navy frigate *Richmond*, who was supposed to be on watch against pirates but could never find any, Fletcher awarded a grant estimated to run forty miles in one direction and thirty in another along the west bank of the Hudson. No one was quite sure of the actual limits. The price was one hundred pounds—and to protect the king's interest, it was made subject to an annual rent of twenty shillings. Henry Beekman, founder of a family that was to figure prominently in the history of New York real estate, received a tract of land running twenty miles along the east bank of the river, which was "as large as the midling county in England." He paid Fletcher about twenty-five pounds and valued the property at five thousand pounds.*

---

* So insatiable was Beekman's appetite for land that there was a joke about a boy who asked if there was land on the moon. An old Dutch farmer replied: "Ask Colonel Beekman, for you may be sure that if there is land there, he has got a patent for the biggest part of it."

Most of the land handed out by Fletcher went to the same group of insiders who had long dominated affairs in the province and filled the seats on his council. Nicholas Bayard received a tract estimated at forty miles long and thirty miles broad. He gave Fletcher 150 pounds and agreed to provide the Crown with an otter skin each year as quit rent, or ten shillings in lieu of it. The chief justice, William Smith, who was not even a lawyer, secured title to a grant on Long Island known as the Manor of St. George for the princely sum of twenty-five pounds. It was said to be the most valuable of all the grants made by Fletcher. Smith, among the most powerful men in the province, all but forced the town of Southampton to accept ten pounds in return for a clear title to almost forty miles of Atlantic beach. In a single year he cleared five hundred pounds from the sale of whales taken there. Peter Schuyler; Godfrey Dellius, a Dutch clergyman; and several associates secured a patent to fifty square miles of the Mohawk Valley valued at twenty-five thousand pounds—an intrusion that enraged the Indians. The land-grabbing preacher also appears to have picked up another seven hundred thousand virgin acres elsewhere. And for a mere pittance, Caleb Heathcote became lord of the manor of Scarsdale in Westchester.

Fletcher disposed of almost three-fourths of the public lands in the province to just thirty men, most of them members of his own council. Fear was widespread that such huge grants would discourage immigration to New York because potential settlers would see no chance to obtain good land for themselves. It was also noted that despite the generous grants made by Fletcher, the rent collected by the Crown suffered a disastrous plunge. Before he began distributing grants, the receipts from this source totaled over three hundred pounds a year. Three years later, with triple the amount of land in private hands, the revenue had dropped to perhaps thirty-five pounds annually. In vivid contrast, Fletcher's take from bribes in return for land grants was thought to be no less than four thousand pounds.[9]

To make certain that there would be no interference with this state of affairs, the governor kept a tight rein on the election of local officials. In 1695, when the magnates feared that voting in New York City might result in the choice of candidates linked to the Leislerians, Fletcher ordered the balloting to take place in an open field under the watchful eye of his troops. A certain Captain William Kidd, a prosperous shipmaster and privateer, later testified that he had seen "Soldiers and seamen with Clubs in the field" and that he had been ordered by the sheriff to bring his crew ashore so they could stuff the ballot boxes. Fletcher denied the charges, saying the only sailors to vote were those who met the qualifications for being freemen of New York. Of course, Fletcher's candidates were easily elected as the Leislerians prudently stayed by their firesides.[10]

Nevertheless, several events combined to bring about the old reprobate's downfall. The Leislerians, successfully working in London to secure a reversal of the bill of attainder against Leisler, spread stories about the graft and corruption rampant in New York. Fletcher also came under attack from the other side, having had a falling out with Robert Livingston, one of the most important of the magnates. The London merchants were angry at the volume of trade with the pirate depots at Madagascar, and they blamed Fletcher for the resulting decline in their own profits. And most importantly, the Tories, who were originally responsible for Fletcher's appointment, had fallen from power.

Orders for Fletcher's replacement, the Earl of Bellomont, were issued on June 18, 1697, but he did not arrive in the province until the following April. The time lag gave Fletcher the opportunity to complete his work just as Samuel Argall had done in Virginia. Among his last transactions was the transfer of a small plot of farmland on the outskirts of town to Caleb Heathcote, one of the large landholders. Although this grant was minuscule, its loss was particularly galling to Bellomont. This tract had been reserved as a farm to fill the new governor's own needs for meat and vegetables.

New Yorkers were flattered at being sent a governor of Bellomont's exalted rank, but he was appalled at what he found.[11] "Corrupted and debauched" were his words for Fletcher's administration. Bellomont was that rare bird, a colonial governor who not only talked about reform but meant it. Ordered to put an end to piracy, he resolved to accomplish nothing less. When offered the governorship, Bellomont reportedly demanded a salary large enough to free himself of the necessity of soliciting bribes. This was an astounding request for the day and was only reluctantly accepted.

Bellomont was in the province only a few days before coming face-to-face with the corruption that permeated the place. Word reached him that a vessel named the *Fortune* had arrived from the East with a cargo valued at twenty thousand pounds, and no attempt had been made by the customs agents to examine her. The merchants, rubbing their hands in gleeful anticipation as her cargo was unloaded, expected Bellomont to share their pleasure just as Fletcher would have. To their amazement, his lordship ordered both the vessel and her cargo seized for nonpayment of duty.

Undoubtedly, the person most surprised by this order was Chidley Brooke, the collector of customs. Under Fletcher, he had amassed a fortune by turning a blind eye when illegal cargoes arrived in port. Brooke was full of excuses.* This was a job for a man-of-war, he did not have a boat, etc., etc. For four days he delayed—long enough to allow all but a thousand pounds or so of the *Fortune*'s cargo to be spirited away to the warehouses of its owners. A chagrined Bellomont dismissed Brooke, but his successor was not much of an improvement. Learning that some contraband was being hidden by a merchant in a garret, the new collector attempted to seize the goods, only to be locked up in the garret. As soon as he was rescued by a file of soldiers, he submitted his resignation.[12]

Bellomont nevertheless pressed ahead with his efforts to clean up New York. Since the Leislerians had opposed Fletcher, he allied himself with them. When Leisler's body was transferred from a traitor's grave to the cemetery of the Dutch church, Bellomont led the torchlit procession. He unearthed a vast amount of evidence regarding his predecessor's sins and ferreted out most

---

* Brooke, who failed to see what all the commotion was about, commented that "the giving of protection to pirates had not formerly been looked upon as so great a matter, and that all the neighboring Governments had done it"—a forerunner of the "Everybody does it" syndrome of our time.

of that connected with illegal trade—pirates, merchants, and members of the government. Corrupt officials were dismissed, including Philipse and Bayard, who lost their seats on the council. Edicts against piracy were issued and substantial bonds were required to guarantee that outward-bound ships did not call at Madagascar or other pirate refuges.*

Bellomont also succeeded in upsetting the most "extravagant" land grants made by Fletcher. Perhaps the most astonishing case nevertheless was the claim of Samuel Allen to the ownership of the entire area of what is now New Hampshire. Allen based this claim on an old and questionable charter which he had bought for 250 pounds. By judicious bribery of those in control of colonial affairs, he had managed to keep it alive. Oblivious to the legal arguments raging over the validity of Allen's charter, settlers spread all over New Hampshire, clearing the land for farms and laying out towns. After they had put down their roots, the crafty Allen claimed the improvements were on his lands and demanded rents totaling twenty-two thousand pounds a year. Rebellion nearly broke out among the angry settlers. Bellomont was called in to investigate because the disputed area lay within his jurisdiction. With only one man between him and the certification of his title, Allen resorted to the methods that had always worked so well in the past. He dangled a ten-thousand-pound bribe before his lordship, not once but several times. "I thank God I had not the least tempting thought to accept," commented Bellomont. He found Allen's title defective and worthless.[13]

---

* The only blot on Bellomont's reputation stems from his association with Captain Kidd. Bellomont, Kidd, and Robert Livingston formed a syndicate before Bellomont's appointment as governor with the aim of apprehending the most notorious Red Sea pirates and confiscating their loot. Bellomont sold his share in the enterprise to several prominent English politicians soon after the syndicate was formed. There is conflicting evidence as to what occurred next. Kidd either turned pirate voluntarily or was forced into it by his crew. In any event, several vessels were seized by Kidd, who later made for New York, where he learned he was now considered a pirate. With the Tories trying to use this case as a weapon to brand his backers as supporters of piracy, he was an embarrassment to both Bellomont and the high-ranking underwriters of the cruise. Kidd was shipped off to England, where he was tried and hanged for murder and piracy. He maintained that the ships he had taken carried French passes which would have made them legitimate prizes. The passes were sent to London, but were never produced at his trial. Thus, Captain Kidd—the epitome of walk-the-plank piracy—may not have been a pirate at all, but merely the unfortunate victim of politicians interested only in protecting their own necks.

Bellomont's only reward for his dedication to the public welfare was unpopularity and hatred. The merchants who had been doing business with the pirates wailed that his restrictions on trade had cost them a hundred thousand pounds a year. There were mutterings of mutiny, and so deep-grained was the opposition to Bellomont's reforms that he was forced to acknowledge to the Lords of Trade that "in plaine termes I must tell your Lordships that I can have nobody prosecuted here than hath ten pieces of eight." In contrast to the splendor that had surrounded Fletcher, Bellomont lived a lonely life in a house with a leaking roof and flooring in an advanced state of decay. There he died on March 5, 1701, worn out by gout and the frustrations of office.

With Bellomont out of the way, the merchants and land barons rushed to sign a petition circulated by Benjamin Fletcher attesting to the prosperity that had prevailed in the province under his rule. They also subscribed to a ten-thousand-pound bond imposed to insure the appearance of Fletcher in London to face charges of malfeasance, mismanagement, and bribery that had been leveled against him by Bellomont.

With a straight face, Fletcher told the Lords of Trade that he had never prosecuted any pirates because no one had ever brought complaints about them to his attention. He also claimed he had never taken a rake-off from illegal trade, never issued privateering commissions or pardons in return for bribes, and, as far as extravagant land grants were concerned, every one that had been made was approved by his council. He was merely an innocent victim of the Earl of Bellomont's vindictiveness and determination to build a reputation at his expense. Their lordships listened to these lame explanations rather coolly and recommended that the case be referred to the attorney general for action. But Fletcher apparently still had friends in high places—perhaps he put the plunder he had brought back from America to good advantage—and was never brought to trial. He disappeared into the mists of history with the ghost of Bellomont pursuing him on gouty legs and calling down curses upon his head.[14]

* * *

Despite the embittered resistance to Bellomont's drive to rid New York of the scourge of piracy, his efforts were so successful that not even Lord Cornbury, his avaricious and grasping successor, dared have any dealings with the buccaneers. Instead, Cornbury resorted to the traditional methods of corruption, such as soliciting bribes and looting the public treasury, to line his pockets. Undoubtedly the most bizarre character to serve as a royal governor anywhere, Cornbury was a transvestite who delighted in flouncing about before his astonished soldiers in women's clothing. He came to America in 1702 with an impressive list of credentials. Cornbury was the grandson of the Earl of Clarendon, Lord Chancellor under King Charles II and the distinguished historian of the English Civil War, and, even more important, was a cousin of Queen Anne.[15]

Even before leaving England, Cornbury revealed the type of administration he planned for the province. His first action was to name Daniel Honan, Fletcher's go-between with the pirates, as his secretary. Appalled by the choice of this grafter and perjurer, the Lords of Trade demanded that Honan be dismissed. It was all a mistake, replied Cornbury, pretending to be chastised. But he kept Honan at his side throughout his administration.

With this auspicious beginning, Cornbury lost little time in aligning himself with the anti-Leislerians just as Fletcher had done a decade before. And for the same reason—he needed money. The new governor arrived to find Nicholas Bayard under sentence of death on charges of treason for inciting opposition to the pro-Leisler interim governor. Ironically, Bayard had fallen afoul of the very same harsh statute he had helped enact for the entrapment of his political enemies after Leisler's execution. Branding Bayard's arrest and conviction as "the most unjust that were ever heard of or known," Cornbury pardoned the old troublemaker. To show their gratitude, the aristocratic faction awarded his lordship a special grant of two thousand pounds, ostensibly to reimburse him for the expense of his voyage to New York, and doubled his six-hundred-pound-a-year salary.

But Cornbury had come to the province burdened with debt,

and his avarice was unrestrained. His salary and legitimate graft were insufficient to maintain him in the lavish style to which he had become accustomed and he even stole the money appropriated by the assembly for the defense of the colony. When a French warship arrived off Sandy Hook in July 1706 and threatened to attack the town, the inhabitants were shocked to discover that Cornbury had embezzled the funds for a fort at the Narrows and squandered them on a vacation home on Governor's Island. Panic swept over the city. Cursing the governor, the citizens sweated under the blazing summer sun with pick and shovel to throw up earthworks to defend their homes. Luckily, the French were driven off, but the affair had an important effect upon the government of New York and all the American colonies.

As soon as the New Yorkers had gotten over their immediate fright, they took action to prevent themselves from again being endangered by the greed and cupidity of a governor. Every level of society grumbled that it was one thing to accept bribes from pirates or to seek gratuities from landowners for services rendered—after all, no one was hurt by this sort of "honest graft"—but it was quite another to play fast and loose with the security of the province with a bloodthirsty enemy in the offing. To replace the funds stolen by Cornbury, the assembly levied a special tax to be used to properly fortify the Narrows. The legislators, convinced that the governor was no longer to be trusted with public funds, insisted upon appointing a treasurer, answerable only to themselves, to spend the money. Cornbury regarded an independent treasurer as an affront to the royal prerogative—as well as to his pocket—and a bitter battle raged for control of the governmental purse. Much to his dismay, the Lords of Trade in London supported the assembly, granting it the power to appoint the treasurer. Inadvertently, Cornbury and corruption had precipitated the beginnings of responsible government in America.

Seemingly oblivious to the storm he had created, Cornbury was frequently seen at night strolling on the ramparts while wearing a voluminous hoop skirt, elaborate headdress, and flourishing a fan. He apparently fancied that this feminine finery heightened his resemblance to his royal cousin.* Only his relationship to Queen Anne kept him from being recalled in disgrace, and finally even that was not enough. After repeated protests to London, he was dismissed with scant ceremony in 1708. The panoply of office removed, Cornbury's covey of creditors, who were owed several thousand pounds and had been hovering about for some time, descended upon him. Cornbury went from the governor's mansion to a debtor's prison, where he remained until his father's death made him Earl of Clarendon. He left America to the jeers of his former subjects and the verdict of a contemporary historian who wrote: "We never had a governor so universally detested."

The Treaty of Utrecht, which ended Queen Anne's War between England and France, as it was known in America, in 1713, resulted in a new outbreak of piracy, particularly off the Carolina coast, where it flourished under the wing of corrupt officials. The peculiar nature of the coast, especially the Cape Fear area, with its shifting sandbars and shallow sounds, seemed made to order for the needs of the buccaneers and their swift-darting craft. They lay hidden in inlets, often under the protection of the local officials who shared their loot, refitting their ships and taking on supplies until ready to sail again in search of fresh prey.[16]

The most notorious of the Carolina pirates was Edward Thatch, alias Teach and better known as Blackbeard. Blackbeard's early life is a mystery, but he is believed to have served on several privateers during the war with the French. With the coming of peace, like many privateersmen, he was said to have chosen piracy rather than unemployment. A tall man with a hulking

* Cornbury was married and his wife, who died in 1706, seems to have been something of a character, too. According to one account, Cornbury had married her because he had fallen in love with one of her ears. After a while, however, the ear no longer pleased him and he began to withhold her pin money. Lady Cornbury then took up begging and stealing to replace the missing funds. Coats and gowns were borrowed and never returned. When her coach was heard approaching, society ladies made haste to hide their valuables. If her ladyship admired a dress or a piece of jewelry, she was certain to send for it the next day. That would be the last the owner would see of it.

physique, Blackbeard went into battle with his huge, matted beard plaited with ribbons and two slow matches burning behind his ears. Although he has come down to us as the very model of piratical brutality, one authority holds that he treated his prisoners humanely and only fought when he could not avoid it.[17]

Blackbeard was not without a macabre sense of humor. Convinced that he and his men were bound for Hell after they died, the pirate chieftain, on one occasion, summoned his crew below deck for a taste of the afterlife. Battening down the hatches, he lit several pots of brimstone and settled down in the choking darkness to see who would last the longest in this homemade purgatory. Almost suffocated and gasping for breath, the sailors risked Blackbeard's wrath by abandoning the inferno and clambering up into the open air. The last to emerge from "Hell," Blackbeard came on deck with a low opinion of the readiness of his men for the next life.

In an effort to halt the ravages of piracy, the British authorities, acting under an Act of Grace (as it was called), allowed the colonial governors to issue pardons to buccaneers who surrendered and promised to abandon their old way of life. Governor Charles Eden of North Carolina and his secretary, Tobias Knight, turned the issuance of pardons into a rewarding racket. Blackbeard and other pirates surrendered to Eden, and in exchange for a share of their plunder, the governor allowed them to enjoy the limited entertainment offered by Bath, the colony's capital, until they were ready to put to sea again. Upon their return, they were given new pardons for a price. As in New York under Fletcher, everybody benefited—the governor, the pirates, the merchants, and the tavern and brothelkeepers.

On at least one occasion, the cooperative Governor Eden convened a vice-admiralty court presided over by Tobias Knight which solemnly condemned one of Blackbeard's victims as a lawfully taken Spanish prize, even though Britain and Spain were not at war. At another time, Blackbeard sailed into Bath with a French prize loaded with sugar and cocoa which he claimed had been found adrift at sea without a crew or identifying papers. Knight swallowed this tall tale and ruled that Blackbeard was entitled to salvage rights. To hide all evidence of a crime in case the French came looking for the vessel, Blackbeard ordered her to be burned—but not before Eden took sixty, and Knight twenty, hogsheads of sugar as their share of the enterprise. Blackbeard lived a lavish life ashore, often entertaining the governor and his secretary at his fine home. When he married a girl of sixteen—provoking a contemporary comment that this was his fourteenth wife, of whom "a dozen might still be living"—Eden attended the ceremony.

Nevertheless, the protection provided by Eden eventually led to Blackbeard's downfall. Insulated by the governor's favor, Blackbeard did not realize that Eden's views on piracy were not shared by every Carolinian. Not everyone was profiting from Blackbeard's depredations, and some people were scandalized by his reckless and arrogant conduct. Fully realizing they would get no satisfaction from Eden, these citizens turned for help to Governor Alexander Spotswood of Virginia, an implacable foe of the pirates.

After being tipped off that Blackbeard was at Ocracoke Inlet, where he was reported to be preparing to transform a nearby sandspit into "another Madagascar," Spotswood disregarded the fact that his authority did not extend into North Carolina and dispatched two small vessels to deal with the buccaneer. They were manned by about fifty-five men under the command of Lieutenant Robert Maynard of the Royal Navy. On November 2, 1718, Maynard cornered Blackbeard, and in bloody, hand-to-hand combat killed the infamous pirate and captured the remnants of his crew. With Blackbeard's severed head stuck on the bowsprit of his vessel as a trophy, Maynard sailed back to Virginia in triumph.

Among the pirate's effects, Maynard discovered a letter from Knight containing a veiled warning of the punitive expedition and advising the buccaneer to make his getaway before it was sighted. The letter also expressed Eden's friendship for Blackbeard. Several of the captured pirates also linked Knight to Blackbeard in an attempt to save their own necks. Spotswood sent the incriminating evidence to Eden and carefully dispatched a report to the Lords of Trade. Eden now faced a dilemma. With the charges against his secretary known in London, he could not ignore them; yet there was the danger that if Knight were placed on trial, he might implicate his master. The governor resolved the problem by turning the matter over to his council, which included Knight among its members. The council quickly found the evidence against their colleague "false and malicious."

Outraged, Edward Mosely and Maurice Moore, two prominent Carolinians who had been among the first to complain to Governor Spotswood about Blackbeard's depredations, sought evidence to tie Eden to the pirates.[18] They went to Knight's office in Bath to inspect the public records only to discover the governor had ordered them sequestered. That night, Mosely and Moore burglarized the place in an attempt to seize the documents, but were arrested by an armed posse dispatched by Eden. "The governor could find men enough to arrest peaceable citizens, but none to arrest thieves and robbers," commented the contemptuous Mosely. Eden saw to it that Mosely and Moore were hauled into the General Court, fined, and barred from holding public office for three years. Blackbeard would have roared with laughter at the irony of it all.

III

Prelude to Revolution

UNBRIDLED KLEPTOMANIA ON both sides of the Atlantic helped
bring on the American Revolution. In fact, it is entirely within the
realm of possibility that had not corruption become one of America's major growth industries, the final break with Britain might
have been avoided—at least for a while. Accelerating expansion
and prosperity had made the American colonies a prime source
of graft by the middle of the eighteenth century. From a perilous
bridgehead on a hostile coast they had grown into a thriving,
soon-to-be independent nation of nearly two million souls.[1] Britain's final victory in 1763 over France in the Great War for Empire had removed the threat of French attack upon the frontier,
and the Americans, thirsting for new worlds to conquer, had
already taken the first tentative steps across the Appalachians
into the unspoiled lands which lay beyond the mountain barrier.
"Westward the course of empire takes its way," intoned Bishop
George Berkeley somewhat majestically—and graft and corruption propelled the settlers on their way.

Unhappily for the Yankees, Britain had been far too successful
in her long struggle with France for control of North America.
The expulsion of the French permitted the more grasping British
politicians to turn their undivided attention to the internal affairs of the colonies. Like the citizens of modern underdeveloped

42

nations, most Americans tolerated a certain level of graft as the necessary price of progress. As long as corruption seemed to show some benefit, they accepted its evils with little more than a shrug. But they were to be dragged into a cesspool of bribery, favoritism, and privilege that had long been a chief feature of British politics—and revolution was the result.

The Treaty of Paris left the Union Jack flying without a rival from Hudson Bay to the Florida Keys and from the Atlantic Coast to the Mississippi. This new empire would have to be protected against any attempt by the French or Spaniards to again try to wrest control of it. Yet Britain had emerged financially exhausted from the long struggle and felt she was unable to assume the total cost of defense. The British national debt had nearly doubled over seven years of war from 72 million pounds to 132 million pounds. Trade was in the doldrums, and the cost of living was soaring. A four-pound loaf of bread, once sold for a penny, had increased two and one-half times in price. Beef and mutton, which had cost about four pence a pound, now commanded up to three times as much. Rampaging mobs of English countrymen had rioted against the imposition of a new tax on cider, closing off an avenue of revenue—and providing the Americans with a vivid lesson in how to nullify an unpopular tax.

For decades, Britain's colonial policy had been one of "salutary neglect." Sir Robert Walpole, the Whig prime minister who had maintained a tight grip on the reins of power from 1721 to 1742 through a mixture of judicious bribery and nimble manipulation, had declined to tax the colonies. He believed unrestricted trade and growth would bring more gold into Britain's coffers than taxes or customs duties. Walpole's successors, however, decided that the Americans should bear the burden of paying for their own defense inasmuch as they derived most of the benefit from it. As long as the French and their Indian allies had terrorized frontier settlements, the Americans had welcomed the security and protection offered by the British army. There were no more vocally loyal subjects of the Crown anywhere. But with the removal of this threat, the Yankees expected less interference from Britain in their affairs—not more. They saw no need to maintain an army of ten thousand men in America and flatly refused to pay their share of the 350,000 pounds a year it cost to support these troops.

George Grenville, the prime minister in the immediate postwar period, resorted to the Acts of Trade and Navigation to make up for the missing revenues. This was a fatal mistake. For decades, the enforcement of these laws—designed to subordinate the economic interests of the colonies to that of Britain—had been purposely lax. The colonists had grown used to either ignoring or evading these regulations. Grenville's determination to put an end to graft and corruption in the collection of customs duties came as a deep shock to Yankee merchants who had come to regard smuggling as a way of life. It was the foundation upon which many a colonial fortune rested, including those of the Hancocks of Boston and the Browns of Providence.

Smuggling had long been permitted by the British officials sent to America to regulate trade. It was reckoned that it cost the British government about eight thousand pounds to collect two thousand pounds in duties. Everyone viewed the government as fair game. Ranking posts in the customs service were regarded as sinecures for political appointees who never left England. Their poorly paid agents were discovered by the colonial merchants to be "needy Wretches who found it easier and more profitable, not only to wink but sleep in their own beds; the Merchants' Pay being more generous than the King's." James Otis, a leader of pre-Revolutionary Boston, noted that "a very small office in the customs in America has raised a man a fortune. . . ." One collector had a visible salary of one hundred pounds a year—but "earned" six thousand Spanish dollars annually.[2]

Smuggling had become so vital to colonial commerce that not even war could halt it. While the merchants mouthed patriotic slogans, they traded with the French. For example, an angry General Edward Braddock was informed in 1755 that as many as forty ships, mostly from New York, Rhode Island, and Boston, had been spotted at one time unloading provisions for the enemy at the fortress of Louisburg on Cape Breton Island in Canada. While Braddock was preparing to lead his troops and their American allies into the wilderness, the French were being supplied with food and forage for the coming campaign. British military officers might brand this traffic as traitorous, but the Yankee merchants merely regarded it as good business. In exchange for flour and meat, they received large quantities of wines, silks, and produce from the French West Indian islands which were sold for high prices. What were the lives of a few rum-soaked soldiers to their profits?

When war was declared against the French in 1756 and it became impossible for ships flying the British flag to sail openly into French ports, the merchants altered their tactics. Products intended for the enemy were now carried to neutral ports, where they were transferred to French ships in exchange for contraband. The illicit trade between Rhode Island and the French was so great that Lord Loudoun, the British commander-in-chief, thundered that the Newport merchants were all "a lawless set of smugglers."

Some crafty Yankee traders wrapped their operations in humanitarianism and resorted to flag-of-truce ships to maintain their trade in contraband. These vessels had special permits to carry a few prisoners that were to be exchanged for captives held by the French, but their main purpose was to exchange colonial products for French goods. Permits were hawked about Newport, New York, and Philadelphia for as much as four hundred guineas each until Governor William Denny of Pennsylvania sold them in wholesale lots for twenty pounds. There is little doubt that this illegal trade sustained the French military and naval effort.[3]

Although the names of those trading with the enemy were widely known, customs officials exhibited a singular inability to lay violators by the heels. The reason was obvious. Trading in contraband was big business; those involved were usually men of wealth and influence, and they often acted in concert with the authorities. The power of the illicit traders is shown by the fate of George Spencer, a patriotic New Yorker who wrote an article for a local paper setting out the facts concerning trade with the enemy. Among those named as participants were two justices of the New York Supreme Court. Spencer was set upon by a mob, pelted with garbage, and finally arrested on a false charge for his trouble.

In an attempt to put an end to this sordid trade which placed profits above patriotism, the British government authorized the use of writs of assistance and singled out Massachusetts for this special treatment. These writs authorized customs officials to call upon sheriffs and other local officers to assist them in their duties, and permitted them to enter private warehouses and homes in search of contraband. An attempt in 1760 by a customs official in Salem to search for smuggled goods stirred a hornet's nest of opposition. The Massachusetts merchants, convinced that they were being unfairly discriminated against because the law was only being applied to them, hired James Otis to take the matter to the courts. The Boston traders were not men to sit idly by while the pious Quakers of Rhode Island piled up fortunes.

To John Adams, who was present in the courtroom, Otis "was a flame of fire" whose very words seemed to rouse his large audience to the point where they were ready "to take up arms against the Writs of Assistance." Otis denounced the statute of Parliament that legalized the writs, raising a fundamental question as to what extent could the British government exercise sovereign powers in the American colonies. The legality of the writs was upheld, but as far as Adams was concerned, "then and there, the child Independence was born." If this is so, most Americans have conveniently forgotten that it was sired by corruption out of cupidity.

George Grenville's abilities as a financier were open to question, but he was truly horrified by the conditions which prevailed in the customs service in America. He moved to put an end to the 700,000-pound-a-year smuggling trade by ordering the Royal Navy to enforce the Navigation Acts. Colonial commerce depended not so much upon violation of these laws as ignoring them, and Grenville's decision to use the navy as a floating customs service caused a shudder of apprehension among the colonial merchants. "Men of war, cutters, marines with their bayonets fixed, judges of admiralty, collectors, comptrollers, searchers . . . with a whole catalogue of pimps are sent hither, not to protect our trade but to distress it," objected a memorial from Boston.

When the navy's efforts to suppress smuggling did little to ease the burden on Britain's treasury, Grenville and his successors resorted to additional—and equally offensive—measures such as the Stamp Act, the Sugar Act, the Townshend duties, and other levies to raise revenues. Even in the best of times, however, these taxes would have been onerous considering the high taxes already being levied in the colonies. The postwar depression brought no relief and tax delinquencies soared. Samuel Adams, one of the Boston tax collectors, ended an eight-year term in office in 1764 with a deficiency of at least eight thousand pounds in his accounts. Some of the more zealous of Adams's Tory detractors later charged that he had pocketed the money. In reality, these arrearages were merely evidence of Adams's inability to collect the taxes because of economic conditions.

But even if the Yankees had been able to pay their taxes and had considered them just, they might still have rebelled, for they were convinced their money was being shoveled into the insatiable maw of a corrupt political system. The youthful King George III came to the throne in 1760 with a determination to regain the authority lost by the apathy of his two predecessors. He brought to power as predatory a cabal as ever seen in the annals of British politics. Known as the "Bloomsbury gang," from the section of London being developed by its chief, the grossly corrupt Duke of Bedford, this group became the king's instrument to humble the Whig oligarchy that had held the reins of power since the death of Queen Anne in 1714.

The structure of politics at the time suited the king's purpose. Parties were rudimentary and based less upon ideology or principle than upon personality and the prospect for loot. Prime ministers maintained slush funds to buy the votes of their party members for measures to which they were supposedly pledged. "Rotten boroughs"—districts actually owned by magnates who told the handful of eligible voters how to cast their ballots—were a common political phenomenon. In some cases, seats in Parliament were openly advertised for sale by the small groups of electors who controlled them. They pocketed the fees and turned out on the hustings to hear themselves described as the bulwark of the British Constitution. During the election of 1768, Benjamin Franklin, then in London, sourly observed: "Four thousand pounds is now the market price for a borough. In short, this whole venal nation is now at market, [and] will be sold for about two millions, and might be bought out of the hands of the present bidders (if he would offer half a million more) by the very Devil himself."*

Offices, pensions, and perquisites were the weapons used by George III to achieve his goal of dominating Parliament. Those who supported the king received their share of the "great plum pudding"; recalcitrants were shorn of sinecures and cast out. The system worked to perfection. A party of royal favorites—the "King's Friends"—became the major force in Parliament. Operating independently of both Whigs and Tories, they served the prejudices and obsessions of their master. As Bernard Bailyn has pointed out, the conviction took root among the colonists that there was a deliberate and sinister conspiracy to upset the balance of the Constitution, and to at least severely restrict—if not completely subvert—the liberties to which they were entitled as freeborn Englishmen. And the handmaiden of this conspiracy was the corruption coursing through every vein of British politics. It was a parody of a constant theme of American thought— American innocence as opposed to European decadence.

To their utter dismay, the Americans noted that for the first time there was a sufficient number of posts in the colonial service worthy of the attention of persons of influence in England. The ministry needed jobs to maintain its majority in Parliament, so it was feared that the colonies would be flooded with jobholders who, as Franklin said, would come "only to make money as fast as they can." Not only did this mean that control of colonial graft would pass out of the hands of the Americans themselves, it also raised the threat that the "baneful harpies" who would replace them might be merciless in their enforcement of oppressive trade laws and taxes—or equally rapacious in their demands for bribes to look the other way. They would be "like dogs of prey thirsting after the fortunes of worthy and wealthy men." Creeping corruption thus became one of the most potent forces unifying Ameri-

* For once, the good doctor was wrong. That year a three-way contest for a pair of seats representing Northampton cost the enormous sum of 160,000 pounds—or about eighty pounds for every vote cast.

cans, tugging them toward opposition to the policies of the Crown and eventual independence.[4]

The reaction to these fundamental and almost universal grievances was fanned to fever heat by such radicals as Sam Adams, who was in the process of creating a new kind of political power. Everyone knew of William Pitt, who had controlled Parliament through eloquence. They knew of Walpole, who had dominated British politics through graft. And now they were to learn of the power of political organization. Adams had been left comfortably fixed upon the death of his father, a psalm-singing merchant and brewer who had no qualms about drawing rents from properties used as brothels and waterfront dives. His son, however, lacked the old man's knack for making money, and rapidly dissipated his inheritance in a hapless series of commercial misadventures. Unable to manage his own affairs with any degree of success, Adams turned to politics and the management of the affairs of others. Revolution soon became his business, and it was the only successful enterprise he ever undertook.

Adams owed his political success to his affinity for the ordinary folk of Boston. He had a wide acquaintance among the town's carpenters, blacksmiths, and tradesmen which had been broadened by his years as a tax collector. By the 1750s, the growing number of freemen in Boston, led by skilled manipulators such as Adams, took the town meeting out of the hands of the gentry and ran it as a branch of the Caucus Club which they controlled. Adams's younger cousin, John, reported that the club met in the garret of Tom Dawes's house on Purchase Street. "There they smoke tobacco, till you cannot see from one End of the Garret to the other. There they drink Phlip . . . and there selectmen, Assessors, Collectors, Wardens, Firewards, and representatives, are Regularly chosen before they are chosen in the town."[5] The smoke-filled room has a long tradition in American politics.

Adams had decided upon eventual independence for the colonies as his goal long before this bold idea crossed the minds of other colonial leaders. He shrewdly converted the Caucus Club and its interest in political spoils into an engine of revolution. Strange alliances resulted—none odder than that formed between Adams and John Hancock, the wealthiest merchant in Massachusetts. Orphaned early in life, Hancock had been adopted by his uncle, Thomas Hancock, who had amassed a fortune through a deft disregard of the Navigation Acts. In 1764, the old man died, and at the age of twenty-seven, John Hancock became a millionaire. He not only inherited his uncle's penchant for smuggling but believed that it was his inalienable right to pay no taxes to the Crown on the goods brought to Boston by his large fleet of ships. Thus, he showed his patriotic principles—and saved himself a considerable sum in duties. "King" Hancock, as the Tories dubbed him, was none too bright, and as Adams soon discovered, had a pathetic desire to be liked. In return for the plaudits of the Caucus Club and the radical Sons of Liberty—all carefully orchestrated by Adams—Hancock became the financial angel and front man for the revolutionary movement in Massachusetts.

This combination of Machiavellian political agitator and millionaire smuggler soon touched off an explosion. The crisis occurred in June 1768, when the Boston customs officials got wind of the fact that Hancock had smuggled a valuable cargo of wine into the port in one of his ships. The customs men boarded the *Liberty* and demanded to inspect her cargo. Showing scant respect for the king's agents, the crew locked them below deck, and with the aid of scores of volunteers unloaded the wine. When this work was done, the agents were tossed overboard amid the cheers of a sizable crowd that had gathered to watch the fun. The mob then went on a rampage. The hapless customs officials decided that the time had come to flee to Castle William in the harbor, putting three miles of open water between themselves and the mob.

Boston was not alone in defending its right to enjoy French wines and other fruits of smuggling. The merchants of Providence and Newport, who had grown wealthy through illicit trade, were disconcerted in March 1772, when the armed British schooner *Gaspée*, commanded by Lieutenant William Dudingston, appeared off the Rhode Island coast. Dudingston was something new in the experience of the Rhode Island smugglers—a naval officer who was determined to stamp out illegal trade without regard to the tender sensibilities of the colony's "best families." The *Gaspée* began aggressively patrolling Narragansett Bay, snapping up vessels belonging to the Providence and Newport smugglers with unhappy regularity.

The merchants were so angry that Newport buzzed with rumors that they were planning to send out an armed ship to rescue any vessel taken by the *Gaspée* for violation of the anti-smuggling laws. The opportunity for action presented itself on June 9, 1772, when the schooner ran aground on a shoal near Providence while giving chase to a suspicious-looking craft. That night a lone drummer paraded through the town urging all citizens to join a secret expedition aimed at disposing of the hated *Gaspée* once and for all. Eight longboats, their oars muffled and with crews armed with staves, stones, and a few firearms, slipped silently down the bay to where the stranded vessel lay. Alarmed by the approach of the unidentified boats, Dudingston threatened to fire his cannon into them. Before the order was issued, a Yankee sharpshooter drew a bead on the officer and badly wounded him. The Americans stormed aboard the *Gaspée* and overwhelmed her crew. They stripped the schooner of all valuables, set the painfully wounded captain and his men adrift in a small boat, and put the vessel to the torch. She made a lovely light to guide them as they rowed back to their homes.

If they had been efficiently and honestly collected, quit rents, a form of feudal land tax due to the Crown, would have reduced Britain's reliance on the galling Acts of Trade and Navigation and the accompanying series of nuisance taxes that precipitated the American Revolution.* But so well had generations of greedy royal governors and their American accomplices done their work that quit rents, designed to produce continuing revenue for the Crown, brought in negligible returns. As early as the middle of

---

* Quit rents were not exorbitant and were usually fixed at two shillings for each hundred acres.

the eighteenth century, it was charged that all the fertile and readily accessible land on the eastern slopes of the Appalachians had passed into the hands of a small, avaricious group of land-grabbers. As a result, total quit rents from all the colonies amounted to only sixteen thousand pounds. Virginia alone provided half this sum, while South Carolina, where the rent rolls had long since disappeared, provided nothing.[6]

The amount of land left to grant was so limited that Governor George Clinton of New York complained in 1743 that the value of the post had been grossly misrepresented at the time it was offered him. It would require a decade rather than the two years he had counted upon in which to make his fortune. Clinton appealed to the Lords of Trade to help him out of a bad bargain by increasing his salary and widening his opportunities for legitimate graft. One need shed no tears over Clinton's plight, however. The governor was so corrupt, noted one sardonic observer, that "he would have done anything for you for his bottle and present." In spite of Clinton's impassioned protestations of imminent poverty, he had no trouble in amassing a fortune estimated at over eighty thousand pounds by the time he retired to England.

In the absence of most of the vehicles for investment that we take for granted today, land was the favorite object of speculation in the eighteenth century. The teachings of the French physiocrats, who held that all wealth was ultimately derived from ownership of the soil, had a strong influence on the thinking of Americans. So did their memories of the high land values prevailing in the Old World and of the social prestige automatically enjoyed by the owners of broad acres. All these factors combined to produce an insatiable lust for land in colonial America. Such prominent members of the Revolutionary generation as George Washington, Benjamin Franklin, Patrick Henry, and Robert Morris were all deeply involved in land speculation.[7]

Concentration of the lands to the east of the Appalachians in fewer and fewer hands directed the covetous eyes of the land speculators toward the vast unsettled areas west of the mountains. The prospects for clever operators were dazzling. The initial investment didn't have to be lavish, as the land was not bought but secured from the Crown or the colonial governments for the asking—as long as one knew who to ask and had greased the way with well-placed bribes. After all, reasoned the speculators, land was worthless without settlers, and they promised to populate the land. Settlement would bring rising prices—and profits to the speculators. Thus, for the expenditure of only a few hundred pounds in bribes and a promise of a generous share of the boodle to interested British and colonial officials, grants often totaling several hundred thousand acres in size were handed out.

In the mid-eighteenth century, fingers of settlement already poked into the heartland of the continent along a dozen rivers and streams from the Merrimack to the Savannah, but the West was still largely the realm of the Indian, the fur trapper, the trader, and the soldier. Serious problems would have to be overcome before the speculators could gain control of this virgin territory. Not only did the usual dangers of the frontier have to be met, but the very title to the area was in doubt. It wasn't that anybody cared about the Indians. Enunciating a policy that Americans were to follow for the next century and a half, Lord Jeffrey Amherst described the Indians as "more nearly allied to the Brute than to Human Creation. I am fully resolved whenever they give me an occasion to extirpate them root and branch."

The basic problem was that most of the colonies had no fixed boundaries and claimed a share of the West as part of their original charter grants. Inasmuch as these limits could not for the most part be pinpointed with any degree of certainty, claims conflicted and overlapped. Disputes often flared up among the colonies and between the competing land companies over the ownership of various tracts and the right to exploit them. For example, the same grants were claimed by Pennsylvania and Virginia, while South Carolina, Virginia, and Maryland were rivals for identical western lands. Two Virginia companies—the Ohio Company and the Loyal Company—were in conflict as to the site of their patents. The claims of the London grafters had to be taken into account, too. Parliament insisted that the West belonged to the Crown—to be distributed only as the king or his advisors thought best. Thus there was always the threat that Parliament might uphold a grant made by one colony over another—or it might even rule that all claims were invalid, and the land belonged to the Crown. Settlers moving west found themselves venturing into a minefield sown with greed, deception, and illegality.

One of the most notorious of the speculative land operations was the Susquehanna Company, organized in 1753 by a group of Connecticut entrepreneurs that included the governor, Roger Walcott. Having run out of land in their own colony, they took advantage of Connecticut's broad charter, which invested it with "all land westward to the South Sea," to try to obtain title to some two hundred square miles along the Susquehanna River. The fact that this tract was clearly within the confines of the Wyoming Valley in Pennsylvania did not daunt this tight little band of ambitious land-grabbers. Lawyers, politicians, and clergymen eagerly snapped up shares in the enterprise despite its questionable beginnings. Among them was the Reverend Ezra Stiles, later president of Yale College, who saw nothing wrong with a little claim-jumping.

Although the promoters didn't have a shred of legal sanction, they boldly announced that they would form a new province in the Susquehanna area. John Henry Lydius, a Dutch trader with a shady reputation, was employed to "buy" the land from the Indians. He proceeded to invite several chiefs from the Six Nations to his home in Albany, got them gloriously drunk, and then pushed a deed under their noses. Not until settlers began edging into their hunting grounds did the chiefs realize what they had signed. "That man is the devil and has stole our lands!" cried an Indian spokesman, pointing an accusatory finger at Lydius as the tribes sought redress from Sir William Johnson, the Superintendent of Indian Affairs. "He takes Indians slyly by the blanket one at a time, and when they are drunk puts money in their bosoms and persuades them to sign deeds for our lands upon the Susquehanna, which we will not ratify nor suffer to be settled by any means."

As usual, Indian eloquence and anger failed to prevail against the avarice of white land-grabbers. The Connecticut speculators sold tracts in their new territory as fast as settlers would buy them—and left the purchasers to learn at their own peril of the opposition of the Indians and the Pennsylvanians to their presence. Not only did the unwitting settlers have to contend with the danger of being scalped by hostile Indians, they also had to be ready to fight pitched battles with the Pennsylvanians, who resisted their intrusions with arms. But the speculators did not care. While smoke rose from burning cabins up and down the Wyoming Valley, they raked in profits from the sale of questionable land titles. So bitter was the struggle between Connecticut and Pennsylvania that when the French and Indian War broke out, the two colonies seemed more likely to fight each other than the French.[8]

Land-jobbing was big business. Between 1743 and 1760, the Virginia authorities alone granted over three million acres of western lands to groups and individuals—a sizable portion of it in conflicting claims or under the control of the French. For example, the Ohio Company, formed in 1748 by representatives of the leading tidewater Virginia families (including the Washingtons, the Dinwiddies, the Lees, the Carters, and the Fairfaxes), received a grant of 500,000 acres west of the Alleghenies adjacent to Virginia. The next year, another group of equally distinguished Virginians formed the Loyal Company which claimed 800,000 acres nearby. The rival companies set about securing their grants by sending surveyors to the western lands and lobbyists to London to obtain the British government's sanction for their land-grabbing schemes. The way was smoothed for such approval by scattering shares in the companies among the officials involved.

French reaction to the efforts of the English to extend their control was swift. They reinforced their troops in the Ohio region. Alarmed at what he considered to be an invasion of Virginia's boundaries, Governor Robert Dinwiddie dispatched a twenty-one-year-old land surveyor named George Washington to warn the French that they were trespassing on British soil—the territory reserved for the Ohio Company, in which both the governor and his messenger had a stake. Land-jobbing had set in motion the events which were to result in the eventual expulsion of the French from their holdings in North America.

The French and Indian War only temporarily interrupted the fertile schemes of the speculators to gain control of the West. As soon as the Treaty of Paris ending the war was signed in 1763, they were once again eager for new acquisitions. No one had more ambitious plans than the young Washington, who was destined not only to become first in war and first in peace, but also first in land speculation. "Land is the most permanent estate and the most likely to increase in value," he declared as he turned his eyes westward. Later in life, Washington professed to be disdainful of land speculation. "From long experience of many years," he wrote in 1794, "I have found distant property in land more pregnant of perplexities than profit." But this was said well after he had laid the foundations for one of the largest fortunes in America through practices which have aroused considerable controversy ever since.

The exultations of the land-jobbers at the end of the French and Indian War were rudely interrupted by the news that the Indians, led by Chief Pontiac, had taken to the warpath. Fearing that they were to be driven from their hunting grounds by the advancing line of white settlement, they fell upon the outlying settlements with fire and tomahawk. To placate the Indians, the British government hastily issued the Proclamation of 1763, which established a line of demarcation—roughly along the summit of the Alleghenies—beyond which no one could settle or purchase land. Squatters who were already west of the line were ordered to move forthwith, and lands promised by Governor Dinwiddie as a bounty to veterans of the French and Indian War were withdrawn.

While the land speculators and frontiersmen objected to the restrictions, they did not believe at first that the proclamation represented a permanent British policy. Sooner or later, they were convinced, the West would again be opened to settlement. Their primary fear, however, was that during the period in which the proclamation was in effect, British promoters would bribe the corrupt ministers to grant them the most desirable lands in the area—and beat them to it. "One half of England is now land mad and everybody there has their eye fixed on this country," observed George Croghan, a leading American land speculator. No self-respecting Yankee was going to allow himself to be deprived of rich land that lay ready for the taking by a mere scrap of paper issued by a pack of corrupt officials lolling in the safety of their London clubs.

George Washington was no exception. Although the proclamation dashed the plans of Washington and other shareholders in a newly formed Mississippi Company that tried to secure a grant of two and a half million acres near the junction of the Ohio and Mississippi Rivers, it did not dampen his enthusiasm for speculation in western lands. Washington was so convinced of the temporary nature of the restrictions on settlement of the West that he secretly dispatched a land surveyor named William Crawford to the back country with instructions to search out and preempt the best locations. "Any person . . . who neglects the present opportunity of hunting out good lands, and in some way marking and distinguishing them for his own, in order to keep others from settling them, will never regain it," he told Crawford. "I would recommend that you keep this whole matter a secret . . . because I might be censured for the opinion I have given in respect to the King's proclamation, and then, if the scheme I am now proposing to you were known, it might give the alarm to others." With a deviousness that would have astounded Parson Weems, the creator of the cherry-tree legend, he added: "All this may be avoided by silent management, and the operation snugly carried on by you under the guise of hunting other game."

In 1768, as Washington had predicted, the proclamation line was modified, and the West was again thrown open to settlement. Washington went to work, as one biographer has said, "like a man with twenty hands" to make certain that he got a large share of the new lands.[9] Almost immediately, he began wheeling and dealing for immediate distribution of 200,000 acres of bounty land which Governor Dinwiddie promised to the volunteers who had followed him into the wilderness in 1754. Historians are still debating whether Washington was entitled to any of this land or if by sharp practice he gained a significant part of a grant that was clearly intended for his soldiers. Bernhard Knollenberg, who devoted considerable study to Washington's acquisition of the bounty lands, believes that Washington was not entitled to a single acre of the property that became the foundation of his fortune.[10]

It is Knollenberg's argument that this land was earmarked as a reward only for the enlisted men of the First Virginia Regiment, and as their colonel, Washington was to have no share it.* He points out that the title of Dinwiddie's proclamation—"A Proclamation for Encouraging Men to enlist in his Majesty's Service for the Defense and Security of this Colony"—indicates that it was intended as an incentive for men to enlist rather than to persuade officers to accept commissions. He feels that the intention to include the enlisted men is also made plain by the statement that the land was to be "granted to such Persons who by their voluntary Engagement and good Behaviour in the said Service shall deserve the same ... in a Proportion due to their respective Merit, as shall be represented to me by their Officers." This, according to Knollenberg, implies that the officers themselves were not to share in the bounty land.

Yet, when Washington submitted a petition to the governor of Virginia and his council in 1769 requesting distribution of the lands promised the veterans by Dinwiddie, he not only included the soldiers but himself and the other officers as well. By this means, observes Knollenberg, he managed to obtain in excess of twenty thousand acres to which he was not originally entitled.† As the guiding hand in the plan to obtain the land, Washington was ordered by the Virginia authorities to publish notices alerting the claimants to the forthcoming distribution and to arrange for a survey to be paid for by the petitioners. He gave this appointment to William Crawford, who had been secretly earmarking land in

---

* It should be noted, however, that James T. Flexner, one of Washington's leading biographers, states Knollenberg has erred in holding that officers were barred from obtaining land under Dinwiddie's proclamation.

† Washington and two other field-grade officers each received 15,000 acres. Washington also obtained 5,147 acres through claims purchased from others. Privates received 400 acres each.

the Ohio country for him. Washington received as his share what he later frankly acknowledged to be "the cream of the country"— including most of the rich bottomland.

As soon as the other officers had the opportunity to inspect their grants, there were apparent objections to their former commander's land-grabbing activities. Crawford notified Washington that some of the officers were "a good deal shagreened" to discover that he had appropriated the best of the bottom land. Washington imperiously shrugged off these complaints. He said that he had borne "the greater part of the expense attending this business" and "if it had not been for my unremitting attention . . . not a single acre of land would ever have been obtained." To one complainant, a Major George Muse, who charged that he had not been given his rightful share of land, Washington wrote a scathing letter which must have scorched the hands of the recipient: "I would advise you to be more cautious in writing me a second [letter] of the same tenour; for though I understand you were drunk when you did it, yet give me leave to tell you that drunkness is no excuse for rudeness; and that, but for your stupidity and sotishness you might have known, by attending to the public Gazettes . . . that you had your full quantity of ten thousand acres of Land allowed you." As a parting blow, Washington advised the major that he was sorry that he had ever agreed to help "so ungrateful and dirty a fellow as you are."

Instead of long concerning himself with such irritations, however, Washington was laying plans for the settlement of his lands with tenants in the mold of the English aristocracy rather than selling them to small farmers. Although he offered farms rent-free at first, no one accepted because the leases would expire after "three lives." Thus, the tenant's great-grandchildren would have to hand back the land, including all improvements, to Washington's heirs. No one wished to risk their lives and labor under such an arrangement when freeholds could be found elsewhere. So, the man who was to lead the embattled small farmers of America in battle for their rights was forced to turn to recruiting indentured servants in Germany, Scotland, and Ireland for his own lands.

Before Washington could populate his acres, however, several legal obstacles threatened to cost him his holdings, according to Knollenberg. It was discovered that Crawford had not taken the oath of office required by surveyors of Crown land. This meant his surveys would be declared void. On April 3, 1775, just two weeks before Lexington and Concord, a worried Washington wrote Lord Dunmore, Virginia's governor, that if the patents were voided and new surveys required, all those who had received land would suffer severe hardship. Knollenberg notes that Washington tried to insinuate that all the grantees would suffer alike if Crawford's surveys were tossed out. But in reality, he points out, "the officers, other than Washington himself . . . stood to benefit if a new survey were required since they would then be in a position to insist on receiving a proportionate share of the valuable bottom lands granted to Washington . . . on the basis of Crawford's surveys."

Knollenberg adds that Washington had another reason not shared by the other landholders for opposing a resurvey. By including only rich bottomland in Washington's tract, Crawford violated a Virginia law requiring that grants of Crown land be in tracts not more than three times as long as they were broad. It was obvious that Washington's patents violated this statute in order to include the bottomland. "If new surveys were made by a surveyor who had taken the oaths of office," remarks Knollenberg, "he presumably would be unwilling to perjure himself by submitting surveys which violated the law."

Lord Dunmore notified Washington on April 18, 1775, that the patents would be declared null and void, but the whole issue was rendered moot by the outbreak of the Revolution. It remained in limbo for three years—until 1778, when the Virginia legislature approved a law upholding the original surveys and grants. "No matter how vulnerable they may have been before," notes Knollenberg, "the patents issued to Washington on the basis of Crawford's surveys would now be validated if the people of Virginia succeeded in establishing the independence for which they were fighting."

The Proclamation of 1763, that bane of the land speculators, was also a source of Washington's vast western land holdings. In addition to its other provisions, the proclamation had provided for the distribution of Crown lands to "reduced" officers who had served in America until the end of the French and Indian War. Knollenberg maintains that the term *reduced officers* meant those who had remained with their regiments until they were disbanded. Washington was not included in this category as he had resigned his commission long before his regiment furled its colors. This did not stop him from plotting to obtain a share of the land, however. Acting as deviously as he had when he had sent out Crawford before the modification of the proclamation line, Washington suggested to his brother Charles that he buy up the rights of some of the soldiers for him. "I should be glad if you would (in a joking way, rather than in earnest, at first) see what value they set upon their lands." At the same time, Washington somehow persuaded Lord Dunmore to include him in the distribution of land. In 1773, he received a grant of five thousand acres, the amount allowed "reduced" colonels. Thus, as Knollenberg points out, Washington—who had no rights at all to bounty lands— secured twenty thousand acres on his own, plus those he purchased from others. At the time of his death, in 1799, land in the Ohio Valley constituted more than 40 percent of the total appraised value of his estate of $488,339.[11]

Knollenberg's conclusions regarding Washington's ethics in his speculative operations in western lands have raised the hackles of idolators. He found there was apparently some foundation for a hostile contemporary biographical sketch which called Washington "avaricious under the specious appearance of disinterestedness—particularly eager in engrossing large tracts of land." Knollenberg is particularly harsh in his condemnation of Washington's acquisitions of lands which were actually due to his men under Dinwiddie's proclamation of 1754. "The more he got of the 200,000 acres, the less was available for the enlisted men to whom it was promised," the historian remarks. "Furthermore, Washington's engrossing of the land at the expense of the officers who contributed to the cost of employing Crawford to make the surveys for this joint account is difficult to defend." Such opinions are not confined to iconoclasts. Even so passionate and articulate a defender of Washington's reputation as James T. Flexner is forced to acknowledge "it cannot be denied that . . . in

this one aspect of his career he acted as an oversharp businessman."[12]

Nothing so angered the land speculators and made these basically conservative gentlemen as susceptible to the siren song of
independence as the cynical refusal of British politicos to provide
fair value in return for the bribes they had extracted. After all,
reasoned the speculators, an independent government, which
they stood a fair chance to dominate, would probably cast a
benevolent eye on their schemes. A graphic illustration of the
English grafters' wolfish delight in exploiting the hopes—and
pocketbooks—of Yankee land-jobbers is the story of the Grand
Ohio Company and its efforts to establish a fourteenth colony in
the western wilderness.[13]

This ambitious enterprise had its roots in the claims of a group
of Indian traders for reparations for losses sustained during
Pontiac's uprising in 1763. Under the leadership of Samuel
Wharton of the Philadelphia firm of Baynton, Wharton & Morgan, the so-called "suffering traders" banded together into the
Indiana Company to obtain a tract of a million and a half acres
west of the Ohio River from the British government. Benjamin
Franklin was persuaded to support the project by his illegitimate
son, William, the governor of New Jersey. In exchange for a share
of the profits, the old man became an eager promoter of one of
the largest land deals ever concocted on the American continent.
Franklin, in London at the time, won the support of the Earl of
Shelburne, the official concerned with colonial affairs, but before
anything could be accomplished, the vagaries of British politics
brought in a ministry less sympathetic to the Americans.

Discouraged from obtaining the grant from the Crown, the
speculators altered their plans. Instead of winning the approval
of the British government and getting land from the Indians
later, they decided to negotiate with the Indians first and then
seek confirmation of the treaty in London. In 1768, Sir William
Johnson, the British government's Indian agent and a shareholder in the Indiana Company, called the northern tribes together for a giant powwow at Fort Stanwix, near the present site

of Rome, New York. After two months of nightly feasting and the draining of countless barrels of rum, a treaty was signed. It not only modified the western limits of the colonies as established by the Proclamation of 1763, but also resulted in the sale by the Indians of some two and a half million acres to a syndicate representing the "suffering traders." The price for a tract that later made up most of the state of West Virginia was 10,460 pounds.

Armed with this agreement—which at least gave the traders a better title to their proposed grant than most speculative companies possessed—Samuel Wharton arrived in London early in 1769 to lobby for royal confirmation. The way had been prepared for the Quaker merchant by Benjamin Franklin. No one was more closely attuned to the actual workings of the British political system than Franklin; no one was better at calculating the exact price at which a given official could be bought. Franklin fully understood that the most powerful weapon in Wharton's arsenal was that he provided an opportunity for the politicians to make fortunes at no expense to themselves. Under Franklin's tutelage, Wharton sought out members of the "Bloomsbury gang" and other political factions and presented them with shares in the enterprise. Thomas Walpole—a London financier, member of Parliament, and nephew of Sir Robert Walpole—became the front man and did his work so well that the project became known as "Walpole Associates."

With the machinery of government duly greased, Wharton made his pitch for confirmation of the grant to Lord Hillsborough, the head of the Board of Trade and Secretary of State for the American Department.* Hillsborough was anti-American and opposed to speculative land schemes in the West, fearing that the ready availability of land there would lead to the depopulation of his estates in Ireland. But to the surprise of Wharton and Franklin, his lordship was all smiles and ready with an astound-

---

* Until 1768, British policy overseas was made by two secretaries of state. Between them they divided responsibility for foreign and military policy in Europe and America. In that year, a secretary was appointed to head the American Department, prompting Edmund Burke to remark that "the two secretaries are doing nothing so a third was appointed to help them."

ing idea: Why limit their request to two and a half million acres? Why not ask for enough land for a province?

This seemed such an attractive proposal that, as 1769 drew to a close, Wharton, Walpole, Franklin, and several prominent British politicians gathered at the Crown and Anchor Tavern in London for the creation of a new organization to be known as the Grand Ohio Company. Its goal was to carve out a new colony of twenty million acres encompassing the present states of Ohio and West Virginia, as well as sizable sections of Pennsylvania, Indiana, Kentucky, Virginia, and North Carolina. In return for this grant, the company would pay 10,460 pounds and a quit rent to begin in twenty years of two shillings for every hundred acres of arable ground. Shares were doled out to several influential British politicians.

The new colony was to be called Vandalia in hopes of gaining the favor of King George's German wife, Queen Charlotte, who claimed to be descended from the kings of the Vandals. Later, Wharton may have believed that the line of descent included the gang of noble boodlers who surrounded him with outstretched palms at every turn. The Grand Ohio Company also financed a flood of propaganda about the great national benefits it would confer. One might have thought it a charitable project like Georgia, which had been established to alleviate the plight of English debtors, rather than a moneymaking scheme for its promoters.

The question of approval of the grant went back to Hillsborough, where it was expected to have clear sailing. After all, hadn't he suggested that the promoters ask for enough land for a province? Yet for a year Hillsborough delayed sending in the petition to the Privy Council. Gradually it dawned on Franklin and Wharton that they had been deceived. Hillsborough had obviously hoped to lure them into seeking too large a grant so as to arouse the opposition of the other speculative companies with claims to the same area. This proved to be true, but after lengthy negotiations, all claims—including those of such magnates as the Washingtons and Lees—were merged into that of the Grand Ohio Company. Franklin's resentment at this example of official double-dealing knew no bounds. "Witness his [Hillsborough's] duplicity," he angrily wrote his son, "in encouraging us to ask for more land, pretending to befriend our application."

Faced with this setback, Wharton drew more bills on the credit of the so-called "suffering" Indian traders back in Philadelphia who had originated the project and were now really suffering from the cost of trying to do business in England. The money went to propitiate secretaries, assorted clerks, and obscure but influential gentlemen. Although he maintained his sober Quaker dress and manner, Wharton had become an expert on the seamier aspects of political behavior. Through an elaborate system of contacts, he even reached the ear of George III. William Strahan, a shareholder in the Grand Ohio Company and publisher of David Hume, wrote to the philosopher. Hume, who had once been secretary to Lord Hertford, the lord chamberlain, wrote to him, and Hertford, in turn, talked to the king. The king then asked Hillsborough when the company's petition would be ready for submission to the Privy Council.

Unable to delay any longer, in March 1772 Hillsborough forwarded the petition to the council—but with an adverse recommendation. Hillsborough contended that such a large grant would lead to trouble with the Indians, and the formation of large inland colonies in America was contrary to the interests of the Crown. Let the restless Yankees populate Nova Scotia and Florida, where they would export their produce directly to Britain and buy British goods. Wharton countered with bogus petitions from individuals wishing to settle on land earmarked for the Grand Ohio Company. He told the Privy Council that five thousand families had already settled in the area and that there were an additional twenty-five thousand families in the trans-Appalachian West. Letters from such "disinterested" parties as William Franklin were produced, requesting protection for these settlers and contending that only the company could provide it.

Hillsborough was replaced as colonial secretary by the Earl of Dartmouth, looked upon as a friend by the Americans who had named an Indian school in New Hampshire for him. Still the Grand Ohio grant was not approved. "The affairs of the grant goes on but slowly," observed Franklin somewhat wearily in April

1773. "I do not clearly yet see land. I begin to be a little of the sailor's mind when they were handling a cable out of a store into a ship, and one of 'em said: 'Tis a long heavy cable. I wish we could see the end of it.' 'D———n me,' says another, 'if I believe it has any end; somebody has cut it off.' "

By the close of the year, however, the end of the cable was at last in sight. Conditional approval of the Vandalia grant was given by the king—and Wharton's years of toil and an estimated ten thousand pounds in bribes and other expenses appeared to have borne fruit at last. But events in America were conspiring against the establishment of new colonies, or for that matter, retention by Britain of the old ones.

To keep the East India Company from bankruptcy resulting from the corruption and mismanagement of its directors, Parliament had granted it a monopoly for supplying tea to the American colonies. Part of the company's problems lay in the refusal of the Yankees to buy British tea because it was taxed. Instead, they drank an immense amount of smuggled Dutch tea, depriving both the East India Company and the Crown of revenue. Believing that the colonists would prize cheap tea more than principle, Lord North, the British prime minister, gave the company the right to sell its product directly to the American consumer, cutting out the middleman. This made the price lower than that charged by the smugglers, even with a three-penny tax on each pound. But it soon became apparent that Sam Adams and his allies were more interested in brewing trouble than tea.

The tea monopoly succeeded in uniting the smugglers, the legal merchants, and the radical Sons of Liberty. The smugglers were afraid of being driven out of business by cheap tea; the lawful businessmen feared the East India Company's monopoly might be extended to other goods; and the radicals regarded the tea tax as one more violation of their rights as British citizens. Tea became the symbol of corruption in the management of colonial affairs. In some ports it was allowed to rot in damp cellars, while in others it was not even permitted ashore. And in Boston on the night of December 16, 1773, a group of men sketchily disguised as Mohawk Indians boarded three tea ships and emptied the chests into the harbor.

The events that led to the breakup of the old British Empire followed in quick succession, culminating in the clashes at Lexington and Concord. Wharton received his land charter as the first shots of the Revolution resounded around the world. Vandalia was doomed to remain only a name in forgotten archives, a victim of the greed and inertia of a tiny band of corrupt men who ruled Britain with little thought of what the future might bring.

IV

Nobody Here
but Us Patriots

"THE TRUE HISTORY of the American Revolution cannot be written," the aged John Jay said in a moment of frankness long after the war. "A great many people in those days were not all what they seemed; nor what they are generally believed to have been."[1] Legend has it that every American was a patriot who abandoned the plow to take musket in hand and answer the clarion call of Lexington and Concord. In truth, however, probably more Americans were indifferent to independence, or actually opposed to the cause, than supported it. While tattered uniforms and a lean and hungry look were the badges of the Continental soldier, the war was regarded by many citizens as little more than an enormous pork barrel from which they hoped to extract their fortunes.

In the beginning, however, the Puritan virtues of self-denial were extolled. "Let us eat potatoes and drink water," declared John Adams. "Let us wear canvas and undressed sheepskins rather than submit to the unrighteous and ignominious domination that is prepared for us." Public fasts were proclaimed by Congress and the individual colonial governments. Instead of drinking coffee or tea, many Americans followed Adams's suggestion of a glass of milk for breakfast. Horse racing, gambling, and public balls were banned. Benjamin Franklin was under the happy impression that his countrymen would gird themselves for battle with the maxims of Poor Richard. On all sides, orators stirred cheers with talk of dying for freedom—with others doing the dying, of course. Yankee patriots delighted in drawing comparisons between the corrupt, vice-ridden mother country and a vigorous, virtuous new nation uninfected by the sicknesses which had enfeebled the Old World.[2]

This mode of Spartan restraint was short-lived. Never before had so many Americans enjoyed such ripe opportunities for getting rich quick. Clever men soon grasped the opportunities that lay at hand. Corrupt contractors, greedy speculators, and artful swindlers exploited the critical need for provisions and tools of war for a quick profit. As was to be expected, the soldier in the field was the principal victim. By withholding supplies from the market—or forestalling, as it was called—profiteers and speculators boosted the price of necessities. Even when food, clothing, shoes, guns, and powder were in abundant supply, the troops often went without them, because money could not be found to pay the exorbitant prices demanded.

Safe behind the lines, speculators had no scruples about holding up the government for high prices, though they knew that this added to the misery of the starving, ragged, and homesick soldiers. Government purchasing agents were forced to bid against private speculators for scarce supplies—and the government usually came away with empty hands. On one occasion, iron was cornered by the speculators and none could be procured for casting artillery and making cannonballs for the army. When a ship arrived in port, the get-rich-quick gentry swarmed to the waterfront to buy up her cargo and hold it off the market until prices had reached levels they desired. "Such a dearth of public spirit, and want of virtue, and stock-jobbing, a fertility in all the low arts to obtain advantage, of one kind or another, I never saw before and pray God I may never be witness to again," exclaimed George Washington early in the war. "Could I have foreseen what I have, and am likely to experience, no consideration upon earth should have induced me to accept this command."[3]

So oblivious were the speculators to the needs of the army that in November 1776, when they cornered the supply of shoes and warm clothing, the Continental Congress was forced to appeal to the citizens of Philadelphia to contribute blankets and warm clothing for the troops. A few years later, some merchants were asking—and getting—one hundred dollars for goods that had cost them less than five dollars. Washington's wartime correspondence is filled with angry fulminations against this "tribe of black hearted gentry" who put their pocketbooks before the welfare of his men.

Laboring to hold his army together, he charged that the profiteers and speculators were more dangerous than the entire military might of Britain. "These murderers of our cause" ought to be "hunted . . . down as pests of society, and the greatest Enemys to the happiness of America," he declared. "I would to God that one of the most attrocious of each State was hung . . . upon a gallows five times as high as the one prepared for Haman." No punishment was too severe, in Washington's opinion, for those who preyed "upon our very vitals, and, for the sake of a little dirty pelf, are putting the rights and liberties of the country into the most imminent danger."[4]

But instead of decorating gibbets, the speculators made a dazzling display of their new wealth. They rode in fine carriages, lived in great houses, and, in general, disported themselves as if the war were being fought primarily for their benefit. In 1779, an awed guest in Philadelphia reported that he had sat down to a dinner consisting of 169 dishes. At the same time, Washington's army was starving at Morristown in winter quarters far worse but less publicized than Valley Forge. This did not seem to effect the appetites of either host or guests. With nothing in law or custom to curb their cupidity, profiteers seemed beyond punishment. The state governments, which had been established after the royal governors fled to the safety of British ships, were too weak and insecure to prevent speculation and profiteering. Besides, some of the politicians were engaged in the same practices. Only the army—which occasionally seized supplies at the point of a bayonet—and the rampaging mobs of the cities—which sometimes broke into warehouses and took provisions by force—gave the speculators cause for alarm.

To be sure, not all businessmen engaged in questionable activities. William Gray, a wealthy Boston merchant, marched off to Lexington with a musket on his shoulder, and Haym Salomon, a Polish-born financier, lent money to the government when it was in dire straits—money which was never repaid. One merchant pledged all his property to support the war; he said everything would be worthless if the struggle were to be lost. But, by and large, business support of the American cause was mixed. The merchants declared that the war was being fought to end British interference in their business, so why should they accept meddling from the new government. Trading with the enemy, smuggling, and other illicit forms of trade that had become common business practice under British rule were hard habits to break. "Almost open Trade is carried on from here with the Rebels," noted a British officer in New York. "At least both close one eye. Passionately anxious for gold and silver, they [the Americans] brought us cattle and other provisions."[5] Even though there was a ban on trade with England throughout the war, some Yankee merchants evaded it. English manufactures "are so much to be preferred that America now winks at every importation of their goods," reported a Virginian in 1779. There was also a significant flow of English goods to America by way of the West Indies and Nova Scotia.

Under the circumstances, it was only natural that there should be suspicion of the merchants as men who put profits above patriotism. "The merchants are generally a people whose good is gain and their whole plan of policy is to bring publick measures to square with their private interest," declared General Nathanael Greene. John Adams was of the opinion that the spirit of business was "incompatible with that purity of Heart and Greatness of Soul which is necessary for an happy Republic." But despite radical objections to making profit the polestar of the new nation, the merchants were called in to provide the sinews of war.

Only they had the necessary experience in foreign trade to provide the arms and supplies so badly needed by the Continental Army. Gunpowder was so short at the beginning of the war that Washington, laying siege to Boston, dared not fire a morning or sunset gun for fear that it would touch off a British bombardment which couldn't be answered. And pickets guarding the roads leading out of the town were often issued pikes and spears instead of muskets. Benjamin Franklin suggested that the army be supplied with bows and arrows, reasoning that a man could shoot four arrows in the time it took to load and fire a musket just once.

Robert Morris, a member of Congress from Pennsylvania and a partner in the great Philadelphia mercantile house of Willing, Morris & Company, soon became the most important figure in procuring supplies for the Continental Army. He did his job so well—while lining his own pockets—that he emerged from the war as the richest man in America. Morris was a controversial figure about whom legends cluster. He pursued wealth with audacity and skill, only to end up in a debtors' prison. As one historian has observed, the myth persists that Robert Morris financed the Revolution out of his own pocket, while in reality it is "the other way around—the Revolution financed Robert Morris."[6]

Morris was born in Liverpool in 1734, lived for a time in the small town of Oxford on Maryland's Eastern Shore, and then was apprenticed to Thomas Willing, of Philadelphia. Within a few years he had become a partner in a firm that owned ships which carried goods to all parts of the globe, bought and sold merchandise, and engaged in banking and brokerage. Unlike many wealthy merchants who had helped precipitate the conflict with Britain in an attempt to reduce parliamentary restrictions on trade and then had drawn back in fright at radical domination of the cause, Morris was an ardent patriot.[7]

From the very beginning, his colleagues in Congress put his financial and commercial acumen to work. Like most businessmen of the eighteenth century, Morris saw no reason why public service could not be mixed with private profit. Although he served the new nation well, he obliged it to pay handsomely for his time and effort. He made no secret of retaining his rights as a businessman to use his official position to further his own enterprises. In 1775, for example, Morris entered into a contract with Congress to supply powder to the government. It ensured Willing and Morris a clear profit of $60,000 without risk or loss. Congress was obliged to pay a flat price of $14 a barrel, whether the powder came safely through the British blockade or not. At another point, Morris disclosed to an associate, with no apparent feelings of guilt, that he was withholding a recent shipment of powder from the market until prices improved, since the army had no immediate need for it. "There never has been so fair an opportunity of making a large fortune since I have been conversant in the World," he declared—and advised his fellow businessmen to seize that opportunity.

Along toward the end of 1775, Congress decided to systemize the haphazard procurement of military supplies and appointed a committee to deal with the matter. The Secret Committee, which became the Committee of Commerce in 1777, was given wide powers and could draw upon sizable sums of money to be advanced to contractors. It conducted its business behind closed doors and most of its records were never made public. The committee's duties were soon broadened to include the importation of supplies of all kinds: medicines, surgical instruments, blankets, cotton goods, and various metals. When privateering was formally authorized in April 1776, the committee was given authority to arm and man ships in foreign countries. For the duration of its life, the committee was controlled by Willing and Morris—and, in fact, was operated almost as a subsidiary of the firm. Thomas Willing was its first chairman, and was succeeded within a few months by Morris. The original members also included Benjamin Franklin, Silas Deane, Robert R. Livingston, John Alsop, John Dickinson, Thomas Mckean, John Langdon, and Samuel Ward—all men with considerable experience in foreign business operations.

The line between the public and private interest was often a thin one. Several committee members, particularly Morris and Deane, had been deeply involved in importing arms and powder, both for Congress and their own account, before the committee was called into existence. After its organization, most of the contracts were awarded to Willing and Morris, to Deane's friends and relatives, and to concerns with which the other committee members had some connection. From 1775 to 1777, when the value of Continental currency was nearly equal to hard cash, the committee expended over two million dollars. Nearly a fourth of the disbursements—or $483,000—went directly to Willing and Morris. At one time, Morris reported that his firm had twenty ships carrying supplies for the Secret Committee and five others in which it had an interest. In sorting out his public and private operations, Morris was hazy. He often shipped goods belonging to his company in vessels whose charter and insurance were being paid by the government. And in 1781, when he was appointed Superintendent of Finance and given the task of salvaging what was left of the Continental finances after years of unrestricted issuances of paper money, Morris insisted he be allowed to continue his private business and control the personnel of his department. It was, as has been remarked, as if he had combined the office of Secretary of the Treasury with the leadership of Tammany Hall.

Other merchants also discovered a good thing in the importation of supplies for the Secret Committee. The Browns of Providence, Rhode Island, were given an advance of $20,000 in December 1775 to import munitions with a commission of 2½ percent on their dealings abroad. One voyage alone resulted in a net profit of 1,400 pounds. One of the committee's more questionable operations was launched in January 1776. Congress had voted 40,000 pounds to import presents to bribe the Indians to keep them from joining the British, and the four contracting merchants were allowed a commission of 5 percent on the transaction. The government also insured their ships against loss. The contract ended up in the hands of three members of the Secret Committee—Morris, Alsop, and Francis Lewis, a new member—while the fourth contractor was Livingston's cousin.

Was Morris consciously corrupt? His contemporaries were of mixed mind on this issue, and historians have debated it with considerable intensity over the years. No government official of the Revolutionary era was under greater suspicion by his fellow citizens of having enriched himself at their expense. None was investigated more often and more thoroughly than Morris. Periodically, he was savagely attacked by Thomas Paine, the great propagandist and self-appointed incorruptible conscience of the Revolution. As far as Paine was concerned, Morris was one of the chief practitioners of those "low dirty Tricks" by which speculators and profiteers amassed their fortunes. Yet no one was able to legally pin any wrongdoing upon him. Either Morris was too wily for his critics or he skirted the line between mere sharp practice and actual dishonesty without tumbling over it.

There were times, however, when it appeared as if he had gone too far. On one occasion, he was charged with shifting the ownership of a cargo of about 470 hogsheads of tobacco, originally reported to belong to Willing and Morris, to the public account after the ship was captured by the British. Morris immediately entered a claim upon the public treasury for the value of the cargo, saying it all belonged to the government, except for 50 hogsheads which were the property of his firm. This placed the major loss upon Congress, and not Willing and Morris. A lengthy investigation followed. Morris explained that he had purchased the tobacco on the public account, but had used his firm's name to avoid the usual exorbitant prices charged when the government made purchases in the open market. He was absolved— and no one mentioned the 50 hogsheads belonging to Morris that had been shipped at the public expense.

Morris's accounts were particularly suspect. Repeated demands were made for an examination of his books—and suspicion of wrongdoing was heightened when Morris first refused to make them public. Then, after months of "stonewalling" he acknowledged that the records were in such a tangled state that not even he could unravel them. So, while no irrefutable proof exists that Morris was engaged in corrupt practices, the suspicion remains. He may not have been dishonest in the eighteenth-century sense of governmental morality, but his operations made dishonesty possible—and easy.

*   *   *

Morris's official position enabled him to build a commercial empire that extended across the seas. He played a leading role in the selection of diplomatic and commercial agents to represent the new nation abroad—and did not neglect the opportunities available for his own gain. Silas Deane was sent to France to obtain clothing and munitions for the army and to ascertain French intentions toward the United States. Even Deane acknowledged that a better choice might have been made, for as he told his wife, "people here, members of Congress and others, have unhappily and erroneously thought me a schemer."* More important to Morris's pocket was the decision to send William Bingham, a young business associate, to the French Caribbean island of Martinique. The island was the pivotal point in a network of West Indian ports where supplies and ammunition from Europe were exchanged for American tobacco, indigo and naval stores, and then transshipped to the mainland in small, fast ships which attempted to escape patrolling British cruisers.[8]

Morris told Bingham that, like Deane in Paris, he was to go to Martinique as a private merchant interested only in the shipment of goods to and from the West Indies. He was to carry on a private business "in the mercantile line" with Willing and Morris for their mutual profit as a cover for his intelligence and diplomatic operations. Morris also suggested two commercial ventures—the importation of powder and the purchase of linens—that could be shipped back on the *Reprisal*, a Continental man-of-war that was to take him to the island. Bingham invested five hundred pounds of his own money in these operations, and, like his mentor, saw nothing wrong in using Continental ships or business to make a profit. "We shall be ready to transact rich business," Morris cheerfully informed the young man as the preparations for his voyage were being made.

And so began William Bingham's profitable four-year stay on Martinique. The *Reprisal* returned not only with a cargo of five

---

* Fearful of British spies, Deane adopted the name Jones, wrote his letters in invisible ink, and vowed that in the presence of English-speaking people he would use only French. This prompted the Comte de Vergennes, the French foreign minister, to remark: "He must be the most silent man in France, for I defy him to say six consecutive words in French."

hundred muskets and a small amount of powder, but also with a shipment of linens and other goods suggested by Morris. Bingham's share of the profits totaled about seven hundred and fifty pounds. He began to buy supplies on commission for the Secret Committee, commissioned privateers, and procured cargoes for the private sale of Morris and himself. Bingham also engaged in privateering ventures with Morris that were so successful the older man was once moved to declare "we shall make a fine hand of it." One prize cargo fetched almost fourteen thousand pounds at sale; medicines captured aboard another ship were sold "for the highest prices ever given." To this day, no one knows for certain how much Bingham realized from this judicious mixture of patriotism and profit. When he returned to the mainland, Bingham had amassed enough of a fortune to marry the beautiful Ann Willing, daughter of Morris's old partner, Thomas Willing. And he was well on his way to becoming one of the richest men in America well before he had turned forty.

Although the Americans had long railed against the corruption of English politicians, members of the Continental Congress were always ready to scrape up a few more crumbs for their own friends, supporters, and relatives. No better example of the influence of "interest"—the eighteenth century's version of political patronage—exists than the circumstances surrounding the organization of the Continental Navy.[9] Because many Americans thought it would be suicidal to try to resist the Royal Navy, then the world's most powerful fleet, the formation of a navy had lagged well behind that of an army. Not until late in 1775 did Congress, acting upon the recommendation of its Naval Committee, authorize the purchase of four lumbering merchantmen to be converted into warships, and begin the commissioning of officers and the enlistment of seamen and marines.

The officers were chosen under the same principles of nepotism and preferment that had long been the bane of the British military services. Esek Hopkins, a fifty-seven-year-old former privateersman from Rhode Island who was named commodore of the tiny fleet, was the brother of Stephan Hopkins, chairman of the Naval Committee. Dudley Saltonstall, the senior captain, was Silas Deane's brother-in-law. Abraham Whipple, the next-ranking captain, was a member by marriage of the influential Hopkins clan. He was followed by Nicholas Biddle, of Phila-delphia, whose brother, Edward, was a member of the congres-sional delegation from Pennsylvania, and by John Burroughs Hopkins, the commodore's son. John Paul Jones, an ex-slaver and merchant skipper, was appointed a lieutenant with the backing of Joseph Hewes, a North Carolina congressman and shipowner whom he had asked for a job.

Esek Hopkins's incompetence and the sectional rivalries which plagued Congress all during the war brought about his dismissal and replacement by another commodore, James Nicholson, of Maryland, who owed his appointment solely to politics. He also turned out to be a lackluster naval officer—rightfully accused at one time of being "a commodore safe in port." But he had the support of the influential Lee family of Virginia and other South-erners, and that would prove much more important than mere professional skill and ability. Nicholson was to lose two Continen-tal frigates during the war—one of them under particularly disgraceful circumstances—but he never lost his political clout. His influence was so great that the Nicholson family eventually supplanted the Hopkinses' dominant role in naval affairs.

Political influence also played a vital role in the choice of where the Continental Navy's ships were to be built and who was to receive the lucrative contracts to build them. On December 13, 1775, Congress authorized the construction of thirteen frigates which were to be ready for sea in three months. Completion of these ships according to schedule would have provided the Conti-nental Navy with a considerable array of strength in record time, for these vessels were not converted merchantmen, like those already in commission, but built-from-the-keel-up men-of-war. Two of them were to be built in Rhode Island, two in Massa-chusetts, two in New York, four in Pennsylvania, and one each in New Hampshire, Connecticut, and Maryland—locations that were chosen as a result of the political clout of the congressional delegates from those states rather than their shipbuilding capa-bilities.

Selection of the builders had been left in the hands of the Marine Committee, which had been organized by Congress to take over from the Naval Committee. It consisted of one member from each of the thirteen colonies—undoubtedly to ensure that each would get an equal share of the gravy. The contracts were used, by and large, to reward political friends. John Langdon, a former member of Congress from New Hampshire, was placed in charge of building the frigate assigned there. Thomas Cushing, a political crony of John Hancock, then president of Congress, was given the two ships to be built in Massachusetts. Rhode Island set up an eleven-man committee to oversee construction of its two vessels, and Esek Hopkins charged they turned it into a political clambake in which supplies were diverted to privateers building in private shipyards. Silas Deane saw to it that Connecticut's contribution was built under the supervision of his brother, Barnabas. Cost overruns and repeated delays resulted. Some of the builders were so inefficient that a number of the frigates never got to sea. They were captured by the British or were destroyed to prevent them from falling into enemy hands.

One by one, examples of corruption, graft, and human greed march before us like so many soldiers on parade. And even when there is no dishonesty involved—only questionable judgment— doubts were aroused. There are reports that some members of the Continental Congress accepted gifts and loans from the French minister after an alliance was formed between the two countries in 1778. A few naval officers took a rake-off on the prize money earned by their crews. Thomas Mifflin, the army's Quartermaster General, doled out government contracts to his brother and his mercantile associates in Philadelphia. Jeremiah Wadsworth, the Commissary General, intermixed government accounts with his own. The Clothier General, James Mease, was a flagrant speculator. Dr. William Shippen, head of the Hospital Department, dealt in medical supplies.

Even so well-regarded a soldier as Nathanael Greene engaged in activities while Thomas Mifflin's successor as Quartermaster General that raised serious questions about the propriety of his conduct. Greene entered into a secret partnership with his brother, Jacob, in a firm which sold supplies to the army. While the general vehemently protested his innocence of any wrongdoing, suspicion still attaches itself to the transactions. Greene tried to convince others—and perhaps himself—that the business was legitimate and that he had clothed his interest in secrecy only because it might arouse gossip. "This is a murmuring age and everybody that handles money must expect to be subject to some degree of reproach," he once declared. Despite Greene's protestations, however, even a sympathetic biographer concludes: "One may lament that avarice got the better of Greene and that . . . his conduct as quartermaster was not always above reproach. . . . That [his] company did relatively little business with the army does not excuse him or lessen the impropriety."[10]

Although Timothy Pickering, Greene's successor, may have exaggerated when he said that the Continental debt was nearly doubled as a result of malfeasance in the purchase of supplies and other equipment for the army, he expressed the popular opinion. Speculation was so widespread that even combat officers engaged in it. In justice to them, it should be emphasized that it was the only way they could protect themselves against the cancer of inflation. As the value of Continental paper money sank, their salaries became all but worthless, and they were unable to buy even the barest necessities. One marine officer lamented that he was not only slow in receiving his monthly pay but "when we wished to spend it, it would not pay for a pair of shoes." Following the example of the more prosperous civilians, officers compensated themselves somewhat for the shrinking value of their salaries by trading in military stores. Unless the army's officers were adequately and promptly paid, observed Pickering rather matter-of-factly, "they will find means to help themselves."

Henry Laurens, an acid-tongued president of Congress, was so aroused by the prevailing miasma of corruption that he wrote a friend during the summer of 1778: "Were I to unfold to you [the] scenes of venality, peculation and fraud which I have discovered, the disclosure would astonish you." Laurens's bitter words may have been inspired by an event that had recently occurred. Not satisfied with the more or less legitimate forms of graft at hand, at least one member of Congress—Samuel Chase, who had signed the Declaration of Independence for Maryland—made use of his official position to line his pockets.

Few Americans had been louder in their attacks on the alleged injustices suffered by the colonists at the hands of King George and his corrupt minions than Chase. This hulking Annapolis lawyer was so active in the affairs of the local Sons of Liberty that the authorities characterized him as a "busy, restless incendiary, a ring leader of mobs, a foul-mouthed and inflaming son of discord." When the break with Britain came, it was obvious that he should represent Maryland in Congress. Returning from an unsuccessful diplomatic mission to Canada in June 1776, Chase learned that the Maryland Assembly had instructed its delegates in Philadelphia to vote against independence. He immediately sped off to Annapolis, where he almost single-handedly bullied and prodded the assembly into rescinding its previous instructions and ordering its delegates to vote for independence. Then he mounted his horse and covered the 150 miles of bad roads to Philadelphia in two days, arriving on the eve of the decisive vote.

For all his red-hot patriotism, however, Chase was not one to ignore an opportunity to make a financial killing; love of country evidently did not interfere with his love of profit. Taking advantage of secret information that Congress planned to purchase vast quantities of grain for the use of a French fleet expected momentarily off Philadelphia, Chase organized a scheme to corner the flour market. Dr. Samuel Johnson could have had Chase in mind when he observed that "patriotism is the last resort of a scoundrel."*

Only a few months earlier, Washington's scarecrow army had frozen at Valley Forge without food and clothing—in part as a result of actions such as those taken by Chase and his friends. Today, Valley Forge stirs noble images of ragged sentries freezing at their posts and of bloody footsteps in the snow, but the winter of 1777–1778 was a mild one, and much of the suffering needless. The prosperous farmers of Pennsylvania preferred to sell their produce to the British Army in Philadelphia for hard cash

---

* Chase appeared, however, to have a sense of humor. Upon one occasion he regaled Congress with a three-hour discussion of the beauties of brown eyes vs. black eyes.

rather than to their countrymen for nearly worthless Continental paper currency. The merchants of Boston demanded profits of 1,000 percent for clothing in their warehouses. "It was an old tale, one of graft, speculation, meanness, selfishness, and gross mismanagement," comments one authority with complete and utter disgust.[11]

Chase's plot to corner the flour market miscarried—probably because Robert Morris was willing to sell flour to the French for only a 50 percent markup. And even though Chase had carefully hidden his involvement behind a screen of agents and intermediaries, his participation in the affair leaked out. Alexander Hamilton, then an ambitious young officer on Washington's staff with a reputation to make, launched an attack on the would-be profiteer. In those days, Hamilton—like most soldiers—professed to despise money-grubbing tradesmen and their lack of ideals. Honor, patriotism, and self-sacrifice were the qualities to be sought in his countrymen, according to Hamilton, while avarice and other selfish passions were regarded as the ruin of the new nation. Only a few years later, however, Hamilton would come to regard avarice and self-aggrandizement as the means of salvation of the nation—and Samuel Chase was to be a formidable ally in his work.

Writing under the pseudonym Publius, the same he was to use in publishing the Federalist papers, Hamilton savaged Chase in a series of open letters printed in an upstate New York newspaper addressed to "The Honorable_____, Esq." His model was Junius, the anonymous master of the poison pen who a few years before had both startled and delighted England with his unbridled attacks on the ministry of the Duke of Grafton. Hamilton opened up with a scathing denunciation of "that tribe who, taking advantage of the times, have carried the spirit of monopoly and extortion to an excess which scarcely admits of a parallel." A member of Congress who turned "the knowledge of secrets to which his office gave him access to the purposes of private profit by employing emissaries to engross an article of immediate necessity to the public service . . . ought to feel the utmost rigor of public resentment, and to be detested as a traitor of the worst and most dangerous kind."[12]

Chase was easily identified as the target of this floodtide of invective, even though his name had not been mentioned. It created a sensation. He and his friends made desperate efforts to determine the author of the letters, but the newspaper held its secret well. Chase's opponents in Maryland seized upon the charges in an attempt to bring him down, finally forcing the State assembly to hold formal hearings. Chase's followers controlled the legislature, so, with the same fastidiousness it has shown in our own day, that body whitewashed him on a strictly partisan vote. Years later, as Hamilton had predicted, Chase was to be "immortalized in infamy." His high-handed conduct as an associate justice of the Supreme Court—often bullying and terrorizing lawyers and clients with business before him—resulted in an impeachment attempt in 1804.

V

A More Perfect Union

SOMEHOW IT SEEMS particularly fitting that a portrait of Alexander Hamilton should grace the ten-dollar bill. No man did more to establish the credit and the finances of the United States—and no one was more adroit in mustering the positive power of corruption. Like Sir Robert Walpole, Hamilton brilliantly exploited the greed and self-interest of others for his own ends. He was not personally corrupt; if anything, the evidence indicates otherwise, but his political philosophy determined his financial policies. Hamilton's objective was the creation of a strong and vigorous central government that would guarantee the future stability and prosperity of the nation. To achieve this goal, he was convinced that government must have the support of the rich and well-born—and he was perfectly willing to purchase their backing. As long as Hamilton was secretary of the Treasury, the merchants, the shipowners, the manufacturers, and the speculators did not have to buy favors from the government—they were offered a piece of the action.

Like most of the plutocracy spawned by the struggle for independence, Hamilton was an offspring of revolution who quickly forgot his origins. He profoundly distrusted the political capacity of the ordinary citizen and regarded the people as "a great beast" whose riotous spirit must be curbed if the new republic were to

succeed. Inasmuch as only the propertied class had the wisdom
and skill to rule, they should be given a monopoly on the government. "Our prevailing passions are ambition and interest," Hamilton noted, "and it will ever be the duty of wise government to
avail itself of these passions in order to make them subservient to
the public good."[1] Appealing to the self-interest of the rich and
well-born, Hamilton welded them to the government with a policy that openly supported and advanced their interests. English
society, "bottomed on corruption," was his model. What was good
for the rich, he reasoned, was good for the country.

Much of Hamilton's compelling devotion to a strong national
union may have resulted from the fact that of all the nation's
leaders he alone was born outside the continental limits of what
had become the United States.[2] Unlike Washington, Jefferson,
Madison, and the Adamses, he felt no surge of sentiment for an
individual state or section, which sometimes tended to weaken
their loyalty to the national government. Hamilton was born on
the West Indian island of Nevis—in John Adams's sneering
phrase "the bastard brat of a Scotch pedlar." As is often the case
where genius is concerned, it has been suggested that his father
was not James Hamilton, a n'er-do-well sprig of a Scottish noble
family, but some better man. George Washington, who developed
a great attachment to Hamilton, is among those thought to be
Hamilton's real father. Washington, it seems, visited Barbados at
the time Hamilton's mother was living there. But in truth, all
Washington got on the island was smallpox.[3]

The circumstances of Hamilton's birth only made him more
ambitious. Deserted by his father, and with his mother dead, at
the age of fifteen he was successfully conducting a business for a
benefactor. Two years later, he was a student at King's College, in
New York City, and an active and eloquent revolutionary orator
and pamphleteer. At twenty-two, he was a lieutenant colonel on
Washington's staff, the scourge of profiteers like Samuel Chase,
and a certified war hero. His marriage to Elizabeth Schuyler won
him entrance into one of New York's oldest and most influential
families. When the war ended, he hung out his lawyer's shingle on
Wall Street and was quickly acknowledged by the business community as one of the city's cleverest advocates. The Schuyler

connection sent him to the postwar Congress, where he observed at first hand the inadequacies of the new nation's weak and divided government.

For eight years, from 1781 until the inauguration of Washington in 1789, the United States was not so much governed as maintained in a sort of caretaker status under a loosely drawn series of laws known as the Articles of Confederation. Chaos, confusion, and governmental paralysis reigned supreme. Congress functioned as little more than a council of ambassadors of an uneasy league of thirteen more-or-less sovereign republics. The "imbecility" of the Confederation, as Hamilton was quick to point out, resulted from a "rage for liberty" that seemed to possess the American people. Fearful that a strong government might reimpose a hated tyranny similar to that of Britain, they narrowly limited the powers of Congress and made the states the dominant force in government.

Acrimonious debates flared among these semi-independent satrapies over access to the western lands. Some states imposed duties on the commerce of their neighbors which almost precipitated armed conflicts. All but destitute, Congress was periodically forced to beg the states for money. Most of these appeals were ignored. Hamilton shook his head at the sight of his adopted country floundering in disorder and declared: "A nation without a national government, is in my view, an awful spectacle."

The merchants, the speculators, and businessmen of all kinds readily agreed, for the United States had begun its independence with a depression. The wartime boom had been followed by a dizzying descent from riches to rags. Men who had borrowed when money was cheap and the economy flush now found themselves pressed to pay debts and taxes in hard cash. Thousands of small farmers, tradesmen, and craftsmen were faced with the loss of everything they owned. An ugly, rebellious spirit stalked the land. Civil war flared in Massachusetts, where debtors were unable to persuade the legislature to enact laws for their relief. In the autumn of 1786, a mob of farmers under the leadership of a former army captain named Daniel Shays, forcibly prevented local authorities from seizing cattle and farms to satisfy unpaid taxes and debts.

From the safety of Paris, where he was serving as American minister, Thomas Jefferson looked on approvingly. "A little rebellion now and then is a good thing," he observed. "The tree of liberty must be refreshed from time to time with the blood of patriots and tyrants." But the Massachusetts merchants and creditors, fearing that any blood shed might be theirs, took a less philosophical view. They financed a loyal militia to put down the insurrection. Armed for the most part with only pitchforks and clubs, Shays's followers were routed with dispatch and mercilessly hunted down through the backwoods like wild game.

Shays's "little rebellion" had a profound effect on the making of the Constitution. As James Madison noted, the shock-waves from this blind lurch toward radicalism contributed more to the Constitution than any of the political or economic inadequacies of the Articles of Confederation. For some time, Hamilton had been issuing Isaiahlike warnings that only a strong national government could effectively control the passions of mankind and preserve the sanctity of property and contract. His ideas now fell upon sympathetic ears in the business community. No doubt with a deep sigh of relief at their narrow escape from the clutches of anarchy, the representatives of America's new aristocracy trooped off to a Constitutional Convention in Philadelphia to form "a more perfect union"—and to make the nation safe for profits and property.

Time and tradition have elevated the fifty-five men who drifted into the familiar surroundings of the Pennsylvania State House in the latter part of May 1787 into demigods. Legend has endowed these Founding Fathers with Olympian wisdom and virtue. Their sole objective is said to be the enhancement of liberty and improvement of the welfare of their fellow citizens. The delegates would be hard put to recognize themselves in this portrait, however. Basically conservative in background and outlook, they were hard-headed realists who had come to Philadelphia to protect their own interests and those of their class. They labored, in Madison's words, to cure the "defects, the deformities, the diseases" of the Confederation, not to legislate for all time.

While the Constitution was proclaimed in the name of "We the people," the ordinary citizen had precious little to do with it. The document was primarily the work of the Eastern aristocracy—merchants, shipowners, budding industrialists, speculators, slaveholders, moneylenders, and their lawyers. Conspicuously absent were spokesmen for the small farmer, the urban laborer, the debtor, and the expanding West. As John D. Hicks has written, the delegates "had little faith in democracy; indeed, one might almost say that it was their fear of democracy that brought them together."[4]

Their cardinal objective was to preserve and protect their own interests and those of their class and sections. As Charles A. Beard pointed out in his *Economic Interpretation of the Constitution*, "the overwhelming majority of the members, at least five-sixths, were immediately, directly and personally interested in the outcome of their labors in Philadelphia and were to a greater or lesser extent economic beneficiaries from the adoption of the Constitution."

Beard's survey of the overlapping economic interests of the delegates to the convention disclosed that forty of them held public securities, twenty-four in amounts in excess of five thousand dollars, and at least fourteen were land speculators. Twenty-four representatives had money on loan at interest, and eleven were involved in mercantile, manufacturing, and shipping enterprises. All these interests were certain to benefit from the establishment of a strong and stable national government, notes Beard, so the delegates cannot be called disinterested in the outcome of their labors. For example, Benjamin Franklin, who had lent the government three thousand pounds and had accepted 6 percent promissory notes in return, observed in February 1788 that "such Certificates are low in Value at present, but we hope and believe they will mend when our new Constitutional Government is established."[5]

Beard erred, however, in regarding the economic interests represented at the Constitutional Convention as monolithic. The making of the Constitution was a much more subtle, ambiguous, and complex process. Throughout the stifling hot summer of 1787, debate raged as the various elements struggled for advantage at the expense of the others—the shipowners against the manufacturers, the planters against the merchants, the large states against the small states. Behind the surface veneer of fine phrases and discussions of the philosophy of Locke and Montesquieu raged a naked struggle for power. "The present Constitution was dictated by commercial necessity more than any other cause," declared Fisher Ames, a spokesman for New England's businessmen. "The want of an efficient Government to secure the manufacturing interests, and advance our commerce, was long seen by men of judgment."[6]

Despite their conflicting interests, the delegates wanted a stable government badly enough to submerge their differences in compromise. They produced a document with which all the contending economic and sectional interests represented could live. Hamilton, for example, abandoned his insistence on something resembling a constitutional monarchy which resulted from his fear and loathing of popular government. Even though he regarded the proposed Constitution as dangerously weak, he worked unremittingly for ratification. The result was a reasonable distribution of power amid all the competing forces. The delegates had produced a government which in Hicks's description was "democratic enough to be adopted but not so democratic as to constitute any menace to upper-class control." The federal government was given control of taxation, the making of war, the issuance of money, interstate commerce, and the western lands. The states got what was left. All in all, the Constitution advanced the interests of the moneyed class while practically ignoring the rights and wishes of the common man. It charted the course for the establishment of a business civilization in which property in all its myriad forms was to reign supreme.

On the morning of April 30, 1789, George Washington climbed into an open coach drawn by four matched horses and was driven through the crowded streets of New York to his inauguration as the first president of the United States. Inauguration day had dawned cloudy and overcast, but the sky soon brightened. This was regarded as a good omen for the future. Escorted by bands and jangling troops of cavalry, the coach moved slowly through the cheering multitude, its occupant bowing ever so slightly— now to the right and then to the left. The city which met Washington's eyes had vastly changed since 1776, when it had been the scene of one of the worst disasters of his military career. Fire had destroyed most of the remnants of the old Dutch town and the streets were now lined with new brick buildings. New York was already the largest city in the United States with a population of about thirty thousand. There was a fresh spirit of enterprise everywhere. New wharves and warehouses crowded the waterfront, and the harbor was filled with ships that had sailed around Cape Horn to China and returned with rich cargoes of silks and tea. In the counting houses of lower Manhattan, the speculators quietly calculated the effects of the new government on their fortunes.

The first problem to which Washington addressed himself after taking the oath to faithfully carry out his duties in accord with the Constitution was the selection of men to help him run the executive branch. Like everything else involving the new government, there were no precedents for the president to follow, so Washington created them as he went along. There were five major posts to be filled—the heads of the departments of State, Treasury, War, and Post Office, as well as an attorney general to be appointed. The State Department and the Treasury—foreign relations and finances—were the most important. John Jay, who had conducted the nation's foreign affairs under the Confederation and was still serving during the transition, was the natural choice for Secretary of State. But Jay had grown weary of the post and desired appointment as Chief Justice of the United States, a position he regarded as a sinecure. Benjamin Franklin and John Adams, the two other Americans with the most diplomatic experience, were unavailable—Franklin because of age and illness, and Adams because he had been elected vice-president. Washington next made overtures to Thomas Jefferson, still serving in Paris as American minister. He accepted the post reluctantly, and only after considerable persuasion by the president.

Robert Morris was the leading choice for Secretary of the

Treasury. Although his personal integrity had been questioned during the war, no one else matched his experience in the conduct of government finance. On his way to New York, Washington had visited Morris's elaborate home in Philadelphia and offered him the post. Morris declined, however, citing the press of business—in reality a new scheme for land speculation which was to eventually send him to debtors' prison. In his place, Morris recommended Hamilton, with whom he had been in correspondence on financial matters since the Revolution. Hamilton accepted with alacrity, and the money men gleefully rubbed their hands in anticipation.

Even while the new government was taking shape, finagling was making an early bow. Congress convened on March 4, 1789, and had only been in session a few weeks before it was discovered that some members were already using their positions to line their pockets. To provide funds to meet the immediate requirements of the government, it had been agreed after a process of give and take worthy of the Constitutional Convention that a tariff should be imposed upon imports coming into the country. Yet for some unexplained reason, final congressional action had been stalled for some time. No one seemed to know why. William Maclay, a fiercely democratic senator from western Pennsylvania, began to delve into the mystery. The reason why everyone was so close-mouthed about the affair soon became apparent.

Maclay found that the bill was being obstructed by some members of Congress who were deeply involved in seaborne commerce. They hoped to delay final approval of the measure until their ships had returned safely from current voyages and the cargoes unloaded into their warehouses—free of duty, of course. The merchants had already raised the price of goods on hand to cover the duties which hadn't been paid, but that was the public's worry. Maclay was pained to discover that his colleague, Thomas Fitzsimons of Philadelphia, a leading shipowner and vigorous spokesman for commercial interests in Congress, was one of the culprits. He noted unhappily in his journal that when a man acted in the double capacity of both merchant and congressman, "you will always find the merchant uppermost."[7]

Rampant conflict of interest and open evasion of customs duties by the people's representatives were merely schoolboy pranks compared to what was brewing. Ever since the appointment of Hamilton as secretary of the Treasury, the ever-vigilant Senator Maclay had noted that strange gyrations were occurring in the price of government certificates. Surprisingly the value of the seemingly worthless paper that had been issued by Congress during the Revolution and the Confederation to pay its debts was mounting every day. There was feverish activity in the counting houses of Boston, New York, and Philadelphia, as speculators fought for the certificates. The mystery was resolved on January 14, 1790, when Hamilton unveiled his plan for establishing the nation's credit and finances on a firm foundation. "A committee of speculators in certificates could not have formed it more for their advantage,"[8] observed Maclay bitterly.

Brilliant, tireless, and plausible, Hamilton was, at thirty-five, entering the brightest phase of his career. Still slim and boyish, he was an elegant dresser with a taste for good living and the attentions of women. His plan for magically transforming the crushing burden of debt inherited by the new nation transported the speculators into paroxysms of delight. Hamilton had proposed nothing less than a refunding of the national debt—or payment at face value plus accrued interest—and the assumption by the federal government of the debts of the various states.

Unable to raise money to finance the government, the Continental Congress and the state legislatures had issued millions of dollars' worth of paper certificates which they promised to redeem at full value at some future date. Washington had also persuaded his mutinous troops to accept similar certificates in lieu of back pay when the army had been disbanded. When the interest on the debt fell due, more paper money was pyramided on top of that already in existence. The exact amount in circulation was sheer guesswork because the wartime Quartermaster and Commissary departments had showered a storm of paper upon the country when requisitioning supplies for which they had no money.

Only the foreign debt could be readily calculated—$10 million plus another $1.6 million in unpaid interest. Hamilton estimated that the domestic debt was about $27 million with $13 million in back-due interest. State debts may have totaled perhaps another $30 million or so, which meant that Hamilton proposed to provide for payment on a consolidated debt of perhaps $80 million—a dizzying sum at that time. This great mass of certificates, notes, and indents had gravitated into the hands of speculators who now stood to make fortunes if Hamilton's plan was approved. Impoverished and hard-pressed for cash, the soldiers and small holders had sold their paper for a fraction of its face value to speculators with ready cash and steady nerves. "The public debt affords the best field in the world for speculation," acknowledged Andrew Craigie, a Boston financier, as he went to work with a will.[9]

Hamilton was more high-minded—at least in public. He regarded the debt as "the price of liberty." The credit of the nation would be firmly established only if it were paid. "States, like individuals, who observe their engagements are respected and trusted, while the reverse is the fate of those who pursue an opposite conduct," he told Congress.[10] "The proper funding of the present debt will render it a national blessing," he added, making one of those statements that politicians live to regret. Obviously, the United States did not have money to redeem the mountain of outstanding paper, so the secretary suggested that it all be called and new certificates—or bonds—be issued. These would be backed by government revenues specially earmarked for the payment of interest and eventually the entire principal. Hamilton's elaborate scheme had another refinement that particularly appealed to the speculators: full payment would be made to those who held the certificates at the time of redemption, not the original owners.

Bits and pieces of gossip about the wave of speculation that had preceded Hamilton's announcement reached the alert ears of Senator Maclay, who carefully set everything he heard down in his journal.[11] "I walked out this evening," he wrote, and "I call not at a single house or go into any company but traces of speculation in certificates appear." There were rumors that Hamilton's relatives, friends, and some members of Congress had been tipped off in advance about the funding plan and had hastened to purchase certificates before the general public learned of the momentous decision. Robert Morris, Maclay's fellow senator from Pennsylvania, and the ubiquitous Thomas Fitzsimons were said to be so deeply involved in speculation that they had delayed in attending the new session of Congress so they could spend more time buying paper at bargain prices. Representative James Wadsworth of Connecticut, a former business partner of Hamilton's, sent two swift sailing ships to the South in order to buy up all the available certificates before their holders learned the good news. Other speculators rushed horsemen with money-packed saddlebags to the backwoods of North Carolina for the same purpose. General Henry Knox, the secretary of war, and William Bingham, Robert Morris's former agent in Martinique, also plunged deeply into the securities market. William Constable, another Morris partner and Hamilton associate, raised more than five million dollars from Dutch bankers to purchase American securities. Convinced that the treasury secretary had leaked the information to a favored few, Maclay bitterly declared that the affair would "damn the character of Hamilton as a minister forever."

Events had made Maclay so suspicious of everyone linked to Hamilton that he even suspected George Washington of having a hand in the frenzied wave of speculation. An invitation to dinner with the president and some friendly attention from the chief executive set him to brooding. "He knows how rigid a republican I am," Maclay confided to his journal that night. "I can not think that he considers it worth while to soften me. It is not worth his while."

Just how much truth is there in the charges leveled against Hamilton? Nathan Schachner, a sympathetic biographer, states that the secretary "did not own or deal in a single share of the public debt, and when he left the Treasury he was poorer than when he entered it."[12] Nevertheless, Schachner concedes that Hamilton's Schuyler in-laws profited handsomely from their speculations in certificates. Old Philip Schuyler, the head of the clan and Hamilton's father-in-law, was so active a speculator that by 1791 he had accumulated $67,000 worth of securities. "Even more damning," in Schachner's view, was the case of John Barker Church, Hamilton's brother-in-law. As he was in England at the time that the funding scheme was announced, Hamilton agreed to act as his agent in the purchase of securities so Church would not miss this golden opportunity to line his pockets. He engaged in business on Church's behalf with Thomas Willing, Robert Morris's old partner. An astonished Maclay claimed that Willing had openly declared that he had seen Hamilton's entire plan before it was publicly presented.[13]

So, even though Hamilton may not have enriched himself through his plans for funding the debt, he was, at best, remarkably indiscreet. Hamilton doesn't appear to have been overly concerned by the speculators' ready access to inside information or even the use to which they put it. They were part of the moneyed interest that he wished to establish as the nation's ruling class. Perhaps, like many of the speculators themselves, he thought they should be amply rewarded for their touching demonstration of faith in the paper issued by the federal and state governments.

The best that can be said for Hamilton is that he did not use his office to personally enrich himself, but the same cannot be said of his assistant, William Duer. Known as "the Prince of Speculators," Duer blithely disregarded all charges of conflict of interest and used his position as an insider to indulge in a monumental maze of shady financial manipulations.[14] Andrew Craigie, the Boston stock jobber, once noted that he knew of "no way of making safe speculations but by being associated with people who from their official situation knew all the present and can aid future arrangements either for or against the funds." One of the persons he selected to be "associated with" was Duer. It was a wise choice.

The "Vice-Secretary of the Treasury," as Duer was called, was an Englishman who, after attending Eton, had sought his fortune in both India and the West Indies before coming to America. During the Revolution, he actively supported the Yankee cause and had grown rich by furnishing supplies to the army at the usual handsome profit. The ambitious Duer soon rivaled Robert Morris in the lavishness of his life-style and in the amounts of certificates and speculative options on western lands he held. Along the way, he married the daughter of the late General William Alexander, who claimed the title of Lord Stirling. She, in turn, was known as "Lady Kitty" and was related through her mother to the Schuylers and Hamilton. George Washington gave the bride away. In 1786, Duer had been named to the Treasury Board under the Confederation and lost no time in using this strategic post to benefit himself and his friends.

One of his grander schemes was to purchase the entire Continental debt from France and then sell it to the American government—of which Duer was an official! Duer worked hand in glove with speculators such as the agile Craigie, who profited immensely from the association. Duer was so liberal with vital information that when Theophile Cazenove, a Dutch agent, arrived in the United States, he was immediately introduced to Duer by a friend. He told Duer that Cazenove "is to settle himself in America, and I believe to make some speculations in your funds. I am sure, knowing your obliging temper, you'll give him good information about his speculations." Duer also appears to have demanded a rake-off on government contracts. He tried to shake down a contractor who was trying to sell some copper to the government for a $10,000 share of the proceeds. This would ensure that the contract would proceed without a hitch. "Tho I did not want his assistance, I wished him not interested against me," allowed the unhappy contractor.

These activities occurred before Duer received his appointment as Hamilton's assistant, but he maintained a similar style of operations even after joining the Treasury. Among the most active speculators in the nation, he borrowed money from anyone he could, pyramiding his purchases of government paper to massive proportions. Before an outraged public opinion finally forced Hamilton to ask for his resignation, Duer even used notes that were on deposit with the Treasury to build up his own fortune. Later, Duer's accounts for the period in which he served on the Treasury Board under the Confederation were found to be

$230,000 short, and he was clapped into debtors' prison, where he died—but not before precipitating the nation's first financial panic in 1792.

There can be no doubt that Hamilton was fully aware of Duer's reputation at the time he named him as his assistant, for Duer had offered him a share in the plan to purchase control of the French debt, which Hamilton declined. The only explanation possible for the appointment is that Hamilton didn't care. Family connection, personal friendship, and Duer's vaunted financial skill and business contacts probably outweighed all other considerations in the secretary's mind.

Shortly before Hamilton submitted his report on public credit to Congress, President Washington had been congratulating himself upon the spirit of goodwill and unanimity prevailing throughout the country. But the fight over the funding of the national debt—tainted as it was by corruption—touched off a monumental struggle which almost tore the nation asunder. Formal debate on Hamilton's proposal was slow in beginning, however, which set Senator Maclay to suspecting that some of his colleagues were deliberately stalling so they would have more time to buy up paper at bargain prices. "I really fear that members of Congress are deeper into this business than any other," he wrote.

Much to Hamilton's surprise, the assault upon his funding plan, when it was finally unleashed in the House, came from his friend James Madison. Although Hamilton and Madison had differing political philosophies and outlooks on life, they had worked closely together for the ratification of the Constitution and each had a profound respect for the abilities of the other. So, in preparing his report on the public credit, Hamilton had solicited the views of the little Virginian as to the best means to deal with the national debt. Madison's reply was carefully worded. He talked of the necessity for paying off the nation's foreign and domestic creditors—or extinguishing the debt, as he put it—and suggested the sale of western lands held by the federal government to obtain the revenues needed to accomplish this objective.

Madison did not disagree with Hamilton over the importance of economic self-interest in politics. In fact, he had formulated a theory in No. 10 of *The Federalist* that was later to inspire Charles Beard.[15] "The most common and durable source of factions has been the various and unequal distribution of property," Madison had written in words that antedate Karl Marx's theories of class warfare by well over half a century. "Those who hold and those who are without property have ever formed distinct interests in society." Madison's disagreement with Hamilton centered about which economic interest should profit from the operations of the government. Like his mentor, Jefferson, Madison was a Virginia landowner, suspicious of speculators and all those who made their fortunes from manipulating money rather than from the soil. He had no confidence in a government that depended upon the greed of the business class for its support. It was inevitable that these interests—and men—should eventually clash.

The Senate adjourned so the members could go to the House to hear Madison. The crowded galleries strained to catch his thin, reedy voice as he poured vitriol on Hamilton's plan. He dwelt at length on the sad plight of the impoverished widows, orphans, and veterans who had been robbed by the greedy speculators. Rather than pay off the public debt, Hamilton's scheme would merely perpetuate it. Far from being the national blessing that Hamilton had described, the debt would be "a public curse" that would mortgage the future to enrich the speculators. Of course, the federal debt must be paid because it had been contracted for the national welfare—but who was to be repaid? Should the speculators be allowed to reap a rich harvest at the expense of the original holders, who had freely given their support to the government in a time of grave crisis? Madison found it inadmissible that America should "erect . . . monuments of her gratitude, not to those who saved her liberties, but to those who had enriched themselves in her funds."

The Virginian proposed a compromise in which the government would discriminate between the original holders of its certificates and persons who had bought them later. Thus, those who had originally been issued certificates would share in the profits rather than have everything go to the speculators.

Alarmed, Hamilton's supporters leaped to the offensive and the secretary himself, according to Maclay, "spent most of his time in running from place to place among the members" of Congress to keep his forces in line. Madison's proposal was denounced as uneconomical and unworkable. If it were approved, confusion and corruption—as if there already had not been plenty of both—would follow. The sacred rights of property would be violated. It would be impossible to determine the original owners of vast amounts of paper without an exhaustive search of the records. In the end, Madison's proposal was defeated. Long afterward, it was discovered that the voting had been rife with conflict of interest. Of the sixty-five members of the House, twenty-nine held certificates which were to be funded under the plan.*

The bitterest battle was yet to come, however. This was the struggle over the assumption of some thirty million dollars in state debts by the federal government. To the casual observer, it must have appeared strange that all the states did not enthusiastically welcome a proposition designed to relieve them of a crushing fiscal burden. The problem resulted from the fact that the Southern states, with the conspicuous exception of South Carolina, had paid off most of their war debts and were vehemently opposed to being taxed to pay the debts of those states that had not been as thrifty. The New England states, particularly Massachusetts, had done little toward paying their creditors, and were eager to dump their debts into the lap of the national government—further aggravating the North–South split which had plagued the nation since its founding. Adding to the bitterness among the Southerners was their conviction that most of the certificates to be redeemed had fallen into the hands of Northern money sharks. It was also feared that if Hamilton had his way, the states would be reduced to little more than rowboats following in the wake of a federal man-of-war. "The Secretary's [Hamilton's] people scarce

---

* Plans by the anti-Hamilton forces to examine the records of the Treasury Department after Jefferson's inauguration as president in 1801 were blocked by a fortuitous fire which destroyed most of the documents. Suspicions of conflict of interest were confirmed a century later when scholars examined the federal records on file in the various states.

disguise their design, which is to create a mass of debts which will justify them seizing all the sources of Government, thus annihilating the State Legislatures and creating an empire on the basis of consolidation," Maclay declared.[16]

The debate raged for five months—from February 23 until July 26, 1790. Realizing that the opposition to assumption was much greater than it had been to his funding scheme, Hamilton mobilized every resource at his disposal. Maclay, upon being told that one member of Congress had been offered a thousand guineas for his vote, sardonically replied that he doubted it, as the fellow could be bought "for a tenth part of that sum." While the senator reported that he did not know for certain if bribes had been offered by proponents of assumption, "I am certain that every other kind of management has been practised and every tool at work that could be thought of."[17] Clergymen, members of the government, and of the Order of the Cincinnati, an organization of officers who had served in the Revolution of which Hamilton was a founder, were all mobilized to bring pressure on Congress.

Yet the torrent of words continued and the price of state certificates tobogganed, as the speculators grew frightened and unloaded their holdings. The strength of the opposition dismayed Hamilton's "Senatorial Gladiators," as Maclay called them. "I never observed so drooping an aspect, so turgid and forlorn an appearance as overspread the partisans of the Secretary," he said after six weeks of debate. Some paced back and forth in the Senate chamber and others were even more agitated. Rufus King, the senator from Massachusetts, "looked like a boy who had been whipped, and General Schuyler's hair stood on end as if the Indians had fired at him."[18]

Finally, when chances seemed favorable, a vote was risked in the House on April 12, 1790. As the members of the Senate, who had adjourned for the occasion, and a gallery packed with speculators looked on, national assumption failed by a mere two votes. Hamilton's followers were stunned. Once again, Maclay gleefully described the scene:

Fitzsimons reddened like scarlet; his eyes were brimful. Clymer's color, always pale, now verged to a deadly white; his lips quivered,

and his nether jaw shook with convulsive motions . . . Benson bungled . . . Ames's aspect was truly hippocratic—a total change of face
and features; he sat torpid, as if his faculties had been benumbed
. . . Wadsworth hid his grief under the rim of a round hat. Bou-
dinot's wrinkles rose in ridges and the angles of his mouth were
depressed and assumed a curve resembling a horse's shoe.
Fitzsimons first recovered recollection and endeavored to rally the
discomforted and disheartened heroes. . . . The Secretary's group
pricked up their ears, and Speculation wiped the tear from either
eye. . . .[19]

Disappointed, but not yet ready to admit defeat, Hamilton
looked about for a way to pick up the handful of votes needed to
reverse the decision, while his hard-core New England and South
Carolina supporters kept assumption barely alive through skillful
parliamentary maneuvers. He fully understood that failure to
gain approval of assumption would jeopardize the chances of
success for his entire fiscal program. At this point, a solution
presented itself in the gangling figure of Thomas Jefferson.

Jefferson arrived in New York early in the spring of 1790 to
become Secretary of State and found two struggles under way:
the fierce battle over assumption of the state debts and an only
slightly less confused conflict over the location of the nation's
capital. New York was only the temporary home of the government, and all sections of the nation wanted the honor of being its
permanent host. Proposed locations included almost every town
of any size from New York to the Potomac River. Distances were
long and travel rigorous in those days, so officials from all sections
wished the capital near their homes. New Englanders would settle
for New York or Philadelphia; New Yorkers, of course, wanted
the capital to remain where it was; Pennsylvanians wanted Philadelphia or perhaps a central location in their state; Southerners,
who wished a capital away from the speculators and stock jobbers
of "Hamiltonople," as they called New York, wanted Baltimore or
a site on the Potomac, as did George Washington, who owned
land in the area.
    Hamilton, owing loyalty to no section, probably didn't care how

the question of "residence," as it was known, was resolved—if it ever were. Fisher Ames undoubtedly expressed his viewpoint, when he said: "I care little where Congress may sit. . . . This despicable grog-shop contest, whether the taverns of New York or Philadelphia shall get the custom of Congress keeps us in discord and covers us all with disgrace."[20] A brilliant idea soon struck Hamilton. Why not trade off the location of the capital for the necessary votes for assumption? If his fellow New Yorkers dissented, they could console themselves by the profits of their redeemed state certificates.

The Pennsylvanians were approached first. Maclay would hear nothing of such a proposition, but Robert Morris was amenable. Locating the capital at Germantown or on the Susquehanna River sounded like a fine idea to him, but he would have to convince the state's other representatives to vote for assumption. That would take time. In the meantime, Hamilton went elsewhere. Jefferson relates what happened next:

> Going to the President's one day I met Hamilton as I approached the door. His look was sombre, haggard, and dejected beyond description. Even his dress was uncouth and neglected. He asked to speak with me. We stood in the street near the door. He opened the subject of the assumption of the state debts, the necessity of it in the general fiscal arrangement and its indispensible necessity towards a preservation of the union: And particularly of the New England states, who had made great expenditures during the war, on expeditions which tho' of their own undertaking were for the common
> · cause; that they considered the assumption of these by the Union so just, and its denial so palpably injurious, that they would make it a *sine qua non* of a continuance of the Union.[21]

Hamilton added, as they walked back and forth in front of Washington's mansion on Broadway, that if the measure did not pass, he would resign. For the good of the country as a whole, he suggested that Jefferson persuade some of his Southern friends to switch their votes and support assumption. Undoubtedly, he meant Madison. For his part, Jefferson allowed that he had been out of the country for a long time and was not completely knowledgeable about affairs at home. But what he had learned of assumption "struck me in an unfavorable light," although he was willing to consider the treasury secretary's arguments.

A few days later, according to Jefferson's account, he invited Hamilton and Madison to "a friendly discussion"—probably over a tasty dinner and fine bottle of wine for which the Virginian was to become famous. Perhaps impressed by Hamilton's concern over the possible breakup of the nation, Madison agreed to switch enough Southern votes to pass the assumption bill, although he could not bring himself to vote for it. He noted, however, that inasmuch "as the pill would be a bitter one to the Southern states, something should be done to soothe them." Doctor Hamilton was ready with the soothing syrup. He quickly agreed to trade Southern votes for assumption for Northern votes for a Southern capital—and a marsh beside the Potomac not far from Washington's beloved Mount Vernon was designated as the new seat of government. To placate the Pennsylvanians in case outraged cries of double cross should issue from that quarter, the capital was to be moved temporarily to Philadelphia. It would remain there for ten years while the new seat of government was under construction. Jefferson and Madison then turned their powers of persuasion upon likely candidates for conversion to the cause of assumption.

It was not long before Jefferson began to suspect that he had been outfoxed by Hamilton. He came to strongly regret his part in presiding over the deal and considered it a monumental mistake. His later protestations of ignorance about the true state of affairs in the nation at the time he met Hamilton on Washington's doorstep have the appearance of a cover-up. Jefferson's professions of guilessness do not suit his reputation as a seasoned diplomat who had just returned from five years at the sophisticated French court, and he had assured a group of Dutch bankers while serving abroad that it was safe to buy American state certificates as they would be redeemed at full value.[22]

This conflict was the opening gun in what was to develop into a bitter contest between Hamilton and Jefferson not only for control of the government but also to establish rival political philosophies. Hamilton believed in a strong central government, Jefferson in a minimum of government. Hamilton was the spokesman for the banker and manufacturer; Jefferson for the yeoman farmer. Hamilton welcomed an urbanized and industrialized America; Jefferson held aloft a vision of a nation devoted to the arts and agriculture. Enactment of Hamilton's schemes for funding, for assumption, and for the establishment of a Bank of the United States convinced Jefferson that Hamilton was the chieftain of a well-organized "corrupt squadron" of cheats and embezzlers who dominated the government while honest men looked on helplessly. He sincerely believed that "the credit and fate of the nation seemed to hang on the desperate throws and plunges of gambling scoundrels."

As for Hamilton, he could hardly have cared less. His "system" was aimed at putting the country on its financial feet, and morality was secondary. If speculators piled up fortunes by means of shady maneuvers and the plutocrats ruled the nation, that was all to the good. Like John Jay, he felt that "the people who own the country ought to govern it."[23] The soaring prices of government securities were eloquent testimony to his success, as were rising land prices, particularly near the newly designated capital. No one realized this more than George Washington. Although there is no hard evidence that he had a hand in choosing the site, he was quick to take advantage of it. On December 24, 1795, he wrote a tenant that rents would have to be raised because "lands in this Country generally, and particularly in the vicinity of the federal City, have risen so much in their price. . . ."[24]

VI

To the Victors

YOU HAVE PROBABLY never heard of Samuel Swartout, but he deserves a place in the front rank of any gallery of notable rascals. He was the first man to steal more than a million dollars from the United States Government and get away with it. And Swartout had the good fortune to make off with his instant million in the 1830s—long before inflation had devalued the proceeds of such determined energy and enterprise. A graduate of New York's Tammany knee-in-the-groin, thumb-in-the-eye school of politics, Swartout was typical of the army of spoilsmen who descended upon Washington in the weeks preceding the inauguration of Andrew Jackson on March 4, 1829, with the rallying cry of "To the victors belong the spoils!"

In its brief history, the capital had never seen such revelry. Tennessee backwoodsmen, farmers from the Northwest, laborers and mechanics from the cities of the East, politicians of every stripe, and old soldiers with tales of how they had stood shoulder-to-shoulder with Andy Jackson at New Orleans—all jostled each other in the straggling town on the Potomac mud flats as if some mysterious force had suddenly tipped the continent in that direction. On almost every street corner, Old Hickory's victory over John Quincy Adams was boozily trumpeted as tantamount to revolution. At last the people had won over the decaying forces of privilege and aristocracy. Now the time had come for a division of the spoils—some eleven thousand jobs, including postmaster-ships, that lay within the jurisdiction of the new president.

Sam Swartout had a head start on most of his fellow job-seekers. A long-time follower of Aaron Burr, as a young man Swartout had played a key role in Burr's ill-fated attempt to establish a Western empire. When the scheme was betrayed by General James Wilkinson,* to save his own neck, Swartout stoutly resisted every attempt to force him to testify against his chief. Following Burr's acquittal on charges of treason, Swartout tried to provoke a duel with Wilkinson. When this failed, he publicly posted the general as a coward. Such sterling conduct brought him to the attention of Jackson, who had been on the fringes of the Burr conspiracy. From this time on, Swartout's fortunes were linked with those of Jackson. As he awaited his reward for years of devotion, Swartout zestfully wrote a friend: "No damned rascal who made use of his office or its profits for the purpose of keeping Mr. Adams in, and Gen. Jackson out of power, is entitled to the least lenity or mercy, save that of hanging. . . . Whether or not I shall get any thing in the general scramble for plunder remains to be proven; but I rather guess I shall."[1]

The rest of the invading horde of job-seekers roamed the muddy streets of Washington and surged about the barrooms in a frenzy of celebration. Such a huge amount of whiskey was consumed that a shortage was feared. Hotels and boarding houses were so packed that the visitors were glad to sleep five to a bed or on floors and billiard tables, if they slept at all. Barbers who advertised "hair-cutting in the Jackson-style," and haber-dashers who sold "Jackson stocks" copied from the old-fashioned neckware favored by the president-elect, did a brisk business. Some office-seekers toured the various government departments scattered about the sprawling town to earmark jobs in which they might be interested—terrorizing the clerks who held them out of their wits.

---

* Few men have had as long a history of dishonesty as Wilkinson. While Clothier General of the Continental Army during the Revolution, he had taken a rake-off on supplies which passed through his hands. After the war, he was on the payroll of the Spanish governor at New Orleans while in command of American troops in the West.

Night and day, job-seekers crowded the lobby and corridors of Gadsby's Hotel on Pennsylvania Avenue, where Jackson was staying, in desperate hopes of catching the ear of the president-elect or one of his bustling aides. Martin Van Buren, the urbane New York political manipulator chosen by Jackson as his secretary of state, had no sooner alighted from his stagecoach than he was surrounded by a swarm of office-seekers. As a leader of the "Albany Regency" which ran the Empire State, the "Little Magician" was well-schooled in the spoils system. The job-seekers trooped after Van Buren, grouping themselves about as he threw himself upon a couch to rest in his hotel room. One fellow pressed for anything that would yield from $300 to $3,000 a year as long as it wasn't a clerkship. Asked why he would refuse this type of employment, the job-seeker replied that he couldn't read or write.

Jackson's inauguration was without pomp or pageantry, as he had requested. Thin patches of snow still lingered on the slopes of Capitol Hill, but the day was brightened by a weak sun. Dressed in black, and with his hawk's face bearing a look of determination, Jackson walked from Gadsby's to the Capitol accompanied only by a few friends. His eyes were sad and his heart empty as he mourned the death only a few weeks before of his beloved wife, Rachel. Heated passions aroused by the savage campaign that preceded the election still swirled about the city, casting a shadow over the ceremony. The incoming and outgoing presidents disliked each other with such intensity that there had been no exchange of courtesy visits. Adams had already departed from the White House a bitter and frustrated man.

To avoid the huge crowds awaiting him, Jackson scaled a low wall around the Capitol and entered the building through the basement. Reappearing on the East Portico, he bowed for a moment to acknowledge the cheers of his partisans as a brisk wind ruffled his mane of white hair. Most of his inaugural address was carried away, but one sentence would have incited wild applause from the job-seekers if they had heard it: "The recent demonstration of public sentiment [the election] inscribed on the list of Executive duties, in characters too legible to be overlooked, the task of reform. . . ." *Reform* was the Jacksonian code word for "Throw the rascals out!"

With this formality out of the way, the new president cantered down Pennsylvania Avenue to the White House on horseback, followed by a motley cavalcade of carriages, farm wagons, and horsemen as well as a shouting, laughing throng of men, women, and children of all ages, colors, and position. The mob in Jackson's wake swept through the gates of the White House and into the East Room, where long tables had been spread with cakes, punch, and ice cream. Women screamed and fainted in the melee, clothing was torn, and broken glasses and plates were trampled into the expensive carpeting. Some people stood on the chairs in muddy boots to get a better view of the president. It was "a regular saturnalia," declared one witness. He added that it would have pleased William Wilberforce, the English abolitionist, "to have seen a stout black wench eating a jelley with a gold spoon in the President's House." Jackson finally escaped through a window, and the crowd was decoyed out of the mansion by placing tubs of punch on the lawn. Polite Washington society shuddered and that Sunday a prominent churchman preached a sermon with the text "When Christ drew near the city he wept over it."[2]

And so began the reign of Jacksonian Democracy which established patterns of political behavior that with remarkably few changes have persisted into modern times. It represented the triumph of a new generation of recently enfranchised voters over the corpse of a semiaristocratic Jeffersonian Republicanism that had ruled the nation for nearly thirty years. On all sides the old barriers were tumbling down. One by one, the states had allowed a popular vote for presidential electors. Nominating conventions were soon to replace the congressional caucus as the way of selecting candidates for high office. And in 1828, a president was elected who had been a man of the soil.

Yet Andrew Jackson was no frontier democrat, as he is popularly portrayed. True, he had been born poor and had little education, but he possessed a sizable number of slaves, owned a large plantation, and lived in baronial style. Proud and individualistic, he had been a lawyer, horse trader, judge, land speculator, cotton planter, and soldier—and in no way was he a common man in the mold of those he represented. Like most self-made men, Jackson was basically conservative in his economic, political, and social outlook. He was intolerant, undisciplined, and contemptuous of intellectuals. Despite the efforts of later liberal writers to portray him as a premature New Dealer, Jackson was a frontier aristocrat and a firm believer in laissez-faire economics and a noninterventionist state.[3]

There is one place, however, where Jackson's views and those of his supporters completely coincided, and that was in "rotation of office." He was convinced that one man was as well qualified as another to fill public office. "The duties of all public offices are ... so plain and simple," he declared, "no one man has any more intrinsic right to official station than another." From this view springs one of the great myths of American history—that Jackson originated the spoils system as part of the process of democratization of the electoral system. Certainly, Jackson made loyalty and service to the Democratic party the chief qualification of appointment to public office. But the dubious honor of applying the spoils system to national politics belongs to Thomas Jefferson, who may well have been the shiftiest politician ever to occupy the White House. Proportionately speaking, Jackson probably axed fewer federal appointees for political reasons than did Jefferson. In fact, Jackson cannot even be credited with originating the battle cry of his supporters, "To the victors belong the spoils!" That statement was made by Senator William L. Marcy of New York.

Upon taking power in 1801, Jefferson issued an eloquent appeal for an end to the bitter partisan warfare that threatened to destroy the new nation. "We are all Republicans—we are all Federalists," he declared. But these conciliatory words apparently did not extend to the Federalist jobholders who had dominated the bureaucracy since the founding of the republic. When George Washington had been sworn in as president, he kept most of those who held posts under the Confederation in office. His standards for appointment were extraordinarily high, far above the levels which had been established in Britain or in France, or, for that matter, what his successors were able to maintain.[4] Competence and loyalty to the Constitution were Washington's first criteria for federal employment. But as partisanship developed, emphasis was placed on faithfulness to the Federalist party. John Adams went even further. He made appointments solely on a partisan basis, and to prevent Jefferson from filling vacant jobs, signed a stack of last-minute commissions in the waning hours of his administration that became known as the "midnight appointments."

Jefferson soon found that few jobholders died and none resigned.[5] "If a due participation of office is a matter of right, how can vacancies be obtained?" he asked. To make room for deserving Republicans, he axed as many Federalists as he could. Jefferson called his job "the office of executioner, that of lopping off" the heads of Federalist jobholders. Despite his expressed antipathy for the role of patronage boss, of the 316 offices that fell within his appointive power, only 130 were still held by Federalists two years after Jefferson took office. Even so, he was unable to keep up with the insatiable appetite of his followers. "You would find yourself in most cases with one loaf and ten wanting bread," Jefferson complained. "Nine must be disappointed, perhaps become secret, if not open enemies."

The three presidents who followed Jefferson—James Madison, James Monroe, and John Quincy Adams—inherited a public service which remained almost unchanged, except in size, until the advent of Jackson. With the Federalists fading away as a political force, there was no need to periodically revise the distribution of loaves and fishes. Fossilized over a thirty-year period, the bureaucracy was dominated by a semiaristocracy that believed it owned the jobs it held. Some families gained so firm a control over certain offices that they passed them along from father to son. It was a situation made to order for incompetence, if not corruption.

The War of 1812, occurring almost at midpoint in this period, was marked by the usual graft and profiteering, particularly by the New England merchants who opposed the war in the first place. Perhaps, as has been remarked, a completely honest bureaucracy might have driven the Yankees to actually going through with their repeated threats to break up the Union.[6] The prospects of lining their pockets at the expense of the government kept the New Englanders more or less loyal, but did not prevent them from trading with the British. So brisk was this commerce that the enemy depended upon American suppliers for a large part of their needs. Some Americans drove cattle and other supplies from the interior to border areas on the pretense that the herds were destined for the American army. At night, cattle were driven over to the Canadian side and sold to the British at a satisfying profit.[7]

While the navy did far better than expected against the might of Britain with its handful of ships, the war on land was a comic-opera fiasco. Political generals and superannuated veterans of the Revolution blithely led the army from disaster to disaster. James Wilkinson, despite the long history of double-dealing that trailed after him, was appointed to a top post. As was to be expected, he so badly mismanaged his forces that he was dismissed. There were others less corrupt, but no one more competent.

Graft almost cost Andrew Jackson his victory at New Orleans. Preparing for a British attack, his ill-equipped and poorly trained army of backwoods riflemen, regular troops, militiamen, and temporarily reformed pirates was desperately in need of reinforcements. On January 4, 1815, only four days before the onslaught of the Duke of Wellington's veterans, a long-awaited Kentucky division arrived in the American camp. The cheers which greeted them were short-lived. To his utter consternation, Jackson found the men almost completely unarmed, with only seven hundred guns for nearly twenty-four hundred men. "I don't believe it!" roared the general. "I have never seen a Kentuckian without a gun, a pack of cards, and bottle of whisky in my life!"

Barely able to control his anger, Jackson wrote the secretary of war that "the Arms I have been so long expecting have not yet Arrived. All we hear of them is that . . . the man . . . entrusted with their transportation has halted on the way for the purpose of private speculations. . . . This negligence . . . [threatens] the defeat of our armies." Scraping up some rusty fowling pieces from the citizens of New Orleans, Jackson sent the Kentuckians to man the breastworks he had ordered erected along the Mississippi and won the battle. Probably the government agent with the arms, hearing rumors of the imminence of peace—a treaty had in fact been signed by the United States and Britain in Ghent, Belgium, on Christmas Eve—had stopped off to buy cotton at bargain prices before the news had a chance to spread.[8]

The Peace of Ghent marked not only the end of the war between America and Britain but also of the quarter-century of global conflict that had been touched off by the French Revolution. This struggle had broken the old restraints upon society, and mankind threw off the shackles of the past. As always, there were clever men on hand ready to use technological change and demographic revolution to make a fast buck. Nowhere did this phenomenon have a greater effect than in the United States. Within the three decades from 1800 to 1830, the nation's population soared from a little more than four million people to nearly thirteen million. Through the acquisition of Florida and the Louisiana Purchase, the size of the nation was more than doubled. The simple agrarian economy of the age of Jefferson gave way to the Industrial Revolution. In the first two decades of the nineteenth century, twelve hundred miles of turnpike were built. Canals were dug that brought the products of western farms to the eastern cities cheaply and reliably. Rights of way were cleared for the first steam railroads. Cotton and woolen mills were opened and smoke billowed from countless factory chimneys. Thousands of Americans crossed the Appalachians each year to establish settlements on a frontier that was being pushed ever westward. Eleven new states had already been added to the original thirteen, and more were in the offing.

This transformation from a simple agrarian society to a business economy was aided by an alliance between politics and private enterprise that played a great part in the rapid development of the nation. All too frequently, expansion was marked by dubious promotions, scheming, pirated inventions, speculation and outright corruption of the political process. As industrial activity played a more significant role in the nation's economic life, businessmen grasped the wisdom of influencing the government in their favor. They saw that the decisions made by bureaucracy on such issues as trade and tariffs effected their own enterprises. Therefore, it was to their own interest to exact whatever influence they could over the process of government. "The control of public office often meant control of the political and economic destiny of, if not the nation, a great portion, thereof," states one authority.[9]

Businessmen needed look no further than the shipping industry to see the validity of this statement. From 1789 to 1823, reports Gustavus Myers, the government lost some $250 million in customs duties which the men who ran the American shipping companies had not paid.[10] Some shipping tycoons, including John Jacob Astor, practically financed their operations with money they owed the government. Rather than pay duties on their cargoes, the shipmasters used these funds to finance new ventures. Sometimes they would have the interest-free use of money for years before they deigned to pay the government. Myers estimated that Astor alone enjoyed the interest-free use of over five million dollars in public funds over a period of nearly twenty years.

Much was to be learned from Astor, for no one had more experience in turning the government to his own use and profit.[11] A German butcher's son, Astor had come to America with a few dollars in his pocket and a driving ambition to strike it rich. Shortly after his arrival in New York, he obtained employment in the store of a fur merchant at two dollars a week. There he learned all that was to be known about the fur trade, and with the $300 that his wife brought him as a dowry set himself up in his own business. It was a good time to be in the fur trade. The abandonment by the British of a string of forts that had blocked Yankee expansion into the West and the Louisiana Purchase opened vast tracts of virgin territory to the traders. With a talent for bargaining and by "giving the least and getting the most," Astor was, by the end of the War of 1812—in which it was whispered he had added to his riches by trading with the enemy—the undisputed master of the international fur trade. He was also a shipping tycoon, a merchandising magnate, the owner of more real estate than any other person in New York— and a multimillionaire.

The methods through which Astor amassed this fortune were not very pretty. To obtain furs from the Indians at the lowest possible price, the agents of his American Fur Company exploited the savages mercilessly. Despite government edicts forbidding it, the Indians were plied with cheap liquor and swindled out of their catch while they were befuddled. Enormous profits were also made on the whiskey itself, which was traded to the Indians in exchange for furs. Colonel Josiah Snelling, the commander of the garrison at Detroit, reported that "the neighborhood of the trading houses where whisky is sold, presents a disgusting scene of drunkenness, debauchery and misery; it is the fruitful source of all our difficulties, and nearly all the murders committed in the Indian country. . . . I have daily opportunities of seeing the road strewed with the bodies of men, women and children, in the last stages of brutal intoxication."

The treatment which Astor accorded his own employees was as cold-blooded as that meted out to the hapless Indians. He ruthlessly drove down the already miserable wages paid the trappers, boatmen, and laborers who risked their lives in the wilderness to enrich their master. The wages of these men, which were about $100 annually, were steadily reduced until they were paid $250 for three years' service. At the same time they were cheated and overcharged at the company stores where they bought supplies. It was not uncommon for a trapper to finish three years in Astor's service so deeply in debt that he was forced to sign on for another tour of duty. Even if the men completed their contracts without owing Astor money, they had no assurance of receiving what was due them. Some of Astor's agents were not above having a man murdered to save a few hundred dollars. "It remains a terrifying commentary on the lengths to which men are forced to go in quest of a livelihood, and the benumbing effects on their sensibilities, that the fur traders should find a host of men ready to seduce the Indians into a state of drunkenness, cheat and rob them, and all this only to get robbed and perhaps murdered in turn," declares one historian.

The political clout amassed by Astor along with his enormous wealth placed him beyond the reach of the law. President James Madison and James Monroe, Madison's secretary of state and successor in the White House, were among his personal friends. In fact, Monroe was indebted to Astor to the tune of $5,000, a sum not repaid until after he became president. In Congress, Astor's unqualified champion was Senator Thomas Hart Benton, a Missouri Democrat, who, like several other congressmen, was easily identified by the weight of the moneybags he carried. Not for nothing was Benton known as "Old Bullion." In the West, Governor Lewis Cass of the Michigan Territory, whose domain included much of the area where the fur traders were active, was on Astor's payroll. The American Fur Company's books show that he received at least $35,000 for unstated services. The money was well invested; later as secretary of war, Cass was in a good position to head off any government probe into charges of corruption that might be brought against the company.

Sharp business practices, threats, and violence forced most of Astor's rivals either out of business or to merge with him. But this was not enough. Astor desired a complete monopoly of the fur trade. There were, however, two major stumbling blocks to his scheme for supremacy. He had to find a way to prevent British and Canadian traders from doing business within the territorial limits of the United States, and put an end to the competition from the government's own trading posts or factories. Astor decided to first get rid of his foreign rivals. Monroe and other well-placed friends of the American Fur Company in Washington were informed of the threat to the sovereignty of the United States and legitimate American business by the uncontrolled activities of the foreigners. No further hints were required. In 1816, Congress passed a bill reserving the fur trade for American citizens.

The problem of the government factories was a bit more difficult to deal with. These posts had been opened as part of a humanitarian effort to protect the Indians against the worst excesses of the fur traders. Goods which the Indians wanted were to be sold to them at far lower markups than those charged by the private traders. Fair dealing was to be emphasized and the sale of liquor banned. There can be no argument that the most noble motives had inspired this policy, but like many liberal programs, it was oversold, underfunded, and badly administered. With Senator Benton leading the way, the fur traders' representatives in Congress charged that the government factories were hopelessly inefficient and mismanaged. What was even worse was that they were monopolistic. Benton got himself appointed chairman of a Senate investigating committee which promptly recommended that the government trading posts be closed.

In March 1822, a bill was introduced that abolished the factories. Benton led the fight with a stem-winding speech in which he recited poetry, read from balance sheets, and quoted statements from Astor's agents and other such disinterested parties in an effort to prove the factories were a drain on the Treasury. The posts were also condemned as a public monopoly which barred private enterprise from a legitimate area of operation. "Nothing but individual enterprise, individual industry and attention" would serve to make America great. The bill passed the Senate on May 2, 1822, and sailed through the House two days later. The fur trade and the Indians were now left to the tender mercies of John Jacob Astor.

One of Astor's aides exuberantly wrote to Benton: "I hasten to congratulate you on your decisive victory. . . . The result is the best possible proof of the value to the country of your talents, intelligence, perseverance, and you deserve the unqualified thanks of the community for destroying the pious monster. . . ." A few months later, Astor expressed his own gratitude in a more concrete manner by employing Benton as attorney for the American Fur Company. By then, the senator was at work trying to force the government to divest itself of some publicly owned lead mines, so they could be taken over by another group of would-be tycoons.

Democratization of the political process and the corresponding expansion of business interest in politics encouraged a degree of professionalism—and opportunities for corruption—greater than had ever been seen before. Until the election of 1828, campaign costs had been minimal and organization rudimentary. As long as the right to vote was tightly restricted, most campaigns could be fought in the usually partisan newspapers and at public rallies with limited funds furnished by the candidates and their friends. Now, all that had suddenly changed. Winning a popular majority among an electorate that had been increased to a million voters almost overnight required money and organizational talent. For example, sums ranging from $5,000 to $10,000 were sought in 1828 on behalf of a gubernatorial candidate in Kentucky, indicating that even larger amounts were involved in the presidential campaign. Contributions often came stuffed in carpetbags with no questions asked. In 1839, the Whig political boss, Thurlow Weed, raised $8,000 from a group of New York merchants. The money arrived wrapped in a bandana—and no one thought this unusual.[12]

Mass participation in elections also required the technical skills of political professionals and their machines, such as Tammany Hall, to get out the vote. The price of an uncommitted vote in New York City in 1832 was about five dollars, which was several days' pay for the average laborer. During a mayoralty race in 1838, the price skyrocketed to thirty dollars a head. Both the Democrats and Whigs imported floaters and repeaters from Philadelphia to vote early and vote often.* The hired Whigs wore pins on their left sleeves so that poll watchers would not challenge their own men. Tammany, not to be outdone, put ink marks on the ears of its voters.

Tammany was almost as old as the Constitution, having been founded three weeks before that document went into effect. It was soon an important factor not only in the politics of New York City but in national affairs as well. In the beginning, it was primarily a social and patriotic organization that had been established by the enlisted men of the Revolutionary Army as a counterweight to the aristocratic Society of the Cincinnati, formed by

---

* Floaters sold their votes to the highest bidder while repeaters voted as many times as they could get away with.

ex-officers under the leadership of Alexander Hamilton. Inasmuch as the Society of St. Tammany, as it was formally known, took its name from a chief of the Delaware tribe, it adopted an Indian ritual, calling its leaders sachems and its headquarters the Wigwam. Aaron Burr was among the first to sense that the Tammany Society could be used for political purposes, and put it to work in the campaign of 1800 from which he emerged as Jefferson's vice-president.

Early on, Tammany's leaders sought patronage jobs as a reward for their political efforts and developed sophisticated techniques for manipulating these positions for their own benefit. In 1806, a Tammany sachem was removed from the office of city comptroller because he had appropriated some municipal land without paying for it. There was the almshouse supervisor fired in 1809 after it was discovered his expenses were running four times his salary. The first sachems of Tammany did not limit themselves to legitimate graft, however. As early as 1838, it was estimated that as much as $600,000 a year was extorted from dives, gambling dens, houses of prostitution, and prisoners in the Tombs. Even in those days, extortion was considered "an established custom."[13]

It was only natural in such an atmosphere that charges of corruption should be freely bandied about. In fact, one of the major weapons in Jackson's arsenal during the campaign of 1828 was the alleged corruption of the Adams administration. The Jacksonians claimed that Adams had come to power through a "corrupt bargain" with Henry Clay four years before. In 1824, Jackson had run for the presidency against Adams and Clay but had lost when none of the candidates received a majority in the electoral college, and the choice was thrown into the House of Representatives. Clay, who controlled the votes of three states, swung them to Adams, giving him enough votes to win by the narrow margin.

Outraged, Jackson's partisans charged that a deal had been arranged in which Adams promised to make Clay his secretary of state in exchange for the Kentuckian's votes. Clay and Adams stoutly denied everything, but when the appointment was actually offered and accepted, Jackson's men claimed this was irrefutable proof that the nation's highest office had been bargained away. John Randolph of Roanoke, no admirer of either Clay or Adams, characterized the agreement as "the coalition of Blifil and Black George—the combination unheard of till then, of the Puritan and the blackleg." If nothing else, his picturesque language sent political observers scurrying in search of copies of *Tom Jones.**

"Dirty tricks" were already a mainstay of American politics, and the personal reputations of the candidates were fair game. Adams, a dour and straitlaced man, was accused of having pocketed enormous sums of public money while in office—without the public being told that the total had been arrived at by adding up the entire salary and expenses he had received over thirty years of distinguished service. It was charged that he had purchased "gambling tables and gambling furniture" with federal funds. This turned out to be a billiard table for the White House. Of course, it was useless for Adams's supporters to point out that of the $25,000 that Congress had voted to refurbish the Executive Mansion, the frugal president had spent only $6,000—and had paid for the billiard table out of his own pocket.

There were a number of attempts to smear Jackson, too. He was charged with executing militiamen serving under him during the Florida campaign without trial and faked court-martial documents were circulated. And there was the usual raking over of the irregularities surrounding his marriage to a woman who had not yet obtained a valid divorce from her first husband. Jackson was convinced that the revival of this old scandal had helped cause the death of his wife, and he never forgave Adams for the dirty work of his henchmen.

Nevertheless, it was possible to fight slander, as the indomitable John C. Calhoun proved. Late in 1826, Calhoun, then vice-president under Adams, found himself the subject of a letter from a contractor named Elijah Mix that had been published in

---

* Clay challenged Randolph to a duel as a result of the remark. They met on April 8, 1826, on the Virginia side of the Potomac after Randolph insisted on fighting there rather than at the usual Washington dueling ground at Bladensburg, in Maryland. If he fell it would be on the sacred soil of his native state. Honor was satisfied when both men fired twice—and missed.

an Alexandria newspaper. Mix charged that Calhoun, while secretary of war, had personally profited from a contract for fortifications at Old Point Comfort, Virginia. The next day, a message from the vice-president was dropped on the desk of the Speaker of the House of Representatives demanding a full and immediate inquiry into the charges. Although he was fully aware that the accusation was part of a plot by his political enemies to discredit him, the fiery Calhoun wrote:

> In claiming the investigation of the House, I am sensible, that under our free and happy institutions, the conduct of public servants is a fair subject for the closest scrutiny and the freest remarks. . . . But when such attacks assume the character of impeachable offenses, and become, in some degree official, by being placed among the public records, an officer thus assailed, however base the instrument used, if conscious of innocence, can look for refuge only to the Hall of the immediate Representatives of the People.[14]

At first it looked as if Calhoun had committed a fatal blunder by falling into the trap set for him. For forty days, a seven-member committee of inquiry dominated by the vice-president's political adversaries examined every aspect of his administration of the War Department. They were convinced that Calhoun had called for the probe primarily in the hope of "enlisting public sympathy" and were determined to destroy him. But no matter how hard and deeply it dug, the committee was unable to strike pay dirt. The inquisition ended on February 13, 1827, with the unanimous finding that the vice-president was innocent of having profited from the Mix contract. Calhoun resumed his duties the next day as the presiding officer of the Senate—from which he had voluntarily suspended himself during the inquiry—and never again was his honesty questioned.*

---

* In 1973, Spiro T. Agnew tried to use the Calhoun precedent to stall his eventual resignation as vice-president, after being accused of soliciting and accepting bribes and kickbacks while county executive of Baltimore County and governor of Maryland. This time, the House was wary, and Agnew was forced out of office. Oddly enough, Calhoun was the first vice-president to resign. He stepped down in 1832 after a stormy dispute with Jackson over the tariff to become senator from South Carolina. There, any resemblance between Calhoun and Agnew ends. Calhoun was an honest man.

*   *   *

Like an Old Testament avenging angel, Andrew Jackson set to work immediately after his inauguration to scourge those who had been so wicked as to oppose his election. In his own hand he set out an "Outline of Principles" to be followed in staffing the new administration. It began high-mindedly enough with an admonition to all department heads to determine what retrenchments could be made in the public service to improve economy and efficiency. And then Jackson got down to business. Orders were issued for the immediate dismissal of all those "who were appointed against the manifest will of the people or whose official station, by a subserviency to selfish electioneering purposes, was made to operate against the freedom of elections."

Enough petty grafters were found in the dusty recesses of the government to provide some proof to support Jackson's campaign charges that the Adams administration had been riddled with corruption. He discovered that some Treasury clerks had taken the bankrupt's oath as many as a dozen times and eighty-seven had prison records. Jackson glowed with accomplishment when informed that the embezzlements charged to those who were deposed had totaled at least $280,000.[15]

The subtle hand of Martin Van Buren was prominent in the filling of government jobs with administration supporters. In Albany, he had seen hundreds of public servants vanish from the payroll after each election, as if by magic, to be replaced by others. He wished to apply the same legerdemain in Washington and settled on the Post Office Department as the primary vehicle for building up a national political machine. When John McLean, the postmaster general, refused to be a party to sweeping removals of postmasters solely on political grounds, Van Buren decided that he should be replaced. McLean was kicked upstairs to the Supreme Court. William T. Barry, his successor, did what was expected of him so well that he was later accused of widespread fraud in the handling of mail contracts.

The axes of the spoilsmen flashed all across the nation during the spring of 1829. "I turned out six clerks on Saturday," an official wrote his wife. "Several of them have families and are poor. It was the most painful thing I ever did." Spies abounded in every office. They collected gossip and repeated everything that was in the least bit critical of the removals, the administration, and the president. The identity of these agents was kept a closely guarded secret, so everybody suspected everyone else. Washington was a company town with government its single industry and anything that disrupted the familiar grooves of the bureaucracy created panic. One Treasury clerk went mad at the thought that he might be removed from his usual rut, and another, in the War Department, concealed his insanity long enough to slash his throat from ear to ear.

Jackson's aides and advisors might make proposals on who was to go and who was to remain, but the final decision rested with the president. For example, Van Buren wished to replace the aged Solomon Van Rensselaer, the postmaster at Albany, with a party wheelhorse. Somehow, the old man gained entrance to a White House reception and instead of leaving with the rest of the guests, seated himself on a sofa until noticed by the president. The surprised Jackson was about to engage him in conversation when Van Rensselaer blurted out: "General Jackson, I have come here to talk to you about my office. The politicians want to take it from me, and they know I have nothing else to live upon."

Before the president could reply, the old man began to pull off his coat.

"In heaven's name what are you going to do?" asked the astonished president. "Why do you take off your coat in a public place?"

"Well, sir, I am going to show you my wounds which I received in fighting for my country," said Van Rensselaer, who by now was in shirtsleeves.

"Put on your coat at once, sir!" commanded the president. In a somewhat softer manner, he told his visitor, "I am surprised that a man of your age should make such an exhibition of himself." And with that, he ushered the old fellow out of the White House with the assurance that he would not be replaced as long as Andrew Jackson was president of the United States.

The axe was wielded with such abandon, however, that no one knew where it would fall next. Another elderly bureaucrat, Elbridge Gerry, the son and namesake of a signer of the Declaration of Independence and former vice-president, made a personal plea to the president that he be kept on as surveyor of the port of Boston. Having fallen upon evil times, he pocketed his pride and said the salary was needed to maintain his mother and four unmarried sisters. Although Gerry readily acknowledged that Adams was an old family friend and he had voted for him, Jackson promised that he could remain in his post. Nine months later, learning that he was to be removed, Gerry came to Washington to personally confront the president. Upon being reminded of his promise, Jackson ordered Gerry from the White House in a towering rage for having questioned the presidential word.[16]

Nevertheless, despite Jackson's fulminations about "reform," most of the spoilsmen lingering in Washington in hopes of obtaining jobs were disappointed. Of an approximate total of 612 presidential officers, only 252 were replaced. If postmasterships are included, the number of ousters is greater, for there were from 400 to 600 changeovers in that department.[17] During Jackson's entire eight-year tenure in the White House, only from one-tenth to one-third of all federal officeholders were replaced for political reasons. As has been noted, Jackson probably fired fewer job-holders in proportion to the size of the civil service than had Jefferson in 1801. Why, then, has Jackson's administration become associated with the worst excesses of the spoils system? The answer probably lies in the fact that unlike Jefferson's well-publicized agonizings, the Jacksonians swung their axes with obvious delight and relish.

The result was a civil service that was probably less efficient than the system Jackson had inherited, but much better adapted to the needs and character of the society it served. Alexis de Tocqueville, an astute French observer of Jacksonian America, was surprised upon his arrival in the United States in 1831 "to find so much distinguished talent among the subjects and so little among the heads of the Government." But even though de Tocqueville found the American public officials "frequently unskillful and sometimes contemptible," he readily acknowledged that, in contrast to Europe, they were "uniformly civil, accessible to all the world, attended to all requests and obliging in replies."[18]

They were probably also somewhat more corrupt—with the faithful Sam Swartout accounting for the most swag by far. Swartout had come to Washington with his eye set on the juiciest plum within the gift of the president—the collectorship of the port of New York, with revenues of at least ten million dollars a year. Even Van Buren was appalled at the idea of presenting such a lucrative prospect for plunder to Swartout. Although they were both veterans of New York politics, Van Buren and Swartout represented rival factions—the former the upstate "Albany Regency" while the latter was a Tammany sachem. Besides, Van Buren was convinced that the gregarious Swartout lacked the subtlety that such an important post required. Undoubtedly, Swartout's transparent machinations would quickly embroil the administration in trouble. When the president asked him to pass on the proposed nomination, the secretary of state replied that "the appointment of Mr. Swartout . . . would not be in accordance with public sentiment, the interests of the Country or to the credit of the administration."

But Jackson was not to be denied this boon to one of his favorites. Van Buren, who had no desire to be kicked upstairs to the Supreme Court as had happened to John McLean, the postmaster general who made the mistake of resisting the president's wishes in the field of patronage, acquiesced in the appointment. Privately, Van Buren agreed with the sentiments expressed by C. C. Cambreleng, a New York congressman, who had written him: "If our Collector is not a defaulter in four years, I'll swallow the Treasury if it was all coined in coppers."[19]

Actually, Cambreleng was wrong—it took eight years for Swartout to be caught with his hand in the till. During that whole period, he had been secretly diverting customs duties and deposits to a series of freewheeling speculations in land, canals, banks, and railroads with no one the wiser. Not until he suddenly hopped on a boat to Europe did anyone bother to examine his books. The revelations were sensational. Swartout was found to have embezzled at least $1,225,705.69. He was soon joined in his plush European exile by William M. Price, the U.S. Attorney for the Southern District of New York and a fellow Tammany stalwart. Price's speculations, however, were minor-league stuff—amounting to a mere $72,124.06.

Swartout remained abroad until 1841, when the hue and cry about his raid on the customs house had died down. He then returned to New York—not to be laid by the heels but to learn that he had added a new word to the language. For years afterward, anyone who lined his pockets at the expense of the government was said to have "swartouted." In fact, the only one who seems to have suffered because of Swartout's adventure in graft on a grand scale was Martin Van Buren, who had warned against making the appointment in the first place. He had the bad luck to be in the White House when Swartout departed for more hospitable climes and was saddled with the blame. It helped cost him reelection to the presidency in 1840.

VII

The Eagle Spreads
Its Wings

LEGEND HAS IT that in antebellum times there was an Alabama
congressman who periodically amused himself and his colleagues by turning a somersault or two on the House floor while
proclaiming, "America is a great country! America is a great
country!"[1] This was carrying exuberance a bit far, although at the
midpoint of the nineteenth century the United States was indeed
a great country. In the years immediately preceding the Civil
War, the American people were enjoying the fruits of the richest
and most prolonged boom yet experienced in the history of the
young Republic. The continent fairly oozed wealth. Exploitation
of field, forest, and mineral vein, the weaving of a net of rail lines,
the opening of factories, iron mills, and machine shops—all
promised new roads to riches.

But alongside this wild and free frontier of progress was another world—a shadowy domain of graft and corruption. The
United States was also a land of wirepullers, lobbyists, speculators, huge land grabs, votes bought and sold in Congress, the
open hawking of public offices, political machines that herded
masses of immigrants to the polls, and of state legislatures and

municipal governments that were the best that money could buy. In New York City, the Board of Aldermen, already known as "The Forty Thieves," sold ferry leases and street railway franchises to the highest bidder with impunity. They charged the city $100,000 for land to be used for a paupers' burial ground which had cost less than a third of that amount. Things got so bad that the City Hall—with all its furniture and fittings—was sold at public auction to satisfy a judgment of $196,000 which had been obtained fraudulently. And when the body of Henry Clay, which had been lying in state in New York, was sent off to Albany, the resourceful aldermen billed the taxpayers for $1,400 for cigars and booze consumed on the boat ride up the Hudson.[2]

The love affair between business and politics which had bloomed during the age of Jackson had ripened with the years until the two were inextricably intertwined. The acquisitive spirit had penetrated into almost every level of American society, carrying away in its torrential course most of the moral barriers that had been built into the conscience of preceding generations. To the old temptation of speculation in land was added an appreciation of the profits to be realized from government policies favorable to rapid development. Insistent demands were made for larger appropriations for public improvements, sweeping land grants, and protective tariffs which ran counter to the laissez-faire principles of earlier years. The sale of political influence to businessmen intent on making fortunes from the favors that lay within the gift of the government became an industry in itself. And as the value of the spoils multiplied, the degree of corruption increased apace.

The lasting contribution of Daniel Webster to American politics was his demonstration to the financiers and manufacturers spawned by the Industrial Revolution of the value of an able friend in the Senate. The lesson was so thoroughly digested that the acquisition of lawmakers has been one of the primary objectives of big business ever since. But if a present-day senator were as indiscreet in seeking bribes as was Webster, most lobbyists would probably run for cover. During his long career in public life, he solicited and eagerly accepted gifts totaling hundreds of thousands of dollars that had been gathered by passing the hat among businessmen and financiers. They thought his value to their cause a bargain at any price—which it was.

As a result, Webster's booming oratory, often warmed up with copious doses of brandy, was completely at the disposal of his clients. With an elasticity of conscience, he moved from free trade to protectionism; from support of his native New England's right to secede to championship of a strong Union; from opposition to a national bank to ardent defender of the institution. He seemed to forget that he had already sold his services to the people when he drew his salary as a United States senator, and therefore had no right to sell them again.*

Webster's appearance and histrionic talent rather than the substance of his ideas accounted for his ability to capture the imagination of the people. The most commanding figure in public life, he had eyes that seemed to burn like coals from under a precipice of brows. "The sense in Webster's speeches frequently breaks down, vaporizes and vanishes under analysis, but their sound is superb," comments one biographer.[3] A melodious voice gave distinction to the most banal of platitudes, transforming them into eloquence. Webster's philosophy may well be summed up in a statement attributed to him: "Let Congress take care of the Rich, and the Rich will take care of the Poor." The rich may not have taken care of the poor, but under the prodding of Webster's soaring eloquence, Congress took care of the rich— and, in turn, the rich certainly took good care of the "God-like Daniel."

Even in his own day, Webster's conduct was the subject of gossip. Ralph Waldo Emerson recorded what he said were Webster's

---

* Looking for someone with whom the late Senator Everett McKinley Dirksen, the oleaginous Illinois Republican, could be compared, an unnamed official told *Newsweek* (June 16, 1969) that Dirksen "is the most venal man in American politics today, and perhaps the most venal since Daniel Webster. . . . He has a price for everything." Dirksen himself acknowledged receiving "sustaining funds" to help him maintain his style of living. These, he said, were "helpful contributions from those who recognize the difficulty that public service interposes for you. . . ." Webster probably would have added a fervent "Amen." So oblivious were Dirksen's colleagues to his questionable activities they named a Senate office building after him.

three maxims for living: "(1) Never to pay any debt that can by any possibility be avoided; (2) Never to do anything to-day that can be put off till to-morrow; (3) Never to do anything himself which he can get anybody else to do for him." Washington society chuckled over the story of how Webster, having dined and drunk too well before a performance by Jenny Lind, rose at the end of her first song and bowed majestically when he heard the applause.[4]

Webster's problem was that although he earned large fees as a brilliant advocate, he was incapable of handling his own finances. Worshiping admirers were constantly being bombarded to bail him out of his latest round of money troubles. From the beginning of Webster's political career, he was subsidized by "friends," allegedly to recompense him for the income "lost" while representing them in Washington. As early as 1813, while defending New England's mercantile interests in the House of Representatives, he accepted payments from the merchants who stood to benefit from his efforts. "You must contrive some way for me to get rich as soon as there is peace," Webster wrote one of his supporters. When he began circulating broad hints that he might be forced to leave the Senate because of his need for money, Boston's leading citizens presented him with a sizable trust fund. Not long before, Webster had been working on the floor of the Senate for a protective tariff—an issue in which many of the contributors to the fund had an interest. This fund was replenished with another assessment—for perhaps as much as $100,000—a few years later.

Webster was not above using government funds with the same lightheaded abandonment with which he treated his own money. He attempted to repay one loan of $10,000 by helping the lender secure an appointment as minister to China. Serious questions were also raised about Webster's handling of secret service funds under his supervision while he was secretary of state. Among other things, it was charged that he used some of the money to influence newspapers to support a northeastern boundary settlement he negotiated with the British. And a group of Wall Street financiers who made up a purse for Webster's personal use raked in generous profits from their dealings with the State Department during his tenure in office.

Probably the most open and unblinking conflict of interest was Webster's connection with the Bank of the United States. He was indebted to the bank to the tune of at least $32,000 and was on retainer as its attorney while he was a member of the Senate with a life-and-death vote over the institution as it was locked in a titanic struggle with Andrew Jackson for its very existence. During this battle, he wrote a famous letter to Nicholas Biddle, the president of the embattled bank, unashamedly demanding a payoff: "I believe my retainer has not been renewed or *refreshed* as usual. If it be wished that my relation to the Bank should be continued it may be well to send me the usual retainers."

Webster saw nothing wrong with such a crass attitude. Probably, he thought—if he thought about it at all—that in protecting the interests of big business or the Bank of the United States, he was protecting the interests of the American people. This may have been intellectual dishonesty on his part, but it was not a viewpoint that was restricted solely to Webster. Henry Clay was another member of the stable of "useful and valuable" political attorneys maintained on Biddle's payroll. On one occasion Biddle informed Clay that "your remuneration, liberal as it was designed to be, has been amply earned."

The transformation of the United States from an agrarian to an industrial society not only created new institutions to meet its needs but also generated new forms of corruption. Just as individual owners and simple partnerships retreated before the chartered corporation, the old ways of cheating gave way to more sophisticated and complicated forms of dishonesty. Instead of the explosive rough and tumble antics of the past, corruption now consisted of a shrewd man who sat behind a large desk and manipulated other people's money to his own use. Impressively engraved bank notes and stock certificates that were often not worth the paper they were printed on were rapidly becoming the new symbols of wealth—and corruption.

Banks flourished throughout the nation despite the warnings of past leaders. From his Virginia mountaintop, Thomas Jefferson had claimed that banks would "enrich swindlers at the expense of the honest and industrious part of the nation," while John Adams had warned of "a plague of banks" settling upon the country. But the need for easy credit to finance the continued expansion of commercial and manufacturing enterprise led the states to charter banks. Although bank notes issued by these institutions may not have been the most reliable form of capital, it was the only supply of ready-flowing money in an era when hard cash was scarce.

Nevertheless, Jefferson's bitter words were an apt description of most of the banks that mushroomed across the nation. Any man with an unlimited amount of nerve and a few thousand dollars could usually bribe a state legislature into granting a charter that would transform him into an instant financier. Armed with this document, the newly minted banker could issue paper money as fast as the printing presses could turn it out. Supposedly, these bank notes were secured by gold and silver on deposit in the bank's vault, but more often than not there was nothing behind the paper but the promise of the bank to redeem it.

One bank in Ohio was chartered as an Orphan's Institute; another was founded on the charter of a moribund library association with assets consisting of a few shelves of dog-eared books. There were at least three hundred different kinds of authorized notes, to say nothing of counterfeits. Learning that the state inspectors were due, a bank would accumulate enough specie to satisfy legal requirements. Then the cash would be whisked away to serve the same purpose at another bank. Bank examiners in Michigan complained in 1839 that the same cache had preceded them to so many banks that they recognized some of the coins. "Gold and silver flew about the country with the celerity of magic," they reported. "Its sound was heard in the depths of the forest; yet, like the wind, one knew not whence it came or whither it was going."[5]

When Joseph Smith, the Mormon prophet who then lived in Kirtland, Ohio, needed money to pay his debts, he organized the Kirtland Safety Society Bank Company with a capital stock of "not less than four million dollars." Just as a supply of crisp new bank notes arrived from the printer, word was received that the

Ohio legislature had refused to grant a charter to the bank. Smith was much too resourceful to be halted by such a minor technicality. He immediately renamed the institution the Kirtland Safety Society Anti-Banking Company, and the bank notes, with the name suitably altered with a rubber stamp, were circulated. The bank was said to have been established by a revelation from God, and it would "grow and flourish, and spread from the rivers to the ends of the earth." Doubters were taken by Smith into the vault which was lined with boxes, each marked $1,000, and packed with glistening silver coins. Later, it was disclosed that those boxes were filled with sand, lead, and old iron topped off with a thin layer of half-dollar pieces.[6]

Such operations were known as wildcat banks because the offices where they promised their notes would be redeemed usually lay in some Godforsaken spot, perhaps in a deep forest where wildcats prowled. There were also "saddlebag banks" whose officers wisely kept on the move. One "banker" gave this description of his operation:

> Well, I didn't have much else to do so I rented an empty store building and printed "bank" on the window. The first day I was open for business a man came in and deposited one hundred dollars. The second day another deposited two hundred fifty dollars, and so along about the third day I got confidence enough in the bank to put in a hundred myself.

In 1816, reacting to wild speculation in banks and bank notes, Congress had chartered the Second Bank of the United States with the purpose of creating some sort of order out of financial chaos. The successor of the national bank organized by Alexander Hamilton as part of his scheme to fund the federal debt, the B.U.S., as it was known, was chartered for twenty years and was headquartered in Philadelphia. The institution was capitalized at $35 million, one-fifth of it provided by the government, and was to be the depository of federal funds. As a central bank, it could restrain the flow of paper money from the state banks, and thereby help stem the relentless spiral of inflation.[7]

The original management of the B.U.S. was as weak and as corrupt as that of any of the wildcat banks. A gang of grafters operating out of the Baltimore branch systematically looted the institution. Under the leadership of the branch cashier, James McCulloch, these freebooters practically backed a horse and wagon up to the back door and carted away the bank's deposits. They used the money to buy stock in the bank, and made substantial loans to themselves. McCulloch, who was said to have no assets of his own, cheerfully remedied that situation by lending himself more than $500,000. The frauds ultimately cost the bank over a million and a half dollars and almost forced it to close its doors.

Yet, in the long run, the depredations of the Baltimore conspirators produced favorable consequences. The old management was ousted and replaced by abler men, among them Nicholas Biddle. This suave and brilliant Philadelphia aristocrat first appeared on the scene as a member of the bank's board of directors. Within a few years he was made its president at the age of thirty-six. Even in those days, Biddle was considered something of a genius. He had completed all the work for a degree at the University of Pennsylvania by the time he was thirteen, and when the school piously refused to award him a diploma because he was too young, he went off to Princeton where he earned another degree—this time with honors—within two years.

Urbane and witty, Biddle was more a scholar than a businessman, with an interest in Hellenic civilization that helped inspire the Greek revival movement that flourished in America during the Jackson years. In fact, the bank's main building, built in the form of a graceful Greek temple on Chestnut Street under Biddle's direction, is still considered an architectural gem. According to Bray Hammond, the banker-historian, Biddle was far ahead of his time in using the B.U.S. to manipulate the credit supply and help provide a stable economy. But for all his intelligence and wit, Biddle was no match for Andrew Jackson on a rampage—and he compounded his weakness by convincing himself that he was.

The epic battle between Jackson and the B.U.S. is usually portrayed as a class struggle between the agrarian West and the "money power" of the East—the small farmers and the simple

mechanics arrayed against the "monster" bank. In reality, however, the "Bank War" was a contest between two conflicting crews
of capitalists for control of the nation's economy. On the side of
the bank were the older business interests who wanted a stable
currency and an even flow of credit so that they could maintain
their dominance. On the other side were the new entrepreneurs
lunging for power in both business and politics and impatient
with all limitations on expansion. They demanded an easier flow
of money and credit, freer access to land and an end to monopolies.

Like most Westerners, Jackson was not only suspicious of banks
and bankers on principle but was also convinced that Biddle's
policies severely restricted opportunities to get ahead. "All the
flourishing cities of the West are mortgaged to this money power,"
thundered "Old Bullion" Benton, putting tongue to the fears of
the Jacksonians. "They are in the jaws of the monster! A lump of
butter in the mouth of a dog! One gulp, one swallow, and all is
gone!" The antibank forces also had an unexpected ally: lurking
in the shadows were the moneymen of New York awaiting the
destruction of the B.U.S. and the shift of the center of financial
power from Chestnut Street to Wall Street.

The battle was joined when Henry Clay persuaded Biddle of
the political wisdom of bringing up the rechartering of the bank
during the presidential election campaign of 1832, rather than
waiting another four years for the charter to expire. Clay, the
Whig candidate for president, argued that Jackson would be over
a barrel no matter what he did. The bill was certain to be passed
by Congress. If the president signed it, he would lose the support
of the South and West; if he vetoed it, there would go the East—
particularly Pennsylvania, where the B.U.S. was popular. A furious struggle raged on the floor of Congress and in the newspaper columns. Biddle doled out loans to prominent politicians
and influential editors. At his fingertips were possibilities for
corruption on a grand scale. "I can remove all the constitutional
scruples in the District of Columbia," he bragged to a correspondent. "Half a dozen Presidencies, a dozen Cashierships, fifty
Clerkships, a hundred Directorships"—all lay within his power to

distribute "to worthy friends who have no character and no money."

The recharter bill was finally passed on July 3, 1832. When Biddle made a triumphal appearance in the House of Representatives after the vote, the members crowded around to shake his hand. But from his sickbed, Jackson firmly declared, "The bank . . . is trying to kill me, but I will kill it!" To the surprise of Clay and Biddle, he promptly issued a veto message that burst like a thunderclap over the nation. The "hydra of corruption" was denounced in ringing terms as un-American, unconstitutional, and undemocratic. And who had written this important state paper? Why, Amos Kendall, the Postmaster General who was to become a millionaire through his machinations in state banking charters, and Roger B. Taney, the attorney general and future Chief Justice of the United States, who not only owned shares in state banks but thriftily added to his holdings as he worked on the death warrant of the B.U.S.

Not to be outdone, Biddle spent as much as $80,000 of the bank's funds on propaganda—carefully itemized in accordance with sound banking practices as "stationery and printing." Pro-bank newspapers raised the specter of "the fearful consequences of revolution, anarchy and despotism" which would occur if Jackson won. One New York newspaper, the *Courier and Enquirer*, which had ardently supported the president, suddenly switched sides and began to denounce Jackson. Later, it was revealed that the paper's owners had borrowed $50,000 from the bank and had been given the option of paying up or supporting Biddle.[8] In the end, Jackson's veto was upheld by Congress and reaffirmed by the voters in November when he overwhelmingly defeated Clay for the presidency. The Kentuckian, who had once said "I'd rather be right than President," ended up being neither.

Taney, given the task of shifting federal deposits from the B.U.S. to various state banks, chose those receiving the government's largess with the same care that was reserved for doling out the better jobs under the spoils system. This sudden influx of cash into the economy resulted in a chaotic wave of speculation. A flood tide of wildcat money spewed from the state banks, which grew in number from 506 in 1834 to 788 within three years. The whole shaky edifice came crashing down in 1837, precipitating a financial panic and depression. Thus, Jacksonian fulminations about curbing the "bribery bank" and of an end to special privileges and monopoly, availed the small farmer, the frontiersman and the city mechanic absolutely nothing. If anything, these people were worse off than before. Wall Street eventually picked up the pieces and created a financial dictatorship that was more ruthless and corrupt than anything that had been envisioned by Andrew Jackson.

Railroads added a new dimension to the expansion of the republic—and opened fabulous pathways for corruption. Railroad construction was attended by an unending procession of fraud, bribery, swindles, and double-dealings that unleashed upon the nation a horde of unalloyed rascals of such magnitude as had never been seen before, and, hopefully, will never be seen again. The names of "robber barons" such as Daniel Drew, Russell Sage, Commodore Cornelius Vanderbilt, Jay Gould, Collis Huntington, and Jim Fisk became household words. Nevertheless, there were railroad builders as well as railroad manipulators. Part businessman and part prophet, these men won victories over mountains, snows, and swamps, built bridges over countless rivers, and vanquished Indians, politicians, and business rivals alike.

Puffing locomotives, the smell of hot iron and oil, and a vision of rails vanishing over the horizon excited a fever in the blood of most Americans. The railroads were born, however, not in romance but as a result of a struggle by such cities as Boston, Baltimore, and Charleston to preserve their share of western commerce against the threat of the inland canal. "It became the object of each city to build railroads which would gather up the trade of the back country," remarks one historian, "and funnel it to its own wharves and warehouses."[9]

Soon, any city or town of consequence had to have a railroad, even if it were to start nowhere and end nowhere. Within two decades after the Baltimore & Ohio Railroad began operations on its first thirteen miles of track, or by 1850, a network of short lines stretched from Maine to Georgia and poked its way over the Appalachians. Few places of substantial population in the eastern part of the country were out of earshot of what Walt Whitman called the locomotive's "fierce-throated beauty."[10]

In the beginning, the money to finance the railroads came from small private investors. Merchants, businessmen, and professionals residing in the proposed terminal cities, and farmers living alongside the planned rights of way—many of whom had never seen a locomotive—were persuaded to buy capital stock or bonds out of local pride or the hope of making quick and spectacular profits. But with track costing anywhere from ten to sixty thousand dollars a mile to lay, most communities could not raise this sort of capital. They turned to the government for assistance, and the state legislatures, under voter pressure, were eager to participate. A shower of land grants, bond issues, franchises, and charters flowed from the state houses. Over the fifteen-year period preceding the Civil War, the states kicked in more than $90 million to the railroads.[11] Cities and towns vied with each other in granting monopolies, free rights of way, and depot and pier facilities. The icing on the cake was provided by the federal government, which after 1850 provided substantial land grants for railroad construction.

Such a wide-open system was made to order for venturesome men, unburdened with sensitive consciences and with an urge to make a fast buck at someone else's expense. Although many railroads were honestly built and competently managed, the pattern of corruption that was to be a prominent feature of the post–Civil War period had been firmly established long before Fort Sumter was fired upon. Smooth-talking promoters bilked investors out of their savings with tantalizing visions of the coming of the iron horse; they bribed legislatures and watered stock. Officials who siphoned off company funds into their own pockets were soon commonplace. In various places, travelers reported finding the rusting and abandoned tracks of fly-by-night railroad schemes. Speaking of one railroad promoter, Wendell Phillips, the reformer, declared that "as he trailed his garments across the country, the members of twenty legislatures rustled like dry leaves in a winter's wind." And in 1861, Governor Alexander W. Randall, of Wisconsin, was moved to observe: "In the history of the financial speculations of this country, so bold, open unblushing frauds, taking in a large body of men were never perpetrated."[12]

Railroads were supposed to be run for the benefit of the public which had poured huge amounts of tax money into their construction. In practice, however, the insiders really ran them for their own benefit. The Camden & Amboy, which had been given a profitable monopoly of service between New York and Philadelphia by the New Jersey legislature, cast the mold that was quickly adopted elsewhere. The Stevens family, which controlled the line, used outright bribery, free passes for deserving politicos, and the purchase of newspapers to ensure successive governors and legislators would be subservient to their railroad. "In the fifteen years before 1860, they were the most notorious manipulators of the New Jersey legislature," writes Gustavus Myers. "Time after time, they lobbied bills through, swayed the elections and the courts, ignored or evaded the laws, and bled the public by an illegal system of transportation charges."[13] New Jersey was so deep in the railroad's clutches that it was known as "the Camden & Amboy state."

The promotion of new lines—not the drudgery of operation—was the key to quick riches. "The main idea was to grab all you could and make off with the proceeds before investigating committees, grand juries, and bilked electorates discovered what you were doing under the guise of forwarding white civilization through the wilderness," remarks Richard O'Connor in his book on Western railroads.[14] Railroads had a distinct pattern, according to O'Connor, which would more or less follow this scenario:

Operating with barely enough capital to buy stationery and print up a flamboyant-looking bond issue, a promoter would first set about persuading a state legislature to grant him a charter. These were usually easy enough to obtain: all that seemed to be required was a map showing the proposed route. Within a half-dozen years after the B&O began operations, some two hundred lines had been chartered, most of them swallowing up the savings of the investors without laying so much as a foot of track. In return for passing out part of the bond issue to members of the legislature and other prominent citizens, the promoter would receive a sizable land grant consisting of alternate sections— usually of 640 acres—along the proposed right of way. Without spending a single cent for construction or laying so much as a foot of track, the promoter had suddenly been transformed into a wealthy man. The insiders would now be asked to participate in the establishment of a separate land company to dispose of the acreage that had been bestowed upon them. The actual building would not begin, however, until part of the land had been sold off at handsome prices and the investor-legislators had voted the company a hefty cash subsidy. Bonds would also be peddled in Europe, where investors had a touching faith in the potentialities of Western railroads, despite repeatedly burned fingers. Construction would then be farmed out to another company also formed by the insiders, which would lay the rails at a vastly inflated cost to the shareholders.

When the line was almost completed, advertisements would be run in European newspapers, and emigrants' guides would be printed that painted a glowing picture of conditions along the railroad's right of way. "The backwoodsman of the West has many substantial enjoyments," trumpeted one such guide. "After the fatigue of the journey west, and a short season of privation and danger, he finds himself surrounded with plenty. His cattle, his hogs and poultry supply his table with meat; the forest abounds in game; the fertile soil yields abundant crops. . . ."[15] And, of course, the railroad would bring a ready market for the emigrants' produce right to his door. What was left of the land grant would be sold to these hopeful souls at marked-up prices. If they had no cash left to buy seed or supplies, were unable to cope with the harsh climate or drought, succumbed to cholera and other diseases, or were murdered by angry Indians—that was no worry of the railroad promoter. By then, he had sold out his interest and was operating at full throttle on a grander scheme elsewhere.

* * *

The construction of the Illinois Central Railroad was typical. Through the unstinting efforts of Senator Stephen A. Douglas of Illinois, who profited both personally and politically, the railroad received a vast land grant in 1850 that was valued at $25 million. The first such grant made by the federal government to a railroad, it paid for the construction of the line with about $9 million in profits left over for the insiders. The Illinois Central land grant sparked a speculative fever that spread across the nation. Grenville M. Dodge, then a young surveyor in Illinois and, later, the builder of the Union Pacific, wrote to his father: "I can double any amount of money you've got in six months. . . . Buy a couple of Mexican [War] land warrants, send them out and I'll locate them in places where land is selling at this minute for $2.50 an acre. The warrants for a quarter section each, can be bought back east for about a dollar. . . . Don't tell anybody about it, but get to work."

Demands for vast land grants for railroad construction deluged Congress. One would-be railroad magnate and land baron had a distinct advantage over the others, however. Russell Sage was a congressman from upstate New York, so when he wanted a grant for a railroad planned in Wisconsin, he helped push through a bill which gave the state nearly 2.4 million acres to be distributed to railroad builders. So blatant was the corruption surrounding passage of the bill that three congressmen were expelled from their seats and a House committee reported: "The undersigned believe that it is clearly established by the testimony that money has been liberally used to secure the passage of bills. . . ."16

Such action was par for the course at the time. Samuel Colt, the inventor of the revolver, paid at least $60,000 to obtain approval of a bill extending the life of his patents. A New England woolen-mill owner passed out $87,000 in bribes in hope of having the duty lowered on raw wool and dyes used in his operations. One of the lobbyists involved in this case was Abel R. Corbin, who was to become the brother-in-law of Ulysses S. Grant. Commodore Cornerlius Vanderbilt, E. K. Collins and other steamship line operators handed out hefty bribes to get mail contracts. W. W. Corcoran, the leading Washington banker, was said to have bribed government officials to become middlemen in the handling of funds paid to Mexico as an indemnity for territory seized by the United States during the war between the two nations, Corcoran's bank, conveniently located across the street from the Treasury, was said to have realized at least $500,000 from the transaction. Jay Cooke, another banker, made "large sums" by working hand-in-glove with officials with inside information about the disposition of Texas bonds after the annexation.

The executive branch had its share of scandals, too. Under President James Buchanan navy contracts were handed out on a political basis and Secretary of War John B. Floyd was deeply involved in shady deals. The New York postmaster "swartouted" to Europe with $160,000 in federal funds. And the Public Printer pocketed at least $800,000 siphoned off the cost of the printing of just one session of Congress.[17]

Russell Sage was completely at home in this heady atmosphere. Beginning as a clerk, he worked his way up until at the age of twenty-three, he was a partner in a wholesale grocery business. Even then, Sage was a sharp operator. He swindled his partners out of their shares of the business and with the proceeds won a seat on the city council in Troy, New York. During this period, the twenty-one-mile Troy & Schenectady Railroad was built with $750,000 in public funds. As a member of both the council and of the railroad's board of directors, Sage joined the other insiders in purposely mismanaging the railroad's affairs in preparation for a takeover. When the line was all but bankrupt, he stepped forward as its savior with the offer to buy the railroad for $200,000—$50,000 in cash and the rest spread over fourteen years.

Sage had kept to himself the fact that the Troy & Schenectady, along with several other small upstate lines, was a target for acquisition by the group of capitalists engaged in organizing the New York Central. He quickly sold the railroad to the Central for $900,000. And that was not all. Sage and his accomplices shared in the distribution of $8 million in watered stock passed out as a bonus among the owners of the various roads that had been amalgamated into the Central. Instead of angrily demanding a share of Sage's enormous profits which were won at their expense, the voters of Troy elected him to Congress.[18]

Sage had visited the West several times as part of his early business ventures, so he was familiar with the rich soil of Wisconsin and the prospects for loot in Western railroading. In 1856 he surfaced as the head of the LaCrosse & Milwaukee Railroad which had a charter to lay track across Wisconsin from Lake Michigan to the Mississippi. He first set about gaining a share of the Wisconsin land grant which he had helped obtain from Congress—and wholesale bribery of almost the entire state government was used to pry off the lid. A million-dollar bond issue was printed and handed out to thirteen senators and to seventy members of the assembly. Governor Cole Bashford was presented with a bribe of $50,000 and other influential parties, including newspaper editors, divided $246,000. An investigating committee later reported that "the LaCrosse & Milwaukee Railroad Company has been guilty of numerous and unparalleled acts of mismanagement, gross violations of duty, fraud and plunder. In fact, corruption and wholesale plundering are common features."

In exchange for the bonds, the legislature naturally awarded Sage a grant of a million acres of farm and timber lands later estimated to be worth $17 million. With this princely domain in hand, he organized a construction company to build the railroad at a vastly inflated cost, which was borne by the ordinary stockholders, while Sage and his friends reaped enormous profits. When the railroad had been completely pillaged and its timber lands stripped, the financier and his henchmen moved on to new conquests.

Other men had grander visions. From almost the time the first railroad was opened, there were those who saw the shimmering rails reaching from the Mississippi to the Pacific shore, binding the nation together with bands of steel. This would occur in time—with every step of the way attended by fraud and corruption—but the coming of the Civil War delayed the realization of this dream. Nothing was lost, however, for the conflict opened up opportunities for graft unheard of until then.

VIII

The Battle Cry
of Freedom

THE CIVIL WAR gave the courthouse squares of America their most common landmark—a statue of an infantryman leaning upon a musket. In Dixie, he usually wears a wide-brimmed hat; in the North, a jaunty forage cap. In both North and South, his pedestal bears the names of comrades who did not come back from Bull Run, Gettysburg, or the Wilderness. But a remarkable thing about these monuments is the number of soon-to-be prominent men who managed to avoid taking any chance that their names might be carved there. Jim Fisk, Jay Gould, Pierpont Morgan, Collis Huntington, Andrew Carnegie, and John D. Rockefeller were all of military age during the war, but they were too busy negotiating fat contracts and hatching speculative deals to follow the fife and drum into battle.

Hundreds of thousands of other young men, however, rallied to the colors with cheers and a light heart. Everywhere, great crowds assembled to see the new recruits march off to war, proud of their improvised uniforms and happily unaware of the horrors that lay ahead. Looking back on four years of battle, Abraham Lincoln said in his Second Inaugural Address, "Neither party expected for the war the magnitude or the duration which it has already attained. . . . Each looked for an easier triumph." Not until the first shells exploded over Fort Sumter did Northerners really believe that the South would actually fight. And Southerners deluded themselves that the Yankee farmers and workmen would not go to war to keep them in the Union.

Lincoln's call for volunteers found the North woefully unprepared for war. The regular army consisted of only about sixteen thousand officers and men, most of them deployed against the western Indians. Many of the officers were Southerners who resigned to go with their states. Untrained men to fill the ranks were plentiful, but where were the arms, munitions, uniforms, tents, blankets to outfit them? Where was the barest organization for feeding, training, and transporting the men to the front? Shortages and confusion reigned supreme. All over the country, recruits found that not even the most rudimentary preparations had been made to receive them. Even barracks and camps were lacking. The militia, which turned out to save Washington, was quartered in the Capitol and in other public buildings. One New Yorker found several hundred men stuffed into a building on Broadway and reported, "I never knew before what rankness of stench could be emitted by unwashed humanity."[1]

Such chaotic conditions were made to order for plundering and profiteering, particularly in the North; the Confederacy offered fewer opportunities for large-scale graft and corruption. Alongside the men being mustered to dragoon the recalcitrant rebels back into the Union, there marched another army—one of lobbyists, contractors, and speculators which was never exhausted and was continually on the offensive. Later, the subsidized biographies of the lords of finance would relate how, as private contractors, they patriotically threw all their energies and resources into the war effort. But an angry Union officer took a different view. The contractors were "strangers to every patriotic impulse," he declared. They "saw in the war only an extraordinary opportunity of making a fortune. Every means of obtaining it was a good one to them; so that corruption played a large part in the business of contracting."[2]

Although some contractors served the country well, others

made millions from selling the government defective arms, un-seaworthy ships, rotten foodstuffs, spavined horses, threadbare blankets, uniforms that shredded in the rain and shoes that fell apart on the march. For sugar the government often got sand; for coffee it got rye; and for leather it got cardboard. "Such gross and unblushing frauds would have cost those who participated in them their heads under any system than our own," lamented a congressional investigating committee.[3]

No one individual can be singled out and saddled with the blame for the tidal wave of graft that engulfed every aspect of the Union Army mobilization. Fundamentally, chaos and corruption resulted from the collapse of a system that was never designed to carry such a load. Neither President Lincoln nor Simon Cameron, his secretary of war, had previous administrative experience. In their anxiety to see the Union armed, they were fair game for anyone out to make a fast buck at government expense. But Cameron, the Machiavellian Republican boss of Pennsylvania, contributed much to the pervasive atmosphere of swindle and fraud.

It would have been difficult to find a man more unsuited for a position involving the award of lucrative contracts than Cameron. Known as the "Czar of Pennsylvania," he had been promised a seat in the cabinet in return for swinging the votes he controlled at the Republican convention in 1860 to Lincoln. These had been enough to give the Illinois lawyer the nomination—and eventually the presidency. Cameron was the epitome of the link between business and politics that had prevailed since Jackson's day. Over the years he had moved as circumstances—and his pocketbook—dictated, from Jacksonian Democracy to nativist Know-Nothingism to abolitionist Republicanism. But no matter what his political guise of the moment, Cameron maintained an un-swerving loyalty to the iron and manufacturing interests of Pennsylvania, and their demands for a high protective tariff. As such, he was a master spoilsman and perhaps the most skillful political manipulator in America at the time. The remark that "an honest politican is one who, when he is bought, stays bought," is attributed to Cameron.

Early on, Thaddeus Stevens, a Republican congressman from

Pennsylvania and no admirer of Cameron, warned the President that the War Secretary had light fingers.

"You don't mean to say you think Cameron would steal?" asked Lincoln.

"No," Stevens replied, "I don't think he would steal a red-hot stove."

Amused, Lincoln repeated this to Cameron, perhaps as a diplomatic warning to stay honest. Cameron was angered and said he would demand a retraction from Stevens.

Later, Stevens asked the President, "Why did you tell Cameron what I said to you?"

"I thought it a good joke and didn't think it would make him mad."

"Well, he is very mad and made me promise to retract. I will now do so. I believe I told you he would not steal a red-hot stove. I now take that back."[4]

Nevertheless, Lincoln had gone along with the appointment which had been promised by his managers at the Chicago convention. In matter of fact, Lincoln was one of the most artful practitioners of the spoils system ever to reside in the White House. There were 1,639 jobs within his gift and he removed the holders of 1,457, replacing them with deserving Republicans. This was the most thoroughgoing sweep of jobholders that had ever been made in the history of the Republic, far surpassing the much-publicized removals of Andrew Jackson. The occupants of some jobs changed as many as two or three times before the end of the war, as Lincoln periodically redistributed the loaves and fishes in order to broaden his base of support. Artemus Ward, the humorist, jokingly blamed the hysterical retreat of the Union Army at Bull Run on a rumor that several vacancies existed in the New York customs house.

With so many jobs at his command, Lincoln was the target of office-seekers from all over the nation. They crowded the White House, waiting for the president to pass from his office in one end of the building to his meals in the other so they could present their claims. One fellow tried for a federal judgeship and when told none were available asked for a postmastership. Upon being informed that all were filled, he said he would settle for a place as a lighthouse keeper—anywhere along the Atlantic Coast would be fine. Lincoln often raged in frustration at the demands upon him. Sometimes, he once said, he felt like a man who was renting rooms in one end of his house while the other end was on fire. When he contracted a slight case of smallpox, he told a secretary: "Tell all the office seekers to come at once, for now I have something I can give to all."

Lincoln used patronage as a weapon to unify the diverse elements that made up the Republican party and to attract the allegiance of those outside the party who supported the Union. He made no effort to obtain men who were best suited to perform the duties of the various offices, but filled them instead with those whose appointment would best serve the cause of the party and the Union. For example, when the editor of a formerly Democratic newspaper supported administration policies, Lincoln rewarded the editor's two sons with army commissions, Charles A. Dana, a War Department official and later editor of the New York *Sun*, reported that in order to secure the admission of Nevada as a state, upon which it was thought ratification of the Thirteenth Amendment rested, the president authorized his agents to offer several fat jobs to wavering congressmen to secure their votes. Lincoln was also not above appointing relatives and friends to jobs that might profit them if the appointment did no harm to the country.[5]

"You can sell anything to the government at almost any price you've got the guts to ask," trumpeted Jim Fisk, a gaudy Yankee peddler turned uniform salesman. Living it up to the tune of a thousand dollars a day, Fisk held court in the most lavish suite in Willard's Hotel, near the White House. There, he kept an around-the-clock bar and buffet at which congressmen, generals, purchasing agents, and quartermasters with contracts to be let were always welcome. Beginning with a few thousand mildewed blankets which no one wanted, Fisk sold them to the government at a price several times higher than they were worth. This was parlayed into an operation that handled contracts for hundreds of thousands of dollars' worth of uniforms, blankets, socks, and underwear. Establishing the pattern for those who followed him to Washington with carpetbag and contract in hand, the genial Fisk probably provided more than rollicking entertainment in his suite at Willard's. "It has always been shrewdly guessed that he paid liberally for the favors granted him, knowing that the profits on the transactions would be immense," said one observer.[6]

The foundation of many a new fortune was quarried from contracts allocated by the government for the tools of war without advertising or public bidding, as the law required. An estimated $50 million in arms contracts were let during the opening months of the war. An investigating commission later determined that at least $17 million of this sum was in illegal overcharges.[7] One authority[8] has estimated that during the four years of the Civil War, private contractors of one sort or another received orders valued at at least a billion dollars. Based upon a conservative estimate, he states that they pocketed at least a half of it.

"Five-percenters" and "influence peddlers" had a field day obtaining contracts for a percentage of the total amount. The investigating commission charged that a senator—whom they did not identify—had taken a rake-off of $10,000 for procuring a contract for muskets for the army.[9] Wheeler-dealers promoted contracts at exorbitant prices and then sold them at a discount to subcontractors who were to provide the required supplies or equipment. Often, no attempt was made by contractors to fulfill their obligations. They provided goods that bore only a slight resemblance to what they had agreed to deliver. For example, New York authorities ordered twelve thousand uniforms from one firm at a price of $9.50 each. When delivered, they were found to be made of shoddy material and of a strange design—without buttons or pockets.* Protests availed nothing—and the public soon had its attention diverted by other scandals.

A good proportion of such frauds might have been prevented had Cameron not proved to be an incompetent—as well as a

---

* The term *shoddy* seems to have been derived from the cheap cloth used by corrupt contractors for uniforms, blankets, and tents. It was described as "a villainous compound, the refuse stuff and sweepings of the shop, pounded, rolled, glued and smoothed to the external form and gloss of cloth but no more like the genuine article than the substance."

corrupt—secretary of war. For thirty-five years he had gloried in the title of General—he was adjutant general of Pennsylvania—but his knowledge of military affairs was abysmal. Even a friendly biographer states that his performance was that of "a nervous, confused, embarrassed executive who had completely lost control of the situation."[10] Hordes of contractors, office-seekers, local political hacks, and influence peddlers besieged him. All got equal time and most came away with a bone to chew on—adding to the list of those who owed him favors in return. Cameron's methods of doing business were unabashedly slipshod. One disgusted visitor came away with the following tale: "What was the last action I took on your case?" Cameron had asked the man. "You borrowed my pencil, took a note, put my pencil in your pocket, and lost the paper," was the caustic reply.

Perhaps the most unsavory episode in the veteran spoilsman's administration of the War Department was the establishment of an independent purchasing agency in New York with $2 million to its credit. Although there were competent military officers in New York, Cameron delegated authority to buy arms and equipment to Alexander Cummins, an old political lieutenant, and Governor Edwin D. Morgan. The governor, in turn, delegated his power to George D. Morgan, a relative and business partner, who was also the brother-in-law of Secretary of the Navy Gideon Welles. Employing a clerk recommended by Thurlow Weed, the well-known New York political fixer, Cummins and Morgan piled up within a few weeks a $250,000 stock that included Scotch ale, London porter, Dutch herring, and twenty-three barrels of pickles. Perhaps they thought the army was going on a picnic. They also spent $21,000 for linen pantaloons and straw hats. A firm that made several loans to Cummins received a contract for 75,000 pairs of shoes at a substantial profit. And Cummins never did account for $160,000 of the government's money which he had deposited in his own private account.[11]

In the meantime, George Morgan had moved on to bigger things. Navy Secretary Welles, usually regarded as a competent administrator, gave him the authority to hire and purchase vessels for military use and to take a 2.5 percent commission on the funds paid out. Business was so good that within a few months

Morgan pocketed $90,000, and congressional investigators called the arrangement "unwise and pernicious."[12] The case of the steamer *Stars and Stripes* seems to have been typical of Morgan's operations. The vessel cost $36,000 to build and was briefly chartered to the government for $15,000. She was later purchased at Morgan's order for $55,000—$19,000 more than the original cost of construction. Several other cases were cited in which Morgan paid more for ships for government use than their owners had asked of private buyers.

Denouncing the employment of Morgan, Representative Charles H. Van Wyck, chairman of the investigating committee, told Congress that it was not enough for Welles to protest that his brother-in-law had served the nation well.

> It is no answer to say that Mr. Morgan is honest. Grant it. Mr. Morgan is fond of money, or he would not, he could not, consent to take nearly ninety thousand dollars of the money which had been paid him in about five months. A man who is this greedy of gain evidently is more zealous of his own than his country's interests.[13]

The purchase and charter of vessels for the War Department developed into an even bigger racket. Corrupt agents bought a pair of ferryboats for $90,000 more than they cost to build, despite warnings from marine experts that the craft were totally unfit for service. One foundered at sea on her first voyage and the other was so badly damaged that she was condemned as soon as she reached port. On another occasion, an agent purchased a steamer even though it had been condemned by the navy as unseaworthy. This vessel also sank on her first voyage in the War Department's service.

Congressional investigators determined that many vessels were taken under charter and remained safely at anchor while the government paid out exorbitant fees for their use. One ship ran up charter fees of $135,000 without ever having left Boston. When she finally got to sea, the vessel earned nearly a million dollars for her owners. After having sold a ship to the government for far more than it was worth, an official of one company pocketed $8,000 of the fee rather than turning it over to his partners.

The aura of corruption was so thick that he got away with it by claiming that he had to use the money to pay off an ex-congressman who had allegedly set up the deal. Summing up, the angry congressional investigators declared that the testimony "discloses a gross abuse of trust and profligate expenditure of money in this regard."[14]

Nevertheless, the shipping frauds continued unabated, with the rapacious old Cornelius Vanderbilt leading the pack. The commodore was sixty-seven years of age when the Civil War broke out and had amassed a fortune of well over $11 million, but the fires of acquisition still burned brightly within him. A native of Staten Island, Vanderbilt had gotten his start at seventeen by persuading his mother to lend him a hundred dollars to buy an old barge to transport goods and passengers from the island to Manhattan. From this beginning, he developed his own shipping line, driving his competitors out of business by slashing charges. Having bankrupted them and obtained a monopoly, Vanderbilt then proceeded to charge shippers exorbitant rates. Historian Gustavus Myers claims that Vanderbilt undermined his competitors by bribing the New York aldermen to give him exclusive use of docking facilities while refusing them to others. Once he got control of coastal shipping, Vanderbilt branched out into transatlantic service—and the blackmailing of his competitors for much of the funds they received from government in mail subsidies. "What do I care about the law?" he told critics. "Haint I got the power?"

The outbreak of fighting and the activities of Confederate commerce raiders quickly convinced the commodore that the time had come to dispose of his shipping business. He turned his attention to more profitable ventures such as railroads. He had only one ship left and it was tied up, earning him no profits, so Vanderbilt "lent" her to the government. He was promptly hailed as a great patriot, but much to his chagrin, Congress regarded the vessel as a gift and kept her without payment. In 1862, the War Department, no doubt in recognition of Vanderbilt's patriotic services, placed him in charge of rounding up transports for a seaborne expedition against New Orleans. Vanderbilt operated through an agent named T. J. Southard and refused to charter or purchase any vessel unless the owner made arrangements with

Southard. Southard took a rake-off of from 5 to 10 percent of the purchase price after agreeing to pay enormous sums for the vessels, often as much as $800 to $900 a day. "It is obvious that [Vanderbilt] was in collusion with Southard, and received the greater part of the plunder," according to Myers.

Under normal circumstances, Vanderbilt's actions would have been greeted with a shrug and looked upon as ordinary business practices. But this time the old man had gone too far. Many of the vessels he chartered or bought were worn out and unsafe river steamers that were completely unsuited for travel on the high seas crowded with troops. Built to carry perhaps 300 passengers, some carried as many as 900 soldiers, and they did not have skilled navigators or adequate charts for the long voyage south. The worst craft of this flotilla of misfits was the old lake steamer *Niagara*, for which Vanderbilt paid $10,000. "In perfectly smooth weather," reported Senator James W. Grimes, of Iowa, after a congressional investigation of Vanderbilt's operations, "with a calm sea, the planks were ripped out of her, and exhibited to the gaze of the indignant soldiers on board, showing that her timbers were rotten." Grimes added that the committee had in its possession "a large sample of one of the beams of this vessel to show that it has not the slightest capacity to hold a nail." Grimes asked the commodore and others why navigators and charts were not supplied for the vessels. He was told the insurance companies and owners of the ships assumed all risks "as though the Government had no risk in the lives of its valiant men whom it has enlisted under its banner and set out in an expedition of this kind."

No attempt was made to bring Vanderbilt or Southard to book for corruption or for endangering the lives of the soldiers. Of course, a resolution was introduced in the Senate censuring them as "guilty of negligence," but the old man used his political clout to have his name removed, leaving Southard holding the bag. When the war was over, the commodore was among a group of distinguished citizens to whom a grateful Congress presented medals for loyal, patriotic, and meritorious service. By then, he was the only American worth more than $20 million.[15]

*   *   *

The Civil War was the first conflict in which railroads played a major role. In fact, the superiority of the North's rail network, which allowed troops and supplies to be easily shifted between threatened points, was an important factor in its final victory. But a high price was extracted for this contribution. The rail barons ran their trains full throttle through the Treasury. The railroads had been largely built with taxpayers' money, but that didn't prevent unmerciful gouging of the government. The pattern of victimization was set early in the war by Simon Cameron himself. The war secretary was deeply involved in the ownership and management of the Pennsylvania Central and the Northern Central railroads, which carried the bulk of military traffic during the opening months of the Civil War. The Northern Central was commonly called "Cameron's road."

Cameron had lost little time in securing the interests of the railroads. Among his first appointments was that of Thomas A. Scott, vice-president of the Pennsylvania Central, to be Superintendent of Railroads, and, after August 1861, Assistant Secretary of War. There is no question about Scott's abilities, for he was a first-class railroad man. Nevertheless, as congressional investigations emphasized, there was a clear conflict of interest which Scott usually resolved in favor of the railroads. Scott kept his position as vice-president of the railroad during his entire period of government service, and collected his salary of $4,000 a year until he became Assistant Secretary. Sharply critical of the appointment, the congressional committee reported:

> It will be readily seen that in view of the vast amount of transportation which might and probably would be required of these roads, as well as others in the United States, an agent should have been selected ... having no interest hostile to the government and no railroad interest to serve. The people had a right to demand this; common honesty would have suggested it. The employment therefore of Mr. Scott by the Secretary of War would have been inexcusable even if Mr. Scott had been able to overlook the interests of the two great roads with which he was connected.

And it was the opinion of the committee that Scott had not overlooked the interests of the Pennsylvania and Northern

Central. He immediately established tariffs which the War Department would pay the railroads for the transportation of men and munitions that were branded as "outrageous and indefensible." The prices fixed by this schedule were over a third more than those charged private shippers for goods carried over the same distance. One railroad man, not in on the graft, testified that the overcharges really ranged in the area of 50 percent or more.

Under the benevolent gaze of Scott and Cameron, it was charged that the Pennsylvania and Northern Central piled up an "immense and unnecessary profit which was spirited from the government. . . ." The annual report of the Pennsylvania Railroad issued on February 3, 1862, showed that net earnings for the year were $3,646,938—an increase of $1,350,235 over the preceding period, or about 40 percent. The earnings of the Northern Central from July 1861 to July 1862 were estimated at more than double those reported for the previous year.

Surveying the widespread graft and corruption in the transport of the army, the committee declared, "the government, in consequence of the mercenary interests of public officials, has been made the victim of extreme injustice." And the investigators left no doubt as to the identity of these public officials. "Within reasonable limits, a just and fair competition between the various railroads would not only have resulted in reasonable prices," they said, "but would have prevented the corrupt and dishonorable feelings which were instigated by the extraordinary prices fixed by the Secretary of War, through Mr. Scott, for railroad transportation."[16]

Initial confusion, hectic demands, improvisation, and corruption permeated the actual arming of the Union forces. When war came, there were about 350,000 small arms in Northern armories and arsenals. But what guns! Only about eight in a hundred were modern rifled weapons, the rest were antiquated smooth bores that ranged in quality from adequate to wretched. One officer thought it would be "a master stroke of policy" to allow the rebels to capture the lot that were sent to his regiment. They were "infinitely more dangerous to a friend than enemy [and] will kick further than they will shoot." Not untypical of the poorly armed regiments was the Thirtieth Illinois, whose 773 men took to the field with a mixture of 273 serviceable weapons and 357 guns of poor quality. The remaining 121 men had no arms at all—and some of the Illinois regiments that were mobilized in the spring of 1861 did not get them until Christmas.[17]

The demand for arms for the troops produced a near panic. Purchasing agents for the states, local defense committees, political generals, newly minted colonels, and the federal government were all engaged in frenzied bidding against each other for the available weapons. The market was soon plagued with middlemen who knew almost nothing about guns but could smell a lucrative opportunity. They landed fat contracts, and then went in search of arms. The trade quickly spread to Europe, where modernization programs had emptied the arsenals of weapons that had been manufactured as long ago as the Napoleonic wars. The trade was so hectic it was reported that five speculators took the same boat to England and were soon bidding against each other. They snapped up whatever relics were available and shipped them home to sell at exorbitant prices. An investigating committee said that "in many cases these unserviceable arms were paid for at rates which, under a system of vigilance and obedience to law, would have procured improved rifles of the first class."[18]

Just how bad most of the arms were can only be judged through the testimony of the soldiers to whom they were issued. A shipment of guns which had been purchased in Austria for $166,000 were particularly detested. Heavy and clumsy, the Austrian muskets fired at a rate that was so slow as to endanger the lives of the men unfortunate enough to use them. General Grant, then serving in Missouri, said these guns would often misfire; when they did go off they had an extremely heavy recoil. "Men would hold them very tight, shut their eyes and brace themselves to prepare for the shock. . . ."[19] Fortunately, reported another officer, the soldiers had the "hardihood or ingenuity to loose them," which would at least give them hope of being issued something better. A batch of Belgian muskets were even worse.

The soldiers called them "pumpkin slingers" and because so many had crooked barrels, said they were well adapted for shooting around corners.

Middlemen also stood ready to lend a helping hand to manufacturers having difficulties landing fat contracts. The Colt Arms Company, which had excellent contacts in the War Department, sold revolvers for $25 each that would have ordinarily sold in the open market for $14.50. In only a year, Colt made $325,000 in excess profits. One authority holds that the contract was probably obtained corruptly since the Remington Company, which had been offering revolvers of equal quality for $15 each, could only get a contract for five thousand—less than one-sixth of the order given Colt at a substantially higher price.[20] Another firm was told that its pistols did not meet the army's requirements. Yet, as soon as it hired a go-between who had offered his services, the company received a contract for thousands of revolvers at $20 each. There had been no change in the quality of the firm's guns—but $10,000 had been passed to the middleman for distribution as he saw fit.

Out of this maze of confusion and corruption emerged the notorious Hall carbine affair that has set generations of writers to splashing tubs of printers' ink upon one another.[21] The basic facts of the case are simple enough, however. In May of 1861, during the frenzied search for arms of any sort, Arthur Eastman, a Yankee tinkerer and sometime munitions dealer, sought a way to turn the emergency to his own ends. Learning that the government had in storage in New York some five thousand Hall breechloading carbines which nobody seemed to want, he put in a bid for them at a bargain price of $3.50 each. These weapons were obsolescent, having originally been placed in service in the 1830s. Those purchased by Eastman, however, were mostly new, of an improved pattern, and had never been removed from their packing cases except for cleaning and oiling. Eastman obtained a contract to buy 4,996 of them at a cost of $17,486—a monstrous blunder on the part of the War Department, considering the shortage of weapons. It was a blunder that was to be repeated and compounded.

Eastman now had a valuable contract for arms, but lacked the money to pay for the guns, and the government was insisting on cash on the barrelhead before the carbines would be delivered to him. He had to find someone to buy them from him before he took possession of the weapons himself. At this point, a shrewd operator named Simon Stevens entered the picture. Stevens was a political henchman, although not a relative, of Thaddeus Stevens. As a deserving Republican, after the election of Lincoln in 1860, he had grabbed off a share of the seemingly inexhaustible supply of graft that flowed from the New York customs house. He had been in New York only a few months when he worked out a deal with Eastman for the carbines, offering $12.50 each for the guns. The price was reduced to $11.50, when Stevens learned that they were smoothbores without modern rifled barrels. Payment was to be made in two installments—$20,000 within five days and the remaining $37,500 within a few weeks.

Although the carbines were still in the possession of the government, Stevens sought a customer for them. He did not have far to look. Out in St. Louis, Major General John C. Frémont, the newly appointed commander of the Department of the West, was frantic for arms of any sort and at any price. To make matters even easier for Stevens, he and Frémont were old political friends. Known as the "Pathfinder" because of his daring explorations of the West as a young officer, Frémont was a romantic figure who had captured the public imagination. He was also an ardent abolitionist and in 1856—when he apparently first made Stevens's acquaintance—had been the first presidential candidate fielded by the fledgling Republican party.

Aware of Frémont's desperate need for arms, Stevens telegraphed an offer to sell him five thousand rifled Hall carbines at $22 each. Frémont, who had carried a Hall carbine during his explorations and liked it, immediately wired an acceptance. And so one branch of the government had agreed to buy guns for $22 each that another branch had sold only a few weeks before for $3.50—and still had in its possession.

The story now grows more complex. Stevens needed $20,000 to pay off Eastman before he could obtain the guns. He turned for the cash to J. Pierpont Morgan, a hulking young man of twenty-four who had recently set himself up in business just off Wall Street. Morgan put up the money, took the arms as collateral, and stipulated that when Stevens sold the guns, the bills should be made out in his name so that he would be reimbursed out of the first payment received. He laid out the money for the rifling and other modifications to the carbines as part of the agreement. On September 14, 1861, Morgan received payment from Frémont of $55,000 for the first twenty-five hundred carbines shipped to St. Louis—just thirty-eight days after having entered the agreement. He deducted $26,343.54—of which $5,556, or better than 25 percent, was commission and interest—and gave the remainder to Stevens. This was a tidy profit on an investment of $20,000 for little more than a month, considering that the yearly salary of the vice-president of the Pennsylvania Railroad was $4,000.

Even so, Morgan refused another loan to tide Stevens over until all the carbines had been shipped and paid for. Stevens, pressed by Eastman for full payment of the money owed him, secured a new loan from Morris Ketchum, another Wall Street banker with pliable ethics.* Word of the deal soon leaked out— perhaps Stevens bragged too loudly of the "killing" he had made—and in the resultant hue and cry about profiteering and corruption, there were investigations by a congressional committee and a special War Department commission. Stating that the price charged for the arms "was not fair or reasonable, but manifestly exorbitant," the commission held that Stevens and Ketchum were entitled to only a price of $13.31 each. They appealed to the Court of Claims after the war—and were awarded the full price of $22 for each carbine.

---

* In 1863, Morgan and Edward Ketchum, Morris's son, worked out a deal in which they made $160,000 by speculating in gold and indirectly attacking the credit structure of the embattled government. That same year the draft was instituted and young Morgan, who had suddenly developed fainting spells, hired a substitute to serve in his place in the ranks. A few years later, Edward Ketchum fled to Europe after stealing securities worth about $2.5 million and forging gold certificates for $1,250,000.

For a half century, the affair was pretty much unknown until the indefatigable Gustavus Myers dredged it up in his *History of the Great American Fortune*, which was published in 1909. He portrayed Morgan and Stevens as fellow conspirators in an un-principled plot to swindle the government by selling it "con-demned" guns. Myers further embroidered the story by claiming that the carbines would blow off the thumbs of soldiers firing them. With some embellishments, the same story has appeared in several later accounts. On the other hand, R. Gordon Wasson, a Morgan partner, later wrote *The Hall Carbine Affair*, which com-pletely exonerates the founder of the firm of all wrongdoing. The truth, in all probability, lies somewhere between the interpreta-tions of Myers and Wasson.

Wasson contends there was no conspiracy between Morgan and Stevens because the two men had not known each other, or only had a slight acquaintance before August 1861, when Stevens came to Morgan to borrow the $20,000. Stevens knew of Morgan, Wasson says, because Stevens's sister had once been one of Mor-gan's teachers, and his brother had been one of the leading members of the American colony in London at the time Morgan had lived there. Under these circumstances, he continues, it was only natural for Stevens to go to Morgan to borrow money after arranging a deal with Frémont. It is also his contention that Morgan did not know of the sale at the time he entered the transaction. When he sensed a scandal brewing, he abandoned the project as soon as he had protected his investment. "Morgan was a mute and minor character," argues Wasson, who was pushed to the front of the stage by Myers for dramatic effect.

Yet, in spite of Myers's obvious exaggeration of Morgan's role, it is difficult to completely accept the explanation of the financier's part in the affair offered by Wasson. It stands or falls upon the acceptance of the curious proposition that Morgan was a poor businessman. We have to convince ourselves that Morgan knew absolutely nothing about the nature of the transaction or of the man with whom he was involved. I find it difficult to believe that he was so inept a businessman as to lend $20,000 to someone he did not know for purposes of which he had no knowledge. Even Frederick Lewis Allen, a Morgan biographer who accepts

Wasson's version of the affair, remarks: "It was an ugly thing to have been involved in, however inadvertently."

Through all these scandals, President Lincoln had defended Simon Cameron, but by the end of 1861, even this patient man had had enough of the secretary's maladministration and incompetence. John Nicolay, the president's secretary, recorded Lincoln's thoughts on Cameron: "Utterly ignorant and regardless of the course of things, and the probable result. Selfish and openly discourteous. . . . Obnoxious to the country. Incapable of either organizing details, conceiving and executing general plans." Lincoln was seeking an opportunity to gracefully rid himself of a man who had proven such a liability, when Cameron, almost as if by design, presented it to him.

Just as the year was drawing to a close, the secretary had issued a report defending the operation of his department. Errors had occasionally been made, he acknowledged, and extravagant prices had been paid for vital arms and munitions. Cameron claimed that this was only the result of the need for "haste and the pressure of rapid events." Despite all the difficulties, a well-equipped force had been put into the field "at so small an expense." Cameron then dropped a bombshell. He suggested that slaves residing in the areas occupied by the Union army be armed and used against their former masters. Some critics suspected that this was a ploy by the wily Cameron to divert attention from the charges of corruption leveled against him. What was worse, he leaked a copy of the report to the press before sending it along to the president. Lincoln was furious. The war, as far as he was concerned, was still a war to maintain the Union, and not to free the slaves. Early in the new year, he found just the place to pack off Cameron—to Russia as American minister. Congress sent him on his way with a resolution of censure for acts "highly injurious to the public service," but it made no specific charges.[22]

In Cameron's place, Lincoln named Edwin M. Stanton. Stanton was dictatorial, vindictive, and often unreasonable, but he was a great improvement over his predecessor. He was efficient, and woe betide anyone whom he found with a hand in the public till. If anyone deserves the title "Organizer of Victory" in the Civil War, it is Stanton. But not even he was able to completely stem the flood tide of corruption. As the war progressed, and the Union army built up a satisfactory reserve of arms and equipment, sharp operators sought new fields of plunder. They soon turned toward the lower Mississippi Valley where vast stockpiles of cotton urgently needed by Northern mill owners had accumulated.[23]

"I am greatly afraid that in some quarters the movements of our armies have been directed more with a view to carry on trade and to procure the productions of the southern country than to strike down the rebels," declared Senator John C. Ten Eyck of New Jersey after an investigation of the cotton trade in 1864.[24] Charles Dana reported to Stanton that "the mania for sudden fortunes made in cotton . . . has to an alarming extent corrupted and demoralized the army. Every colonel, captain or quartermaster is in secret partnership with some operator in cotton; every soldier dreams of adding a bale of cotton to his monthly pay."

Trade between the Northern and Southern states had officially ceased with the outbreak of the war, but almost from the very beginning this ban was evaded. The demands of mill owners combined with the soaring price of cotton on the world market and the need of the Confederacy for vital supplies and medicines led to a brisk and profitable trade. In 1862, the government, recognizing a situation that already existed, authorized a limited commerce with the South under the eye of special Treasury agents. These watchdogs were to make certain that those who held permits did not exchange contraband for cotton. But they soon succumbed to the temptation for a fast buck, and either were bribed to look the other way when wagonloads of salt, quinine, powder, and arms moved south, or took part in the trade themselves. Senator Ten Eyck uncovered a brisk commerce in which not only greenbacks and gold were exchanged for cotton "but bullets and powder instruments of death which our heroic soldiers have been compelled to face and meet on every field of battle."

Memphis and New Orleans were the focal points of the illicit trade. A traffic estimated at a half-million dollars a day passed through the lines along the Mississippi, and Memphis was described as "a regular depot for rebel supplies." The town was said to be more valuable to the Confederates after its capture by the Yankees than it had been before. "My experience in West Tennessee has convinced me that any trade whatever with the rebellious states is weakening to us of at thirty-three per cent of our force," declared General Grant in demanding an end to the trade. And General C. C. Washburn, commanding at Memphis, was of the opinion that the "wretched system" which allowed commerce with the enemy had contributed much "toward pro-longing the war."

General Benjamin F. Butler, the cross-eyed Yankee commander at New Orleans, is believed to have piled up a multimillion-dollar fortune through trade with the enemy. Acting with his brother, Andrew, a colonel on his staff, Butler even pressed steamboats belonging to the government into carrying salt and other supplies to the rebels up the Mississippi. They returned with cargoes of cotton that were disposed of at fat profits. On one occasion, a new officer halted one of the vessels in the belief that it was engaged in smuggling. Butler immediately ordered the vessel released and detailed armed guards to go along with the boats to protect them against such interference in the future.

Complaints about Colonel Butler's activities soon reached Washington, but he had a ready defender in his brother, who had been a well-placed Massachusetts politician before the war. Ben Butler contended that the colonel was engaged in a "legitimate business" in which he had no interest. Colonel Butler's profits were less than $200,000, he said, although rumor had it that the "take" amassed by the Butler brothers was closer to $2 million. Ben Butler was finally removed from his command, though not for engaging in wholesale corruption, and was given a post at Fort Monroe, near Norfolk, Virginia. There he was soon up to his old tricks, this time hand-in-hand with his brother-in-law. Large quantities of medicines, shoes, bacon, and other supplies were shipped off to the Confederates, and back came substantial quantities of cotton. Matters got so bad that General Grant finally sought his dismissal. "I have put a stop to supplies going out through Norfolk to Lee's army," Grant noted with satisfaction following Butler's departure.

After the war, it was estimated that when Ben Butler had gone to New Orleans in 1862, he owned property worth about $150,000. A few years later, his fortune was said to have grown to $3 million. Butler was never questioned about the suspicious multiplication of his assets. Instead, he was elected to Congress, helped manage the impeachment trial of Andrew Johnson, and in 1884 ran for president—on a reform ticket.

IX

Of Grant, Gould,
and Gold

SEVERAL YEARS AGO Bill Moyers said that he had once asked a
distinguished historian why Ulysses S. Grant appears so sad in all
his pictures. "If you had his friends, you'd look glum, too," was
the reply. Saddled with the blame for the misdeeds of the men
around him, Grant left his name on what, until the Reagan years
at least, has been regarded as the most corrupt presidential
administration in American history. Grant's personal tragedy was
that, after playing a magnificent role in preserving the Union, the
country thrust upon him its greatest reward, for which he was
entirely unsuited. In the end, it was a curse. "I did not want the
presidency, and have never quite forgiven myself for resigning
command of the Army to accept it," Grant declared after leaving
the White House. "But it could not be helped. I owed my honors
and opportunities to the Republican party and if my name could
aid it I was bound to accept."

The old soldier's frank appraisal was supported by Senator
George F. Hoar of Massachusetts. "Selfish men and ambitious
men got the ear of that simple man," he said. "They studied
Grant, some of them, as the shoemaker measures the foot of his

customer." These "selfish men" were the managers and operators of a spoils machine that subordinated every department of the federal government to their own devious ends in the years following the Civil War. The hapless president soon became their tool. To the politically unsophisticated Grant—he had voted in a presidential election only once, and that was for James Buchanan, a Democrat—these men were not crooks but the leaders of the Republican party to which he owed his "honors and opportunities." As a result, the spoilsmen, the grafters, and the sharpers ran the country—treating it like a melon patch to be divided among a limited and favored few.

In recent years, some historians have challenged the conventional view of the post–Civil War Gilded Age as a period of unparalleled corruption.[1] They suggest that corruption was little worse than usual, and contend there was so much talk about it because Grant and others were seriously trying to make improvements. For example, the president is credited with establishing the first civil service board with the intention of ending the worst excesses of the spoils system. Grant has received such a bad press, it is argued, because an extremely articulate band of reformers stood ready to let loose geysers of indignation at any alleged injustice, and their spectacularly lurid portrayal of the era has unduly influenced our thinking. This may be so, but even if these mitigating factors are taken into account, there was still plenty for the reformers to complain about.

Yet it would be a mistake to blame everything on Grant. The Civil War had given the North not only victory, but unprecedented power and prosperity. The Southern plantocracy, which had played a key role in ruling the nation and in setting its standards since Jefferson's day, had been swept away. A new class of men replaced them—pushing, hardened, cynical men who had piled up fortunes by furnishing shoddy goods to the government, by speculation in necessities, and by other schemes in which the public had been plucked. As soon as the war was over, this crew had turned their attention to business and politics, where they operated with the same unalloyed ruthlessness and greed. Looking on with distaste, Edwin L. Godkin, the editor of the *Nation*, declared: "Every man at present may be said literally to live by his wits;

hardly anybody lives by tradition, or authority, or under the dominion of habits acquired in youth. The result is a kind of moral anarchy." And the scientist Simon Newcomb wrote, "The decay in the public sense of delicacy and propriety . . . is striking."[2]

The deterioration of morals which the reformers perceived was not limited to the White House or Capitol Hill. These institutions were but a faithful mirror of the nation as a whole. The triumph of business and the emergence of an age of enterprise produced powerful industrialists and unprincipled speculators who made corrupt alliances with the politicians to protect and enlarge their economic stake. Charles Darwin's new theory of the evolution of the species, with its emphasis on struggle and victory of the strongest, tempted the successful to believe that their accomplishments were both meritorious and socially desirable. Moreover, Americans were weary of great causes like the crusade against slavery before the war, the battle to maintain the Union during the war, and the struggle to reconstruct the nation after the war. The failure of these struggles, along with the sacrifice of so much blood and treasure to solve the problems of sectionalism and race relations, produced a general disillusionment that led many Americans to mistrust any form of idealism.

On the surface, society was governed by a severe Victorian moral code, but selfish passions raged behind the scenes. Piety seemed to walk hand-in-hand with double dealing. The Reverend Henry Ward Beecher, the country's leading divine and self-appointed keeper of the public morals, was discovered to have had astonishing success in seducing his female parishioners. Senator Roscoe Conkling conducted a long-time love affair with Kate Chase Sprague, the comely wife of one of his colleagues, that ended on an absurd note when the lady's aggrieved husband ran him off at the point of a shotgun. Old Commodore Vanderbilt gleefully cheated his son, William, in a manure-hauling contract and shipped his wife off to an insane asylum for several months to still her objections to moving to a new home. And the paragon of business morality was Daniel Drew, whose soul, it was said, bore the exact shape of a dollar sign and who knew more Scripture and less charity than any man on Wall Street.

Corruption was confined to no one party or region. Alternately at the mercy of the carpetbaggers and the avenging Ku Klux Klan, the Southern states were the most obvious example of excess. State treasuries across the South were looted. Legend places the blame for corruption upon the ignorant blacks who supposedly dominated local governments after the Civil War. The truth of the matter is that the worst crimes during Reconstruction were committed by white carpetbaggers and their Southern allies, who were known as scalawags. Henry Clay Warmoth, the carpetbag governor of Louisiana, demonstrated how a yearly salary of $8,000 could be run up into a million dollars in four years. Louisiana's chief justice helped sell a railroad in which the state had invested $2 million for $50,000 to his friends. Other incidents piled up like autumn leaves.

But in the East and West where there were no grasping carpetbaggers or uneducated blacks in the state legislatures, political thievery was as rampant as in Dixie. Most of the nation's large cities were held captive by political rings such as that run by Boss Tweed in New York and the Gas House Ring in Philadelphia. In 1868, the *Nation* cried out that "there is hardly a legislature in the country that is not suspected of corruption; there is hardly a court over which the same suspicion does not hang."

Simon Cameron returned to America after a brief exile in Russia and held sway over Pennsylvania for another dozen years. He developed what became known as the "Pennsylvania idea"—a conviction that big business should use its funds to help the Republican party stay in power, even if this meant buying votes and bribing legislators to get what it wanted. After the old man's retirement, his son, Don, carried on his work. In the West, the record was just as bad. The Illinois legislature indulged in 1867 in an orgy of boodle, in which from ten to twelve million dollars was voted into the pockets of the corporations, contractors, and speculators. In Iowa, some light-fingered soul made off with the entire treasury of the State Agricultural College. And in Kansas, a member of the state legislature confounded his colleagues by refusing a $7,000 bribe and openly charging that it had been offered him in exchange for his vote during a senatorial election. The candidate who offered the bribe emerged later as the presidential nominee of the Prohibition party.[3]

Such conditions required a president of considerable moral stamina to keep his administration on a straight and narrow path, and Ulysses S. Grant was not up to the job. Whatever fires had raged within the man during the Civil War seemed to have flickered and died by the time he entered the White House. Before the war, he had been all but forced out of the army after an undistinguished career, and was completely unsuccessful as a farmer and as a businessman. One Christmas Eve, he was reduced to pawning his watch in order to provide his family with a few gifts. The war came to his rescue, sweeping him from a shabby $50-a-month clerkship in his father's leather store to the command of a regiment of newly mustered volunteers.

Even after his success during the war and his election to the presidency, these years of poverty and humiliation still haunted Grant. In the presence of men of learning, talent or culture, he had a tendency to freeze up and cover what he felt was his own inadequacy. These men, awed in turn by Grant's reputation and position, found it almost impossible to break down the barrier. An uncomfortable standoff usually resulted. The president sought companionship and understanding among men with backgrounds like his own—army friends from the war and among the Republican party's professionals, the practical spoilsmen who were known as Stalwarts. They flattered him, told him what he wanted to hear, and filled his mind with their own pet schemes. "Through his obtuseness, trustfulness and responsiveness to flattery, Grant had little capacity for self-protection," states one historian.[4] "He did not understand a fraud, 'game' or plot."

Grant came to power amid hope that he would launch an administration of conciliation and reform. As a national hero, he owed nothing to the politicians for his election. Thus, it was reasoned, he would have a free hand to surround himself with able men rather than spoilsmen, and adopt policies in the spirit of his eloquent statement of acceptance of the Republican nomination, "Let us have peace." Young Henry Adams was typical of those who expected great things from the new President. "Grant represented order. He was a great soldier, and the soldier always represented order," thought Adams. "A general who had organized and commanded half a million or a million men in the field must know how to administer."

Disillusion came as soon as the names of the members of Grant's cabinet were announced. Late in life, Adams said he "was to hear a long list of cabinet announcements not much weaker or more futile than that of Grant, and none of them made him blush, while Grant's nominations had the singular effect of making the hearer ashamed, not so much of Grant, as of himself."[5] With the exception of one or two men of ability, Grant's choice of advisors seemed based mostly on the desire to have no one about who would overshadow him. During the eight years in which he served as president, cabinet officers came and went with unsettling rapidity—and the abler they were the faster they left. With the notable exception of Hamilton Fish, the secretary of state, who stayed the course, the President was surrounded mostly by nonentities and downright crooks.

Roscoe Conkling, New York's incredibly flamboyant Republican boss—who favored white flannel trousers, florid vests, and a "turkey gobbler strut"—became the administration's spokesman in the Senate. Michigan's facile Senator Zachariah Chandler managed its backroom operations. They were assisted by Senator Oliver Morton of Indiana, a masterful practitioner of the politics of spoils. Old Simon Cameron was one of Grant's favorite fishing companions, and Ben Butler, forgiven for his wartime transgressions, was also included in the president's inner circle.

Like Ronald Reagan's after him, Grant's spectacular naïveté placed him in the hands of men who were ready to exploit their association with the president to the hilt. Through them, he became involved in a running series of scandals that completely tainted his administration. Lincoln's crusty secretary of the navy, Gideon Welles, was not surprised when the new president got into trouble. Grant "does not intend to labor like a drudge in office, does not propose to study public affairs, has no taste for books or intellectual employment," he confided to his diary. "The appointment of his friends to office is the extent of his ideas of administration." While most of the corruption that gave the Grant era its notoriety was not exposed until the closing years of his second term, an affair occurred in his very first months in office—the "Black Friday" gold corner conspiracy—that should have put him on the strictest guard against some of the men around him.

Early in the summer of 1869, Jim Fisk and Jay Gould, who had already set the bulls and bears of Wall Street bellowing and growling in anguish, evolved a scheme to corner the gold market which would, if successful, bring them millions. For Fisk, such a grandiose plan was a long way from his days as a back-country peddler and Civil War profiteer. With the coming of peace, he had gone into Wall Street, where he was eventually taken on as a protégé by Daniel Drew, one of the first of the robber barons.* Fisk rode Drew's coattails to a fortune as the old man staged a coup that ambushed Commodore Vanderbilt and gave him control of the Erie Railroad.

The Erie had passed from hand to hand so often that the line was known as the "Scarlet Woman of Wall Street." More often than not, the men who consorted with the hussy were not interested in the Erie as a transportation system but in the manipulation of its assets for selfish ends. An engineer characterized its tracks, which ran from Jersey City to Buffalo, as "two thin streaks of rust." Service was notoriously poor. "Another accident on the Erie," noted a diarist in 1868.[6] "Scores of people smashed, burned to death, or maimed for life. We shall never travel safely until some pious, wealthy and much beloved railroad director has been hanged for murder, with a conductor on each side of him. Drew or Vanderbilt would do to begin with." Soon, the names of Fisk and Gould would top any such list.

Despite Fisk's success on Wall Street, he shocked its staid denizens. The hypocritical cant and the funeral garb favored by

---

* Drew was the originator of the financial term *watered stock*. As a young man he had been a cattle drover and followed the practice of salting the stock as they were being driven to market. Just before delivering them for weighing, he would permit the beasts to drink all the water they wanted—adding considerably, if only momentarily, to their weight. On Wall Street, the term was soon applied to shares in a company issued by insiders that were pegged at a price far higher than the value of the firm's entire assets.

Daniel Drew as he went about fleecing his fellows and a random selection of widows and orphans was not for Fisk. He advertised himself with costumes which looked as if they had been run up for a race-track tout and sported a dazzling array of diamonds. Fisk openly flaunted his mistress, a sometime actress named Josie Mansfield, while his wife looked on from Boston. One observer of Fisk's riotous antics said he had come "bounding into the Wall Street circus like a star acrobat, fresh, exuberant, glittering with spangles and turning double summersets. . . ."[7]

No one ever accused Jay Gould of being fresh or exuberant, except possibly when he was plotting a raid on Wall Street. A slight, coldly calculating young man of thirty—a year younger than Fisk—Gould had suffered through a poverty-stricken childhood in upstate New York. One of his schoolboy literary efforts had been an essay entitled "Honesty Is the Best Policy"— sentiments which were promptly forgotten as he shouldered himself into Wall Street through a felicitous mixture of fraud and swindle. To his enemies, there was a touch of the Mephistophelian about Gould; some even professed to detect a whiff of brimstone as he passed by. Joseph Pulitzer, publisher of the New York *World*, regarded him as "one of the most sinister figures that ever flitted bat-like across the vision of the American people."

Fisk and Gould were a strange pair of allies. The basic differences in their outlooks could be summed up by an incident that occurred one day when they were strolling together and were stopped by a panhandler. Gould took out a roll of bills and began searching for one of a small denomination. Fisk grabbed the entire roll from him and handed it over to the beggar, saying, "Jay, never count charity." Perhaps the best explanation of their alliance is that with his clownlike caperings, Fisk diverted attention from Gould's infinite capacity for conspiracy. While the public was laughing at Fisk, Gould was picking their pockets.

Soon, this strange pair were ready to strike out on their own. The result was the "Erie War," an affair without parallel in the annals of finance and corruption.[8] This wild ride down the tracks began in 1867 with a three-cornered fight for control of the railroad.

Drew, Fisk, and Gould were ranged on one side, a group of Boston financiers was on another, and Commodore Vanderbilt was at the head of a third faction. The Bostonians convinced the commodore to throw in with them, and Drew was squeezed off the board of directors, though Fisk and Gould kept their seats. Vanderbilt quickly had second thoughts, however. He reasoned that Drew would probably be less dangerous on the board than off it, and restored him to membership over the protests of the Bostonians. Embittered by this double-cross, they decided to give old Vanderbilt a taste of his own medicine. They joined a secret alliance with Drew and his cohorts, while Vanderbilt was allowed to believe that he still controlled the Erie.

As soon as he figured out what had happened, the commodore thundered that if the other side wanted war, then he would let them have it. Orders were issued to his brokers—"Buy Erie, and keep on buying it!" Vanderbilt had decided to grab a majority interest in the railroad and dictate the selection of a new board of directors at the next meeting, scheduled for March 1868. His entire fortune of $30 million was placed behind the effort. But something strange seemed to be happening. The more Erie stock the commodore bought, the more seemed to come on the market. Not until he had poured out $8 million did Vanderbilt unravel the mystery. Fisk and Gould had discovered a printing press in the basement of Erie headquarters and turned out a paper storm of shares. "If this damned printing press doesn't break down, we'll give the old hog all he wants of Erie," Fisk gleefully declared.

Facing defeat on Wall Street, Vanderbilt turned to the law. Judge George G. Bernard, of the New York Supreme Court, who owed his appointment to Boss Tweed, obliged the commodore with an injunction forbidding Gould and Fisk to issue further stock. They, in turn, got another judge to set aside this order—an easy enough accomplishment in an era in which robber barons and major politicos all but kept judges on retainer. In the meantime, Fisk's printing press rolled on.

On March 11, 1868, the Erie triumvirate gathered to perform a joyous task—the counting of the loot they had taken from Vanderbilt. They were busy tying greenbacks into stacks and

stuffing them into sacks when word reached them that Judge
Bernard had issued an order for their arrest on charges of contempt. One jump ahead of the sheriff, Drew, Gould, and Fisk
transferred their base of operations across the Hudson to Jersey
City, where the arm of Judge Bernard did not extend. Barricaded in Taylor's Hotel—so heavily guarded by an army of hired
thugs and a brace of cannon borrowed from the local militia that
it was known as "Fort Taylor"—the masters of Erie settled down
to see what would happen next. "Commodore Vanderbilt owns
New York," Fisk told the squads of delighted Manhattan reporters assigned to the story as he passed out champagne and cigars.
"We saw there was no chance for us to expand in your city, so we
came over here to Jersey to grow up with the country."

Realizing that this stalemate could not long remain unre-
solved, Gould decided that the best course was to get the New
York legislature to legalize all the stock that gushed from the
basement of the Erie building. He stuffed a valise with $500,000
in greenbacks from what was called "the India Rubber Account,"
and was off to the state capital. The commodore's men were
already there and had him arrested. But this was only a minor
inconvenience. Freed on bail and in the custody of a friendly
deputy, Gould continued his machinations from a suite in the
Delevan House, Albany's leading hotel.

The most corrupt members of the legislature were known as
the "Black Horse Cavalry" and both Gould and Boss Tweed, who
was leading the Vanderbilt forces in his role as a state senator,
outbid each other in trying to buy the troop. With characteristic
enterprise, most legislators took money from both sides. One
fellow was said to have been bought by Vanderbilt for $75,000
and later sold out to Gould for $100,000. Tweed held court in the
same hotel on the floor above Gould's suite, and kept six bars
going while he doled out $180,000 to persuade legislators of the
righteousness of Vanderbilt's cause. Having availed themselves of
Tweed's hospitality, they descended to see what delights Gould
offered. He was so lavish with the Erie's money that when a
Vanderbilt agent arrived with a fresh supply of cash, Gould gave
him $70,000 to do a vanishing act with the money. In the end,
Gould was victorious. It was later estimated that he had paid out

nearly a million dollars to buy legislative approval of the law legalizing the watered Erie stock. There was still the problem of Vanderbilt's legal bloodhounds, however. The commodore offered to call them off if Gould and Fisk, who had long since deposed Drew, would buy back some of the stock they had dumped on him. An agreement was reached and the "Erie War" was over.

To celebrate the victory, Gould and Fisk, who had become president and vice-president of the Erie, purchased Pike's Opera House at Eighth Avenue and Twenty-third Street in New York and turned it into the railroad's offices. It was bought with $820,000 of the Erie's money, and then leased back to the company for $75,000 a month. The idea was that of the flamboyant Fisk, and the fact that Gould went along with it is a measure of his confidence in his partner's abilities. Three floors above the theater where Fisk played impresario, he maintained a lavish apartment where he could "interview" actresses, singers, and ballet dancers while seeking relief from the everyday cares of the business world. The Spartanlike Gould, however, spent his time in spinning out a plot to corner the nation's entire gold supply. And he was even prepared to argue that such a move would benefit the country as a whole.

During the Civil War, the government had issued a flood of paper greenbacks to finance its operations and this sent the price of gold soaring. At one point, it took $241 in currency to buy $100 in gold. Four years after Appomattox, prosperity had created such confidence that the price of $100 in gold cost $131 in greenbacks. It was at this low price that Gould quietly purchased about $7 million worth of gold—almost half the $15 million in circulation in New York. Therefore, it was to his advantage to drive up the price of the metal. But Gould proclaimed himself above mere selfish interests. An upward movement in the price of gold would reduce the value of the paper dollar. The resulting inflation would make Western wheat cheaper in European markets and send it flowing over the Erie's rails to Eastern ports in a golden cascade. Farmers and workers would benefit—and an era of prosperity such as the nation had never seen would surely follow. All in all, it was a delightful prospect.[9]

Yet there was a problem. With the resources of the Erie behind him, Gould knew he would have no trouble buying up the loose gold, but what about the $100 million in gold that the Treasury had in its reserves? How could he make certain that the government would not open the sluice gates and pour it into the market? Gould was still trying to puzzle out a solution to this problem when events played into his hands. Soon after Grant's inauguration, the president's middle-aged sister, Virginia, had married Abel R. Corbin, a long-time speculator and lobbyist who had been involved before the war in bribing congressmen to give favorable treatment to his clients. As a business acquaintance of Corbin, Gould hastened to visit the newlyweds, who had recently set up housekeeping in New York.

When he got Corbin alone, Gould made his pitch, and the old rascal must have whistled to himself at the audacity of Gould's scheme. He was even more impressed when his visitor said it would be his pleasure to purchase in Corbin's name as much as $2 million in gold. Corbin was to claim he had declined this offer, but later accepted it "for the sake of a lady, my wife."[10] Yes, indeed, Corbin conceded, Gould had certainly found the key to national prosperity. Of course, he would take the necessary steps to inform his brother-in-law of this marvelous plan. Corbin would warn Grant against permitting the sale of the government's gold, which would interfere with the sale of American agricultural products in the world market.

A month later, on June 15, 1869, President Grant and his family stopped over at the Corbins' home while on their way to a glittering Peace Jubilee in Boston. Corbin furnished an opportunity for Gould and Fisk to meet him and to offer the use of one of their steamers, the *Providence*, to transport the First Family to the celebration in style. One of the more intriguing questions, considering what came next, is why Grant consorted openly with two such certified rascals as Fisk and Gould and accepted repeated favors from them. While the president probably looked forward to a pleasant and relaxing voyage up Long Island Sound, the conspirators were elated at the idea of having the Chief

Executive as a captive audience overnight. After a lavish dinner had been eaten, and cigars and brandy passed around, Gould, as he later told a congressional investigating committee, launched into a spirited discussion of the price of gold and its link to prosperity. Grant, never a loquacious man, seemed content to puff on his Havana and to listen to the ideas of the others at the table.

Finally, Fisk pressed the president for his thoughts on the matter. Grant's answer must have sent chills down the spines of the conspirators. "There was a certain amount of fictitousness about the prosperity of the country," he was quoted as saying, "and that bubble might as well be tapped in one way as another."[11] These remarks, which Gould interpreted as meaning that Grant would not look with favor upon his scheme, threw such a wet blanket over the conspirators that the next day some of Gould's allies telegraphed orders to New York for the sale of their gold holdings.

Jay Gould was not one to give up so easily when millions were to be made. He continued to quietly buy gold and had Corbin write an article indicating that the new president would follow an inflationary financial policy, which Gould planted in *The New York Times.* The conspirators also had a stroke of good fortune when the important post of Assistant Treasurer in charge of Subtreasury in New York became vacant. Could Corbin use his influence with Grant to name a friendly person to fill the position? Corbin said he could, and General Daniel Butterfield, an old soldier who combined a need for money with a scrupulous dishonesty, received the appointment forthwith. Butterfield was provided with an account—similar to the one given Corbin—which held $1.5 million in gold from which he would receive the profits when gold prices advanced. Butterfield's appointment to the Subtreasury apparently convinced Gould of old Corbin's influence with the president, and he stepped up his purchases of gold through the use of spurious certified checks on the Tenth National Bank, which he controlled.

Gold prices began to edge upward slightly, but Gould was still worried about the president's intentions. On September 2, Grant, on his way to Saratoga, stopped over at his sister-in-law's home, and at breakfast Corbin again sang the old refrain about national prosperity and high gold prices. One would imagine that Grant would have grown suspicious of these constant and obvious attempts to influence him on the matter. Be that as it may, he decided that morning to write Treasury Secretary George S. Boutwell, instructing him not to sell any gold until further orders. And he told Corbin about it. Gould, who was lurking in an adjoining room, was elated—and went out and bought more gold. Everything seemed to be falling into place.

Gould now decided that the time had come to bring Fisk, who had kept his distance, into the conspiracy. But Fisk was leery, saying the scheme would fail because the government would sell gold if the price got too high. Fisk later claimed that Gould had assured him that all the bigwigs were in on the plot "beginning with President Grant and ending with the doorkeepers in Congress." Gould supposedly added: "This matter is all fixed up; Butterfield is all right; Corbin has got Butterfield all right, and, Corbin has got Grant fixed all right." According to this tale, Mrs. Julia Grant, the wife of the president, and General Horace Porter, a presidential secretary, were also in on the plot. Each was said to have $500,000 in gold in their names, and $25,000 in profits had already been forwarded by Corbin to Mrs. Grant. Fisk said Corbin confirmed what he had been told by Gould, and Mrs. Corbin had added: "I know there will be no gold sold by the government; I am quite positive there will be no gold sold . . . this is a chance of a lifetime for us. . . ."

Someone was lying—either Gould or Fisk or the Corbins, or perhaps all of them. Gould did give Corbin $25,000, but instead of going to Mrs. Grant, the check was traced to his own bank account. And General Porter, upon being informed by Gould that $500,000 in gold had been purchased for his account, bluntly replied: "I have not authorized any purchase of gold and request that none be made on my account. I am unable to enter into any speculation, whatever." Even so, Fisk plunged into the market with a bullish roar, spreading the word of Grant's involvement. He bought $8 million worth of "phantom" gold—gold that was not available in New York, but which the sellers promised to provide at a later date. The price began to soar, closing at $141 on September 22 and still going up. With every penny's rise in the price of gold, Corbin made $15,000.[12]

That evening, Gould got an urgent message to come to the Corbin home. Five days before, the nervous Gould, with purchases of $50 million in gold hanging over him, had persuaded Corbin to again write the president, who was vacationing in western Pennsylvania,* urging him to withhold the Treasury's gold. The letter had been delivered by a special messenger. After being told there was no reply, the messenger hurried to the nearest telegraph office and sent this dispatch to Gould: "Letter delivered all right." The conspirators interpreted this to mean that Grant had agreed to everything in the letter, rather than the fact that it had been safely delivered.[13] They plunged ahead with their purchases of gold and all seemed to be going well. Without warning, Corbin suddenly received alarming news from the summer White House.

The urgent tone of Corbin's letter must have finally set off an alarm bell in the president's mind. The newspapers had been full of reports of his brother-in-law's involvement in the gold conspiracy, and no doubt General Porter informed him of Gould's offer to him. At the president's suggestion, Mrs. Grant wrote a letter to Mrs. Corbin signed *Sis*, warning the Corbins to "disengage" themselves from the plot at once. This letter arrived at the Corbin house late one night, and the sentence that leaped out at Gould read as follows: "Tell Mr. Corbin that the President is very much distressed by your speculations and you must close them as quickly as you can."[14]

Gould could now see his whole plan crumbling before his very eyes. The letter could mean only one thing—that Grant would order Boutwell to start selling gold. Unless he could keep the letter secret and act fast, he would be ruined. Corbin and Gould circled each other cautiously, looking for an opening. The con-

* He had traveled there in a special railroad car furnished by Gould free of charge.

gressional committee, in its report, painted a vivid picture of the scene: "Shut up in the library, near midnight, Corbin was bending over the table and straining with dim eyes to decipher and read the contents of a letter, written in pencil to his wife, while the great gold gambler, looking over his shoulder, caught with sharper vision every word."[15]

Corbin, holding the advantage of being able to threaten Gould with immediate disclosure of Mrs. Grant's note, used the time to spin a new plan aimed at salvaging his profits. He demanded that Gould immediately pay him at least $100,000, in addition to the $25,000 already received. Gould stalled for time after obtaining a pledge of secrecy, and by morning had evolved a plan of his own. He told Corbin a check for $100,000 would be forthcoming, but never sent it—and decided to let Jim Fisk bear the brunt of whatever losses would be taken.[16] Gambling on the expectation that the president would delay the order to Boutwell to sell gold until Corbin had had time to get out of the market, Gould allowed Fisk to go on buying gold while he secretly sold off his holdings. He may have regretted the necessity of throwing his old partner to the wolves—but business was business.

Oblivious to what was happening, Fisk dashed to the Gold Exchange as soon as it opened on September 23, bellowing orders to buy, buy, buy. He struck terror in the hearts of the bears who were frantically trying to cover their short sales by proclaiming, "I'll bet anyone $50,000 that gold will go over 145!" In the meantime, Gould sat quietly in his office at the Opera House, methodically tearing strips of paper into confetti, which was the only way in which he revealed tension and strain. His brokers had their orders. Buy small amounts of gold to make it appear that he was still a bull, while secretly unloading as much of his horde as they could without depressing the market.[17] Hourly, he sent special messengers to Butterfield at the Subtreasury to find out if the order had yet been received from Boutwell to sell gold from the government reserve. As he had expected, it did not come during the day, and he was able to partially disentangle himself.

The next day—September 24, 1869—was bright and clear, but it has gone down in financial history as Black Friday. Hundreds of persons had gathered on the floor of the Gold Exchange and milled about outside its doors, where peddlers sold toy bulls and bears. Thousands of others awaited developments at telegraphic indicators in the city and throughout the nation. Business was paralyzed from coast to coast as the country awaited the final scene of the drama. Gold opened at 143 and shot upward to 145 ... 147 ... 150. ...

A newspaper reporter on the scene described what happened next:

> The usually surging, bustling, shouting mass of humanity crowded there was held silent, almost motionless as by a magic spell. 150 is now bid and despair suddenly gives back life to many. They rush eagerly to bid and buy. Orders come in by telegraph to buy at any price. Messengers from all parts of the city, the great bankers, the merchant princes, from up-town and down-town, force their way in through the crush, and give back to the brokers the sense of reality which they seem to have lost amid the dreamlike terror. The stillness is suddenly succeeded by frantic excitement. Transactions of enormous magnitude are made amid the wildest confusion and the most unearthly screaming of men, always excitable, now driven to the verge of temporary insanity by the consciousness of ruin, or the delusive dream of immense wealth. But amid all the noise and confusion the penetrating voices of the leading brokers of the clique are still heard advancing the price at each bid ... until at last, with a voice overtopping the bedlam below, the memorable bid did burst forth, "160 for any part of five millions." Again, the noise was hushed. Terror became depicted on every countenance. Cool, sober men looked at one another, and noted the ashy paleness that spread over all. Even those who had but little or no interest at stake were seized with the infection of fear, and were conscious of a great evil approaching. And from the silence again came forth that shrieking bid, "160 for five millions," and no answer; "161 for five millions;" "162 for five millions," still no answer; "162 for any part of five millions. ..."[18]

While this spectacle worthy of Dante's *Inferno* was taking place, Gould and Fisk were holed up in a nearby brokerage office. Fisk had arrived in style in an open carriage with two actresses from the Opera House on his arms, and immediately issued orders to buy. As the price of gold rose implacably, he offered to bet

$50,000 that it would hit 200 before the end of the day. Gould sat in a corner, tearing small pieces of paper into even tinier bits. "Do nothing but sell—only don't sell to Fisk's brokers," had been his secret command. It was the only sign of consideration that he showed for his duped partner. Screaming, hoarse-voiced men overflowed the floor of the Gold Exchange, and spilled out into the street. The situation looked so dangerous that a militia detachment was called upon to stand by to "quell the riot in Wall Street." Shortly before noon, Gould received the word he had been expecting momentarily from Butterfield*—Grant had ordered Boutwell to sell $4 million in gold from the Treasury reserves. Gould used his twenty-five-minute advance warning to unload everything he had left.

This sudden influx of gold into the market broke the price.

> Dimly it dawned upon the quicker-witted ones that for some reason or other the game was up. As if by magnetic sympathy the same thought passed through the crowd at once. . . . In an instant the rumor was abroad, the Treasury is selling. . . . All who had bought were mad to sell at any price, but there were no buyers. In less time than it takes to write about it, the price fell from 162 to 135. The great gigantic gold bubble had burst, and half Wall Street was involved in ruin.[19]

As soon as the ruined speculators had recovered their senses, they howled for the blood of Gould and Fisk, but the pair made their escape out a back door. In a closed carriage, they dashed uptown to the Opera House and barricaded themselves inside. Gould was so haggard from the strain that Fisk said there was nothing "left of him but a pair of eyes and a suit of clothes"—and the $11 million he had made in the last few days by selling gold short.[20] It is a wonder that Fisk didn't tear him limb from limb when he learned of the trick that had been played on him. But Gould was ever resourceful. Following the suggestion of his partner, Fisk simply repudiated all the agreements he had made to buy gold. The Tammany judges, George Bernard and Albert Cardozo, issued a raft of writs that completely tied up his credi-

* Butterfield made $35,000 that day by selling short.

tors, who never collected so much as a dime, while Fisk and Gould divided up the ample loot.

From the safety of the Opera House, Fisk issued a series of statements to the press implicating Grant and his wife in the scandal. These touched off a demand for a congressional investigation of the events leading up to Black Friday. Under the chairmanship of Representative James A. Garfield of Ohio, the inquiry accumulated hundreds of pages of testimony but carefully skirted the question of presidential involvement. Neither the president, Mrs. Grant, nor Mrs. Corbin was called upon to testify, and the probe was carefully limited to the events concerning the Gold Exchange rather than to the link between the conspirators and the federal government. Although a Democratic member of the committee moved that Grant be "summoned" to testify, he was voted down on strict party lines, and the exact role of the presidential family in the scandal was left forever in doubt. "Every one dreaded to press [the] inquiry," said Henry Adams.[21] Perhaps they "feared finding out too much."

X

The Great Train Robbery and Other Holdups

ON THE MORNING of May 10, 1869, two locomotives—one coming from the East and the other from the West—eased toward each other on a single track at Promontory Point, near Ogden, Utah. As a boisterous crowd of Irish and Chinese workmen, train crews, prostitutes, and Mormon saints cheered, Governor Leland Stanford of California raised a silver sledge hammer to drive the golden spike that would mark the long-awaited completion of the transcontinental railroad linking the Atlantic and Pacific coasts. A telegraph wire attached to a spike was to carry the impact of Stanford's blow to Washington. There, a magnetic ball would drop from a pole on the dome of the Capitol, setting off celebrations in cities and towns across America. Rearing back, Stanford took a hefty swing—and missed. Alert for just such a mishap, a telegraph operator jammed down on his key to simulate the stroke of the sledge. So, even at the very end, fraud attended the building of the transcontinental railroad—just as it had nearly every step of the way.

The completion of this nation-spanning railroad after five years of arduous toil was considered by most Americans as the wonder of the age, the crowning achievement of the post–Civil War era. General William T. Sherman,[2] who knew more about wrecking railroads than building them, hailed the project as the "work of giants." And the California poet Joaquin Miller proclaimed "there is more poetry in the rush of a single railroad across the continent than in all the gory story of the burning of Troy." But the laying of every mile of track was accompanied by thievery and human greed that belied the noble intentions of those who first envisioned a transcontinental railroad.

Dreamed of for a generation, but blocked by sectional bickering and rivalry over the route to be followed, legislation authorizing the construction of a railroad across America was finally pushed through Congress in 1862. The Pacific Railway Act provided that the railroad would be constructed by two companies— the Union Pacific to build westward from Omaha, and the Central Pacific building eastward from Sacramento. The Union Pacific was chartered with a capital of $100 million and was given a right of way 200 feet wide through the public domain as well as alternating sections of land twenty miles wide along the entire line. This extravagant handout was further sweetened by Congress in 1864—after nearly $450,000 in bribes was passed out.[1] Government subsidies ranging from $16,000 to $48,000 a mile, depending on topography, were provided, and the land grant was expanded from twenty to forty miles in width until it finally reached the enormous total of twelve million acres. It was "the greatest legislative crime in history," cried Representative Elihu Washburne of Illinois, but no one was listening.

With such an elaborate free lunch spread before them, the buccaneers who dominated the railroad business before the war seized control of the Union Pacific company. Dr. Thomas C. Durant, better known for his skill in stock manipulation than for his railroading abilities, was named vice-president and operating chief. An independent company was established to construct the line—and fill the pockets of insiders. It bore the euphonious name of Credit Mobilier of America.[2] The Credit Mobilier had its origins in a corporation formed under the name of the Pennsylvania Fiscal Company in 1859. George Francis Train, one of the leading promoters of the Union Pacific, saw the possibilities inherent in this now-dormant Pennsylvania charter and purchased it. The company took its new name from a well-known French corporation, which incidentally fleeced a number of its investors.

Fantastically profitable construction contracts were awarded by the Union Pacific's directors to this companion firm. Peter A. Dey, the railroad's chief engineer, believed that each mile of track could be laid for $30,000, but was forced by Durant to increase his estimate. He upped it to $50,000, but even this was not enough. Dey was soon replaced by General Grenville M. Dodge, as capable an engineer but wiser in the ways of railroad promoters. The contracts were finally let for $60,000 a mile. One 200-mile stretch of track alone cost $6 million. As a result of this "great train robbery," the Union Pacific was forced to the edge of bankruptcy, while the Credit Mobilier paid dividends ranging upward of 350 percent a year. It was later determined that the Union Pacific cost about $50 million to build, while the Credit Mobilier charged nearly $94 million.[3]

Fearing that these enormous profits might cause Congress, which had chartered the railroad, to launch an inquiry, Oakes Ames, a Credit Mobilier director and Massachusetts congressman, suggested in 1867 that a large block of Credit Mobilier shares be distributed among his colleagues where they "will do the most good to us." After all, Ames observed, "there is no difficulty in getting men to look after their own property." A quantity of shares was distributed so generously as to raise suspicions of wholesale bribery. Schuyler Colfax, then the Speaker of the House and vice-president during Grant's first term; Senator Henry Wilson of Massachusetts, who was to be his successor; Senator J. W. Patterson of New Hampshire; and such ranking members of the House as James Garfield and James G. Blaine were let in on what Ames cheerfully called "a diamond mine."

In the meantime, the hard-driving Dodge mobilized an army of ten thousand men and pushed the tracks westward. Ex-soldiers, newly freed blacks, and Irish immigrants worked under the harsh prairie sun and froze in the mountain passes. Across Nebraska, Colorado, Wyoming, and into Utah, they graded roadbeds, built bridges, and laid out curves that spiraled around mountainsides. Some died in accidents; others were killed in drunken brawls. The casualty rate was so high that it was said there was an Irishman buried beneath each tie. The survivors pressed onward, laying an average of four rails a minute. Despite the graft, greed, and lust that accompanied the building of the Union Pacific, it was, indeed, an American epic.[4]

Carbine and six-shooter were kept as ready to hand as pick and shovel, while the railroad moved through Indian country. "No particular danger need to be apprehended from the Indians," the sardonic General Sherman had said. "So large a number of workmen distributed along the line will introduce enough whiskey to kill off all the Indians within three hundred miles of the road." But the Indians, sensing perhaps that their way of life was making its last stand, fought desperately to preserve the buffalo country from the encroachment of the Iron Horse. They won some local successes, but all to no avail. The U.S. Army worked with the railroads—an early version of the military-industrial complex—and the Indians were eventually herded onto reservations, where, broken in spirit and culturally emasculated, they were all but finished off by corruption and disease.

As the Union Pacific's tracks marched across the Continental Divide, the Central Pacific was working its way eastward. The idea of a railroad running from the Pacific Coast was the brainchild of a young engineer named Theodore D. Judah. Although some experts said it was impossible to build a line over the forbidding Sierra Nevada range and dubbed him "Crazy Judah," the engineer managed to attract the support of a quartet of tightfisted Sacramento merchants who saw the rich possibilities in his plan. To be known to history as the "Big Four," they were an oddly assorted group. Leland Stanford was a wholesale grocer with a taste for politics; Charles Crocker was a hulking ex-gold-miner turned dry-goods merchant; while Collis P. Huntington and Mark Hopkins were partners in a hardware store. "In later life," Oscar Lewis, their joint biographer, has written, they "accepted easily the roles of men of vision, who had perceived a matchless opportunity and grasped it with courage. It was a role that none of them deserved."[5] They furnished the cash for Judah's lobbying activities in Washington which were climaxed by the choice in 1862 of the Central Pacific to build the western end of the transcontinental railroad. "We have drawn the elephant," Judah telegraphed his partners in triumph. "Now let us see if we can harness him up."

This was easier said than done. No sooner was construction underway than the "Big Four" were insisting that Judah follow the same piratical pattern that had been laid down by Durant for the Union Pacific. For example, they wanted to take advantage of the law allowing a higher government subsidy for tracks laid in the Sierra, by claiming that the territory just to the east of Sacramento was part of the mountain range which was twenty-five miles away. So what if the land was as flat as a table? It was of the same geological structure as the Sierra, wasn't it? Why, then, shouldn't the government pay $48,000 for each mile of track rather than a mere $16,000? Like Peter Dey, Judah refused to go along, and his partners bought him out for $100,000. Stanford, who had been elected governor of California, got a state geologist to proclaim that there was "a regular and continuous ascent" only seven miles east of Sacramento. In Washington, President Lincoln, under pressure from California congressmen, accepted the geologist's opinions. "My pertinacity and Abraham's faith moved mountains," declared one legislator. The miracle cost the taxpayers an additional $800,000.[6]

The Central Pacific also had its version of the Credit Mobilier. It was called the Contract & Finance Company, which operated with the usual skulduggery. As many as seven bills sailed through the California legislature in a single session, doling out millions in public funds for railroad construction, which were siphoned off by the "Big Four." Just how much they put in their own pockets remains a mystery, because the books of the enterprise conveniently disappeared when a government investigation loomed in the offing. Gustavus Myers estimated that the haul may have reached $50 million.[7] From this beginning developed a corporate empire unparalleled in the nation's history for the pervasiveness of its economic and political power. For nearly a half-century, the Southern Pacific, the merged offshoot of the original line, dominated all phases of life in California with the arbitrariness of an absolute dictatorship. Operating under a Kentucky charter that gave it every power except that of operating in Kentucky, it kept the politicians of both parties in happy bondage.

Persistent rumors about the orgy of corruption surrounding the construction of the Union Pacific circulated freely, but all remained comparatively quiet until the closing days of President Grant's campaign for re-election in 1872. But those who knew what was happening below the surface were in despair. "It looks as though the Republican party is going to the dogs," mused former Senator James W. Grimes of Iowa. "It has become corrupt, and I believe that it is today the [most] corrupt and debauched political party that ever existed." The skeleton came tumbling out of the closet at last when Henry S. McComb, a disgruntled Credit Mobilier stockholder, charged that he had been cheated and filed suit. Secret court papers fell into the hands of Charles A. Dana, the editor of the New York *Sun*. He splashed them across six columns of the paper's front page on September 4, 1872, under a headline proclaiming:

THE KING OF FRAUDS

HOW THE CREDIT MOBILIER BOUGHT
ITS WAY THROUGH CONGRESS

Colossal Bribery

The revelations contained in the sworn testimony accompanying this need no explanatory introduction. It is the most damaging exhibition of official and private villainy and corruption ever laid bare to the gaze of the world. The Vice-President of the United States, the Speaker of the House of Representatives, the chosen candidate of a great party for the second highest office in the gift of the people, the chairman of almost every important committee in the House of Representatives—all of them are proven by irrefutable evidence to have been bribed. . . .

Everyone who was named denied everything. Most voters discounted the story as one concocted for campaign purposes—in the same way a future generation was to ignore the Watergate allegations exactly a century later. Grant buried the hapless

Horace Greeley in a landslide. This time the *Sun*'s headlines read FOUR YEARS MORE OF FRAUD AND CORRUPTION. But the force of public opinion was too strong to brush aside the charges of wholesale bribery. As soon as Congress reconvened on December 2, 1872, the House created a special committee, headed by Luke V. Poland, a Republican congressman from Vermont and former judge, to investigate the charges. The Senate also launched a parallel inquiry, but most of the attention centered on the Poland Committee.

Under the fascinated gaze of the public—the hearing room was packed with the cream of Washington society—a bizarre tale began to unfold in which Schuyler Colfax, the outgoing vice-president, was pushed onto the center of the stage. Such a fate was not the one that Colfax had forecast for himself. Connected through his mother with the Schuyler clan, he was born in New York in 1823. His family moved to Indiana, where Colfax became a newspaper publisher and helped found the Republican party in that state. In 1855, he was elected to the House of Representatives, where his amiability earned him the nickname "Smiler" Colfax. After eight years' service, he was elected Speaker of the House with the support of the radicals who favored a hard line toward the rebellious Southern states. Colfax was forty-six years old and had been Speaker for six years when the Republicans chose him to run as Grant's vice-president. He looked forward with confidence to fulfilling his ambition of one day moving into the White House. Things did not go as smoothly as planned, and after alienating the party leadership, Colfax was denied re-nomination and replaced by Henry Wilson as the vice-presidential candidate in 1872.

In his testimony before the Poland Committee, Colfax claimed he had received neither Credit Mobilier stock nor dividends from Ames. But Ames produced a little black book in which he had conveniently kept a record of his transactions and it listed a payment of $1,200 in dividends to Colfax. The vice-president's bank account also showed a deposit of $1,000 at about the same time. Floundering in an attempt to explain this coincidence, Colfax only succeeded in getting himself deeper into the mire. Not until the committee had concluded its hearings did he suddenly recall on February 19, 1873, where the money had come from. Colfax came before a specially convened session of the inquiry to report that the cash had been sent to him through the mail in the form of a $1,000 bill to be used in the 1868 campaign. It had been supplied by George F. Nesbit, a stationer and printer, who admired him. Could Mr. Nesbit be called upon to support this statement? Alas, he had recently died. And what had the generous stationer sought in return, Colfax was asked by Ames, who took part in the interrogation.[8]

"The only favor he ever asked me was to get tickets for his family to see the inauguration," replied the vice-president.

"He must have been a singular man," observed Ames.

"He was a very large-hearted man," Colfax answered.

"No doubt about it," murmured Ames.

Later it was discovered that the "large-hearted" Nesbit had been awarded a $4,000 government contract for envelopes while Colfax had been chairman of the House Post Office Committee.

The Poland Committee recommended that only Ames and James Brooks, a New York congressman and the only Democrat involved in the scandal, be expelled from Congress for offering bribes. As the session had only a few more days to run, this was modified to a vote of censure. Noting that he was being punished for offering a bribe while those who took one got off scot-free, Ames complained: "It's like the man who committed adultery, and the jury brought in a verdict that he was as guilty as the devil, but the woman was innocent as an angel."

The charges against Colfax were referred to the House Judiciary Committee to see if there were any grounds for impeachment proceedings. After deliberating four days, the committee held that he was not liable to impeachment for his misconduct since impeachment could not be used to punish an elected official for acts committed before he entered office. But this was cold comfort to Colfax, as he was ruined politically. The others involved emerged with a coat of hastily applied whitewash. Henry Wilson became vice-president but did not live out his term. James Garfield became president in 1881, but was assassinated within a few months of taking office. James Blaine, who was to be involved in other scandals, never completely cleared himself of the taint of corruption and was denied the presidency despite several attempts to win it.

In less than three years after completion of the transcontinental railroad, this symbol of national progress and pride was tarnished beyond repair. It had become synonomous with graft and the corrupt collaboration of businessmen and politicians. Summing up, Senator George Hoar declared:

> I have seen our national triumph and exhultation turned to bitterness and shame by the unanimous reports of three committees of Congress . . . that every step of that mighty enterprise had been taken in fraud. I have heard in highest places the shameless doctrine avowed by men grown old in public office that the way by which power should be gained in the Republic is to bribe the people with the offices created for their service and the true end for which it should be used when gained is the promotion of selfish ambition and the gratification of personal revenge. I have heard that suspicion haunts the footsteps of the trusted companions of the President.[9]

Although Grant was innocent of any connection with the Credit Mobilier, he was blamed just the same. Reformers proclaimed that this notorious affair was an outgrowth of the easy morality prevailing in Washington.[10] Many people agreed with a cabinet officer who told Henry Adams: "You can't reason with a Congressman! A Congressman is a hog! you must take a stick and hit him on the snout." As if to reinforce the charges of reformers, scandals exploded with bewildering regularity in all parts of Grant's administration.

Sometimes it must have seemed to the confused Grant that no sooner had one scandal subsided than another mushroomed to take its place. After the congressional election of 1874, when the Democrats captured control of the House, he charged that most of the investigations were inspired by a desire to win partisan advantage. He was only partially correct. Certainly, the Democrats were avidly digging for pay dirt in the expectation that it would help them in the presidential election of 1876. But it is also a fact that they found much in the tangled affairs of the Grant administration to warrant inquiry.

Almost every department of the government was honey-combed with corruption. Ironically, the first scandals broke out in the domain of Secretary of State Hamilton Fish, one of the few honorable men in the cabinet. Lincoln had appointed Colonel James Watson Webb, the bellicose publisher of the New York *Courier and Enquirer*, as minister to Brazil and he had been kept on by Grant. Word soon leaked out that Webb had extorted nearly $100,000 from the Brazilian government for a claim later ruled invalid, and diverted more than a third of the money to his own pocket. Outraged, Fish demanded an explanation and resti-tution, but Webb fled to England, leaving the U.S. government to make good his theft.

This sorry tale was followed by that of General T. B. Van Buren, an old friend of Grant, who had been appointed by the president to take charge of the American exhibition at an inter-national fair held in Vienna in 1873. Van Buren and his associ-ates promptly turned the appointment into a lucrative business. They sold places on the American delegation for as much as $6,000 and shook down concessionaires. The European press was delighted to give the scandalous conduct of the Americans full coverage, and the chagrined secretary of state was forced to recall them.

Far more serious was the misconduct of Robert C. Schenck, Grant's choice as minister to Great Britain. Shortly after his ar-rival in London in 1871, the British press criticized Schenck for allowing his name to be used in advertisements touting shares in the Emma Silver Mine in Utah. "The advertisement of the name of a diplomatic representative of the government, as director of a company seeking to dispose of its shares in the country to which he is accredited, is ill-advised and unfortunate," Fish wrote Schenck, ordering him to either resign as American minister or as a company director. Schenck dropped his association with the mine, but delayed in publicly announcing it until his fellow in-siders had time to cushion themselves from any shock wave result-ing from his resignation. After paying high dividends for a short time, the mine "played out" and the price of the stock took a nosedive. Hornswoggled English investors charged that the American minister had been party to a fraud. It was learned that

Schenck had been given 10,000 pounds worth of stock for the use of his name by the promoters of the Emma mine, and he had made a financial killing by selling his shares before the English investors learned the mine was exhausted. Ordered home in disgrace, he was forced to plead diplomatic immunity to avoid an English court writ against him.

An investigation of the Navy Department under the steward-ship of George M. Robeson also revealed widespread corruption. A House inquiry determined that the navy secretary, an unsuc-cessful attorney, had amassed a fortune in excess of $320,000 over a four-year period by shaking down contractors doing busi-ness with his department. One provided him with an oceanside home at Long Branch, New Jersey, where the Grant family usu-ally spent the summer. Exorbitant contracts were let for refitting ships left over from the Civil War, but the work was not done. It was hardly safe to send a ship to sea in Robeson's day. Neverthe-less, the president refused to demand Robeson's resignation, and a committee suggestion that he be impeached was lost in the confusion of other breaking scandals.

Early in 1875, a congressional inquiry turned up "uncon-tradicted evidence" of malfeasance by William W. Belknap, the Secretary of War. Belknap, another of Grant's ubiquitous military comrades, had been named to the cabinet in 1869, and appears to have almost immediately begun lining his pockets. Belknap was married to a woman of social ambition and found his yearly salary of $8,000 inadequate to meet the demands of a luxurious household and extravagant entertaining. As it turned out, how-ever, Mrs. Belknap knew a wealthy New York contractor named Caleb P. Marsh. She offered him a lucrative tradership at the Indian post at Fort Sill in exchange for part of the profits. But John S. Evans, who held the tradership, had made a heavy invest-ment in it which he did not wish to lose. He offered Marsh a yearly payment of $12,000 to be left alone. The astute Marsh accepted and agreed to give Mrs. Belknap half of it. The pay-ments arrived with regularity until Mrs. Belknap died; then they went to her husband.

In February 1876, the New York *Herald* exposed Belknap's link not only to the Marsh case but to the widespread sale of Indian post traderships that brought in graft totaling as much as $100,000 a year. It was also charged that President Grant's brother, Orville, was in on the loot. "Let the President send for his own brother," the paper stated, "and question him about the money that was made in the Sioux country by starving the squaws and children." When Orville Grant acknowledged to the investigating committee that he had been given partnerships in four Indian post traderships in return for the use of his name, the *Nation* caustically commented that the basic difference between the president and the secretary of war was "that while Belknap allowed his wife to sell traderships and apply the money to his household expenses, the President allowed his brother to sell them and keep the money himself."

Alarmed that the congressional investigators would recommend that he be impeached, Belknap raced to the White House early on March 2, 1876, to submit his resignation during a tearful scene. Grant immediately wrote a one-sentence letter accepting the resignation "with great regret." The president and Belknap obviously hoped that the resignation would forestall the impending impeachment. But the angry congressmen went ahead with it anyway. The trial before the Senate dragged on all through the summer, but in the end, the Senate voted 37 to 24 to acquit Belknap. All but one of those voting for aquittal said they had done so not out of any belief in Belknap's innocence but because they felt the Senate no longer had jurisdiction as a result of Belknap's resignation. Grant's speedy acceptance of the resignation had saved him from the disgrace of a guilty verdict.

The president's mistaken sense of loyalty also played a decisive role in submitting the District of Columbia to the brigandage of Alexander R. Shepherd, who threw the local government into virtual bankruptcy.[11] Although Shepherd was only the vice-president of the Board of Works, the newly created administrative body of the capital, he used this position to run the government in the same manner in which Boss Tweed ran New York. A much-needed program of public improvements was instituted which transformed the ramshackle city into a beautiful and impressive capital. In the process, a debt of some $17 million was piled up— along with charges of extravagance and graft. Shepherd was said to have made a fortune through what were euphemistically called "real estate speculations." The outcry from the city's hapless residents was so loud that the president of the Board of Works was forced to resign. And who did Grant appoint in his place? Why, Boss Shepherd himself. Later, it was discovered that Shepherd and his associates—known as District Ring—had also looted the Freedman's Bank. Designed as a philanthropic venture, the institution turned out to be a fraud which swept away the savings of thousands of poor blacks. Yet, public memory was so short that a statue of Shepherd was erected in front of the District Office Building on Pennsylvania Avenue not far from the White House, where it stood for many years.

Columbus Delano, who had been named secretary of the interior replacing a corrupt predecessor, was found to have solicited bribes to enter fraudulent land grants in the records. When Hamilton Fish suggested that Delano resign, the president replied, "it would be retreating under fire and be accepted as an admission of the charges." Grant did not force Delano to step down for another four months and then tried to keep it a secret. And Treasury Secretary William A. Richardson was found to have connived with John D. Sanborn, a Massachusetts politico and agent of Ben Butler in his wartime cotton speculations, to turn the collection of delinquent taxes into a racket. Nevertheless, it was only with some difficulty that Grant could be persuaded to demand Richardson's resignation. And even that blow was cushioned by appointing him to the Court of Claims.

Surprisingly, the forced resignation of Richardson had a positive effect, for Benjamin H. Bristow became Secretary of the Treasury in 1874. This tall, energetic Kentuckian had a zeal for reform and justice that extended back to his days as a federal prosecutor in his home state. In an area where few men opposed the excesses of the Ku Klux Klan, he had acted with courage to combat an antiblack terror campaign. Bristow's aggressiveness brought him national attention, and when Congress, in 1870, created the office of Solicitor General, Grant offered him the post. Four years later, with his administration awash with corruption, the president sought for the Treasury someone who could help restore confidence in the government. He settled upon Bristow—and got far more than he had bargained for.

From the time of his appointment, Bristow took an interest in the activities of the notorious Whiskey Ring, which had defrauded the Treasury of millions of dollars in revenues and seemed to have tentacles reaching into the highest levels of government.[12] The Ring had been operating without hindrance since the Civil War, but the government had shown a remarkable reluctance to investigate the charges of graft and corruption in the collection of taxes that were periodically leveled by opposition newspapers and disgruntled politicians. Western distillers working with Internal Revenue agents on the scene and ranking officials in Washington had reaped enormous profits from the sale of untaxed whiskey that often bore forged revenue stamps. "Crooked whiskey," as it was known, flowed freely from the distilleries of St. Louis, Chicago, Peoria, Milwaukee, and Indianapolis.

In St. Louis, where John A. McDonald, an illiterate former cotton speculator, had been named as Supervisor of Internal Revenue by Grant, it was estimated that the government was cheated out of $2.8 million in six years—$1.2 million during 1874 alone. Nearly half the loot went to officials in the Treasury Department and the Bureau of Internal Revenue. Sizable contributions were also filtered into the war chests of various Republican campaign committees, including those that had supported the president's reelection. The profits were so great that McDonald, whose annual salary never exceeded $3,000, picked up the tab for a presidential visit to St. Louis and presented Grant with a matched team of horses and harness worth nearly $2,000. No questions were asked. General Orville E. Babcock, a presidential secretary, was given a $2,400 diamond shirt stud. When Babcock complained that the stone was flawed, McDonald hastily replaced it with one that was more expensive.

Early in 1875, Bristow got the break that he had been hoping for. Statistics issued by the St. Louis Merchants' Exchange aimed at trumpeting the commercial advantages of the city, showed that only about a third of the whiskey produced there had been taxed.

In addition, George W. Fishback, publisher of the St. Louis *Democrat*, sent the secretary a letter that read:

> There has been much talk of late of the fraudulent whiskey traffic in the West. If the Secretary wants to break up the powerful ring which exists here, I can give him the name of a man who, if he receives the necessary authority and is assured of absolute secrecy about the matter, will undertake to do it, and I will guarantee success.

The man referred to was Myron Colony, the commercial editor of the *Democrat*, who pinpointed the leaders of the Ring, and disclosed which officials were being paid off by them. Because the Treasury was so riddled with corruption, Bristow flooded the city with special agents chosen from outside the department. New codes were devised and agents gathered information that was marked for the eyes of the Treasury secretary alone. Over the next few months, evidence was accumulated by similar methods in other cities.

At last, on May 10, 1875, Bristow was ready to strike. But in spite of the care taken to maintain secrecy, news of the impending raids leaked out. Ring members in St. Louis received telegrams from Washington that read: "The plague is advancing west. Advise our friends." Some of the culprits scurried to Canada, but enough evidence was seized in the way of books and records to obtain 250 indictments—and to implicate Babcock. A few days later Secretary of State Hamilton Fish confided to his diary: "Bristow tells me that Babcock is as deep as any in the Whiskey Ring; that he has most positive evidence, he will not say of actual fraud, but of intimate relations and confidential correspondence with the very worst of them."

Grant's reaction to the raids must have made Bristow wince. "Well, Mr. Bristow," the president said, according to Fish, "there is at least one honest man in St. Louis on whom we can rely—John McDonald. I know that because he is an intimate acquaintance and confidential friend of Babcock's." Bristow's reply was short and to the point. "Mr. President, McDonald is the head and centre of all the frauds. He is at this very time in New York ready to take a steamer on the first indication of any effort to arrest him." Eventually, McDonald was arrested and sentenced to three years in prison, but not before claiming that Babcock had been on his payroll to the tune of $25,000. On one occasion McDonald said he had sent the presidential secretary a $1,000 bill in a box of fine cigars. He also claimed that Grant was involved with the Ring, but could produce no evidence to back up the charge.

Thus far, the president had given the fullest support to the prosecution. When Bristow provided evidence of Babcock's involvement—including telegrams written in Babcock's hand-writing warning the leaders of the Ring of the pending investigation—Grant had written on the back of the letter, "Let no guilty man escape. . . . No personal consideration should stand in the way of performing a public duty." And he said that "if Babcock is guilty there is no man who wants him so proven guilty as I do, for it is the greatest piece of traitorism to me that a man could possibly produce." Nevertheless, it was noted that despite the mounting evidence against Babcock, he continued to occupy his White House office and was still a close confidant of the president.

As time went on, the smooth-talking Babcock managed to convince Grant that the charges against him were part of a plot by Bristow to advance his own political interests at the expense of the administration. He was aided by Republican leaders who claimed that Bristow's investigations were "ruining the party." They demanded that the case be taken out of the hands of the secretary of the Treasury, who handled all tax fraud cases, and that it be given to the more pliable attorney general, Edwards Pierrepont. These charges had the anticipated effect. Soon, the president was convinced that the entire probe was the work of reformers interested only in discrediting his administration, and blocking him from running for a third term—an eventuality that was being seriously considered.

Grant was also angered by unsubstantiated newspaper stories claiming that his brother, Orville, and his son, Fred, were in-volved with the Whiskey Ring. Unwilling to believe anything evil about his associates—especially old wartime comrades like

Babcock—he turned his full ire upon those who were trying to clean up the mess. When former Senator John B. Henderson of Missouri, who had been named special prosecutor, tried to link the White House to the case, he was dismissed by an angry Grant—much in the way that Elliott Richardson and Archibald Cox were to be axed during a White House cover-up a century later.*

But the president was unable to prevent the indictment of Babcock on charges of "conspiracy to defraud the revenue." Babcock still had one last card left to play, however. On January 26, 1876, Grant, obviously acting upon Babcock's advice, ordered the attorney general to forbid federal prosecutors in St. Louis, Chicago, and Milwaukee from offering immunity to any of the conspirators who were willing to testify for the prosecution. Five days later, the order was leaked to the press—apparently after having been filched off the president's desk by Babcock. The effect was immediate. In Chicago, where fifty of the minor conspirators were ready to plead guilty and testify against the major figures in return for immunity, the case fell apart after the president's order was published. And in St. Louis, where important testimony was expected from the Ring's chief paymaster, little new was revealed. "It was unquestionably at Babcock's instigation that Grant thus crippled the prosecution," observes Allan Nevins in his biography of Hamilton Fish. "But no one can doubt that the President knew precisely what he was doing."

Babcock's trial opened in St. Louis on February 8, 1876. "The general public are somewhat surprised at the bold confidence with which the prosecution asserted its readiness to trace Ring money directly to the hands of Babcock," reported *The New York Times*. During the prosecution's opening statement, it was noted that Babcock "showed unusual excitement, nervously twitching his moustache and moving uneasily in his seat." Babcock's uneasiness was transmitted to the White House where the president hastily convened a cabinet meeting. Grant was extremely excited, wrote Fish. He complained that "the prosecution was aimed at

---

* While in the Senate, Henderson had been one of seven Republicans who had voted to acquit President Andrew Johnson when he had been impeached seven years before.

himself, and they were putting him on trial; that he was confident as he lived of Babcock's innocence."

And then Grant made an extraordinary announcement—he intended to go to St. Louis to testify on behalf of his embattled secretary. Appalled at the spectacle of the president racing halfway across the country to testify in a criminal trial, the cabinet persuaded him to reconsider. Instead, he made a sworn deposition to the Chief Justice of the United States, Morrison R. Waite, attesting to Babcock's good character, which was sent to the defendant's lawyers for use as they saw fit.

Despite the damaging evidence against Babcock, Grant's strong deposition and obvious eagerness for an acquittal had great weight with the jury. On February 24, it brought in a not guilty verdict. The news was hailed as a victory for the Republican party, and friends of the administration hastily pledged $30,000 to pay for Babcock's defense. But when Babcock tried returning to his desk at the White House, Grant, bowing to public opinion, was forced to shunt him aside to the inspectorship of lighthouses. Babcock was the only one of those indicted in the Whiskey Ring prosecutions who was found innocent. The verdict of history, however, is less charitable. "Though the judge and jury did not believe that a legal case had been made against Babcock, no real doubt can remain that he shared in the profits of the Ring," says James Ford Rhodes in his *History of the United States.*

As for the zealous Bristow, his resignation from the cabinet was virtually forced by President Grant. Although he tried to win the Republican presidential nomination in 1876, the conservative wing of the party opposed him, and he never again held an important political office. The men whom he had worked so hard to put behind bars soon received presidential pardons.

XI

Who Stole the People's Money?

SQUATTING AMONG THE soaring towers of lower Manhattan just behind New York's graceful City Hall is a low-lying building that time seems to have passed by. In a city that takes a strange pride in destroying and rebuilding itself every twenty-five years or so, it is ironic that this structure should have escaped the wrecker's ball for more than a century. There is something of the ugly duckling about the building, as if it had been purposely tucked out of sight. Even the City Hall faces in the opposite direction, averting its eyes from its raffish neighbor. Inside, behind Corinthian columns and marble walls, the three floors of high-ceilinged rooms and long corridors echo the footsteps of the random passers-by. This is the old New York Courthouse—the Versailles of the Tweed Ring and a masterpiece of civic corruption.

Big Bill Tweed and his henchmen perverted the construction of this palace of justice into a carnival of graft that eventually cost the taxpayers enough to buy all of Alaska almost twice over. In the end, these excesses helped destroy the Ring, but the Boss's ghost is probably having the last laugh. A century after his fall, he would be delighted to learn, architectural historians and preservationists were hailing his often denounced creation as "one of our city's treasures" and "the finest public building in the Anglo-Italian Classical [style] in the country."[1] At one time, it also housed the city's Board of Ethics.

Plans for the courthouse were first approved in 1858, and $250,000 was earmarked for construction, a respectable sum in those days. This, however, was "only the acorn which was planted to methodically raise a great oak of fraud," observed *The New York Times*, Tweed's bitter enemy.[2] Actual work was delayed until 1862, when, perhaps not coincidentally, Tweed had been elevated to the presidency of the Board of Supervisors, the legatees of the "Forty Thieves" who had long plundered the city. That year, an additional million dollars was voted for the completion of the courthouse. It was not enough. Two years later, $800,000 more was required, and another $300,000 was needed the following year. But this still wasn't enough. In 1866, a further $500,000 was appropriated for the job.

Growing suspicious at last, a group of reformers demanded an investigation of the project. Tweed was delighted to oblige. The supervisors appointed a Special Committee to Investigate the Courthouse—which, not unexpectedly, required little time to determine that the construction of the building was remarkably free of fraud. The Special Committee then submitted its expenses for twelve days of deliberation. The bills included $2,938 for stenographic services, $900 for legal fees, $205 for meals, and $14,107.75 to companies owned by Tweed for printing the record and report—for a grand total of $18,460.35.[3]

All the while, demands for money to complete the courthouse continued unabated. In 1867, $800,000 was earmarked for the project, followed by an equal amount the next year. In 1869 and 1870, $1.2 million was swallowed up, to be followed by $750,000 in 1871. The entire amount spent was in excess of $13 million. "Just imagine," commented the *Times*, "the untiring industry, the wear and tear of muscle, the anxiety of mind, the weary days and the sleepless nights that it must have cost the 'Boss' to procure all these sums of money and superintend their economical outlay in order that the people might have a temple of justice worthy of the great judicial luminaries, Bernard and Cardozo."[4] One observer noted that the cost of the courthouse exceeded more than four times the money spent on the construction of the Houses of Parliament in London, which were completed at about the same time.

Strangely enough, the building needed extensive repairs before it was even finished, which added $2 million to the job. That was just the beginning, for as a disenchanted reformer said, bills presented by the contractors hired by the Tweed Ring were "not merely monstrous, they are manifestly fabulous." Take the case of Andrew J. Garvey, a plastering contractor, who handed in a bill of $2.8 million for nine months' work. "Generations of plasterers yet unborn will take off their hats to his memory!" declared one writer. Garvey was dubbed "the Prince of Plasterers" by the *Times*, which described the payment of $133,187 to him for two days work as worthy of the *Arabian Nights*. John Keyser charged nearly $1.5 million for plumbing and gas fixtures—payments that would probably be the envy of even his royally paid descendants of today. Repairs for woodwork totaled $750,000 and lumber not worth $48,000 cost the city $460,000.

The bill for carpets, shades, and curtains came to $675,534.44. One of the favorite pastimes of New Yorkers was to try to compute how far such a quantity of carpeting would reach. It was noted that about the same time, Tweed's son opened the Metropolitan Hotel, which featured gorgeous carpets and elaborate furniture. Awnings cost $41,746.83; "brooms, etc.," $41,190.95; locks, $2,676.75; and thermometers, $7,500. A businessman who kept a private bar in his office where Tweed and his aides could refresh themselves with the best liquor and wine sent in a bill for $404,347.72. The city was also charged for work that probably wasn't done. On December 27, 1869, a check was drawn to the order of one Fillippo Donaruma for $33,283. It came back endorsed "Phillip F. Dummey." A couple of days later, another check, this one for $33,129.89, was made out to Donaruma—and came back endorsed "Fillip Dummin." Both were countersigned by Garvey. Sometimes, items were double-billed. On July 2, 1869, $42,506.64 was paid for furniture; two weeks later, an additional $94,083.13 was doled out in payment for the same account. Two other checks—for a total of $64,090—were made out to the order of "T. C. Cashman." No one could say the Tweed Ring did not have a sense of humor.[5]

Tweed did not overlook the opportunity provided by the opening of a new courthouse to reap a rich harvest of patronage, notes Alexander B. Callow, Jr., who has made the most thorough study of the Ring's operations. A prizefighter called "Maneater" Jim Cusick "graduated" from Sing Sing to a court clerkship. "Pudding" Long, who could neither read nor write and spent most of his time looking after the Boss's kennel, was made an "interpreter." The names of dead men abounded on the payroll—but there was always someone on hand to pick up their pay. Thirty-two men were hired to maintain the building's heating equipment, a job which could be performed by one.[6] All in all, the New York County Courthouse, was, in the words of the *Times*, a "fit and appropriate monument to the Boss."

If ever an American city belonged to one man, it was New York during the heyday of William Marcy Tweed. Just how much Tweed and his allies stole during their reign, which lasted from the end of the Civil War until 1871, will probably never be known. Estimates range from a low of $20 million to a high of $200 million, if fraudulent bonds are included. Under Tweed's stewardship, New York City's debt nearly tripled—from $34.4 million as of the end of 1869 to $97.2 million on September 4, 1871. During virtually the same period, the debt of the United States actually *declined* by about $212 million.[7]

To the Tweed Ring belongs the distinction of having put corruption on an orderly and businesslike basis. Before the rise of Tweed, local government in most American towns and cities had remained almost entirely within the realm of what could best be described as talented amateurs. Usually, they were men whose personal and business affairs were in such good order that they could take time to concern themselves with the affairs of their communities. They were careful to protect their own interests and those of their class, but there was an air of noblesse oblige about them, as well as more than a trace of benevolent dictatorship.

The rise of Tweed and others like him represented a distinct phase in the revolt against this essentially upper-middle-class and aristocratic domination of local government. The triumph of big business in the post-Civil War era, the astounding growth of the urban lower class as a result of the repeated waves of immigration, and the rise of professional politicians of humble origin who could appeal to the masses, all sounded the death knell of the old forms of government. These factors were not understood by the reformers who battled against Tweed and his successors. Well-educated, affluent, patronizingly virtuous and insufferably priggish, they sought to preserve the values of an older, simpler, and less urban America that had already all but vanished.

The reformers attacked corruption, but they did not provide a remedy for it that appealed to the average American. Good government could be provided only by the "best" people—men like themselves—which left no place for the ordinary citizen. To the reformers, the spoils system, municipal graft, and election fraud were moral delinquencies—which, of course, they were—but they failed to comprehend that these offenses were not merely signs of the depravity of the lower classes. When they discovered that industry and big business, the rich and well-born, the people who supported reform publications often worked with Tweed and other bosses and were engaged in similar malpractices to protect and advance their own interests, the reformers were bewildered and frustrated.

Tweed, however, understood the realities of the political system. The end of upper-class control of politics had created a vacuum that was being filled by professionals like himself who served as middlemen between the contending forces—and lined their pockets with plunder. "Steeped in the logistics of grass-roots practical politics," the professional politician "organized the bleak, sprawling areas of the poor into political strongholds, and devoted himself to the mundane business of building and entrenching a political organization," observes Alexander Callow.[8] Under Tweed's dominance, Tammany Hall was the pioneering city "machine"—a permanent, all-embracing, finely articulated political organization that operated for its own ends rather than serving as a vehicle for expressing an ideological point of view. It was not an uplift society, but a blunt instrument for seizing and using power. Sizable amounts of graft and patronage were needed to keep such an organization going. As Tweed later explained, "money was distributed around in every way to everybody. . . ."

Nevertheless, at no time during its days of glory did the Tweed Ring control a majority of the city's voters. Part of its success, of course, came from cheating—seeing that loyalists voted early and voted often. But Tweed did not have to rely solely on political chicanery to win elections. He was Grand Sachem of Tammany Hall and Tammany was the heart of the Democratic party in New York City. Thus, it got the votes of all those who supported the party out of idealism, habit, or conviction that a Republican victory would be tantamount to the visitation of the biblical plagues upon Egypt. For the same reasons, Republican voters in Philadelphia supported an equally corrupt organization, the Gas House Ring, whose handiwork caused the town to be dubbed "The City of Brotherly Loot."

Big businessmen were friendly with Boss Tweed because they could get anything they wanted from either the state or city government as long as they were willing to pay for it. Some of them distrusted reformers because they might not be able to bribe honest politicians. The Ring tacked up a big "For Sale" sign on the city. When Commodore Vanderbilt wanted a traction franchise for a line running from the Battery to 42nd Street, Tweed was the man to see. When John Jacob Astor wanted land he owned that was under water to be filled in, Tweed was the man to contact. Shopkeepers, tradesmen, and ordinary citizens supported Tammany in hopes of receiving favors in return for their loyalty. Others were frightened of its powers of extortion and of retribution. Too often, they had seen dissenters ruined by a sudden refusal of a municipal permit to do business, or the unheralded arrival of city inspectors and even hired thugs.

The Ring also had the support of the thousands of immigrants flooding into the city. Until the 1840s, most immigrants to the United States had arrived with some small means, perhaps with an occupation, or enough capital to enable them to seize the opportunities available in the cities or to move on to the frontier.

The failure of the potato crop in Ireland drastically altered the pattern of immigration. Now, the vast majority of the new arrivals were ignorant peasants without money or readily marketable skills. They crowded into urban tenements and hovels with only the most menial and dirty jobs open to them—when they could find work. For their women, there was only domestic service or prostitution.*

For the most part, the bewildered immigrants met only hostility and contempt from native-born Americans. But Tammany, dominated as it was by Irish Catholics—although Tweed was of Scottish descent and a Presbyterian to boot—had learned the value of ethnic politics. The foreign vote was a vital factor in a city where close to one-half the voters were naturalized citizens. When the immigrant ships unloaded their unhappy cargoes at Castle Garden at the tip of Manhattan, Tammany runners were on hand to offer the newcomer advice, a meal and help in finding a place to live. Perhaps there might be a job or a place on the public payroll if the immigrant seemed a particularly likely-looking prospect. Tammany also operated offices where foreigners could obtain naturalization papers for as little as $2.00, and witnesses were available who would swear that they had been in the United States long enough to become citizens. All that Tammany required in return for such service was the newly minted citizen's vote.[9]

Tweed's men—and particularly the Boss himself—were generous with charity. During the savage winter of 1870, for example, when women and children were freezing and starving in the streets, Tweed donated $50,000 to buy groceries for the poor. This gift won him some praise even though Thomas Nast, whose savage cartoons were to play a major role in putting Tweed behind bars, celebrated the incident with a drawing showing the Boss and a cohort emptying a city safe saying, "Let's blind them with this and then take some more." District leaders also chipped in $1,000 each to buy coal, although it was remarked that few of the poor had cellars to store it. Even after Tweed's fall, when the

---

* In 1870, it was estimated that there were 10,000 prostitutes in New York City, which then had a population of about 950,000.

enormity of his thefts became public knowledge, there were those who said: "Well, if Tweed stole, he was at least good to the poor." Long before the New Deal, Tammany had its own social welfare programs. Hospitals, orphanages, homes for the aged, and religious institutions of all faiths and denominations participated in the Ring's largesse. During the years from 1869 to 1871, the Catholic charities and schools were given $1.4 million from the city's coffers; those of the Episcopal Church, about $57,000; the Jews got $25,800, and the Methodists, $7,300.[10]

But even if the Ring may have stolen from the rich and given to the poor, observes Callow, it also stole from the poor as well. A few dollars' worth of groceries at Christmas or a bushel of coal did nothing to improve the overall conditions of the poor. In fact, they suffered more from the plundering of the city than did the rich. Foul, rat-infested slums; rotting, rickety tenements; high rents; garbage-filled streets; sickness; disease; crime; and violence were not the concern of Tammany Hall. Money appropriated to provide municipal services to alleviate these evils usually ended up in the pockets of Tweed and his associates. Inspectors whose job it was to prevent such conditions were paid off. The *Times* compared the Tweed Ring to the robber barons of medieval Europe "who swept a man's land of his crops, and then gave him a crust of dry bread."

At the height of his power, Bill Tweed commanded respect by his imperial presence.[11] He stood just under six feet tall and weighed nearly three hundred pounds. Usually, he sparkled and gleamed as he moved about, weighed down with numerous diamonds and pieces of jewelry. His most prominent features were an egg-shaped head and a long nose that Thomas Nast used brilliantly to caricature him as a vulture. Born in 1823, Tweed had begun his career as a chairmaker in his father's shop on Cherry Street, but he was far too clever a fellow to spend his time in such a workaday fashion. Quick at figures—a talent that would come in handy in later years—Tweed studied bookkeeping as a young man, but spent most of his time "running" with the Americus, or "Big Six," volunteer fire company.

In those days, New York City had no regular fire department and whatever protection there was against the periodic conflagrations that devastated the town came from volunteers. Fiercely proud of their glittering equipment and their prowess, the various companies were bitter rivals. Often, they halted to fight among each other for supremacy at the scene of a fire, and forgot about the blazing building. As soon as a fire bell sounded, crowds gathered in the streets to see the firemen race by on foot, cheering their favorite company as if it were an athletic team. In dealing with a rival company, Tweed's bulk was an asset and he soon became foreman of "Big Six." The company's talisman was a snarling tiger, and when Nast sought a symbol for the ferocity of Tammany Hall under Tweed's sway, he remembered it and created the Tammany tiger.

Volunteer fire companies had considerable political clout, so the popular and jovial Tweed entered politics. In 1852, he was elected to the Board of Aldermen—the "Forty Thieves." Tweed's political credo was simple. "New York politics were always dishonest—long before my time," he later declared. "There never was a time when you couldn't buy the Board of Aldermen. A politician in coming forward takes things as they are. . . . [New York] . . . is too hopelessly split up into races and factions to govern it under universal suffrage, except by the bribery of patronage or corruption."[12] Two years later, he went to Congress. Always a taciturn man willing to let others do the talking, Tweed was bored by all the palaver about tariffs and free soil and "contracts to carry the mail from Paducah to Schoharie." Returning to New York with relief, he was elected in 1857 to the Board of Supervisors, which had control of public improvements, taxation, and expenditures. Five years later, he became president and took over the roles of Commissioner of Public Works and Deputy Street Commissioner, which offered rich opportunities for graft and patronage. And in 1867, Tweed extended his sway to include Albany, where as a state senator he was a leader of the Black Horse Cavalry, as the most corrupt members of the legislature were known.

In addition, he found time to hold positions in banks, railroads, printing, gas and insurance companies—all of which realized the advantage of having on their boards of directors the man one newspaper referred to as "Mr. Supervisor-Senator-Street Commissioner Tweed." In his climb to this exalted position, the Boss became the third largest owner of real estate in New York, and accumulated a fortune estimated at $12 million, although he claimed it had never topped a quarter of that. Tweed built a mansion among the Astors and Vanderbilts at Fifth Avenue and Forty-third Street that cost an estimated $350,000. When his daughter, Mary Amelia, married on May 31, 1871, in Trinity Chapel, the wedding gifts were valued at $700,000. The Boss must have been pleased when the *Herald* observed that the display was the most dazzling seen since the marriage of the daughter of the Khedive of Egypt. Tweed also had an estate in Greenwich, Connecticut, where Andrew Garvey, the "Prince of Plasterers," was in charge of decorating the grounds with statues. One day, the master of the manor spotted a strange-looking figure with winged feet and asked Garvey, "Who the hell is that?"

"That is Mercury, the god of merchants and thieves," was the reply.

"Good! That's bully!" exclaimed Tweed. "Put him over the front door."

In a lighter moment, an opposition newspaper once defined the Tweed Ring as "a hard band in which there is gold all round and without end." Besides the Boss himself, the ranking members were Peter B. Sweeny, Richard B. Connolly, and A. Oakey Hall. Like any modern corporate management, they operated under a system of division of labor. While Tweed served as chief executive with overall control of the Ring's activities, the other members of this quartet were specialists in dealing with a particular part of its operation.[13]

Sweeny, whose name was often printed in the papers as "$weeny," was the most important member after Tweed. He was the opposite of the Boss in almost every respect. Slightly built, sinister-looking, and secretive, he was considered the Ring's brains and served as its backstage manipulator and wirepuller. Sweeny was entrusted with the task of arranging political deals, picking candidates for office and seeing to it that they were

elected. It was said no one in Tammany Hall was more expert
than he at gauging the exact strength and weakness of a given
candidate. Because of his reserved manner, Sweeny did not hold
elected office, but contented himself with appointment as City
Chamberlain, or treasurer, and Commissioner of Parks. In the
latter role, he managed in just one year to spend—or so his books
said—$8 million of the taxpayers' money for the maintenance of
newly developed Central Park. The year before, his predecessor
had performed the same task with only $250,000.

Abraham Oakey Hall—"the Elegant Oakey" as he was known
because of the magnificence of his attire and his manner—was,
as a lawyer, the Ring's advisor on legislation and legal matters. A
consummate showman, he was elected mayor of New York, and
helped divert public attention from the devious doings of his
colleagues. With a flair for bizarre and colorful costumes, Hall
was described as "the best-dressed man in the annals of Mayor-
dom. He wears a different tie every day." The mayor outdid
himself one St. Patrick's Day, when he turned up to review the
annual parade dressed entirely in varying shades of green. His
catering to his Irish and German constituents was so obvious that
he was jokingly referred to as "Mayor Von O'Hall." At one time,
Hall had been district attorney, a period in which ten thousand
criminal indictments were "pigeonholed." Asked to give the reason for his success in politics, the mayor, who could not resist a
pun, declared, "Few persons have so many tried friends as I
have." During a speech on the Chinese problem, he was moved to
declare: "We could very well say tonight—on this hot night of
June—that the coolie question was a very good one to talk about."
Upon one occasion, however, a newspaperman turned the
mayor's penchant for puns against him. "New York City is
now governed," he wrote, "by Oakey Hall, Tammany Hall, and
Alcohol."

"Slippery Dick" Connolly, the only immigrant among the
Ring's leaders, had come to New York from Ireland as a young
man. Adept at figures, he became a bookkeeper and began a
grass-roots political career in New York's "Bloody Seventh" Ward.
It was said, reports one historian, that "while his neat penman-
ship was much admired, he could not be trusted to count votes

correctly." Connolly amassed considerable influence among the Irish, which brought him to the attention of Tweed and Sweeny when they took over Tammany Hall. Because of his bookkeeping skills, he was a natural for the post of City Comptroller. So well did Connolly perform in this position, that by 1871 he was presumed to be worth at least $6 million. Just a few years before, his annual salary had been $3,600.

Summing up, one writer has described Tweed as "the bold burglar" of the gang; "Sweeny the dark plotter, Connolly the sneak-thief, [and] Hall the dashing bandit."[14] One of the astonishing things about them was the open way in which they operated. The Tweed Ring did not hide behind such modern subterfuges for channeling graft as the dummy corporation, the campaign contribution, or cash laundered through foreign banks. Plunder was accumulated openly and the Ring was contemptuous of its enemies. After all, Tweed and his associates not only controlled the municipal government but their tentacles also extended to Albany and the courts. Governor John T. Hoffman, who had been Oakey Hall's predecessor as mayor, was in Tweed's pocket, and so was a sizable segment of the legislature. And with such leading lights of the judiciary as Judges Bernard and Cardozo on his side, there was nothing to fear from that quarter.

The basic operating technique of the Tweed Ring was simplicity itself.[15] Everyone who wanted a contract with the city, whether for supplies or for work on municipal buildings, had to raise his bills by a fixed percentage and pay off the difference between what the job actually cost and the payment received to the Ring. At first, the amount that the bills were to be padded by was 55 percent. This was later raised to 60 percent, and finally to 65 percent. These transactions were handled by James Watson, the City Auditor, who received the kickbacks and then distributed the plunder to the various members of the Ring. Tweed received from 10 to 25 percent; Connolly from 10 to 20 percent; Sweeny, 10 percent; and Hall, from 5 to 10 percent.

Watson had been launched on his civic career while in the Ludlow Street jail, where he had been imprisoned after funds belonging to a firm for which he worked had mysteriously vanished. A pleasant fellow, he had ingratiated himself with the warden, who put him in charge of the institution's records. On release Watson was appointed, at the suggestion of the warden, as collector in the sheriff's office. He held this position under three sheriffs. When the Ring was formed, he was made City Auditor, a post that paid $1,500 a year. Four years later, he was estimated to be worth close to $3 million. Despite his riches, Watson lived in "ostentatious modesty" so that no suspicion would be aroused by this sudden increase in his wealth. His one indulgence was trotting horses, which would eventually bring about the downfall of his colleagues.

The Ring's greatest coup was staged on May 5, 1870. Tweed, Hall, Sweeny, and Connolly met that day as the city's Board of Audit and stole nearly $5.5 million in one fell swoop—with the aid of a new charter backed by the reformers. Under terms of this reform charter, which concentrated power in the hands of the mayor rather than the Board of Supervisors, the auditors effectively controlled all expenditures made by the city. At its first meeting, the board approved $6.3 million worth of bills, of which all but 10 percent was pure graft. It has been reported that the omnipotent Board of Audit ultimately approved a total of $15,750,000 worth of fraudulent bills which were paid by the city.[16]

No municipal account was safe from the grasp of the Ring, and no opportunity left unexploited. In only two years, $2.3 million was paid out for stationery. A Tweed-owned firm, the New York Printing Company, which was capitalized at $10,000 and did most of its work for the city, paid dividends of from $50,000 to $70,000 a year. Loot from the rental and repair of militia armories ran to $2.9 million in two years. Over one nine-month period, Andrew Garvey was paid $197,330 for plastering work in the armories; John Keyser was given $142,329 for plumbing and another $434,000 was doled out for carpentry. A handful of chairs and tables for the buildings cost $170,729.60. Useless rifles were sold to the militia for $250,000 by a company controlled by Tweed. Businessmen were blackmailed into paying a million dollars a year for franchises. At least $840,000 was realized from the sale of worthless water meters to the city. Fraud also figured in the purchase of school supplies, and teachers were forced to pay bribes to get jobs. Not to be outdone, the Bureau of Permits, under the direct supervision of Oakey Hall, spent $2,842.64 during one month to collect exactly $6.[17]

Even though the Ring's control of New York was all but absolute, there was steady grumbling about its excesses from the reformers. George Jones, publisher of the *Times* and father of Edith Wharton, and Thomas Nast, the brilliant, satiric cartoonist of *Harper's Weekly*, led the fight. Despite all their efforts, however, the Ring grew more powerful and more corrupt almost daily, and most New Yorkers seemed oblivious. Perhaps the major reason for the ineffectiveness of the reformers was that they had little hard evidence of corruption. Even though everyone knew that Tweed and his henchmen were thieves—after all, they made little effort to hide it—it was all but impossible to stir the emotions of the people unless the facts on how much had been stolen could be uncovered. Until then, there was nothing anyone could do. Besides, some citizens hoped the day would come when they would be able to share in the plunder.

Another important factor was that most of New York's newspapers were on the Ring's payroll. On some sheets, it was said, there were six or eight staffers who drew stipends from the city ranging from $2,000 to $2,500 a year.[18] Their job was to write blurbs in the guise of news stories. Some specialized in writing letters to out-of-town papers extolling the accomplishments of Mayor Hall's administration. These were copied in the New York press, creating the desired impression that the city government was admired throughout the nation. Editors and publishers were kept in line through awards of legal and municipal advertising at generous rates. Manton Marble, editor of the *World*, who had once been a bitter enemy of the Ring, became notorious for his support of it. "There is not another municipal government in the world which combines so much character, capacity, experience and energy as are to be found in the city government of New York," he trumpeted on one occasion.

Not long before this, the Ring had pulled off another remarkable coup. Just as the voters were about to go to the polls in November 1870 to elect a new municipal government, the demands of the reformers for a look at Connolly's books had threatened to get out of hand. The *Times* and *Harper's Weekly* claimed that a thorough review would reveal a widespread pattern of fraud and corruption. But once again, Tweed knew how to deal with such demands—just as he had during the outcry over the costs of the courthouse. Mayor Hall appointed a blue-ribbon investigating committee of some of the city's wealthiest and most distinguished citizens headed by John Jacob Astor. It was a committee which not even the reformers could criticize.

Congratulating themselves on their success, the reformers sat back to await the torrent of corruption which the Astor Committee would expose to public view. Proof would finally be provided of all the nefarious doings which Jones and Nast had been relentlessly pursuing over the years. And then, a few days before the election, the committee made its report: "We have come to the conclusion, and certify, that the financial affairs of the city . . . are administered in a correct and faithful manner."

Tammany guffawed and slapped its collective thigh as, once again, the Boss had proven his skill at legerdemain. Outmaneuvered, the reformers could only denounce the report as a blatant "whitewash" and "farce." For what reason had the blue-ribbon committee allowed itself to become a tool of the Ring? There were charges that in return for their cooperation, the members were forgiven their taxes for 1868, 1869, and 1870. Later, it was discovered they had "underestimated" the city's debt by $30 million, and had missed the fact that a check for $35,000 had been "kited" by the recipient to $135,000. By then, of course, it didn't matter, as Oakey Hall had been re-elected by a resounding margin and all Tammany candidates were triumphant, including William M. Tweed, Jr., who was sent to Congress. After it was all over, the Boss challenged New Yorkers with a simple question: "Well, what are you going to do about it?"[19]

As the summer of 1871 began, the Ring was looking around for new fields to conquer. Trial balloons were sent aloft bearing the names of Governor Hoffman for nomination the following year as Democratic candidate for president; that of Oakey Hall for governor, and Tweed, himself, for United States senator. The

Boss, however, privately told friends that while he felt a desire for a change of scenery, London rather than Washington was his chosen destination. If Hoffman were elected president, he had his eye on becoming the American minister to the Court of St. James's.

But this charming reverie was on the verge of being rudely punctured. On the night of January 24, 1871, James Watson, the City Auditor and the Ring's bagman, had been racing one of his fast trotters in the snow near Central Park. Another sleigh careened out of control and in the ensuing melee, Watson was fatally injured. The newspapers reported that he had left his family well provided for, some accounting for his prosperity by saying he had been extremely lucky in Wall Street. There was now the problem of who could be trusted to replace Watson, with access to the Ring's accounts. Connolly promoted Stephen C. Lyons, Jr., who had been a bookkeeper under Watson and could be trusted. He then made two fatal errors, back to back.

Connolly filled the job vacated by Lyons with a well-recommended former newspaperman named Matthew J. O'Rourke. At the same time, William Copeland, a friend of ex-sheriff James O'Brien, who had been on the outs with Tammany but had recently made his peace with the organization, was put to work in the Auditor's office. Both O'Brien and O'Rourke were men with grudges—and therefore dangerous. O'Brien claimed that the Ring owed him $300,000 in fees earned while he had held office, while O'Rourke was the holder of a small unsatisfied claim against the city. Now that the vigilant Watson was gone, those in charge of the city's accounts had grown careless. O'Rourke and Copeland worked long hours at night over their books. Operating independently and without the knowledge of what the other was doing, they made detailed copies of everything they could get their hands on.

As soon as Copeland dropped this political dynamite into his friend's lap, O'Brien passed the word that he wanted a full settlement of his claim. Tweed immediately provided $20,000 and promised the rest in hopes of forestalling a disaster. But O'Brien pocketed the cash, and one night early in July set off without waiting for more to Park Row, the home of most of the city's newspapers. With Copeland's copy of the accounts under his arm, he went first to the *Sun*, but Charles Dana, the paper's guiding genius, was not there. Then he walked over to the *Times*, where Louis Jennings, its editor, sat puzzling about what he could say next about the Ring that would have any effect. He looked up and saw the ex-sheriff, whom he knew, standing in the doorway of his office. O'Brien remarked that it was a warm night.

"Yes, hot," allowed Jennings.

"You and Nast have had a hard fight," O'Brien said.

"Have still."

"I said you have had it," replied O'Brien, as he laid out a pile of papers upon Jennings's desk. "Here are the proofs of all your charges—exact transcripts from Dick Connolly's books. The boys will likely try to murder you when they know you've got 'em, just as they have tried to murder me."[20]

For the rest of the night, the elated Jennings examined the astonishing array of documents that fate had placed in his hands. It was all there—the story of how the Tweed Ring had robbed the people of New York over the years. A couple of days later, O'Rourke delivered to the *Times* the evidence he had collected concerning the leasing and repairs of the armories. As soon as Tweed learned that O'Brien had double-crossed him and the incriminating accounts were now in the hands of George Jones, publisher of the *Times*, he delegated Connolly, whose carelessness had resulted in their loss in the first place, to get them back. A lawyer friendly with the publisher asked Jones to come visit him. When Jones arrived, he was ushered into a private office where he was confronted by "Slippery Dick."[21]

"I do not want to see this man," said the publisher, turning to leave.

"For God's sake!" exclaimed Connolly. "Let me say one word to you."

As Jones halted, Connolly offered him five million dollars not to publish the material in his possession.

"I don't think the devil will ever make a higher bid for me than that," murmured Jones.

Connolly began to plead, and drew a graphic picture of what could be done with five million dollars. "Why, with that sum, you can go to Europe and live like a prince."

"Yes," replied Jones, "but I should know I was a rascal."

Opening their copies of the *Times* on July 22, 1871, New Yorkers were startled to see a three-column headline leap out of the front page at them:

THE SECRET ACCOUNTS

PROOF OF THE UNDOUBTED FRAUD BROUGHT TO LIGHT

Below this headline running on for several columns, line after implacable line, were entries detailing all the fraudulent bills and payments made over the years for the construction, furnishing, and repair of the County Courthouse. Over the next several days, Jones and Jennings gleefully unwrapped further exposures of graft in all branches of the municipal government. Nast followed through with a series of devastating cartoons in *Harper's Weekly*. In one, Tweed, Connolly, Hall, and Sweeny were portrayed standing in a circle pointing accusingly, one at the other, under the caption "Who Stole the People's Money?" Another showed the same group cowering in the shadow of the gallows.

The Ring tried to brush off the newspaper charges. "Never mind, who is going to prosecute?" asked Oakey Hall. And Tweed persuaded himself that everything would eventually "blow over." But the mixture of vitriol and ridicule served up in Nast's cartoons was finally too much even for the Boss's placid temper.

"Let's stop them damned pictures!" he exploded. "I don't care so much what the papers write about me—my constituents can't read. But, damn it, they can see pictures!"[22]

An overt attempt was made to bribe Nast. One day a lawyer acquaintance casually informed the artist that in appreciation of his great efforts, a group of wealthy men were willing to raise a fund to send him abroad to study the great masters and improve his art. Nast replied that he would be delighted to go, but for the moment it was impossible. He had too much unfinished business in New York. The following Sunday, an officer of the Broadway Bank (where the artist had an account) came to his home.

"I hear you have been made an offer to go abroad for art study," said the banker.

"Yes, but I can't go. I haven't time."

"But, they will pay you for your time. I have reason to believe you could get a hundred thousand dollars for the trip."

"Do you think I could get two hundred thousand?" asked Nast, testing to see how far the Ring was prepared to go.

"Well, possibly. I believe from what I have heard in the bank that you might get it. You have a great talent; but you need study and you need rest. Besides, this Ring business will get you into trouble. They own all the judges and jurors and can get you locked up for libel. My advice is to take the money and get away."

Nast paused before answering. Perhaps he thought of what he could do with all that money. It would pay for years of study and make him comfortable for life.

"Don't you think I could get five hundred thousand to make that trip?"

"You can," the banker replied without hesitation. "You can get five hundred thousand dollars in gold to drop this Ring business and get out of the country."

"Well, I don't think I'll do it," said Nast with a chuckle. "I made up my mind not long ago to put some of those fellows behind bars, and I'm going to put them there!"

The banker left with a parting message.

"Only be careful, Mr. Nast, that you don't put yourself in a coffin."[23]

Supplied at last with the documentary evidence of the Ring's corruption, the full fury of the reformers was unleashed. On September 4, 1871, a mass meeting was held in downtown New York at the Cooper Union, which was attended by most of the leading businessmen and merchants of the city. Hundreds of persons unable to gain entrance milled about outside. This audience soon whipped itself into a fine frenzy. "There is no power like the power of the people armed, aroused, and kindled with the enthusiasm of a righteous wrath!" proclaimed one speaker. The rhetorical question, "What are you going to do about these men?" was answered by cries of "Hang them! Hang them!" A Committee of Seventy was organized that night to lead the fight against the Ring, among them Samuel J. Tilden, a secretive legal wizard who had built up an immense fortune through railroad manipulation. Tilden, a rather cold, calculating man, had been a Tammany Democrat as long as it was worthwhile to be one and then had switched sides.

Thoroughly frightened, the members of the Ring turned upon each other. There were demands that one man be chosen as a "vicarious sacrifice" for all—but there were no volunteers. Secretly, Tweed, Hall, and Sweeny put their heads together and nominated Connolly as the fall guy. As part of the plan, Hall agreed to the appointment of a special committee of aldermen and private citizens to examine "Slippery Dick's" records. The night before the committee was to meet, the Comptroller's office was burglarized, and the accounts for 1870 were stolen from several unlocked cupboards. The *Times* sarcastically asked what had happened to the safes that had been bought with the $404,347 supposedly spent upon them. Terrified that his colleagues were about to throw him to the wolves, Connolly consulted with Tilden. He was told to appoint Andrew Green, a member of the Committee of Seventy, as Acting Comptroller and then resign. The reformers now had a beachhead in the County Courthouse—the house that Tweed had built—and they made the most of it.

The Ring was in a shambles.[24] Connolly and Sweeny fled to Europe with their fortunes, while Oakey Hall blustered his way through to the end of his term the following year. Tweed, the major target, refused to flee—perhaps he was too proud, too overconfident, or just too stubborn to run. Not even the resounding defeat suffered by Tammany candidates for the state legislature caused him to abandon the sinking ship. On December 15, 1871, he was indicted on 120 counts of forgery and grand larceny, among other crimes, and was arrested the next day by Sheriff Matthew T. Brennan, who owed his job to Tweed. Bail was set at $1 million. It took two trials to convict the Boss. The first ended with a hung jury amid cries of jury-packing and tampering. Tweed was found guilty at the second, which took place amid the bitterness caused by the Panic of 1873. He was sentenced to twelve years in prison and ordered to pay a fine of $12,000. As he was being booked at the Blackwell's Island penitentiary, Tweed was asked his occupation. "Statesman," he replied.

The elation of the reformers was short-lived. After serving only a year—most of it spent in the comparative comfort of the prison hospital, Tweed was freed on a legal technicality, and his fine was reduced to $250. Chagrined, the reformers had him arrested again, this time to face civil charges of having stolen $6 million from the city. The turncoat Tilden, now governor, saw to it that bail was fixed at $3 million.

Awaiting the slow turning of the wheels of justice, Tweed languished in the Ludlow Street jail, which, as a member of the Board of Supervisors, he had authorized to be built in 1859. He had an opportunity to contemplate the difference in attitude and treatment between himself and some of the businessmen with whom he had been in league. Here he was behind bars while Astor, Vanderbilt, Gould, and others whose thefts were greater than his, were regarded as wizards of finance to be praised and emulated. Eventually Tweed wearied of the game, bribed his way out of jail, and made his way to Cuba and then to Spain.

But once again, Thomas Nast's cartoons were Tweed's nemesis. Spanish immigration officials, on the alert for the fugitive, identified him as he came ashore at Vigo through a drawing ripped from the pages of *Harper's Weekly*. He was extradited to the United States and once again lodged as a paying guest in the warden's quarters at the Ludlow Street jail. His heart weakened by the stress of the past few years, Tweed died there on April 12, 1878, just five days before his fifty-fifth birthday. He was buried in lambskin—the "emblem of innocence."[25]

XII

The Gift of Grab

EMERGING FROM THE bubbling bog of corruption of the Grant years, Americans celebrated the one-hundredth birthday of the Republic in 1876 with a high-spirited, gaudy Centennial Exposition—and the first stolen presidential election in the nation's history. The closing years of the nineteenth century appeared to confirm the sneers of cynics about the low state of American political morality. Commentators spent their time trying to determine what proportion of Congress was on the take. An astute British analyst, James Bryce, estimated that 5 percent of the members actually took bribes while another 15 to 20 percent contented themselves with influence peddling. Henry Adams upped the number of blatantly corrupt members to 10 percent.[1] And Mark Twain wrote with a sardonic twinkle of one lawmaker: "He's only been in Congress a few years and he must be worth a million."

Taking their cue from the captains of industry, the politicians cheerfully regarded politics as merely another form of business enterprise. Public office was not a public trust, but a source of trust funds. As Bryce pointed out in *The American Commonwealth*, "the desire for office and for office as a means of gain" was the glue which held the American political system together. Never before had opportunities for graft been so great, and those with

222

the gift of grab made the most of them. "Steal largely or not at all," was the lesson learned from Wall Street. "He who steals largely . . . shall enter the kingdom of heaven, while to him who confines his stealings to modest peculations shall be opened the doors of Sing Sing."[2]

The "legislative process" in the centennial years was graphically portrayed by Mark Twain and Charles Dudley Warren in *The Gilded Age*:

A Congressional appropriation costs money. Just reflect, for instance. A majority of the House Committee, say $10,000 apiece— $40,000; a majority of the Senate committee, the same each—say $40,000; a little extra to one or two chairmen of one or two committees, say $10,000 each—$20,000; and there's $100,000. . . . Then seven male lobbyists at $3,000 each—$21,000, one female lobbyist, $10,000; a high moral Congressman or Senator here and there— the higher moral ones cost more, because they give tone to a measure—say ten of these at $3,000 each is $30,000; then a lot of small-fry county members who won't vote for anything without pay—say twenty at $500 apiece. . . .

This was intended as satire, but for far too many Americans there was the shock of recognition. In 1873, the same year in which the book was published, an Ohio congressman said, "the House of Representatives was like an auction room where more valuable considerations were disposed of under the Speaker's hammer than in any other place on earth." And corruption was not suddenly exorcised from Washington with the departure of the hapless Grant from the White House. Collis P. Huntington grumpily acknowledged that he had shelled out as much as $500,000 in graft during each congressional session from 1875 to 1885—not so much to generate legislation favorable to the Central Pacific and its offspring as to derail measures designed to limit its imperial ambitions.[3] Huntington divided the Senate into three distinct groups: the "clean," who would run errands for him without pay; the "commercial," who would do his bidding as long as they were paid for it; and the unspeakable "communists," who had the colossal effrontry to resist both his logic and cash.[4]

Politics was little more than a puppet show run by big business.

Tariff advantages, bounties, land grants, subsidies, favorable currency policies and freedom from government regulations were sought—and won—by the capitalists. The spoilsmen were paid off with campaign contributions, bribes, legal fees, railroad passes, and tips on sure-fire investment opportunities. In 1888, Ohio's Senator John Sherman, who had done his share of wheeling and dealing, said the United States had "reached the last stages in the history of the Roman Empire when offices were sold at public auction to the highest bidder." That was the year in which Benjamin Harrison, the victorious Republican presidential candidate, claimed that "Providence has given us this victory." Matt Quay, the Republican boss of Pennsylvania, knew who had really been responsible for Harrison's election. "Providence hadn't a damn thing to do with it," he declared. Harrison probably "would never know how close a number of men were compelled to approach the gates of the penitentiary to make him President."

Politicians still prattled about the glories of competition, as unparalleled power was concentrated in an ever-decreasing number of hands. Big business became monopoly; monopolies became trusts; trusts became supertrusts. "Individualism is gone, never to return," declared John D. Rockefeller, who "rationalized" the tumultuous oil business, not so much by enterprise and risk-taking as by skulduggery. While his competitors put their faith in rugged individualism, Rockefeller compelled the railroads to secretly give him rebates, not only on the petroleum transported from the oil fields to his refineries and on the kerosene he shipped to consumers but also on the shipments of his competition. With such advantages, the Standard Oil trust drove its rivals out of business and raised prices. Individualism was certainly gone, never to return.

Business domination of the political scene was nakedly exposed by Frederick T. Martin in his book, *The Passing of the Idle Rich*. The industrial barons were uninterested in the mundane concerns that commonly occupied the attention of the "statesmen":

> We care absolutely nothing about statehood bills, pension agitation, waterway appropriations, "pork barrels," state rights or any other political question. . . . It matters not one iota which political

party is in power, or what President holds the reins of office. We are not politicians or public thinkers; we are the rich; we own America; we got it God knows how; but we intend to keep it if we can by throwing all the tremendous weight of our support, our influence, our money, our political connections, our purchased senators, our hungry congressmen, our public-speaking demagogues into the scale against any legislation, any political platform, any Presidential campaign that threatens the integrity of our estate. . . .[5]

Business had no permanent friends or enemies—only permanent interests. Money was doled out to both the Democrats and Republicans. Returns were expected on this investment just like any other cash outlay; more often than not, businessmen backed the Republicans because they were more successful. There was certainly little else to distinguish the parties from each other; both carefully straddled the most controversial issues of the day to preserve a precarious balance of power.

Railroad regulation and antitrust legislation were supposedly supported by both parties, but neither gave any serious thought to enactment. Both were unsympathetic to the cause of organized labor. In 1877, the Republicans issued an injunction and called out federal troops to put down a railway worker's strike. Twenty-one years later, the Democrats resorted to the same repressive measures to deal with the Pullman strike. Both parties were allegedly committed to a liberal land policy aimed at assisting the ordinary homesteader, but they allowed these laws to become little more than an empty mockery. Although the Democrats espoused a low tariff policy, they were as reluctant as the Republicans to reduce tariffs when they were in office.

With no visible difference in ideology or ideas separating the parties, politics was a contest for the spoils of office. Even the Republicans were split between the Stalwarts, the old-style boodlers led by New York's Senator Roscoe Conkling, and the Half-Breeds, who owed their allegiance to Senator James G. Blaine of Maine. Political wars were waged on no higher plane than the struggle of rival railroads for new routes and for the control of that running sore of corruption, the New York Customs House.

* * *

If any politician embodied the values—or lack of them—of the Gilded Age, it was Jim Blaine.[6] Member of Congress, Speaker of the House of Representatives, ranking senator, secretary of state, perennial presidential hopeful, and onetime Republican nominee, the "Plumed Knight" was a dominant figure in the councils of the Republican party and in the affairs of the nation. A magnetic leader with eyes that seemed to flash sparks and a voice that hypnotized the galleries, he pursued the voters up and down the byways of the Republic for nearly thirty years. Year after year, election after election, his name echoed across the land from coast to coast like a drumbeat: "Blaine! Blaine! Blaine!"

Blaine's contribution to the art of politics lay not in the laws he drafted or in the bills he shepherded through Congress. Instead, he brought to perfection the alliance between business and politics forged during the Jacksonian era. Conkling and the Stalwarts lent a helping hand to corporations in need of political services in return for a share of the spoils, but they kept their independence. Blaine, on the other hand, voluntarily bound himself to the triumphal chariot of business. He offered his services on a day-to-day basis for a retainer that included stock tips and assurances of campaign financing. So close was this tie to business that a senatorial colleague, observing his operations during a floor fight over railroad financing, said, "It is my opinion that Mr. Blaine acts as attorney for Jay Gould."[7]

But for all the success of his appeals to the business community and his legion of supporters, Blaine could never disabuse a majority of the voters of the conviction that he was a crook. His rival, Conkling, spoke for them when asked to campaign for Blaine, who had at last captured the Republican presidential nomination in 1884. "No thanks," snapped the imperious Roscoe. "I don't engage in criminal practice."[8]

Blaine had been caught red-handed in the Credit Mobilier scandal, but so thick was the whitewash laid upon him that by 1876 he was the front-runner for the Republican presidential nomination. While awed crowds trooped through the Centennial Exposition in Philadelphia to gape at such marvels of modern technology as a Gothic soda fountain and Professor Bell's new-fangled telephone, Republican delegates to the party's convention gathered in Cincinnati. It was expected that they would quickly acclaim Blaine as the party's standard bearer. Shortly before the opening gavel fell, however, rumors about his shady dealings with an Arkansas railroad began to surface. As Blaine's supporters vigorously denied the charges, the Democrats, who controlled the House, happily seized the opportunity to discredit him. A full-dress congressional inquiry was hastily convened.

Blaine, while Speaker of the House, had in April 1869 been instrumental in blocking an amendment to a bill that would have revoked a land grant to the Little Rock and Fort Smith Railroad.[9] At the time he had no financial interest in the project, and his action seemed perfectly above-board. But a few months later the railroad's promoters cut Blaine in on a juicy deal under circumstances that aroused the suspicion he was being rewarded for his legislative assistance. Blaine was offered the opportunity to sell some of the railroad's mortgage bonds to his friends at a fat rakeoff. No doubt with the assurance of the Speaker that they were being let in on the ground floor of a potential gold mine, many of Blaine's friends bought the bonds. Their purchases were further sweetened by the offer of equal amounts of preferred and common stock which ostensibly tripled the value of the bonds. For his efforts, Blaine kept $125,000 worth of land-grant bonds, which should have gone to the investors, and collected another $32,500 as his brokerage fee. "In these transactions," notes the historian James Ford Rhodes, "the Speaker of the House placed himself on a level with unscrupulous promoters on State Street and Wall Street. . . ."

Unfortunately, the railroad turned out to be pretty much of a fraud, and the value of the bonds which Blaine had peddled to his friends plummeted. To placate the angry purchasers, Blaine recompensed them for their losses. Apologists claim this was done to satisfy "a moral claim," but more than likely he feared an open scandal. Besides, if the transaction were made public, Blaine's friends would learn that he had duped them by pocketing the land-grant bonds due them. Blaine got the money to buy them out from the sale of the bonds to three other railroads, including the Union Pacific. And even though the bonds were nearly worthless, Blaine received their book value. Obviously, the purchasers believed that they were buying the goodwill and the influence of the Speaker along with the bonds. All three railroads had land grants and were therefore subject to congressional control.

In the beginning, Blaine's interrogators could find little incriminating evidence against him. One of those who came to his rescue was Thomas A. Scott, at that time the president of the Pennsylvania Railroad. It was he, rather than Blaine, who had sold the bonds to the Union Pacific—or so he testified. For years, this Napoleon of the rails had been scheming to expand the Pennsylvania system clear across the continent, and Blaine was a good ally to have—especially if he were to become president. Scott claimed that he had bought the bonds from a middleman and had not known they were being sold by Blaine. The high price he received for the bonds from the Union Pacific constituted a special bonus for work he had done for the line. With such backing, it looked as if the Democrats had been foiled, and once again Blaine would emerge unscathed from the latest investigation of his financial affairs. But on May 31, 1876, James Mulligan, onetime bookkeeper for one of the Little Rock and Fort Smith promoters, gave testimony that sent a shock wave through the nation.

Mulligan revealed that he had been told by a member of the board of directors of the Union Pacific that the Arkansas railway bonds were bought directly from Blaine, and on terms that were all but regarded as a gift. The witness added that he was in possession of a file of letters between Blaine and his former employer. Visibly shaken, Blaine signaled to a Republican member of the subcommittee for an immediate adjournment. That night, he went to Mulligan's hotel room and tearfully begged for the letters. He claimed that publication of them "would sink him immediately and ruin him forever." Mulligan should consider the effect this would have on his wife and six children. Mulligan was adamant, however, and if the investigators asked for the letters, he would make them available. Blaine asked to read the letters and Mulligan handed them over on condition that they be returned. Instead, Blaine snatched the letters from the surprised bookkeeper and fled.

With the now-famous "Mulligan letters" safely in his hands, Blaine contended they were his personal property, and refused to turn them over to the investigators. But with the Republican convention only two weeks away, refusal to divulge their contents was regarded as tantamount to an admission of guilt. Several states that had instructed their delegates to vote for Blaine were getting restive. Blaine's advisors warned him to do something or he would lose the nomination by default.

At last, on June 5, 1876, Blaine appeared on the floor of the House to break his long silence. With a sense of outraged injustice, he blamed the investigation of his conduct upon the partisanship of the Democrats, downgraded the importance of the evidence against him, and defended the right of privacy of his correspondence. "But, sir, having vindicated that right, standing by it, ready to make any sacrifice in the defense of it . . . I am not afraid to show the letters," Blaine declared, his voice rising with emotion, "Thank God Almighty, I am not afraid to show them!"

Thrusting a hand into an inside pocket of his long black coat, he drew forth a packet of papers and held it aloft over his head. For a moment he stood as still as a statue. And then he slammed the letters down upon his desk with the cry: "There they are!" Inviting "the confidence of 44 million of my countrymen," he undid a string about the packet and began reading from the letters. The crowded chamber was held spellbound by one of the most superb pieces of acting ever seen in the House. Reading what he pleased from the letters, carefully omitting what he wanted and interpolating where he pleased, Blaine seemed to have proved that there was nothing incriminating in the documents. Cheering and applause from the floor and galleries resounded through the House as Blaine sat down surrounded by admirers. As far as they were concerned, he had vindicated himself. The following Sunday, he added a final flourish to this virtuoso performance by collapsing in the doorway of his church—in full view of a sizable crowd.

Nevertheless, the tide of events was running against Blaine. The only hope the Republicans had for keeping possession of the White House after the malodorous scandals of the Grant administration was to nominate a candidate without the slightest blemish. For six ballots, Blaine held firmly to his delegates, even picking up a few. But on each tally, the number of votes cast for Rutherford B. Hayes, the rather colorless three-time governor of Ohio, steadily mounted. On the seventh ballot, the roof caved in on Blaine. His enemies combined to nominate Hayes by just six votes. To Henry Adams, Hayes was "a third-rate nonentity, whose only recommendation is that he is obnoxious to no one." Adams failed to see his one virtue, however—Hayes was clean as a hound's tooth. Two weeks later, the Democrats, meeting in St. Louis, also wrapped themselves in the banner of reform. They nominated Samuel J. Tilden, who had parlayed the persecution of his old friends in the Tweed Ring into a national reputation.

While Hayes and Tilden adhered to the usual practice of making no speeches—in fact, they were mere figureheads—their partisans waged a campaign described as if "not the dirtiest, most marked by undercover chicanery and secret or exposed treachery, fraud and violence in the national history up to then, it was certainly the one most clearly and thoroughly revealed in that character."[10] The Republicans feared that after years of "Grantism," the Democrats would successfully fulfill their promise to "throw the rascals out!" The Democrats, on the other hand, were determined to regain power after a quarter-century in the wilderness and to "redeem" the Southern states from the last vestiges of carpetbag and black rule. Superior skulduggery was counted upon by both sides to provide the margin of victory. Ballot-box stuffing, bribery, perjury, repeating, intimidation of voters, and plain mayhem were common campaign practices in some areas.

"Every man that shot Union soldiers [during the Civil War] was a Democrat!" proclaimed Robert G. Ingersoll, a Republican stemwinder. "The man who assassinated Abraham Lincoln was a Democrat. Soldiers, every scar you have got on your heroic bodies was given you by a Democrat!" In Indiana, John W. Foster, who later became secretary of state,* was assigned the task of raising $35,000 to secretly "finance" a newspaper whose sole aim was to

---

* Foster was also the grandfather of another secretary of state, John Foster Dulles.

persuade soft-money Democrats to desert Tilden for a funny-money third-party candidate. The Republicans poured a minimum of $200,000 into the campaign—a record for the time and worth at least ten times that amount today. Most of these funds—obtained by shaking down federal and state jobholders and from business contributions—were channeled to the key states of New York and Indiana, and into buying votes in the South. The Democrats had a war chest estimated at $150,000, about two-thirds of it supplied by Tilden himself.[11] August Belmont, the American agent of the Rothschilds who had long helped bankroll the Democrats, came up with $10,000 in $500 bills.

The curtain rose on the real drama only after the ballots had been cast on November 7, 1876. Tilden appeared to have won a sweeping victory, carrying New York, New Jersey, Indiana, and apparently the entire South, for a clear majority of electoral votes and a 250,000 plurality. He went to bed convinced that he had won the presidency, a fact agreed upon by most historians. Late that night, however, a group of newspapermen scanning the returns in the office of the pro-Republican *New York Times* discovered that the election might yet be saved for Hayes. The votes of four states—Louisiana, Florida, South Carolina, and Oregon—were so close as to be in doubt. If they were given to Hayes, he would have 185 electoral votes, the exact amount needed to win. The managing editor of the *Times*, John C. Reid, dashed uptown to the Fifth Avenue Hotel, where he roused Zachariah Chandler, the chairman of the Republican National Committee, from his alcohol-befuddled slumber. Telegrams were immediately dispatched to Republican leaders in the doubtful states warning them against conceding, and the next morning Chandler boldly announced that Hayes had been elected.[12]

Even in the harsh light of day, the confidence of diehard Republicans seemed well-founded. Supported by federal troops, Republican carpetbag regimes controlled South Carolina, Louisiana, and Florida—especially the returning boards empowered to review the election returns and to reject ballots judged to have been fraudulently cast. C. Vann Woodward, the foremost historian of the period, states that not only is there ample evidence of the dishonesty and corruption of these boards, but there were

also indications "of irregularities, fraud, intimidation, and violence on the part of both Republicans and Democrats" in the
elections themselves.[13]

Militant white supremacy organizations such as the Red Shirts
in South Carolina, the White League in Louisiana, and similar
groups in Florida frightened newly enfranchised black voters
from going to the polls with threats and, in some cases, actual
violence. The Republicans, on the other hand, operating after
the election through the returning boards, tossed out Democratic votes by the carload to ensure majorities for Hayes. Woodward estimates that in Louisiana alone, the returning board,
dominated by a corrupt carpetbagger regime, ruled that some
13,000 Democratic votes were invalid. This converted what had
been a substantial majority for Tilden into one for Hayes. In
South Carolina, three of the five members of the board who
ultimately gave the state to Hayes were candidates for local office
in the same election. "Flagrant, partisan and arbitrary decisions"
put Florida in the Hayes column even though Tilden had an
obvious majority. In all three states, the Democrats challenged
the findings of the returning boards, and the danger of an open
conflict loomed over the land.[14]

Both sides trafficked in votes, and assorted rogues and ripoff
artists took advantage of the situation. For example, the Democrats claimed that one J. Madison Wells, a cog in the Louisiana
carpetbag machine, had offered to "deliver" the state's recording
board to Tilden in exchange for $200,000. The advantage the
Democrats expected to reap by divulging this tidbit of information was canceled out when the Republicans charged that Colonel
W. T. Pelton, the Democratic candidate's nephew, had been
caught trying to bribe Republican electors in South Carolina and
Florida. Whatever the truth of the charges, states one writer, the
situation was so rife with stories of corruption that not only did
both sides suspect each other of wrongdoing, but "Republicans
also suspected other Republicans, Democrats mistrusted other
Democrats, and numerous key figures changed their stories so
many times that the truth . . . could never be had."[15]

In this poisoned atmosphere, the electors met on December 6
in their respective states to cast their ballots for Hayes or Tilden.

Double sets of electoral certificates were returned from South Carolina, Florida, and Louisiana. How was the deadlock to be resolved? Even though many Americans were convinced the fate of the Republic lay in the balance, the Constitution was of little help in this crisis. It provided that the president of the Senate— then a Republican—should open all certificates in the presence of a joint session of Congress "and the votes shall then be counted." But by whom? If the president of the Senate did the counting, Hayes would be elected, for he would undoubtedly choose the certificates produced by the Republicans. But if Congress, as a whole, which was controlled by the Democrats, did the counting, Tilden was in.

There were mutterings of armed revolt or an attempted coup d'état, banana-republic-style, if Tilden were denied the presidency. "Marse Henry" Watterson, editor of the Louisville *Courier-Journal*, called for a march of a hundred thousand Tilden supporters on Washington. He said the demonstration should be peaceful, but "Tilden or Blood!" and "Tilden or War!" were slogans that were heard with ominous regularity. Such militancy may have been a bluff, but ordinary citizens wondered what would happen on March 4, 1877, when Grant left the White House and no president had been chosen to succeed him.

Nevertheless, behind the scenes, significant movement was taking place. Part of the folklore of Capitol Hill is that Congress abhors a confrontation, so it was no surprise when some of its more conservative members, both Northerners and Southerners, concerned over the drift toward chaos, began searching for an acceptable compromise. Neither side wished to see a new outbreak of civil strife with its useless bloodshed and disruption of the economy. Representative James A. Garfield was among the first to see a way out. "The Democratic businessmen of the country are more anxious for quiet than for Tilden," he told Hayes. "The leading southern Democrats in Congress, especially those who were old Whigs, are saying that they have seen war enough, and don't care to follow the lead of their northern associates who ... were 'invincible in peace and invisible in war.'" Garfield suggested inroads might be made among the Democrats "if in some discreet way, these southern men, who are dissatisfied with

Tilden and his violent followers, could know that the South is going to be treated with kind consideration by you."

"Kind consideration," as far as the Southern Bourbons were concerned, consisted of assurances by Hayes that federal troops would be withdrawn from the "unredeemed" states of Louisiana and South Carolina, and a guarantee of the same sort of subsidies for the construction of Southern railroads that had financed the transcontinental railroad. For their part, the Republicans saw in such an agreement the opportunity to build an alliance between moderate Northern Republicans and old Southern Whigs who had become Democrats because they had no other place to go. Recognition was to be withdrawn from the carpetbaggers, who had ruled the South in the name of Republicanism, and granted to the Southern conservatives. Thus the foundation would be laid for a new Republican party with a solid base in all parts of the country, including the South. To further this Southern strategy, the Bourbons would be given a role in the Hayes administration, perhaps even including a place or two in the cabinet.

One of the most important figures in hammering out what Woodward has called the Great Compromise of 1877, was Tom Scott of the Pennsylvania Railroad. Scott was then at the height of his power and prestige. "There is no power in one State to resist such a giant as the Pennsylvania road," declared Wendell Phillips, the radical agitator. "We have thirty-eight one-horse legislatures in this country; and we have a man like Tom Scott with three hundred and fifty millions in his hands, and if he walks through the States they have no power." Although Scott was a disarmingly amiable man, with a set of muttonchop whiskers that gave him what one writer has described as the benign look of a successful clergyman, he usually got anything he wanted. Upon one occasion, after a surprisingly recalcitrant Pennsylvania legislature had at last succumbed to pressure to pass several measures that aided the railroad, a weary lawmaker asked: "Mr. President, may we now go Scott free?"

Now, Scott's attention was focused on the Southwest. Doubling as the president of the Texas & Pacific as well as the Pennsylvania Railroad, he was the leader of a group of financial adventurers with a plan for a railroad across Texas, New Mexico, and Arizona to San Diego that would break the monopoly of the Union Pacific and the Central Pacific. Congress had approved a federal land grant of some 16 million acres—the last large grant given a railroad—but the proceeds had been quickly swallowed up in a morass that paralleled the Credit Mobilier scandal. Reformers charged that if a similar investigation were made into the affairs of the Texas & Pacific, it would reveal "a large number of members of Congress had become directly or indirectly interested" in the enterprise. No such investigation was ever launched.[16]

If the Texas & Pacific were ever to be finished, fresh federal subsidies were needed. Scott mounted a lobbying campaign in Washington in which railway passes and other inducements were showered upon the fortunate lawmakers. In ordinary times, this would have produced the desired effect, but in the era of post–Credit Mobilier morality, it wasn't enough. The American people were obviously angry about the unraveling skein of rip-offs—at least for the moment—and Congress was skittish. So Scott turned southward for help, a course that would eventually bring him into contact with those working for the election of Hayes.

Southern leaders were convinced that in the years since the Civil War the South had been short-changed. Northern capitalists had received generous federal subsidies for railroads and other improvements, while the South had gotten nothing. They now wanted some of the gravy for themselves. Scott's propagandists played upon these desires, trumpeting the benefits of a Southern transcontinental route. Newspapers, chambers of commerce, and cotton exchanges were all persuaded to join in a well-orchestrated campaign backing construction of the Texas & Pacific. If the strangling grasp of Northern monopoly were broken, Southern ports and towns would boom. Soon, demands for assistance to the railroad overflowed upon Congress like a brook in spring. But Scott was not to be left to work his will alone. Collis Huntington, fending off the threat to his monopoly on trade with the Pacific Coast, decided to build his own Southern line eastward from the Pacific. And so began a monumental battle between the two titans for control of public opinion and for votes in the Southern states and in Congress.

"Scott is prepared to pay, or promises to pay, a large amount of money to pass his bill," allowed Huntington. "But I do not think he can pass it, although I think this coming session of Congress will be composed of the hungriest set of men that ever got together. . . ." The fight centered on the House Railway Committee. The Californian noted that Scott was spending "considerable money" and had "convinced several parties that I thought we had for sure." Throwing all his own resources into the fray, Huntington was soon able to note "it has been a very difficult matter to switch a majority of the committee away from him, but I think it has been done." As a result, by the time that the electoral crisis had come to a boil, the two powerful railroad lobbies had fought each other to a standstill.

The Southerners were determined, however, to have their transcontinental railroad. So well had Scott's men done their job that in the minds of most of them it was one and inseparable from the Texas & Pacific.[17] When the time came to actually get down to bargaining with the Republicans for Southern support of Hayes, Republican backing for the subsidy bill was a basic prerequisite for any deal. Of course, no one mentioned the Texas & Pacific by name—that would have been gauche—but the Republicans came through with a promise of support for "internal improvements of a national character." In turn, Tom Scott threw his block of Southern congressmen to Hayes.

In the meantime, under terms of the Electoral Count Bill passed by Congress on January 27, 1877, the disputed returns had been handed over to a specially constituted Electoral Commission which was to determine who won the election. The commission had fifteen members—five from the House, five from the Senate, and five from the Supreme Court. Originally, it was planned that seven Republicans and seven Democrats would be appointed to the commission, with the fifteenth vote being cast by Supreme Court Justice David Davis, regarded by all as an independent. But within hours after the commission was established, the Illinois legislature elected Davis to the Senate, an event which the angry Democrats charged was no surprise to the Republicans. The four remaining commissioners from the Supreme Court then chose Justice Joseph P. Bradley, a Republican, to fill the vacancy. He was to singlehandedly elect Hayes nineteenth president of the United States.

The electoral commission met all through February and decided every question on a strict eight-to-seven party vote, with Bradley voting with the Republicans. The Democrats hurled charges of bribery and conspiracy. It was claimed that Bradley was in collusion with Tom Scott, but nothing came of the allegations. Tension rose to the point where someone took a shot at Hayes as he sat down to supper one evening in his home in Columbus, Ohio. The Democrats mounted a filibuster to prevent congressional certification of the electoral results. It looked as if the nation would be without a government after March 4.

In the shadows, however, the long-discussed tradeoff between the Republicans and the Southern Democrats was consummated. The finishing touches were placed on the bargain at a conference held in a Washington hotel. Without Southern support, the pro-Tilden filibuster collapsed, and at four o'clock on the morning of March 2, the House certified that Hayes had been elected by one vote. The president-elect received the news of his election while on his way to Washington in a luxurious private railroad car. It belonged to Tom Scott.[18]

Disgruntled Democrats might sneer at Hayes as "Rutherfraud" and "His Fraudulency," but he was president. Within a month after his inauguration, the debts that had been incurred to elect him were paid off. The last troops were withdrawn from Louisiana and South Carolina, and the corrosive decade of Reconstruction was finally over. Deprived of the prop of federal bayonets, the carpetbag governments quickly collapsed, leaving the freed slaves to the tender mercies of their former masters.

Economy and honesty in government were the watchwords of the new state governments, but they found it easier to cut spending than to keep wandering hands out of the public till. No one, however, matched the audacity of Major E. A. Burke, who had helped put together the Great Compromise. In ten years as Louisiana's treasurer, this picturesque rogue outdid his carpet-bagging predecessors by stealing $1.7 million before fleeing with his loot to Honduras, where he became a virtual dictator. Light-fingered state officials from other "redeemed" states either preceded or followed him into plush exile.[19]

XIII

Honest Graft

"THE POLITICIAN WHO steals is worse than a thief. He is a fool. With the grand opportunities all around for the man with political pull, there's no excuse for stealin' a cent." So declared George Washington Plunkitt, the sage of Tammany Hall, from his usual rostrum atop the bootblack stand of the Tweed Courthouse. Few men in the opening years of the twentieth century could speak with greater authority about graft. Leader of New York City's Fifteenth Assembly District, sachem of the Tammany Society and onetime state senator, assemblyman, police magistrate, county supervisor and alderman, Plunkitt boasted of having filled four public offices in the same year—and of drawing the salaries of three of them at the same time. Explaining to a friendly newspaperman how he had become a millionaire from the practice of politics, he said with a disarming directness: "I seen my opportunities and I took 'em."[1]

The overt and unrestrained larcenies of the Tweed Ring were regarded by its successors on both the local and national levels as hopelessly old-fashioned. The cheerful Robin Hood spirit of Tweed and his merry men was replaced by tightlipped politicians who presided over highly centralized operations with the gravity of corporate executives. Clever politicians no longer relied for wealth upon what Plunkitt called "dishonest graft"—the proceeds of "blackmailin' gamblers, saloon-keepers, disorderly people, etc." Instead, they reaped far greater harvests from "honest graft." Plunkitt proudly explained this latest twist in political science:

> My party's in power in the city, and it's going to undertake a lot of public improvements. Well, I'm tipped off, say, that they're going to lay out a new park at a certain place. I see my opportunity and I take it. I go to that place and I buy up all the land I can in the neighborhood. Then the board of this or that makes its plan public, and there is a rush to get my land, which nobody cared particular for before. Ain't it perfectly honest to charge a good price and make a profit on my investment and foresight? Of course, it is. Well, that's honest graft.

Although the ordinary taxpayer whose pocket was being picked might see little difference between "honest" and "dishonest" graft, Plunkitt professed a contempt for "political looters" as compared to "politicians who make a fortune out of politics by keepin' their eyes wide open."

> The difference between a looter and a practical politician is the difference between the Philadelphia Republican gang and Tammany Hall. . . . The Philadelphia crowd runs up against the penal code. Tammany don't. The Philadelphians ain't satisfied with robbin' the bank of all its gold and paper money. They stay to pick up all the nickels and pennies and the cop comes and nabs them. Tammany ain't no such fool. Why, I remember, about fifteen or twenty years ago, a Republican superintendent of the Philadelphia almshouse stole the zinc roof off the buildin' and sold it for junk. That was carryin' things to excess.*[2]

The lesson of Tweed's downfall had been learned so well that "Squire" Richard Croker, one of his immediate successors as boss of Tammany Hall, was able to retire to a stud farm in his native Ireland with a fortune estimated at in excess of five million dollars—without the minions of the law baying at his heels. In the

---

* In contrast, said Plunkitt, a Tammany man would have, if the roof were worn, persuaded the city to put on a new one and bought the old roof at a bargain price.

words of the then-popular song, "How He Did It His Books Don't Show." Croker was an exponent of the sophisticated business politics that flowered in the years following the Compromise of 1877. Under his reign, an alliance was sealed between Tammany and the large corporations that was profitable for all parties. Instead of being subjected to periodic shakedowns, the corporations made payments to the politicians that progressively assumed the character of retainers for regular rather than occasional political services.[3]

Although businessmen had harvested their share of the plunder during the Grant scandals, they had since been alienated by the audacity and the unremitting demands of the politicians. Economic depression had made the continuous clamor for payoffs more burdensome, enlarging the ranks of the disaffected. From time to time throughout the 1870s, businessmen rebelled against the mercenary avarice of the spoilsmen, as in New York when the operations of Tweed became too blatant. In most cases, however, as soon as these movements achieved their limited ends, they collapsed. Paradoxically, the replacement of the spoilsmen as the dominant force in politics by the business politicians was accomplished through the efforts of civil service reformers. The union of money and a highly advanced political professionalism that was to dominate American politics for the next half century was forged on a wave of reform.[4]

Today, it is difficult to recall the incandescent passions stirred by the fight for civil service reform and the simple faith of liberals in its all-encompassing benefits. With an evangelism worthy of medieval crusaders, they believed that politics could be purified and the temptations of office removed by bringing the merit system to government. Civil service reform took on some of the abolitionist zeal of the previous generation.[5] Carl Schurz, the German-born reformer, best expressed the viewpoint of his fellows: "I have long considered the reform of the civil service, the destruction of the corrupting and demoralizing influences of the patronage, the elevation of the moral tone of our political life, as one of the most important problems, second, perhaps to none among those we have to solve for the success and perpetuation of our republican institutions."

Yet, the spoils system which had seemed such a radical innovation in Andrew Jackson's day had become a bulwark of conservatism in the post-Civil War era. The entire machinery of American politics now rested upon it. Party leaders contended that patronage was the mother's milk of politics. Unless the bait of jobs were dangled before the faithful, it would be impossible to muster the armies of workers needed to drum up votes. Each party boss marshaled a force of postal clerks, federal jobholders, and city and county officials who labored for the candidates endorsed by their leader. They were judged not on proficiency in their jobs but on how well they procured votes. Contributions levied on their salaries also helped fill the war chests of the parties. Realists like Roscoe Conkling angrily charged that reformers with their unrelenting demands for "snivel service" had utterly failed to understand that "parties are not built up by deportment, or by ladies' magazines, or by gush. . . ."

The curtain on a struggle that was to bedevil Hayes's administration and divide the Republican party for a decade was raised on April 22, 1877, when the president confided to his diary: "Now for civil service reform." Having followed the suggestions of the party bosses in filling most of the places in his cabinet, Hayes showed a streak of independence by naming Carl Schurz as his secretary of the interior. He followed up this galling nomination by informing Treasury Secretary John Sherman, whose department had furnished a haven for carpetbaggers flocking north after Reconstruction, that henceforth "the collection of the revenues should be free from partisan control." Then came an executive order forbidding federal employees from engaging in partisan politics and barring political assessments on their salaries. Congress flatly ignored Hayes's attempts at reform, however, and he was soon brought into open conflict with Conkling and other prominent spoilsmen.

Control of patronage at that cornucopia of graft, the New York Customs House, became the pivotal issue. For years, businessmen had been complaining that wholesale bribery, extortion, and theft at customs houses in Philadelphia, San Francisco, and New Orleans, as well as New York, had cost them thousands of dollars. "A scandalous system of robbery" was the way Schurz had described it. Prompted by William M. Evarts, his secretary of state and a leading business lawyer, Hayes appointed a citizen's committee to investigate the New York operation which was presided over by two of Conkling's lieutenants, Chester A. Arthur and Alonzo Cornell. The committee, packed with anti-Conklingites, found the custom house rife with graft and inefficiency. Broad hints were dropped that the resignations of Arthur and Cornell would be cheerfully accepted by the president, but the two men stood fast.

The twenty-five hundred jobs available at the New York Customs House were the life's blood of the Conkling organization. The Democrats had swept to control of New York State in 1876, leaving the Republicans with only a few crumbs of federal patronage. If Conkling was to maintain his machine in working order, he had to protect and preserve every job that he could. Hayes's insistence on bringing civil service reform to the customhouse was a challenge to his very existence as a political force. More than a mere desire to apply business principles to the collection of revenues lay behind this attack on Conkling's fortress, however. The president had been angered by Conkling's refusal to support him in 1876, when "Lord Roscoe" had petulantly sat on his hands during the campaign, after failing to win the nomination himself.

Defying the president's order that federal jobholders were not to engage in politics, Cornell, who doubled as chairman of the Republican state committee, summoned a meeting of the state convention. Packed with ward heelers and spoilsmen from all over the state, the convention cheered Conkling's chief henchman, the lean and cadaverous Tom Platt, as he denounced the reformers as "political Pecksniffs and tricksters." But the delegates were really waiting for Conkling—and they were not disappointed. Drawing himself up to his full six feet three inches, and tossing his mane of blond curls, he launched a barrage of invective, sarcasm, and ridicule that seared the reformers. Spotting George William Curtis, one of the reform leaders, out on the floor, Conkling dramatically pointed an accusatory finger and thundered: "When Dr. Johnson defined patriotism as the last refuge of the scoundrel, he was unconscious of the then under-developed capabilities and uses of the word 'Reform!' "

Salivating on cue, the Stalwarts whooped and hollered and stomped their feet upon the floor—but Hayes's answer was to send to the Senate the names of two prominent New York businessmen-politicians to replace Arthur and Cornell. They were Theodore Roosevelt, Sr., father of the future president, and L. Bradford Prince. Undaunted, Conkling took up the challenge and the nation was treated to the spectacle of a leading Republican senator fighting the appointments of his own party's president. Through the use of senatorial courtesy, which traditionally gives a senator veto power over federal appointments made in his state, Conkling managed to block the nominations. Hayes, however, patiently bided his time. "In the language of the press, 'Senator Conkling has won a great victory over the Administration,' " he noted in his diary. "But the end is not yet. I am right, and I shall not give up the contest."

The following summer, in July 1878, after Congress had safely adjourned, the president suspended Arthur and Cornell by executive order. When the Senate reconvened early in the new year, the struggle for control of the New York Customs House raged anew. But this time, the tide was running in the president's favor. Widespread labor unrest capped by a paralyzing railroad strike, economic instability, burgeoning radicalism among the nation's farmers, and resurgent Indian troubles on the frontier all caused the Senate to take a fresh look at the long-running wrangle between Hayes and Conkling. Republicans saw no advantage in prolonging it. Such intraparty bloodletting could only be of aid and comfort to the amused Democrats. Besides, John Sherman, who had been placed in charge of winning approval of the new nominees, made skillful use of the powers of patronage vested in him by the president. Enough Republicans were persuaded by Hayes's arguments—and Sherman's liberal offers of jobs and other loot—to disregard senatorial tradition and join the Democrats in confirming the president's appointees. It was the beginning of the end for the Stalwarts.

*   *   *

Ironically, James A. Garfield, Hayes's successor in the presidency, did more to further the cause of civil service reform by falling victim to an assassin's bullet than by anything he did for the cause while alive. An imposing figure, with a leonine head and a ringing voice, Garfield's major political accomplishment was a marvelous flexibility that led him from the fringes of the Credit Mobilier scandal to the front pew of reform. Even so, throughout the campaign of 1880, the Republican candidate was haunted by the cabalistic figure "329" which appeared almost everywhere— chalked on walls, daubed on rocks, and scratched on doors. It was a reminder of the $329 in dividends from Credit Mobilier stock which Oakes Ames had credited to Garfield's account, although Garfield swore that he had not accepted it. The candidate had a more difficult time, however, in explaining his connection with a shady paving contract engineered by Boss Shepherd, who had looted the treasury of the District of Columbia. In 1871, while chairman of the House Appropriations Committee, Garfield accepted a retainer of $5,000—not an insignificant sum in those days—to represent the paving company as an attorney.[6]

In the beginning, Garfield had taken a rather standoffish attitude toward business. He had complained in 1870 that the Ohio iron manufacturers "want a representative that they can own and carry around in their pantaloons pocket." Under the tutelage of his good friend Jim Blaine, however, he was persuaded of the virtues of an alliance with the more powerful businessmen. A few weeks after Garfield's nomination, he was sounding out a friend in Cleveland about the political intentions of "Mr. Rockafeller." While Garfield was warned that the open support of the notorious Standard Oil tycoon would "cut like a knife in Pennsylvania," he sought and received the assistance of Rockefeller's force of five hundred salesmen located all over the key state of Indiana. With their help—and election day money that "flowed like water"—Garfield carried the state by a margin of 6,625 votes out of nearly half a million cast. It was clear proof that in a close race a fat campaign fund and corporate help could make all the difference. In Garfield, big business had what Horatio Seymour, a Democratic politico, said it desired—a man "who will not steal himself but will not interfere with those who do."[7]

Garfield named Jim Blaine as his secretary of state, an appointment that aroused Conkling's full fury. The Stalwart leader feared that his long-time political rival would become the strongman of the new administration. Conkling was also soon involved in a patronage battle with the president. He claimed that in return for his efforts on behalf of the ticket, which included the choice of his lieutenant, Chester Arthur, as vice-president, he had been promised a veto over the secretary of the Treasury and the right to choose all federal officers appointed in his baliwick. Not so, replied Garfield. Taking office amid all this clamor, Garfield was soon lamenting: "My God! What is there in this place that a man should ever want to get into it?"

Under Blaine's prodding, the president appointed Judge William H. Robertson, a leading rebel against Conkling's control of the New York Republican organization, as Collector of the New York Customs House. Conkling was thunderstruck. If Robertson was confirmed by the Senate, he was ruined. Once again, that body became a battleground where Conkling urged his colleagues to stand fast for tradition and senatorial courtesy. But the old magic was gone. Facing rejection, Conkling resigned his seat in the Senate with the aim of securing vindication through overwhelming re-election by the New York legislature. Tom Platt, now the state's junior senator, followed the lead of his mentor with such alacrity that he was known from then on as "Me Too" Tom Platt. After all, it was only a dramatic gesture. The legislature was certain to send them back to Washington in triumph.

For once the lordly Conkling had miscalculated. Blaine went to New York to command the Half-Breeds, who joined the Democrats in opposing the re-election of Conkling and Platt. For six weeks, Conkling was forced to deal hat-in-hand with men whom he had not long before dismissed with a mere wave of his hand. In the last week of June, Conkling's power as a political boss was broken for good. A group of Half-Breed legislators went one night to Tom Platt's room in the Delavan House and placed a ladder against the door. One by one they peeked through the transom, coming away with leering smirks upon their faces. The unctuously pious Platt had been found in bed with "an unspeakable female" from one of Albany's more fashionable bagnios.

Clacking tongues carried the tale around Albany, and an embarrassed Platt withdrew from the contest on July 2, 1881, so, he said, as not to harm Conkling's chances of re-election. He needn't have bothered, for an event occurred that same day that sounded the death knell of Stalwartism. While Garfield awaited a train at a Washington station, a madman put a bullet into his back. As the stricken president crumpled to the ground, the assassin cried out: "I am a Stalwart and Arthur is President!"

"My God! Chet Arthur!" declared the reformers in dismay, as Conkling's old lieutenant took the oath of office. Certain that "Lord Roscoe" would be the gray eminence of the new administration, they expected that before long the odor of scandal engulfing Washington would be as pervasive as that of the Grant years. But the urbane Arthur was something of a surprise— particularly to Conkling. For a man who had spent most of his life in political backrooms dealing in the spoils of office, he showed a remarkable amount of independence. Obviously, he had begun to look to his place in history. Like Harry S. Truman, who had a similar background, Chester A. Arthur is an example of the politician who grows in office. "For the Vice-Presidency, I was indebted to Mr. Conkling," he once said, "but for the Presidency of the United States my debt is to the Almighty."[8]

Prodded by events, Arthur even became a supporter of civil service reform. Garfield's death at the hands of a self-identified spoilsman had made him a martyr to the cause. Spoils now equaled murder in the eyes of many Americans. From all sides came a storm of petitions, letters, mass meetings, and editorials clamoring for reform; and in his first annual message of December 6, 1881, Arthur asked Congress for legislation to achieve that end. The politicians resisted but reform was an idea whose time had come. And so on January 16, 1883, a president who once had been discharged from his post at the New York Customs House for alleged flagrant patronage abuses, signed the Pendleton Civil Service Act into law. It established a Civil Service Commission, required open competitive examinations in filling government jobs, and placed 10 percent of all workers under the merit system, including about half the postal workers and most custom-house employees. Shaking down government workers for political contributions was barred, and even though the practice was not immediately eliminated, it was curtailed. Over the years, succeeding presidents spread the cloak of civil service to include those they had appointed, until eventually most government employees were covered.

Although federal employees were now protected against assessments, state and municipal jobholders were still routinely told to ante up a share of their salaries for political campaigns. Every Pennsylvania state employee received in 1882 a form letter stating: "Two per cent of your salary is——. Please remit promptly." In Philadelphia, a regular schedule of contributions was in force, which ranged from 3 percent of salaries under $1,200 to 12 percent of those over $10,000; Louisiana state employees kicked in a flat 10 percent of their pay into the ruling party's campaign chest.[9]

One of the major reasons for the sudden collapse of resistance to civil service reform was the Star Route frauds which exploded upon an angry public at the time of Garfield's death. During the period of national expansion following the Civil War, the government had established special postal routes for the delivery of mail in the West. These routes were awarded to private contractors who had submitted low bids and were designated by three stars—and thus became known as Star Routes. The contracts were let for four-year periods, and contained provisions for renegotiation in order to provide higher payments for improved service. Responsibility for contract changes was vested in the hands of Thomas J. Brady, who had been appointed by Grant as Second Assistant Postmaster General, served under Hayes, Garfield, and Arthur—and became one of the most accomplished grafters in American history.[10]

Brady's closest ally was Stephen W. Dorsey, a leading Stalwart Republican who had been a carpetbag senator from Arkansas. In 1880, as secretary of the Republican National Committee, Dorsey was Garfield's virtual campaign manager. Working together with postal and Treasury officials, Dorsey and Brady organized a ring that ultimately defrauded the government of some four million dollars over a five-year period. The ring operated in the following manner: Like defense contractors a century later, members of the ring entered preposterously low bids in order to win contracts to carry the mail, and then petitioned Brady for new rates with the promise of speedier and more efficient service. Such applications were approved without question.

While the public did not learn of the corrupt activities of the Star Route ring until Garfield was in the White House, there was broad suspicion in the later years of the Hayes administration that something was afoot in the postal service. These suspicions were fueled by the appearance of Brady each year before Congress with demands for huge deficit appropriations. Nothing was done, however. More useless routes were launched every year; and even more fraudulent and padded accounts were submitted. The operator of a route with an annual income to the government of $761 was given a $50,000 contract. During a period of thirty-nine days not a single piece of mail was carried over this route. Stephen Dorsey submitted bids of $55,264 which were worth $501,092 to him, and his brother held contracts valued at $14,273 that put $147,273 in his pocket. Dorsey's brother-in-law inflated a $30,396 contract to $218,141. Despite all the rumors, Hayes later contended that he had known nothing of the brewing scandal. "One thing you may be sure of," he told a friend after he was out of office, "I am not a party to covering up anything."

The lid was finally pried off in 1880, when Brady requested that Congress approve a deficit appropriation of two million dollars for the Star Routes. A congressional investigating committee set to work poking into the rumors of fraud and corruption. Brady contended that the deficit was solely the result of the constant importuning of congressmen for the establishment of new Star Routes. Scarcely a day passed, he testified, that some member did not solicit his help in obtaining a new route to mollify his constituents. He contemptuously informed the committee that no matter what it did, he would obtain the funds required—and was proved absolutely correct when Congress approved the appropriation. Newspapers openly speculated about the amounts that had changed hands, while one congressman threatened to make public an affidavit which would name fifteen of his colleagues who had allegedly been bribed to vote for the deficiency bill. With a presidential election in the offing and the apparent involvement of prominent members of both parties becoming all too clear, the investigation was at least temporarily shelved.

Although Brady and Dorsey were under general suspicion for gross corruption, they played a leading role in the election of Garfield. Early in the campaign, the candidate sought the active help of Brady, instructing an aide to tell the postal official "that I hope he will give us all the assistance possible. I think he can help effectively." Whether this was intended as an invitation to squeeze more in the way of campaign funds out of the postal employees, or whether it was a veiled appeal to the Star Route contractors for cash has never been satisfactorily resolved. Be that as it may, on February 11, 1881, Dorsey was honored at a banquet for his efforts on behalf of the victorious Republican ticket. In a puzzlingly elliptical manner, Chester Arthur, then the vice-president-elect, alluded to Dorsey's efforts in Indiana:

> Indiana was really, I suppose, a Democratic State. It has been put down on the books always as a State that might be carried by close and perfect organization and a great deal of . . . [laughter] . . . I see the reporters are present, therefore I will simply say that everybody showed a great deal of interest in the occasion and distributed tracts and political documents all through the State.

The press was now openly hinting that Arthur's remarks meant that Indiana had been "bought" by the Republicans and the Star Route probe halted to protect Dorsey. Embarrassed, Garfield ordered the investigation reopened. "If the inquiry should disclose the fact that any person or persons had been guilty of corruption or fraud, that person or those persons must be handed over to the Department of Justice," he staunchly declared. Little was expected from the inquiry, however, because of close ties between Dorsey and the new president.

Throughout Garfield's brief term of office, the Star Route probe was a source of intense anxiety for the president. All the evidence pointed to the complicity of Dorsey and Brady in the conspiracy. Despite his reluctance to prosecute men who had been instrumental in making him president, Garfield was forced to remove Brady from office shortly after the inauguration. The case of Dorsey was even more troubling. On one occasion, Garfield wrote in his journal that he "was kept up until midnight by business connected with Dorsey's troubles. I have great sympathy for him and some doubts." Pressures to soft-pedal the investigation were heavy, but Garfield managed to overcome his doubts and to press ahead. Only a few days before he was fatally wounded, Garfield had complained that the probe was proceeding far too slowly for justice to be done.

The ascension of Arthur to the White House was greeted by the ring as an unexpected blessing. As an old-line spoilsman, he had been on intimate terms with Brady and Dorsey and others involved in the scandal, and it was hoped that he might quash or hamstring the investigation. At first, it looked as if these hopes might be justified. The inquiry was delayed—ostensibly so the president might become familiar with the facts—and the attorney general, a holdover from the Garfield cabinet, resigned amid implications that the new administration would not energetically prosecute the cases. But once again, Chester Arthur proved something of a surprise. Although the decision must have been repugnant to him, he ordered the prosecution to press ahead "with the utmost vigor of the law." In March 1882, Brady and Dorsey were indicted on charges of conspiracy to defraud the government.

The trial lasted for two months, with the defendants doing their utmost to turn the courtroom into a shambles. Upon the advice of Roscoe Conkling, now back in private legal practice, their lawyers hectored the judge, assailed the grand jury, and challenged the legality of the indictments. Confessions were recanted and government witnesses changed their testimonies or could not be found. The trial finally ended with a hung jury, amid allegations of widespread jury tampering. A second trial was ordered and this time, after six months, the jury found all the defendants not guilty. Public anger generated by the failure to

win convictions despite the obvious guilt of the conspirators
helped prepare the way for the Pendleton Act and other mani-
festations of reform.

Civil service reform touched off a quiet revolution on the American political scene. Extension of the merit system to an ever-
increasing number of federal jobholders resulted in fewer
positions which the politicians could bargain away. Laws protecting public employees from shakedowns meant that the parties
had to find new sources of revenue. At the same time, the costs of
campaigning were taking a quantum leap. The rapid growth of
the country and the corresponding expansion of the size of the
electorate required a much more vigorous effort to shape public
opinion and to influence voters. All this required money, so the
politicians turned increasingly to sympathetic tycoons for cash.
Soon, the donations of Standard Oil, the Pennsylvania Railroad,
the American Sugar Refining Company, and the steel
companies—to list only a few of the corporate donors to political
causes—vastly exceeded the revenues previously raised from
kickbacks on the wages of jobholders. Political leaders found that
sufficient funds were available to those regarded as safe by big
business.

As a result, a fresh and startling concept of government was
unveiled in the closing years of the nineteenth century. A new
crop of political leaders who thought in terms of economic interests rather than old-fashioned geographic sections and political
alliances took control of national politics. They regarded "sugar,"
"iron," and "railroads" as entities deserving representation in the
highest councils of the nation, and embraced the widespread but
unspoken belief that America was a huge profit-making concern.
It was the task of government to assist business in maximizing
profits and seeing that they were distributed with as little interference as possible. While the new generation of political leaders
worked with corrupt party bosses such as Matt Quay, who had
succeeded the Camerons in control of Pennsylvania, mere plunder was no longer the immediate goal of politics. The party in
power could bestow benefits upon business that were far more

valuable than the cash and patronage, government contracts and land grants that were the stock-in-trade of the spoilsmen.[11]

Foremost among these favors was the protective tariff. Big business regarded high tariffs as an integral part of the "American system," necessary for the unparalleled growth of the country's economy. The tariff not only protected infant industries but it was patriotic in that it encouraged domestic prosperity and ensured a high level of wages as compared to those in Europe. Trumpeting for a tariff bill that enacted some of the most prohibitive protective duties in the nation's history, William McKinley, a blandly open-faced Ohio congressman and mouthpiece of his state's manufacturing interests, cast scorn upon the idea of cheap foreign imports. "Cheap is not a word of hope," he declared. "It is not a word of inspiration. It is the badge of poverty; it is the signal of distress."

Business politics received its baptism of fire in the election of 1888. Aroused by antiprotectionist sentiments expressed by Grover Cleveland, the first Democratic president in a quarter-century, businessmen flocked to the support of Benjamin Harrison of Indiana. If they needed any further encouragement to support the Republicans, Levi Morton, one of the country's most important bankers, had been named Harrison's vice-presidential running mate. John Wanamaker, a Philadelphia merchant prince who had dreams of ending his career with a prominent political office, was put to work "frying the fat" out of businessmen as the campaign's finance chairman. He had phenomenal success by applying business methods to politics. One of his first moves was to summon ten prominent Philadelphians to a meeting at which each "fat cat" subscribed $10,000 in little more than ten minutes. Wanamaker, himself, further sweetened the pot with a $50,000 personal donation.

Letters were sent to the country's leading manufacturers informing them of the benefits they could expect from a significant increase in the tariff, and then demanded a percentage to guarantee a Republican victory. Wanamaker organized the country into districts to make collections more efficient. In western Ohio, a Cleveland industrialist named Marcus Alonzo Hanna quickly raised $100,000. In New York, Tom Platt, now the state's Republican boss, called upon a long list of moneymen topped by J. P. Morgan, and came away with a neat pile of $10,000 checks. Republican officials acknowledged having raised a million dollars for campaign expenses, four times the amount reported by the Democrats. There were also rumors of a secret Republican cache of another two million or more. The marriage of the Republican party to big business had turned out to be a bonanza for all concerned.

What was done with the huge sums collected? There were, of course, the usual costs—printed propaganda, attracting editorial support, travel expenses for either bringing the voters to the candidate or the candidate to the voters. But a sizable portion of the money was earmarked for less publicized causes, such as vote buying. Even here, the business politicians added a thrifty touch. In the old days, floaters, whose votes were for sale to the highest bidder, and repeaters, who voted early and often, had been paid in advance, but now they were not given their fee until after they had voted.

Once again, the situation in pivotal Indiana was particularly lurid. Matt Quay was said to have dispatched sizable numbers of loyal supporters of his Pennsylvania machine to that state to ensure victory. And Colonel W. W. Dudley, a one-legged veteran who was both boss of the Indiana machine and treasurer of the Republican National Committee, marshaled his force of "floaters" for action. The "floater" vote in Indiana was estimated to run as high as 20,000 and each cost $15 in gold or $20 in greenbacks. To his lieutenants, Dudley wrote: "Divide the floaters into blocks of five and put a trusted man with the necessary funds in charge of these five and make him responsible that none get away and that all vote our ticket."[12] Such doings were so common that no one raised an eyebrow when a ward heeler shouted across a police line on election day: "Are there any more repeaters out there who want to vote again?"

Dudley's "floaters" were the margin of victory for Harrison in 1888. After upward of $700,000 had been expended, he carried his home state by a mere 2,300 votes. New York, another key state, was won by Harrison by only 12,000 votes out of 1.3 million ballots cast after Platt had bought the support of several Democratic political clubs. So well had Harrison's backers done their work that he later complained that they had left him the mere trappings of office. "When I came into power I found that the party managers had taken it all to themselves," he lamented. "I could not name my own Cabinet. They had sold every place to pay the election expenses."

Until 1888, businessmen had been content to use their money and influence to advance the careers of favored politicians, or to press home issues that affected their pocketbooks. Now, they took a direct role in politics, no doubt reasoning that they could accomplish as much as the professionals at a cheaper cost. Representatives of industry and commerce were so prominent in Harrison's cabinet that it was known as the "Businessman's Cabinet." And topping the list was John Wanamaker, whose reward for his labors on behalf of Harrison—and his $50,000 campaign contribution—was the office of Postmaster General. Redfield Proctor, the marble king of Vermont and a prominent spokesman for the high tariff, was named secretary of war. And Jim Blaine, who had brokered the marriage of the Republican party and big business, was back again as secretary of state.

Soon, opposition cartoonists were portraying Wanamaker with tape measure over his arm, calling out "Cash!," as he held a bargain sale of post office jobs. The portrait was not far off the mark. Although Harrison had declared in his inaugural address that he would enforce the Pendleton Act, which placed federal employees under civil service, "fully and without evasion," Wanamaker and his associates immediately lopped off 15,000 fourth-class postmasters and replaced them with deserving Republicans.

Business leaders were not satisfied with mere representation in the cabinet, and they moved with considerable enthusiasm into the actual seats of power. They took over so many places in the Senate that the body soon became known as the "Millionaire's Club." The unbridled venality of the various state legislatures, which elected United States senators until 1913, contributed to the situation.* With leaders like Matt Quay and Tom Platt in control of the legislatures, ambitious men with enough cash could buy seats. Simon Guggenheim, who had made his fortune in mining, bought a seat outright from the Colorado legislature for $2,500 to $5,000 a vote. In West Virginia, Henry Gassaway Davis, a coal and railroad baron who became Democratic vice-presidential candidate in 1904, and his Republican son-in-law, Stephen B. Elkins, who had grown wealthy by manipulating fraudulent Spanish land grants in New Mexico, did the same.

They were in good company. It has been estimated that by the turn of the century twenty-five multimillionaires sat in the Senate—enough to control all legislation that came before the body by artful use of the committee system. William Allen White, the astute Kansas journalist, observed that a senator "represented something more than a state, more even than a region.

> He represented principalities and powers in business. One senator, for instance, represented the Union Pacific Railway System, another the New York Central, still another the insurance interests of New York and New Jersey. Here, out of the West, came not one but a group representing the Southern Pacific. The Sante Fe divided with the Gould System, an interest in another. Coal and iron owned a coterie from the Middle and Eastern seaport states. Cotton had a half dozen Senators and so it went.[13]

David Graham Phillips, in a slashing piece of muckraking, *The Treason of the Senate*, described that body as "the eager, resourceful, indefatigable agent of interests as hostile to the American people as any invading army."[14] Its leader was Rhode Island's aristocratic Nelson W. Aldrich, whose daughter married the son and heir of John D. Rockefeller.† Aldrich was named by Phillips as the "chief servant of the Money Power" in the Senate. As chairman of the Finance Committee and Republican leader, he manipulated the tariff and other fiscal policies for the benefit of the chosen few. So close were his ties to business that the chief

---

* The Seventeenth Amendment to the Constitution, approved in 1913, provided for popular election of United States senators.

† Thus he was the maternal grandfather and namesake of Vice President Nelson Aldrich Rockefeller.

textile lobbyist had a desk in Aldrich's office. In thirty years of service in the Senate, Aldrich had perfected the process of what came to be called "invisible government." He had but to whisper his commands in the committee rooms of Capitol Hill to have his bidding done. Aldrich's ally was Senator Arthur Pue Gorman, a Maryland Democrat. Together, they brought about a "merger" of the Democratic and Republican parties that successfully protected the interests of business no matter which party was in power.

Phillip's language may have been exaggerated for dramatic effect, but there was a mountain of evidence to support his charges. The partnership of business and government resulted in a flood tide of legislation to protect and enhance the aggregate holdings of the men who paid the bills. For example, the McKinley Tariff of 1890 produced a new concept in tariff policy. It not only provided revenue and protected infant American industries but it was also an instrument of exclusion. Duties were fixed so high that foreign goods could not even enter the country. There was also a further refinement. Prohibitive rates were set on products such as tin plate and wire nails, which were not produced to any extent in the United States, to allow the monopolists to establish a new industry without fear of foreign competition. The profits resulting from this piece of legislative necromancy far exceeded the most dazzling dreams of the old-time spoilsmen.[15]

Business politicians also played a vital role in protecting industry from the sting of regulatory legislation. The experience of the railroads was instructive. In the wake of the Grant scandals, several Western states had passed so-called Granger laws aimed at ending such discriminatory practices as overcharges, pools, and rebates. After a lengthy legal battle, the Supreme Court threw out these laws, ruling that a state could not regulate traffic engaged in interstate commerce even if it passed through its borders. Defeated on the local level, the proponents of railroad regulation next turned to Washington with an insistent demand for federal regulation. The backwash was so strong that the railroad barons realized it would be only a matter of time before even the Senate would be forced to approve a bill establishing a railroad regulatory agency.

It is generally assumed that the railroads resisted the passage of a federal regulatory law as inimical to their interests. In truth they welcomed it.[16] Business politicians succeeded in so weakening the Interstate Commerce Act, which became law in 1887, that it was no threat to the railroads. Between them, Aldrich and Gorman managed matters so well that the Interstate Commerce Commission could not set rates and had no coercive powers. It had to appeal to the federal courts for enforcement of its orders, and conservative judges almost always ruled in favor of the railroads. While passage of the Interstate Commerce Act brought cheers from reformers, Nelson Aldrich knew better. He called it "a delusion and a sham . . . an empty menace to great interests, made to answer the clamor of the ignorant and unreasoning."

To meet a similar "clamor" for regulation of the trusts that seemed to be blossoming everywhere, Congress passed the Sherman Anti-Trust Act in 1890. It declared illegal any business combination in restraint of trade or attempt to create a monopoly, and gave the power of enforcement to the federal courts. Like the Interstate Commerce Act, the business politicians regarded the antitrust law as a sop to the malcontents that was not to be seriously enforced. It eventually became an extremely effective weapon in the hands of business in its fight against labor organizations. As Mr. Dooley observed: "What looks like a stone-wall to a layman is a triumphal arch to a corporation lawyer."[17]

Politicians who did the bidding of business were known as "rope-jumpers," and there was no more skillful rope-turner than Mark Hanna. No one was cleverer in mixing big money and political power. "Politics are one form of business and must be treated strictly as a business," the Cleveland industrialist declared with his usual frankness. Hanna had made a fortune in coal, iron, Great Lakes shipping, and banking, but he had wider ambitions. He craved power and sought it in politics—not by running for office himself but through efficient management of others. Comparatively honest in his personal dealings, Hanna was tolerant of corruption by others. Shrewd and cynical in his management of men, he was capable of deep friendships and abiding loyalties.

Although he never gave speeches, he shouldered his way to becoming the nearest thing to a national "boss" that has ever appeared in American politics.

Few politicians have had a worse image than Hanna.[18] Cartoonists delighted in portraying him as a sinister, toadlike figure wearing a flashy suit spangled with dollar signs. Editorialists lashed out at him as "the evil genius of the plutocracy." In reality, however, he was far more foresighted than the average tycoon. Hanna was basically a Hamiltonian in that he believed that those who owned the country should rule it, but he tempered this conviction with a responsiveness to the needs of ordinary Americans. Hanna unhesitatingly condemned employers who fought against unionization, and regarded reasonable treatment of labor as the best guarantee of industrial peace. He believed that in a new, industrialized America, business and politics were natural allies. Inasmuch as individual and social profits were indistinguishable, there was nothing wrong with business using government to further its interests. The great mission of capitalism was to spread the benefits of prosperity among the American people, and the Republican party was to be the vehicle for that crusade.

In William McKinley, a former Ohio congressman and governor, Hanna found the pitchman of the new politics. For years, Hanna devoted his time and money to making his friend president, an effort that was crowned with success in 1896. In fact, Hanna had a higher ambition for McKinley than McKinley had for himself. An unimaginative party wheel-horse who looked like a bronze statue looking for a pedestal, McKinley was in the words of William Allen White, a "kindly, dull gentleman ... honest enough, brave enough, intelligent enough for politics—and no more so."[19] Another observer said McKinley "had the art ... of throwing a moral gloss over policies which were dubious, if not actually immoral." Hanna and McKinley complemented each other beautifully. While McKinley spouted moralistic platitudes, Hanna was a realist with few illusions about his fellow man. As Margaret Leech, a McKinley biographer, has put it, together they made "one perfect politician."

"God's in his Heaven, all's right with the world!" Hanna proclaimed in triumph after he had put McKinley in the White

House. This was accomplished in a campaign in which the candidate was packaged and marketed like a patent medicine. Estimates of the cost ranged upward to $10 million—the most ever
spent until after World War I. To obtain this huge bankroll,
Hanna preyed upon the fears of the rich that the election of
William Jennings Bryan, a prairie Galahad who demanded the
free coinage of silver, would mean revolution. Standard Oil came
up with $250,000—an amount almost as large as the entire
Democratic campaign chest—J. P. Morgan contributed an equal
amount; the meat-packing industry gave $400,000. The insur-
ance companies were also "liberal contributors" and the banks
were assessed at a rate of one-quarter of one percent of their
capital. Bryan didn't have a chance.[20]

With the scalps of the free silverites dangling from its belt, big
business regarded the election of McKinley as a green light for its
imperial ambitions. The relationship between government and
business became even more intimate and productive than ever
before. Under the benevolent gaze of Hanna, railroad mergers,
industrial combinations, communities of interest, and trusts
flourished. Tariffs were set at ridiculously high rates, and business was guaranteed protection against hostile legislation. As
Lincoln Steffens observed a few years later, "Business and politics
must be one . . . it was natural, inevitable, and—possibly—right
that business should—by bribery, corruption, or—somehow get
and be the government."[21]

XIV

"Gee, How the Money Rolls in!"

EARLY ON THE morning of March 4, 1921, Henry L. Mencken, indulging a whimsical delight in farce in any form, went over to Washington to look in on Warren Harding's inauguration. As the words of the inaugural address trailed out on the frosty air like "a string of wet sponges," Mencken shifted uneasily on a folding chair. He readily confessed having voted for Harding after a night spent, as he put it, on his knees in prayerful meditation, but now he was having second thoughts. That evening, back in Baltimore, Mencken hunched over his old Corona and tapped out a column assessing the new president: "No other such complete and dreadful nitwit is to be found in the pages of American history. . . ."[1]

Until the Reagan era, the scandals associated with Harding's name represented the lowest ebb of American political life in this century. Like the decade after the Civil War, the post-World War I era was one of unrestrained corruption in business and government. In both periods, laissez faire was the official policy, but in practice government was little more than an instrument of business. "American business is everybody's business," declared

261

Harding, while Calvin Coolidge said, "The business of the United States is business."

Although there is no evidence that Harding stole so much as a nickel, friends, associates, and cabinet members were in league with crooked businessmen to plunder the nation. His interior secretary became the first cabinet member to go to jail; his attorney general only narrowly escaped a similar fate, and his secretary of the navy was forced to resign as a result of a mixture of stupidity and criminal negligence. Fraud in the Veterans Bureau, graft in the Office of the Alien Property Custodian, and conspiracy in the Justice Department were all part of Harding's legacy. Yet, the president who presided over these revels "was not a bad man," said Alice Roosevelt Longworth. "He was just a slob."[2]

Few Americans had heard of the easygoing senator from Ohio until he unexpectedly emerged from a smoke-filled room in a Chicago hotel with the Republican nomination in his pocket. Nevertheless, he was elected by the largest popular majority run up by a presidential candidate since well before the Civil War. "It wasn't a landslide," said Joe Tumulty, secretary to outgoing president Woodrow Wilson. "It was an earthquake." Harding's smashing victory was the result of his understanding of the hopes and fears of the average American in an age of kaleidoscopic change.

Earlier in the twentieth century, Theodore Roosevelt and then Woodrow Wilson had attempted to curb the worst aspects of what William Allen White called "the alliance between government and business for the benefit of business." For a decade and a half, they had ridden the crest of a crusade for reform of government and politics. Progressive politicians and muckraking journalists had exposed the interlocking relationship between the trusts and the political machines, and demands for change were running high. Some reforms were made but many of them turned out to be merely cosmetic. Under the pressure for reform, practical men of business and politics curbed the worst aspects of their public behavior, but continued to build—perhaps more discreetly than before but no less effectively—a structure of power and wealth that dominated the country.

America's entry into World War I gave big business the opportunity to not only push aside most of the restrictions placed on its activities by the reformers, it also provided a glorious opportunity for some industrialists and financiers to make a killing out of the slaughter on European battlefields. Although there was less gross corruption and petty graft than that which had bedeviled the North during the Civil War, profiteering flourished on a grand scale. Once again, the American people discovered an old truism—patriotism is no bar to making a fast buck. Profiteering was so pervasive that a year after the United States entered the war, an angry Wilson told Congress that it exceeded "the restraints of conscience and love of country." Secretary of the Navy Josephus Daniels, faced with outrageously inflated prices for armor plate, sarcastically observed: "These steel prices are a wonderful monument to the patriotism of the steel manufacturers."

War's end brought bitter disillusionment with great moral crusades—whether for reform at home or for international order abroad. Weary of Wilson's appeals to idealism and his visionary talk of the nation's mission, the American people wanted to shape their own affairs without interference from the government. Harding's campaign slogan was "back to normalcy"—and it struck a responsive chord.* "There might be no such word in the dictionary," Frederick Lewis Allen has observed, "but normalcy is what [Americans] wanted."[3]

Handsome, silver-thatched, and flashing a high-octane smile, Harding looked like an ideal statesman. In fact, during his Senate days, someone suggested that he was probably the only man in Washington who would look at home in a toga. Harding's elevation to the presidency, says one biographer, was as if "a clothing store model, after years of faithful service in displaying choice garments in the front window, should suddenly find itself manager of the store."[4]

Warren Harding epitomized a predominately small-town and rural America that was already fading before the implacable onslaught of urbanization, standardization, and the Tin Lizzie.

---

* In one of his speeches, Harding had meant to say *normality* but stumbled over the word.

Born in 1865 near the hamlet of Blooming Grove, Ohio, he was the son of a country schoolteacher turned homeopathic physician. Later, there would be unsubstantiated rumors that the Hardings had African blood, but they apparently got along well enough with their neighbors.* Like William McKinley, whom he resembled in background, appearance, and outlook, Harding, after three years of meager high school education, decided to study law. When that endeavor proved to be beyond his capabilities, he tried selling insurance, before turning to journalism. He succeeded so well that he eventually became the owner and editor of a county weekly, the Marion *Star*. At twenty-six, Harding married Florence Kling (the divorced daughter of the town's leading citizen), who was six years older. An ambitious, penny-pinching woman, she is usually credited with pushing her diffident husband much further along than his own ambitions and abilities would have taken him.

Harding was a natural booster and joiner and was soon active in the Kiwanis, the Rotarians, the Masons, and Shriners, as well as the Elks, the Odd Fellows, the Hoo Hoos, and the Moose. He also played the tuba in the town band. Wherever he went, people liked him. He was a frequenter of saloons and bordellos, played poker with skill, and enjoyed cracking dirty jokes among men like himself. Sociability led him into politics, the chief diversion of rural Ohio. Harding was a meandering orator, but his apparent sincerity, combined with a gassy pomposity, made him a welcome speaker at crossroads Republican rallies. It was at one of these meetings that he met Harry M. Daugherty, who was to have an important influence on his life. Harding had delivered his speech and was having his shoes shined when Daugherty, next in line, mused upon what a handsome and genial-looking fellow he was. "Gee, what a President he'd make!" Daugherty said to himself—or so he later claimed.[5]

Harry Daugherty was five years older than Harding and had a similar small-town background, except that he had managed to

---

* When these rumors began to circulate during the 1920 campaign, Harding wanted to issue a denial, but Boies Penrose, the Republican boss of Pennsylvania, suggested otherwise. "From what I hear," he said, "we've been having a lot of trouble holding the nigger vote lately."

become a lawyer. He had been elected to a few minor state offices, but by the time he met Harding, was primarily a lobbyist at the state capitol in Columbus for an assortment of business interests and utilities. Mark Sullivan, a leading journalist who knew Daugherty well, wrote: "Always he knew what wire to pull; always he kept a web of wires running from his office out to all sorts of men who occupied places of leverage; always he knew how to get results."

Ohio had provided the United States with six presidents—Harding was to be the seventh—but the state's politics were a cesspool. Political control of the Republican party was divided between Mark Hanna and "Fire Alarm Joe" Foraker, who was later exposed as having been on the payroll of Standard Oil while serving in the U.S. Senate. In 1899, Harding was elected to the first of two terms in the state senate, where he served with no distinction. He made himself useful to the Foraker faction, and four years later was rewarded for his loyalty with election as lieutenant governor. Andrew Sinclair, who has examined Harding's private papers, states that there is no doubt that, like most Ohio politicos of the day, he accepted graft as part of the system. His correspondence is full of demands for free railroad passes and the columns of his paper were for sale. He accepted stock in a local brewery in return for having puffed it in the paper and was alleged to have taken $10,000 from a farm implement company.[6]

While the nation was being convulsed by the battle over reform, the amiable and complacent Harding served as the dignified front man for the boys in the back room. In 1910 and again in 1912 he ran for governor, only to be beaten both times—the last time by his fellow publisher, James M. Cox—who after three terms as governor was to lose the presidency to him in 1920. In 1914, with progressivism on the wane and the Democrats badly hurt by the business slump resulting from the outbreak of world war, Harding was easily elected to the Senate.

In the Senate, Harding's six years of service were undistinguished even in terms of that rather undistinguished body. There was no "Harding Bill" or even a "Harding Amendment" to attract public attention. Most of the legislation he introduced was of a local nature, designed to provide some petty advantage for a constituent. Harding was comfortable in the Senate. There was nothing to tax his intelligence or his energies. The pay was good—$7,500 annually plus allowances. Combined with the $20,000-or-so a year coming in from the *Star*, he was well off. Most of his colleagues liked him, for he was always ready to do a favor. Mrs. Harding, whom he called "the Duchess," had taken to the Washington social scene while her husband was enjoying the company of a young mistress, Nan Britton, by whom he had had a child. Mark Sullivan wrote that "had his career stopped with the Senate, he would have been only an obscure and forgotten name preserved like thousands of others in old Congressional Directories."[7] Harding's career was so lackluster that political observers looking over the presidential possibilities for 1920 did not even bother to include him in their calculations—except for Harry Daugherty.

Daugherty had never forgotten his first impression of Harding, but his primary task was to persuade Harding he had a chance to win the Republican nomination. In recent years, historians have debated whether Harding was as reluctant a presidential candidate as Daugherty was led to believe. Andrew Sinclair, for one, states that Harding's White House ambitions date back at least from his election to the Senate in 1914 and his repeated denials of interest in the presidency were strictly a cover. On the other hand, Francis Russell, another biographer, contends that unpublished letters between Harding and one of his mistresses make it clear that he had no such early ambition.[8] No matter where the ultimate truth may lie, Daugherty threw himself into his work with enthusiasm. When Harding asked "Am I a big enough man for the race?," he had had a ready answer. "Don't make me laugh!" he told his friend. "The day of greatness in the Presidential chair is over. . . . Greatness in the Presidential chair is largely an illusion."

Daugherty's strategy was a simple one. The front-runners for the nomination—General Leonard Wood and Governor Frank O. Lowdon of Illinois—would tear each other to pieces while Harding angered no one and remained quietly in reserve. As early as February 1920, he confidently predicted how his candidate would win the nomination:

I don't expect Senator Harding to be nominated on the first, second or third ballots, but I think we can afford to take chances that, about eleven minutes after two on Friday morning at the convention, when fifteen or twenty men, somewhat weary, are sitting around a table, some of them will say, "Who will we nominate?" At that decisive time, the friends of Harding can suggest him and can afford to abide by the result.

Later, Daugherty embroidered his prediction to say that the choice of the Republican standard bearer would be made by "fifteen men in a smoke-filled room." Not only did he add a vivid phrase to American political folklore, he turned out to be an amazingly accurate prophet.

Meeting in the awful heat of a Chicago summer, the convention quickly became a maelstrom of conflicting ambitions. Just as Daugherty had said, Wood and Lowdon deadlocked through the fourth ballot. Tempers flaring, nerves rubbed raw, and hotel bills mounting, the convention recessed on Friday night so a solution to the impasse could be worked out off the floor before the party tore itself to pieces. The moment that Harry Daugherty had predicted was at hand. A group of the party's Old Guard gathered in Suite 404–406 in the Blackstone Hotel, which had been rented by Will H. Hays, the Republican national chairman. Party leaders and influential senators wandered in and out as the whiskey flowed and the cigar smoke thickened.

Wood and Lowdon had knocked each other out—that much was agreed upon. But who was to take their place? The names of all the various other possibilities were trotted out: Warren Harding, Herbert Hoover, Calvin Coolidge, Hiram Johnson. One by one they were ruled out until only Harding's name remained. The consensus was that he was the best of the second-raters. He did not arouse any strong opposition among any segment of the party and could be depended upon to take advice rather than give orders. About two o'clock in the morning—close enough to the time prophesied by Daugherty to fit the legend—a stunned Harding was summoned to the "smoke-filled room" and told it was likely he would be nominated when the convention met again. Was there any reason why he could not be president?

"Gentlemen, I should like to be alone for a little while," Harding is reported to have replied. He was ushered into an adjoining room where he spent about ten minutes—thinking perhaps of the whispering campaign that he had black blood, or perhaps of Nan Britton and her child, or even of his own inadequacies. When he reappeared he is supposed to have said, "Gentlemen, there is no reason in the sight of God that I cannot be President of the United States." As soon as the convention reconvened, Harding's share of the votes mounted steadily, although there was no massive immediate shift to his standard. The nomination was not his until the ninth ballot. "We drew to a pair of deuces and filled," he said.

As a result of Daugherty's talk about the "smoke-filled room," a legend was created that Harding's nomination was the handiwork of a cabal of corrupt insiders who foisted him onto the convention. Oil controlled the convention, according to William Allen White. "I have never seen a convention—and I have watched most of them since McKinley's first nomination—so completely dominated by sinister predatory economic forces as was this." It was reported that Leonard Wood had been offered the nod if he would promise the oil interests three places in his cabinet. Nevertheless, one historian states that although the convention was certainly dominated by business and financial interests "who knew what they wanted out of government, and were willing to pay for whatever privileges they got," Harding was not forced upon the delegates by a conspiracy.[9] In reality, he happened to be the candidate who best suited the mood of the convention—and the nation.

The election, itself, was anticlimactic. Harding and his vice-presidential candidate, the equally conservative Governor Calvin Coolidge of Massachusetts, waged a front-porch campaign in the style of McKinley. While James Cox and his running mate, a handsome young Hudson River aristocrat named Franklin Delano Roosevelt, who had served as assistant secretary of the navy under Wilson, tried to make the campaign a referendum on the Wilsonian dream of American participation in the League of Nations, Harding stayed in Marion, Ohio, and mouthed canned platitudes. "Keep Warren at home. . . . Don't let him make any speeches," advised the sardonic Boies Penrose. "If he goes out on tour somebody's sure to ask him questions, and Warren's just the sort of damned fool that will try to answer them." So well was this advice followed that by October it was said that if the election were a prize fight, "the police would interfere on the grounds of brutality."

Years before Harding became president, his father had an inkling of the chain of disasters which lay in the future. "Warren, it's a good thing you wasn't born a girl because you'd be in a family way all the time," allowed the old man. "You can't say no." Friendly and gregarious, Harding brought to Washington as jolly a gang of smalltown sports and back-room fixers as were to be found in any crossroads county courthouse in Ohio. Big-bellied and good-natured, they descended upon the capital as if it were a big rock candy mountain. One observer said the rollicking refrain of "Hail! Hail! The Gang's All Here!" could almost be heard resounding across town on inauguration night.

No doubt recognizing his own limitations, the new president announced that he would appoint a cabinet of the "best minds" in the country. Charles Evans Hughes, unsuccessful Republican candidate for president in 1916, was named secretary of state; Herbert Hoover, who had directed relief operations during the war with distinction, was appointed secretary of commerce, and Andrew W. Mellon, the aluminum tycoon who was reputed to be the second richest man in the nation, became secretary of the Treasury. While these appointments were well received, they were followed by others that inspired cynical jokes about Harding's concept of the "best minds."

With Prohibition getting underway and with several war frauds cases pending, the post of attorney general offered an opportunity for either the utmost integrity or for unprecedented loot. Harding gave the job to Harry Daugherty. To the consternation of conservationists and the delight of the oil barons, he appointed Senator Albert B. Fall of New Mexico as secretary of the interior. Fall, whose opposition to conservation was open and notorious, had been so eager for the job that he signed Daugherty's name to a telegram urging his appointment. The appointment of Edwin N. Denby, a conservative ex-congressman and millionaire, as secretary of the navy was another tragic blunder. Henry Mencken later described Harding's cabinet as "three highly intelligent men of self-interest, six jackasses and one common crook."

Harding's concept of public service was to give a friend a job. Dr. Charles E. Sawyer, a Marion homeopath and favorite of Mrs. Harding, was appointed an army brigadier general and named physician to the president. Daniel R. Crissinger, a boyhood pal whose financial experience consisted of a few months in a small-town bank, was named Comptroller of the Currency, and later, was made governor of the Federal Reserve System, the ranking bank official in the country. Another old crony, Ed Scobey, who had never risen above sheriff of Pickaway County, was made Director of the Mint. The post of Superintendent of Prisons was removed from civil service and went to Heber H. Votaw, Harding's brother-in-law. To head the newly formed Veterans Bureau, the president chose Colonel Charles R. Forbes, a smooth-talking confidence man whom Harding had met while on a senatorial junket to Hawaii.[10]

Daugherty brought with him a curious character named Jess Smith. Large, loose-limbed, and big-bellied, he followed Daugherty about like a friendly puppy. Smith had no official duties in the Department of Justice, but he had an office near Daugherty. What he did there no one seemed to know. The two old friends shared bachelor quarters in the Wardman Park Hotel and were often seen at a house at 1625 K Street near the White House. There, Howard Mannington, an Ohio lobbyist and long-time friend of the attorney general, operated a combination speakeasy, gambling house, brothel, and place where the Ohio Gang could arrange its secret deals. Open for business day and night, the "little green house on K Street" was the place to arrange protection for bootleggers, withdrawal permits for alcohol from federal stockpiles, appointments to office, and the purchase of paroles, pardons, and privileges. Charlie Forbes, the head of the Veterans Bureau, once claimed that he had seen Mannington studying a Justice Department file of applications for federal judgeships which he said had been sent over to be auctioned off to the highest bidders. "Gee, how the money rolls in!" Jess Smith used to hum to himself—and with good reason.[11]

Harding did not attend parties on K Street. Instead, he usually invited the boys over to the White House for a poker session a couple of nights a week. The regulars included Daugherty, Smith, Albert Fall, Charlie Forbes, and "Doc" Sawyer. Sometimes Andy Mellon took a hand and so did Harry F. Sinclair, an oil multimillionaire who was on friendly terms with Fall. Prohibition was the law of the land, but not in the White House. Alice Roosevelt Longworth, certainly no prude, once went to the president's second-floor study while an official reception was going on below. "No rumor could have exceeded the reality," she reported. "The study was filled with cronies . . . the air heavy with tobacco smoke, trays with bottles containing every imaginable brand of whiskey stood about, cards and poker chips ready to hand—a general atmosphere of waistcoat unbuttoned, feet on the desk, and the spitoon alongside."[12]

Harding was soon overwhelmed by the complexity of his office. As Andrew Sinclair has pointed out, the nineteenth-century system of corrupt politics and unrestricted business opportunity in which he had been formed was poor preparation for the duties of the modern presidency.[13] On one occasion when a knotty tax problem had been dropped on his desk, Harding threw up his hands in desperation and told a secretary:

> John, I can't make a damn thing out of this tax problem. I listen to one side and they seem right, and then—God!—I talk to the other side and they seem just as right, and here I am where I started. I know somewhere there is a book that will give me the truth, but hell, I couldn't read the book. I know somewhere there is an economist who knows the truth, and I don't know where to find him and haven't the sense to know and trust him when I find him. God, what a job!

If Harding was confused over the day-to-day decisions of his office, there were those who were ready to guide his hand. In many ways, the slanting of the government during the twenties to support whatever big business wanted was far more scandalous than the picturesque banditry of the Ohio Gang. In the forefront of the "gimme" brigade were the oil barons. They had played an important role in bankrolling Harding's campaign, so it was no surprise that he made it the first order of business to help them expand their operations.

The conversion of the world's navies from coal to oil in the years immediately preceding World War I had placed new emphasis on the importance of petroleum. At the same time, there were widespread if erroneous fears that known oil reserves would soon run out. Britain and other European nations therefore gave vigorous diplomatic support to private companies seeking new oil fields in the Middle East and in Latin America. American companies complained, on the other hand, that they were obliged to go it alone. Led by the Rockefeller interests, American oil men demanded similar backing from their government—and the Harding administration eagerly complied.

Four days after his inauguration, Harding pressed the Senate for ratification of a long-stalled treaty designed to make amends to Colombia for the way in which Theodore Roosevelt had in 1903 engineered the independence of Panama from Colombia and then built a canal across the tiny new country. "I took the Isthmus," Roosevelt had declared with a toothy grin. Jingoism had been fashionable during the era of the "Big Stick" but now Colombian animosity made it difficult for American oilmen to get a foothold in the area. To make the Yanqui apology more acceptable, the deal was sweetened with $25 million of the taxpayers' money. Although the payment was assailed as "an indirect subsidy to the oil interests," it was soon approved by the business-dominated Senate.

Big business had supported Harding with the expectation of lower taxes for the upper brackets, and Andrew Mellon did not long delay in gratifying this wish. The excess profits tax that had been left over from the war was repealed, and surtaxes on high incomes were reduced. But taxes on incomes below $66,000 were unchanged, and to make up for the loss of revenue that had been collected from the wealthy, Mellon suggested two-cent postal cards, a two-cent tax on every check cashed, and a federal license tax on automobiles. Mellon succeeded so well in passing the tax load on to middle- and lower-income Americans that during his tenure in the Treasury, refunds totaling some $3.5 billion were handed out—mostly to large corporations, including those controlled by the Mellons. No wonder businessmen were soon hailing Andrew Mellon as "the greatest Secretary of Treasury since Alexander Hamilton."[14]

Because of the pervasive odor of oil at the Chicago convention and in Harding's administration, it is sometimes thought that the appointment of Albert B. Fall as secretary of the interior was a payoff to the oil interests. Whether or not this was true has never been determined. With his drooping moustache, flowing tie, and wide-brimmed hat, Fall looked like the sheriff in a Western movie. Born in Kentucky in 1861, he had gone west as a youth, becoming, successively, a cowhand, prospector, miner, and self-taught lawyer. Originally a Democrat, he had been appointed a territorial judge in New Mexico by President Grover Cleveland. Removed from the bench when he personally led a posse in hot pursuit of a fleeing bandit, Fall angrily became a Republican. In 1912, when New Mexico was admitted to the Union, he became the state's first U.S. senator. In the clubby atmosphere of the Senate, he was popular with his colleagues. For some unfathomable reason, Harding adopted an extravagant view of his intellectual attainments.*

By 1920, however, serving the people of New Mexico in the Senate was a luxury which Fall could no longer afford. He had retreated to his ranch at Three Rivers and was weighing his alternatives. They were none too bright. The taxes on his place had not been paid in eight years; the house was dilapidated, the fences broken, and the stock depleted. Fall was broke. He was rescued from this bleak prospect by his appointment to the cabi-

---

* In 1920, Fall, as a member of a two-man Senate committee appointed to inquire into the state of President Wilson's health after he had suffered a stroke, had insisted on entering the sickroom.

"I have been praying for you, sir," he told Wilson.

"Which way, Senator?" asked the president.

net. Originally, Harding had wanted to make his old friend secretary of state but was prevailed upon to drop the idea and named him secretary of the interior instead.

It was a curious appointment. Like most Westerners of his generation, Fall had little use for conservation. He believed that the federal government had no right to supervise or control the use of the nation's natural resources, and that the West ought to be developed in the same freewheeling fashion as the Eastern states had been—through individual enterprise and without bureaucratic interference. He was even convinced that as soon as it was possible, the Department of Interior should be abolished. Fall was particularly opposed to the setting aside of certain oil lands as naval petroleum reserves, and thought they ought to be turned over to the private oil companies for development.[15]

These reserves had been established by presidents Taft and Wilson with the intention of providing emergency fuel for the future use of the navy. Naval Petroleum Reserve No. 1 consisted of 36,969 acres at Elk Hills, California; Petroleum Reserve No. 2, with 29,351 acres, was at Buena Vista Hills, California; and Petroleum Reserve No. 3 included 9,481 acres at Teapot Dome in Wyoming. The oil companies tried to gain access to these underground reserves almost from their very establishment. Josephus Daniels, Wilson's secretary of the navy, later wrote: "I remember one night toward the end of a session that Mr. Roosevelt and I remained at the Capitol all night long watching the legislation of closing hours, fearing that some act might be passed that would turn over these invaluable oil reserves to parties who laid claim to them without even decent show of title."

Under the pressure of the oil companies, Congress, in 1920, passed the Oil Land Leasing Act, which permitted the government to lease drilling rights on public lands to private operators. The three naval petroleum reserves were included, with the intent of allowing the tapping of government reserves to prevent them from being drained off by wells on adjoining private lands. Royalties from the oil taken from the reserves under the terms of the 1920 law went into the general revenues—a fact that created considerable unhappiness in the navy. Faced with the increasing power of Japan in the Pacific, naval strategists believed that the

United States must have a two-ocean navy. The admirals wished to build fuel-oil storage facilities at the new base at Pearl Harbor in Hawaii and along both coasts. But an economy-minded Congress, which could see no need to prepare for a war that was not likely to occur, refused to appropriate the money for these installations and barred the navy from using the oil royalties for that purpose.

It was at this point that Albert Fall became secretary of the interior. Almost as soon as he was firmly in the saddle, he launched a vigorous campaign to wrest control of the petroleum reserves from the Navy Department preparatory to fulfilling his plan to lease them to private developers. Fall lost no time in convincing Harding that it would be more efficient to have the reserves administered by his department than by the navy. Thus armed, he turned his attention to Edwin Denby, the navy secretary. Denby, who seems to have had little interest in his department except to administer it with the least possible annoyance to himself, readily acquiesced in the transfer.

On May 31, 1921, after the Harding administration had been in office less than three months, the president signed an executive order placed before him by Fall which transferred control of the petroleum reserves from the navy to the Interior Department. No questions were asked and no explanations were given. News of the order was buried in the inside pages of a few newspapers. With final authority over the petroleum reserves safely in his hands, Fall proceeded to enter into a series of deals that were to make Teapot Dome part of the folklore of American politics.

Two months later, Fall awarded the first drilling contract for offset wells in the Elk Hills reserve to the Pan-American Petroleum and Transport Company, headed by Edward Doheny. The contract was publicly advertised, and although there were some misgivings among conservationists and naval officers, there was no great outcry as the wells were supposedly aimed at preventing drainage from the reserve. Fall and Doheny were old friends. In fact, as young men they had been fellow prospectors. While Fall's luck was bad, Doheny had struck it rich, discovering oil fields in California and Mexico. "There is nothing extraordinary about me," Doheny once proclaimed. "I am just an ordinary, old-time, impulsive, irresponsible, improvident sort of a prospector." Unlike most old prospectors, however, he was worth more than $100 million.

Doheny was soon complaining that the royalties that he had to pay for pumping oil from his wells in Elk Hills were too high. Inasmuch as the payments had been set in public bidding, Fall could not reduce them, but promised his old friend that he would have preferential rights to any additional leases in the California reserves under a scheme soon to be put into effect. To placate the navy for the loss of control of its reserves, Fall produced a plan in which private developers would pay the navy for the crude oil pumped from the reserves with certificates good for fuel oil rather than cash. The companies would also agree to build storage facilities at Pearl Harbor, or on the Atlantic and Pacific coasts, as the navy desired. Thus, the navy would circumvent the annoying legal requirement that all funds received for the sale of government oil be placed in the Treasury.

On November 28, 1921, Doheny made a formal bid to construct storage tanks at Pearl Harbor in exchange for oil from the Elk Hills reserve. The next day, Fall telephoned Doheny in New York and informed him that he "was prepared now to receive that loan." Doheny dispatched his son, Edward L. Doheny, Jr., to Fall's suite in the Wardman Park. The younger Doheny carried a little black bag with him that contained $100,000 in cash. Not long afterward, Doheny was given a fifteen-year lease on the reserve. "We will be in bad luck," said the old prospector, "if we do not get $100 million profit."

Albert Fall's customer for the reserve at Teapot Dome was Harry F. Sinclair, of the Sinclair Consolidated Oil Company. Sinclair was a one-time Kansas pharmacist who had become a swashbuckling international wheeler-dealer with interests in all parts of the globe and a fortune in excess of $300 million. In 1924, Albania asked him to become its ruler and settle its problems. By then, however, Sinclair had his own difficulties.

They began at the end of 1921, when he visited Fall at his ranch and the two men reached a mutually satisfactory settlement concerning the future of the Wyoming petroleum reserve. As a token of friendship, Sinclair ordered some expensive stock shipped from his breeding farm to New Mexico. Even before he returned to Washington on the tycoon's private railroad car, Fall instructed his aides to prepare the necessary documents turning Teapot Dome over to the Mammoth Oil Company, a subsidiary formed by Sinclair solely for the operation of the lease.

This was the second lucrative triumph scored by Sinclair in as many months. Just a few weeks before, on November 21, 1921, a small group of oil barons negotiated a deal that cast a brilliant light on the business ethics of the age—and was to play a vital part in eventually unraveling the Teapot Dome scandal. Those present included Colonel E. A. Humphreys, owner of the newly discovered Mexia oil field in east Texas; H. M. Blackmer, of the Midwest Oil Company; James E. O'Neil of the Prairie Oil Company; Colonel Robert W. Stewart, board chairman of Standard Oil of Indiana; and Harry Sinclair. Humphreys agreed to sell 33,333,333 barrels of oil from his field at $1.50 a barrel, or $50 million, to the other men—but not directly to their companies. Instead, the sale was made to a newly established Canadian firm, the Continental Trading Company, Ltd. Continental then entered into an agreement to sell the oil to the companies represented at the meeting—not at $1.50 a barrel, but for $1.75. Thus, these executives diverted into their own pockets an $8 million windfall which would be paid by their stockholders. These enormous profits were to be paid in Liberty Bonds instead of cash.

The lease granting Mammoth Oil the exclusive right to extract oil and gas from the Teapot Dome reserve for twenty years was signed on April 7, 1922. Fall locked it in his desk, and his subordinates were told to give out no information about it. In return for the lease, Sinclair promised to build oil storage tanks at points along the Atlantic coast designated by the navy and to fill them with fuel oil. Royalty certificates exchanged for Teapot Dome oil were to be used as payment. Sinclair estimated his potential profits as high as $100 million. A month later, Fall sent M. T. Everhart, his son-in-law, to see Sinclair, whose private car was in the Washington rail yards. Sinclair gave him $198,000 in Liberty

Bonds, which were part of the loot realized from the Continental Trading deal. He either overlooked the fact, or possibly he didn't care, that such bonds have serial numbers. Another payment of $35,000 in bonds and about $70,000 in cash followed.

So, in exchange for about $400,000 in cash and bonds, Albert Fall had given away navy petroleum reserves then conservatively valued at $200 million—and worth considerably more.*

Shortly after Fall had been appointed to Harding's cabinet, his neighbors in New Mexico were puzzled to see a rapid change in his fortunes. Back taxes on his ranch were paid, and his house was put into repair. New fences were erected and blooded stock began to appear on his range. Fall also added two sizable parcels of land to his property—one valued at $91,500 and the other at $33,000—bringing his total holdings to 700,000 acres. Such improvements obviously could not be supported on his $12,000-a-year salary. As he had no other source of income to explain his sudden prosperity, suspicions were aroused.

The realization that something was amiss with Fall's stewardship of the naval petroleum reserves dawned upon a number of men in different parts of the country at almost the same time. Harry A. Slattery, a Washington lawyer with a strong interest in conservation, learned from acquaintances in various government agencies that Fall had leased Teapot Dome to Harry Sinclair.[16] Even before the lease had been signed, the rumor mill was at work. "I understand the Interior Department is just about to close a contract to lease Teapot Dome," a Standard Oil of New Jersey official told Albert Lasker, head of the Shipping Board. ". . . You should tell the President that it smells—that he must not permit it to go through." That evening, Lasker told Harding what he had heard. "This isn't the first time that this rumor has come to me," was the president's reply, "but if Albert Fall isn't an honest man, I'm not fit to be President of the United States."

Senator John P. Kenrick of Wyoming, who had been bombarded with letters from his constituents, introduced a resolution

---

* In 1975 the oil in the Elk Hills reserve alone was valued at from $30 to $50 billion.

on April 15, 1922, demanding that the secretaries of interior and navy be instructed to "inform the Senate" as to what was happening at Teapot Dome. Passed without much comment, it was supplemented a week later by a more specific resolution introduced by Senator Robert La Follette of Wisconsin. Supplied with information dredged up by Slattery, the senator demanded a full-scale investigation of the oil leases. La Follette's resolution was passed unanimously—but nothing was done about it for eighteen months.

In the meantime, Fall defended his actions as perfectly legal, and submitted a report to the president claiming the leases were vital to national security. Harding defended his interior secretary's decisions, saying they were "submitted to me prior to the adoption thereof, and the policy decided upon and the subsequent actions have at all times had my entire approval." The Senate resolution ordering an investigation had directed Fall to forward all documents and other information relevant to the inquiry—and he did just that with a vengeance. He must have chuckled to himself as he dictated the letter of transmittal: "My casual estimate of the number of pages being forwarded you is that the aggregate will be between 10 and 15,000 . . . the documents number approximately 2,300. . . ."

Fall remained in the cabinet until he had completed all his plans, resigning on March 4, 1923. Harding told the press that he had offered to appoint him to the Supreme Court, but Fall had declined the honor. The high-minded Herbert Hoover wrote his retiring colleague a cordial note that expressed a hope for his quick return to public life. "In my recollection, that department has never had so constructive and legal headship as you gave it," Hoover said. He would soon regret these words.[17]

XV

Teapot Dome and All That Jazz

ALBERT FALL WAS not alone—he was just the first of Harding's associates to put his hand in the pockets of his countrymen. While he was siphoning off the nation's petroleum reserves to his friends, there were lightning flashes on the horizon of other scandals. The only storm to break while Harding was alive centered about Charlie Forbes, who treated the Veterans Bureau as his personal fiefdom. Into the grasp of his jovial poker partner, the president had delivered an agency with an annual budget of nearly a half billion dollars—larger than that of any other part of the government. To the surprise of practically no one who knew him, Forbes wasted no time in launching a raid on the Treasury.

Forbes's betrayal was particularly bitter to Harding because he had come into the White House determined to do something for the human debris cast up by the war. The partial price of Woodrow Wilson's "war to end all wars" had been some three hundred thousand wounded and disabled veterans. Most desperate were the nearly one hundred thousand mental cases and tuberculosis victims. Shunted to poorhouses, insane asylums, and other inadequate public institutions, some did not receive any care at all. No existing government agency was equipped to deal with a problem of such magnitude, so Harding, a kind and generous man if nothing else, created the Veterans Bureau from a half-dozen or so overlapping and conflicting agencies, including "Doc" Sawyer's Federal Hospitalization Bureau.[1]

The artfully smooth Forbes had no trouble in convincing the President that he was building hospitals at a rapid rate— Congress had appropriated $36 million for this purpose alone— and the men who had served the nation well were now receiving the care that they deserved. On several occasions, Harding cited the progress being made by the Veterans Bureau under the directorship of Forbes as an example of the accomplishments being made by all sectors of his administration.

One of the unanswered questions of the Harding years is why Forbes did not come under suspicion long before he did. Popular with men and alluring to women, he cut a wide swath on the Washington social scene. He gave elaborate dinner parties, and sometimes took over a half floor at the Traymore Hotel in Atlantic City for the lavish entertainment of government officials, Broadway and Hollywood stars, and other celebrities. Conditions were so relaxed in Washington, however, that no one thought it extraordinary that he lived so well on a salary of only $10,000 a year—except for "Doc" Sawyer. The newly minted brigadier hated Forbes for infringing on his territory and found a ready ally in Harry Daugherty. They discovered that Forbes was especially close to Elias A. Mortimer, a lobbyist for the Thompson-Black Construction Company of St. Louis and purveyor of booze to the White House.

In April 1922, Mortimer and his young and attractive wife accompanied Forbes on an inspection tour of sites for a dozen new veterans' hospitals that were to be built at a cost of $17 million. During a stopover in Chicago, Forbes told Mortimer that he needed $5,000 for expenses. Mortimer agreed to get it from his employers. When he returned, the Colonel and Mrs. Mortimer were rolling dice. Mortimer handed over ten crisp $500 bills and Forbes went back to the game and won $220 from Mrs. Mortimer. The trio then moved on to San Francisco, where a man who wanted to sell some land to Forbes took the precaution of sending two dozen quarts of wine to the hotel suite where the visitors were staying. The landowner got $105,000 for property estimated to be worth less than $20,000. During this stopover, Forbes, Mortimer, and Charles F. Hurley, another contractor, entered into an agreement in which they would split the profits on the hospital construction contracts. Although other firms entered low bids, somehow all the contracts seemed to go to the Mortimer and Hurley firms. Later that year, however, Mortimer began to grow suspicious of Forbes's attentions to his wife, and they had a falling out. To protect himself, Mortimer went to Daugherty.

In the meantime, with an unconcern that amounted to bravado, Forbes proceeded to empty fifty warehouses at Perryville, Maryland, that were crammed with badly needed hospital supplies. Having obtained full authority from the president for disposal of what he said were damaged goods, Forbes awarded a contract to a Boston company without advertising for bids. Other firms got wind of the sale and submitted proposals, but they weren't given any consideration. More than 150 box cars full of hospital supplies pulled out of Perryville: pajamas which had cost $1.50 a pair were sold for 30 cents, gauze purchased for $1.33 a roll went for 26 cents, and oiled paper bought at 60 cents a pound sold for 5 cents. A million towels that cost 34 cents each went for 3 cents. New sheets that had cost $1.27 a pair were sold for 27 cents at a time when the Veterans Bureau was buying fresh ones. Some were even sold the same day they arrived in the warehouse. All in all, Forbes disposed of supplies worth between $5 and $7 million for $600,000—while disabled veterans lacked bandages, bedding, and drugs.

Early in 1923, Daugherty informed Harding what was occurring at Perryville. Forbes was summoned to the White House for an explanation. He told the president that the supplies had been sold to cut down on storage expenses, which he overestimated at about twenty-five times above actual costs. Then he gave Harding a false appraisal of the value of the supplies and ignored repeated orders to halt the shipments. Four or five days after one of these meetings, Forbes suddenly departed for Europe without warning.

A visitor to the White House who had an appointment with the president on the same day as Forbes's last encounter with Harding reported that he was directed to the Red Room by mistake.[2] As he approached, he heard a voice from this room which sounded as if it were choking with anger. Entering, he was astonished to see Harding with a tight grip on the throat of a man huddled against the wall.

"You yellow rat!" the President was shouting. "You double-crossing bastard! If you ever—"

The visitor said something in shocked surprise, and Harding whirled about. He immediately loosened his grip on the other man, who staggered out, his face discolored and distorted with fear. To his visitor, the president said curtly: "I am sorry. You have an appointment. Come into the other room."

On his way out of the White House, the caller asked a doorman for the name of the man who had left just after he came in.

"That was Colonel Forbes of the Veterans Bureau, sir."

On February 15, 1923, Forbes sent in his resignation from Europe. Harding seemed satisfied and did nothing more about the affair, but a Senate investigating committee began looking into Forbes's stewardship of the Veterans Bureau. The inquiry took a surprising turn about two weeks later. Charles Cramer, the agency's general counsel who was suspected of having shared in the loot, locked himself into the bathroom of his home and put a bullet into his head. It was the first of the Harding administration suicides. Charlie Forbes was finally brought to book in 1925. A federal court jury found him guilty of conspiracy to defraud the government, and sentenced him to two years in Leavenworth Penitentiary and a $10,000 fine. It was estimated that he had raked in at least $2 million in graft.

Under Harry Daugherty, the Justice Department had become known as the "Department of Easy Virtue." The genial attorney general was regarded by many insiders as the center of a web of graft that extended into all parts of the Harding administration. Among the first charges leveled against Daugherty was that he had favored big business by failing to prosecute war fraud cases. There were rumors that indicted or indictable war profiteers who made the "proper" approach to the attorney general could have their cases settled out of court.

The most notorious case with which Daugherty was linked concerned the Alien Property Bureau, an agency which held in trust property seized from German interests during the war. One of the most valuable trusts administered by Colonel Thomas W. Miller, the Alien Property Custodian, consisted of 49 percent of the shares of the American Metal Company, which had been owned by a German bank. These shares were seized by the government in 1917 and sold on the open market for about $6 million, which had been invested in Liberty Bonds. In 1921, a German-Jewish banking family named Moses, which claimed ownership of American Metal, applied for the return of its assets, now worth almost $7 million.

Richard Merton, a member of the family, was dispatched to the United States to obtain control of the sequestered bonds. Immediately upon his arrival in New York, he went to John Foster Dulles, then a leading Wall Street lawyer, with the flimsy story that American Metal had been transferred to Swiss ownership shortly before the United States entered the war. Dulles was not encouraging, so Merton inquired on Wall Street for the name of someone "who could pave the way" to the Alien Property Custodian. He was referred to John King, a member of the Republican National Committee and a somewhat shady politician-businessman. King brought Jess Smith into the picture and on September 20, 1921, Colonel Miller, the Alien Property Custodian; Smith; Merton; and King met in New York. The very next day, the Alien Property Bureau agreed to accept Merton's claim and two days later, it was approved by the attorney general's office. Within the week, Miller drew checks on the Treasury for a total of $6,453,978.97 and two lots of Liberty Bonds valued at $514,350. These he took to New York for presentation to Merton at an elaborate dinner party provided by the German.

So elated was Merton at the quick action on his claim that he presented each of his guests $200 cigarette cases. This was followed up by more substantial mementos. King received $391,000 in bonds and $50,000 in cash. Of this, $224,000 was given to Jess Smith "for expediting the claim through his acquaintance in

Washington," while Miller got $50,000. Smith deposited $50,000 of the bonds in a joint account with Daugherty maintained in a hometown bank operated by Mal S. Daugherty, the attorney general's brother. Harry Daugherty later claimed that this was an account he had set up in Smith's name to hold funds collected for political purposes. The bonds that Smith deposited were a partial payment for collections made but not turned in until then, he said. Little more was ever learned about this account, as Daugherty burned all the records when the legal bloodhounds began baying at his heels.[3]

So widespread were the rumors of illegality in the Department of Justice that as early as 1922 there were demands for Daugherty's resignation. "I wouldn't have given thirty cents for the office of Attorney General," he told newsmen, "but I wouldn't surrender it for a million dollars." Some cynics said it may have been worth almost as much as that to him. In 1923, the House took up a resolution calling for the impeachment of Daugherty, a move which spurred him to take defensive action. William J. Burns, an erratic private detective who had been brought in by the attorney general to head the Federal Bureau of Investigation, and Gaston B. Means, his disreputable chief operative, were assigned to investigate the investigators. Means later declared that he had been told to dig up damaging information that could be used against Daugherty's chief inquisitor, Senator Burton K. Wheeler, a Montana Republican. Burglaries and telephone taps became commonplace in official Washington, and an attempt was made to frame Wheeler on a morals charge.

Throughout this tense period, Daugherty maintained his equilibrium, but the strain began to tell on Jess Smith. During the middle of May 1923, he visited his ex-wife, Roxy Stinson, in Washington Court House. Usually, he had been gay and full of stories about his success in Washington and the big money he was handling. On one occasion, he had shown her a money belt stuffed with seventy-five thousand-dollar bills. Another time, he told her that he had made $18,000 by arranging for the nationwide showing of the films of the Dempsey–Charpentier fight despite the legal ban on shipment of boxing movies across state lines. Now, she said, he was in a complete state of terror.

Suspicious and jumpy, Smith pleaded with friends to spend the night with him and when Roxy and he went out in the evening, insisted on walking down the middle of the street. Roxy vainly asked him to tell her about his troubles, but he answered, "No, no, no, just cheer me up, just cheer me up!" He asked her to help him destroy his papers—bank notes, records, cancelled checks, and letters. "It was pitiful," she said.

Along toward the end of May, Harry Daugherty came home to Washington Court House, too, and the old friends spent some time together at a fishing shack they jointly owned. One day, in a fit of irritation, Daugherty suddenly exploded at Smith's bumbling and mournful manner. He stormed out of the place, climbed into his car, and threatened to leave Jess there. There was no other way to get back to town except to walk. Daugherty eventually relented and gave his friend a lift. They drove back to town in silence. "Jess got out of Mr. Daugherty's car and walked right to the hardware store and got a gun," recalled Roxy Stinson. "He had made his decision." The day before leaving for Washington, Smith went to the cemetery where his mother was buried and laid a wreath on her grave. "I've been through hell, just plain hell!" he told B. E. Kelley, the city editor of the local paper who had accompanied him. "I don't think I have long to live."

For the next several days, Smith was alone at the Wardman Park apartment he shared with Daugherty while the attorney general was a guest at the White House. In a sudden shift of mood, Daugherty professed concern about his friend and asked Warren F. Martin, his secretary, to stay in the apartment with Smith. Early on the morning of May 30, 1923, Martin heard a loud noise in the adjoining room. He thought it was a door slamming and went back to sleep. Feeling restless, he got up about 6:40 A.M. and went into the sitting room, where he found Smith lying on the floor. His head was in a metal waste basket and he had a pistol in his right hand. A bullet had entered his left temple and come out the right side.

Martin immediately summoned William Burns, who lived on the floor below. Burns took charge of the investigation, and delayed so long in calling the Washington police that he had trouble finding the fatal weapon. He had somehow misplaced it—

or so he claimed. No autopsy was performed and the death was written off as a suicide. But Roxy Stinson insisted that Jess Smith had been right-handed—and it would have been extremely awkward for a right-handed man to shoot himself in the left side of the head.[4]

Just when Harding realized—if ever—that his administration was honeycombed with corruption is unknown. By the summer of 1923, enough evidence had piled up to have aroused questions in the mind of any prudent man. The blatant grafting of Charlie Forbes, the Smith and Cramer suicides, the rumors about Harry Daugherty's activities, and the rumblings from Albert Fall's handling of the oil leases were too much to be ignored. Tired and depressed, Harding sought a remedy that had never before failed him. He would go off on a speaking tour. He had the ability to please an audience and the effect stimulated him. As he put it, he would "go out into the country and 'bloviate.' "

On June 20, the presidential party was off to Alaska. At several places along the way, Harding stopped for speeches and it was noticed that as Washington was left farther behind, the crowds grew in size and enthusiasm. But the shadow of scandal still fell across Harding's path. In Kansas City, Albert Fall's wife requested a private interview with the president. Worried and wan, she was smuggled past the reporters covering the president and spent an hour with him. What they discussed was never revealed, but Harding emerged from the meeting looking agitated. The next day, the president told William Allen White: "In this job I am not worried about my enemies. I can take care of them. It is my friends who are giving me trouble."[5]

In Alaska, Harding heard more complaints about Fall's operations as interior secretary. Conservationists charged that he had been plotting to gain control of the public lands in the territory and turn them over to private developers. Just before leaving Alaska, the president received from Washington a long coded message which plainly upset him. For a day or so he appeared near collapse. On the sea voyage back to the United States, Harding called Herbert Hoover to his cabin and told the secretary of commerce that there was a great scandal brewing within the administration. Should it be aired or covered up? Hoover replied that scandal should be exposed to public view, to "at least get credit for integrity on our side." To fight off the nightmare which haunted him, Harding played bridge day and night. The other players sat in shifts so that one of them might have a break. This went on for so long that Hoover could never again bring himself to play the game.

Harding reached San Francisco worn out in body and mind. He was only fifty-seven, but already he looked and acted like an old man. Resting in his suite in the Palace Hotel on the evening of August 2, 1923, while Mrs. Harding read from a friendly article in the *Saturday Evening Post*, he suddenly shuddered and died. Harding had a history of heart trouble, but before long there were rumors that the President had died of food poisoning. Gaston Means spread an even more lurid tale: The president had been murdered by Mrs. Harding to spare him from public disgrace.

A genuine outpouring of national grief followed Harding's unexpected passing. The American people were still unaware of the scandals brewing behind the façade of his administration, and his popularity was high. As the funeral train moved across the nation to Washington, the tracks were lined with mourners paying their last respects. One night, while the president's body lay in state in the East Room of the White House, Florence Harding sat beside the open coffin. Putting her face close to that of her late husband, she whispered, "No one can hurt you now, Warren."[6]

A few months later, Teapot Dome gushered over, forever burying Harding's reputation in scandal. The long-awaited hearings by the Senate Committee on Public Lands and Surveys into the letting of the oil leases began on October 22, 1923, with Albert Fall as the first major witness. The hearings were held in the cavernous caucus room of the Senate Office Building—a room all marble and glittering chandeliers. Swaggering up to the witness table, Fall bore himself with "something more than his usual touch of quiet arrogance," said Mark Sullivan.[7] Senator Reed Smoot, the Utah Republican who was chairman of the committee, and the other majority members had no desire to embarrass their own administration, so the leadership passed by default to a Democrat, Senator Thomas Walsh of Montana. He was a skilled and doggedly persistent interrogator. The mountain of documents that Fall had submitted to the committee had, as designed, intimidated the other members, but Walsh had penetrated into the paper jungle deep enough to become convinced there was something radically wrong with Fall's activities.

While Fall and Walsh were both products of the same rough-and-tumble frontier environment and both had been elected to the Senate in 1912, there the similarity ended. Fall flamboyantly pursued any course that would line his pockets; Walsh was an austere Western progressive who had entered politics to break the political and economic stranglehold that the copper companies had on Montana. In his fight against corruption in politics and business, he had exhibited patient thoroughness and grim determination that was to be of value in his investigation of the oil leases. Unlike the Watergate and Iran–Contra investigators, who met in this same room, Walsh did not have a special counsel or a team of investigators to look for leads, turn up evidence, and question witnesses. He did it all himself.

Separated from each other by a green-baize–covered table, Fall regarded Walsh with amused arrogance while the Montana senator fixed the former interior secretary with a cold stare. Sparks seemed to fly between the two men. Fall accepted full responsibility for the leasing of the Elk Hills and Teapot Dome reserves and again cited "national security" as a defense for his actions. Angrily, he dismissed charges that his motives had been anything but patriotic and said they were based upon sound business principles. He claimed his plan for the construction of oil storage tanks at Pearl Harbor had more than doubled the fighting capacity of the Pacific fleet. At the conclusion of two days of testimony, Fall issued a categorical denial that he had accepted any compensation from Doheny or Sinclair. The two oil tycoons followed him to the witness chair and steadfastly claimed they had given Fall nothing in exchange for the leases. The arrangements made by

Fall were saving the American people millions of dollars, they said. The great confrontation was over—and most observers agreed that Walsh was pursuing a false trail.

Public interest in the hearings waned and press coverage all but ceased. Walsh was accused of engaging in character assassination and of scandalmongering. Newspapers denounced "the Democratic lynching bee" and said the inquiry smacked of "poison-tongued partisanship, pure malice and twittering hysteria." *The New York Times* found it "humiliating to think that we have come to the point where every idle tale and gratuitous suspicion . . . must be given resounding publicity." Walsh's telephone was tapped, his past was raked over by William Burns's agents, his mail was opened, his office ransacked, and his life threatened. Still, he persisted. Information kept coming in about the improvements made to Fall's ranch despite the hard times suffered by his neighbors, raising two key questions in Walsh's mind: What was the source of Fall's sudden prosperity? Had he, despite the heated denials of all concerned, been paid off by Sinclair and Doheny?

Walsh's digging for facts began to tell on Fall. He took to drink, and by the time Walsh again called him for questioning in December 1923, he was in a state of near-panic. Friends told him he must clear up the source of his money for the sake of his reputation and that of the Harding administration. Fall was too sick to appear in person, his doctors claimed, so the day after Christmas he sent the committee a long, rambling letter in which he said that in order to make improvements to his ranch, he had borrowed $100,000 from Edward B. McLean, with whom he had a "pleasant and close personal relationship." He added that "I have never approached E. L. Doheny or any one connected with him or any of his corporations, or of Mr. H. F. Sinclair or anyone connected with him. . . ."

Ned McLean was just the type of man who would lend a crony such a large sum of money. He had inherited a fortune from his father as well as control of the Cincinnati *Enquirer* and the Washington *Post*. A sportsman and big-time spender, he and his wife, Evalyn Walsh McLean, were close friends of President and Mrs. Harding, and were lavish partygivers. McLean was also friendly with the most raffish members of the administration and the *Post* became known as the "Court Journal." Mrs. McLean was the owner of the famous Hope Diamond, which, according to legend, was accompanied by bad luck—a fact that Ned McLean had reason to remember in later years.

It was later determined that Fall, who had fled to Atlantic City, had begged McLean to visit him on "a matter of life and death." The playboy-publisher, who was planning to go to Palm Beach, Florida, for the winter, diverted his private railway car to Atlantic City. Fall came quickly to the point. Would McLean say that he loaned him $100,000? "It has nothing to do with Harry Sinclair or Teapot Dome," Fall assured McLean. "They are barking up the wrong tree." McLean agreed to say that he had given his friend the money and quickly departed for warmer climes.

Fall's story started to come apart when Senator Walsh noted that McLean seemed to be dodging an appearance before the committee in which he would be asked to verify the ex-secretary's statement. He remained in Florida, and his physicians bombarded the committee with letters contending that it would be injurious to his health for him to come to Washington that winter. Suspicions aroused, Walsh decided to go South himself, to take McLean's testimony in person. McLean had established a network of agents to spy upon the committee and to keep him informed of Walsh's movements. On January 9, 1924, the following coded message was received in Palm Beach:

JAGUAR BAPTISICAL STOWAGE BEADLE 1235 HUFF PULSATOR COMME-
NAL FITFUL. LAMBERT CONATION FECUND HYBRIDIZE.

"Jaguar" was the apt code name for Senator Walsh and he had left on the 12:35 train to Florida. Two days later, McLean gave Walsh a story designed to both protect Fall and save himself from a perjury charge. In December 1921, he said that Fall had come to him and asked for a loan of $100,000. McLean said he had given Fall several checks—he couldn't recall how many—on different banks and Fall had signed a personal note for the amount. Several days later, however, McLean said he had again met Fall, who told him he had made other arrangements and returned the uncashed checks. Unfortunately, he had no check stubs to support his story because it was not his habit to keep them. Walsh put no stock in the tale because he had already inspected McLean's bank account and had found he never kept enough in it to cover a $100,000 check.

As soon as he returned to Washington, the senator told the press that Fall had lied to the committee. This was the turning point of the investigation. Conflicting testimony about oil drainage and storage tanks for the navy was pretty dull stuff, but a cabinet officer who lied to a Senate committee, a playboy who told one story and then another, and a mysterious $100,000 "loan" had all the earmarks of a sensation. Everybody began asking where Fall had gotten the money—and Teapot Dome was suddenly transformed into a household word.[8]

In the midst of these revelations, the hearings produced a moment of hilarity. On January 21, 1924, Archie Roosevelt, one of Theodore Roosevelt's sons, his older brother, Theodore, and his sister, Alice Longworth, all marched into the committee room crammed with the largest crowd since Fall had testified four months before. Archie, who had been prodded by the rest of the clan, came forward to divulge information he had picked up while in the employ of Harry Sinclair. Immediately after learning that McLean had changed his story, Sinclair had suddenly realized he had business in Europe and left on the next boat.

Testifying in a confused and halting manner, Roosevelt said that he had discussed Sinclair's hasty departure with Gustav D. Wahlberg, the tycoon's secretary. He had asked Wahlberg point-blank if he thought their employer had bribed Fall to get the Teapot Dome lease. Bribery is a nasty word, the secretary was said to have answered. As an afterthought he added, "I think somebody may have lent Mr. Fall money." And, according to Roosevelt, Wahlberg said that he was worried about "a payment which was made to a foreman of Mr. Fall's ranch; that amount was $68,000; and that he had the canceled checks." When it came his turn to testify, Wahlberg said that Archie had misunderstood what he had been told. He had been talking about cattle shipped to Fall's ranch—"six or eight cows" not "sixty-eight thous."

With all kinds of rumors afloat in Washington as to the sources of Fall's $100,000, Doheny voluntarily appeared as a witness for the second time on January 24. Yes, he acknowledged, he let Fall have the money in question and had a note signed by the ex-secretary. When the noninterest-bearing note was produced, it was found the signature had been torn off. Doheny said he had done this himself as a precaution so that if he should die unexpectedly his estate would not mistakenly press his old friend for payment. Doheny said that he regretted that he had not told the committee about the loan at his first appearance as a witness but he had regarded it as a private matter having nothing to do with the oil leases. Like Vice-President Rockefeller, who during his confirmation hearing a half-century later was to dismiss inquiries about his large gifts to public officials with an airy wave of the hand, Doheny described the "loan" of $100,000 as a mere bagatelle . . . "no more than $25 or perhaps $50 to the ordinary individual."[9]

"I can appreciate that on your side," Walsh remarked dryly, "but looking at it from Senator Fall's side it was quite a loan." And when another senator asked Doheny about the possibility that Fall was bound to favor him in awarding leases as a result of the loan, the witness replied: "I don't think he is more than human"—a remark greeted by a wave of laughter from the assembled newsmen and spectators. Bristling under the barrage of questions, Doheny dropped another bombshell. When asked if he had employed any cabinet officers subsequent to their retirement, Doheny acknowledged that he had.

"Who?"

"Well, I am trying to think now. . . . At the time when our properties were greatly menaced in Mexico by the hostile attitude of the Mexican government, I employed ex-Secretary McAdoo."

With a shout, the reporters rushed from the room to a bank of telephones. William G. McAdoo was Woodrow Wilson's son-in-law and had served as his secretary of the Treasury. At this very moment, he was the front-runner for the Democratic nomination. Doheny claimed to have paid him $250,000 for legal services. McAdoo immediately demanded to appear before the committee, and testified that his law firm had been retained by Doheny for a much smaller sum and in matters that had nothing to do with the oil leases. But the damage was done. So pervasive was the smell of corruption that anyone remotely connected with oil was in the public mind automatically guilty. At a tumultuous Democratic convention later that year, McAdoo's name was greeted with cries of "Oil! Oil! Oil!" and he fell by the wayside.[10]

In the meantime, Albert Fall had come before the committee a second time. His lawyers attempted to avoid the confrontation by claiming that he was too sick to testify. At best, they suggested that a few members of the committee visit him, saying there was ample precedent. Walsh, however, no doubt remembering Fall's own insistence in 1920 upon intruding into President Wilson's sickroom, refused the suggestion. He thought it would probably backfire and create sympathy for Fall. Instead, the committee sent its own physicians to examine the witness. They certified that he was in condition to testify and a subpoena was issued forthwith.

The hearing room was filled to capacity on February 2, 1924, when Fall, leaning upon a cane and the arm of his attorney, made his way through a crush of spectators. There were few traces of the flamboyant land baron in this scarecrow figure in a wrinkled blue suit. From his pocket he produced a statement and began to read in a flat voice. The opening words were familiar to every lawyer in the room: "I decline . . . to answer any questions, on the ground that it may tend to incriminate me." When he had finished, he pulled himself to his feet, and avoiding the eyes of his former colleagues left the room. The tapping of his cane could be heard as he shuffled down the marble corridor and it was a long time before the sound was gone.[11]

On the same day that Fall was making this pathetic appearance before the committee, Congress approved a joint resolution calling upon Calvin Coolidge, who had succeeded Harding in the White House, to appoint a special counsel independent of Harry Daugherty's Department of Justice to bring suit for the cancellation of the oil leases to Doheny and Sinclair. A few days later, there was talk of impeachment against Edwin Denby, the blundering navy secretary who had turned the petroleum reserves over to Fall. Senator Walsh, however, opposed such action against

Denby. "Stupidity is not a ground of impeachment, so far as I can learn," he declared.

Coolidge was in a quandary. Although he had hoped that the scandals would blow over without action on his part, he realized that if he wanted to win the presidency in his own right, he would have to free himself of the embarrassments inherited from his predecessor. The electoral prospects of the Republicans were so dim in 1924 that one senator observed: "The question is not so much whether the Republican party will be defeated as to whether it will survive." Perhaps in jest, a Democratic leader suggested that the party run on a platform emblazoned "Thou Shalt Not Steal."

At the end of February, Coolidge finally made his move. He got rid of Denby and stepped up pressure on Daugherty to resign from the cabinet. Even more important, he appointed two special co-counsel to look into every aspect of the oil frauds: Owen J. Roberts, a Republican and a former professor at the University of Pennsylvania Law School, who would one day be a Supreme Court justice, and Atlee Pomerene, onetime Democratic senator from Ohio. Now wrapped in pristine Yankee virtue, Coolidge went on to win the presidential election from the bitterly divided Democrats that November.

Roberts was the junior counsel, but before long he took over the actual control of the investigation and prosecution of the oil cases. Roberts and Pomerene did not realize the magnitude of the task before them, however. With the exception of the trials, they thought their work could be completed in perhaps three months. A half-dozen years later, they were still trying to unravel all the threads of the Harding scandals.

Harry Daugherty was finally forced out of the cabinet in March 1924. A request by Senator Wheeler's committee that Daugherty allow one of its staff members to examine Department of Justice records gave Daugherty his final shove. He refused to countenance what he said was a "fishing expedition" into his files despite a direct order from the President. Coolidge followed it up with a demand for his resignation. Wheeler ultimately uncovered evidence that seemed to link Daugherty to the American Metal Company case, and the former Attorney General and Thomas Miller, the Alien Property Custodian, were brought to trial in New York in 1926 on charges of conspiracy to defraud the government.

Daugherty claimed that, except for signing his name to a ruling already made by others, he had nothing to do with the American Metal case. Lower-echelon officials in both the Department of Justice and the Alien Property Bureau supported his statements, saying they took full responsibility for the release of the firm's assets. Nevertheless, the disclosure that Daugherty had personally burned all the records pertaining to the special account Jess Smith had kept in his brother's bank raised ugly implications that could only be refuted by his own testimony. But instead of taking the stand, Daugherty produced a handwritten statement that sent a tremor through the nation:

> Having been personal attorney for Warren G. Harding before he was Senator from Ohio and while he was Senator, and thereafter until his death . . .
>
> And having been Attorney General of the United States during the time President Harding served as President . . .
>
> I refuse to testify and answer questions put to me, because: The answer I might give or make and the testimony I might give might tend to incriminate me. . . .

Daugherty's reasons for refusing to testify suggested to most people that Harding was personally involved in the scandal, and his old friend was protecting his memory. These suspicions were further heightened when Max D. Steuer, Daugherty's attorney, later declared that "if the jury knew the real reason for destroying the ledger sheets [of the special account] they would commend rather than condemn Mr. Daugherty."

The question remains, however, whether Daugherty wished to create the impression that he was protecting Harding's name in order to protect himself. If so, the scheme worked. After deliberating sixty-five hours, the jury convicted Miller, who served thirteen months in prison, but failed to agree on a verdict on

Daugherty. As the *Nation* observed, "The jury decided that a President's good name was at stake." In 1927, Daugherty was tried once more; again he refused to take the stand, and again the jury disagreed. Daugherty could say "no charge against me was ever proven in any court"—but it was a hollow victory. He had escaped punishment only at the cost of Harding's reputation.[12]

Senator Walsh's investigation had uncovered the fact that Doheny had given Fall $100,000, but there was still no proof that Sinclair had paid off the secretary. To find the missing link between Sinclair and Fall, Roberts put a four-man team of Secret Service men to combing banks all across the West for accounts in Fall's name. The investigators struck pay dirt in a bank in Pueblo, Colorado after a lengthy search. Records on file disclosed that two years before, $233,500 in Liberty Bonds with consecutive serial numbers had passed through an account bearing Fall's name. These numbers were checked against records in the Treasury and ultimately led to a Toronto bank and then by devious paths to the mysterious Continental Trading Company—and Harry Sinclair.

Sinclair was also in trouble on another front. Summoned to appear before the Senate committee for the sixth time, he refused to answer questions—but not on Fifth Amendment grounds like Fall and Daugherty. He contended that the committee had no right to question him because the government had filed suit for cancellation of the oil leases and the cases were pending in the courts. By a vote of 72 to 1, the Senate cited Sinclair for contempt.* After a long, drawn-out court battle, he was fined $1,000 and sentenced to three months in the District of Columbia jail.[13]

The legal proceedings to which Sinclair referred were civil suits in which the government contended the leases should be canceled on grounds that they had been clouded by bribery and collusion. They were a part of a carefully thought out strategy

* The only senator to vote against the citation was Davis Elkins of West Virginia, who had been the only senator to vote against a resolution calling for an investigation of Daugherty's operations. Elkins, as it turned out, had speculated heavily in Sinclair stock.

evolved by Roberts and Pomerene. Once the fraud was firmly established in the civil courts, the special counsel would then seek criminal indictments of the conspirators. The first of these cases, involving the Elk Hills lease, was tried in Los Angeles in October 1924. While this suit was still under adjudication, the counterpart suit to annul the Teapot Dome lease was heard in Cheyenne in March 1925. A month and a half later, the Elk Hills lease was ordered canceled on grounds that it had been tainted with fraud. Judge Paul J. McCormick said that Doheny's payment of $100,000 to Fall was against good morals and public policy. "The injury that has been done the nation, as well as the distrust of public officers that it has caused, cannot be overestimated," he declared.

But only a few weeks later, Judge T. Blake Kennedy held that the Teapot Dome lease was valid. Doheny immediately appealed the decision in the Elk Hills case, while the government appealed Kennedy's ruling on the Teapot Dome lease. Roberts had the satisfaction of seeing the ruling against Doheny upheld and the verdict favoring Sinclair reversed. In a scathing decision reversing Judge Kennedy, a United States Circuit Court of Appeals concluded that "the entire transaction is tainted with favoritism, collusion, and corruption, defeating the proper and lawful functions of government."[14] Doheny and Sinclair were ultimately forced to pay the government some $35 million for the oil taken from the two reserves.

With the first part of their strategy successful, Roberts and Pomerene now shifted their efforts to the criminal courts. On November 28, 1926, Fall and Doheny went on trial in Washington on charges of conspiracy to defraud the government. The jury was ordered sequestered, prompting some newspapers to caustically observe that the jurors were the only people who had been locked up so far. Fall was frail and trembling as he faced the jury, while Doheny was the picture of outraged honesty. Frank J. Hogan, his attorney, dwelt at length on his patriotic gesture in building the storage tanks at Pearl Harbor, and how they had strengthened the fleet in the face of threats from Japan. He also painted a sentimental picture of two old prospecting pals, one who had struck it rich and had generously come to the assistance of his less fortunate friend in a time of great need.

Having wrapped the flag about Doheny, Hogan proceeded to drape Fall in Harding's shroud. Fall, he said, had been selected for the cabinet "by the able and lovable and as fine-hearted a President as we have ever had, or will ever have." The cash that Doheny had given Fall was described as "the cleanest money that ever passed from the hands of one man to another." After deliberating overnight, the jury brought in a verdict of innocent for both parties. Fall and Doheny expressed profound admiration of the jury system, but Senator "Tom-Tom" Heflin of Alabama expressed the opinion of many Americans when he said they were "two of the most high-handed highwaymen the country has ever produced."[15]

Undismayed at the setback, Roberts and Pomerene pressed ahead with the trial of Fall and Sinclair on similar conspiracy charges. Shortly before the trial opened on October 17, 1927, the Supreme Court upheld the reversal of Judge Kennedy's ruling on the validity of the Teapot Dome lease. Justice Pierce Butler, speaking for the majority, branded Fall a faithless public servant "willing to conspire against the public interest." With these strong words on the record, the defense could not rely on invoking the flag, a war scare in the Pacific, and Harding's ghost. More practical methods for ensuring a favorable verdict were needed. William Burns, now back at his private detective agency after being ousted from the F.B.I. and replaced by his assistant, a young bureaucrat named J. Edgar Hoover, was given the task of supplying this insurance.

Within a few days after the start of the trial, the Washington *Herald* received a tip that one of the jurors—who had not been locked up this time—had told a friend that the case would end with a hung jury. "If I don't get an automobile as long as this block, I will be very much disappointed," the tipster quoted the juror as having said. The story was confirmed by a reporter. The information was passed on to Roberts, who had also learned that Burns's detectives were shadowing the jury with the intention of making it appear that the surveillance was being conducted by the prosecution. A mistrial was declared, and one more sensation was piled upon the plethora of scandals that had gushed from Teapot Dome. Sinclair and Burns were tried for criminal contempt. Despite the efforts of fifteen lawyers, Sinclair was convicted and sentenced to six months in the Washington jail. He had the dubious honor of being found in contempt of both the Senate and federal courts.[16]

While Roberts and Pomerene prepared for a new trial for Fall and Sinclair, Senator Walsh was following the trail of another batch of the Liberty bonds that had been Sinclair's share of the Continental Trading Company loot. Some of the bonds were traced into the coffers of the Republican National Committee. Will Hays, who had been postmaster general under Harding and chairman of the National Committee, was summoned to provide an explanation. Squirming under Walsh's questions and sometimes so rattled that he leaped out of the witness chair, Hays was forced to admit that in 1923, after the Teapot Dome scandal had broken, he had asked Sinclair to help him settle the $1.2 million deficit left over from the 1920 election campaign.

Sinclair, in need of as many political friends as he could find, "loaned" Hays $260,000 in Liberty Bonds. Hays had then peddled them to prominent Republicans in exchange for cash contributions. Some slips of paper found among the effects of the late John T. Pratt, a long-time Republican "fat cat" bearing the scrawled names of those who had come to the aid of the party were introduced into evidence. An official of the Pratt estate was called upon to read off the names. With the aid of a magnifying glass, he determined the first one was "Weeks."

"What is the next one?"

"I am trying to read it," replied the witness. "See if that is 'Candy.' "

" 'Candy?' Might it not be 'Andy?' "

Agreeing that indeed the name might well be "Andy," the witness then said he had not the slightest idea who "Andy," could be. A gale of laughter swept the room, for everyone present had immediately identified "Andy" as Andrew Mellon, the secretary of the Treasury.

Mellon came dashing up to Capitol Hill from the other end of

Pennsylvania Avenue to testify he had received $50,000 in Liberty bonds from Hays but had returned them. Instead, he had made a no-strings donation to the party of an equal amount. Of course, he knew that Harry Sinclair was the source of the bonds, but professed to see no connection between his fellow tycoon's developing legal problems and his sudden generosity to the Republican party.[17]

Sinclair went on trial again in April 1928 for conspiring to defraud the government. Fall, whose doctors said he was too sick to stand the strain of a trial, was to be tried later. It was a decision he was to regret, for after deliberating less than two hours, the jury found Sinclair not guilty. Eleven months later, all appeals exhausted, Harry Sinclair began serving his two terms for contempt in the District of Columbia jail. With time off for good behavior, he was out in seven and a half months proclaiming "I was railroaded to jail in violation of common sense and common fairness." The same day that Sinclair had gone to jail, Fall's ranch, up for sale because its owner could not keep up the payments, was bought at auction by Doheny for $168,250. He allowed his old friend to continue to live there without charge.

Fall did not go on trial until October 7, 1929. This time he had taken the precaution of having the flamboyant Frank Hogan as his attorney. Hogan made his client's entry into the courtroom a pathetic scene guaranteed to wring a tear from the most hardened juror. Haggard and gasping for breath, Fall arrived in a wheelchair, clutching a cane and wearing a shirt collar three sizes too big for him. After the first day of the trial, the prosecution said it would move for a mistrial unless the jury was absent until Fall was lifted from his wheelchair, tucked into a large leather chair, and covered by blankets and shawls. Hogan pleaded with the jury to send this dying man "back to the sunshine of New Mexico," which prompted Judge William Hitz to observe with some asperity: "Neither you nor I have anything to do with sunshine. We are here to decide this case on the evidence and nothing else." The jury agreed. Fall was found guilty and sentenced to serve a year in jail and pay a fine of $100,000. Nevertheless, another jury refused to convict Doheny of having given the bribe for which Fall was jailed.[18]

On July 18, 1931, Albert B. Fall achieved the distinction of being the first cabinet officer in American history to go to prison.* More than a decade had passed since, at Fall's insistence, the unthinking Harding had signed an executive order transferring control of the naval petroleum reserves to the secretary of the interior. The easy money and loose morality of the age of "normalcy" had been swallowed up by the Great Depression, and the exact details of the Harding scandals had faded. Nevertheless, the name Teapot Dome still evoked emotion and controversy.

Some time after Warren Harding's death, a special committee chosen to select a design for his memorial met to consider a proposal submitted by John Russell Pope, a distinguished architect. Arriving late, one member took a glance at the model and threw up his hands.

"My God, gentlemen! You aren't going to take *this*?"

"Why not?" demanded the chairman.

"Stick a handle on here, and what have you got? A teapot!"[19]

---

* Fall served his full term in the New Mexico State Penitentiary at Santa Fe, except for time off for good behavior. Pleading poverty, he never paid the $100,000 fine. Although his lawyers had claimed he was at death's door, he recovered his health with remarkable speed, and lived on for another dozen years before dying in 1944 at the age of eighty-three. In 1935, Doheny died and his executors evicted Fall and his wife from the ranch. They moved to a shabby house in El Paso, Texas, where Mrs. Fall supported them both by running a small lunchroom.

XVI

Rounding Up the Usual Suspects

FRANKLIN D. ROOSEVELT put it best. Campaigning in Chicago for re-election in 1936, he boasted of the honesty with which his administration had managed the massive programs of emergency relief aimed at mitigating the worst aspects of the Great Depression. "In spite of all the demands for speed, the complexity of the problem and the vast sums of money involved, we have had no Teapot Dome," he declared. The verdict of history seems to bear him out, for it would have been difficult to hide any trace of corruption that might exist; Roosevelt was president longer than anyone else and his regime was subjected to microscopic scrutiny. "No scandal produced the conviction, indictment, or even the forced resignation of a member of the White House staff or any major New Deal administrator," according to one study.[1]

The reason for this phenomenon, so strikingly at variance with the traditional American political experience, was that Roosevelt held office at a time when the nation was undergoing one of its periodic reform binges. The stock market crash of 1929 and the ensuing depression not only wrecked the economy but also soured the public on the free-and-easy relationships of business and politics that had been omnipresent since the Civil War. American business leadership had been discredited by the crash and its inability to find solutions as all across the country factories closed, banks failed and farmers poured unsalable milk out on the highways.

The New Deal also brought with it the New Dealer. "At his best," says Arthur Schlesinger, Jr., "he was the ablest, most intelligent, and most disinterested public servant the United States has ever had."[2] Cut off by the Depression from such normal outlets for their talent as the prominent law firms and top universities, an army of bright young men—and a few women—swarmed to Washington. They drafted the legislation that put the Roosevelt Revolution into effect and manned the alphabet soup of government agencies spawned to administer it. Power passed from the paneled board rooms of Wall Street to the warren of offices crammed with battered furniture that suddenly sprang up all over Washington.

Unlike their predecessors, the New Dealers were uninterested in the usual rewards of public service, such as payoffs and kickbacks. Hardboiled, arrogant, and often jauntily cynical, they made a great show of avoiding the gushing sentimentality they attributed to earlier reformers. To them, reform meant nothing less than the redistribution of wealth. Most New Dealers adopted the easy amorality that the end justifies the means and worked in tandem with the political bosses—as long as the politicians cooperated in attaining national goals.

With some justification, Republicans charged that New Dealers "played politics with relief." The vast pool of jobs and the huge sums available for the taking were too much of a temptation for politicians from Roosevelt on down to the most insignificant ward heeler. By the 1936 campaign, relief "scandals" were common fodder for the newspapers and congressional investigators. But in proportion to the amount of money being bandied about—the then unheard-of sum of $20 billion was expended by New Deal welfare programs over seven years—the actual amount of graft was minor.

"How many ... employees have been involved, even in the

charges?" asked Harry Hopkins, the one time social worker, who directed these programs. "How many have you read about? One hundred? Two hundred? Two hundred and fifty? If it is 250, the total is exactly one one-hundredth of one percent of the people in the program. That makes us 99.99 percent pure. . . ."

Smoke was still rising from the battered ships of what had been the U.S. Pacific Fleet when President Roosevelt told a press conference shortly after the Japanese attack on Pearl Harbor that "old Dr. New Deal" had been replaced by "Dr. Win-the-War." Under the pressure of World War II, representatives of big business, who had regained confidence under ministrations of the much-criticized New Deal, pressed to the fore to offer their services. New Dealers made way for dollar-a-year and Without Compensation men (known as WOCs) who received no pay from the government but continued to draw salaries from their private employers. It was a situation fraught with the possibility of conflict of interest and favoritism.

Donald Nelson, the Sears, Roebuck executive named to direct the nation's industrial mobilization, defended the practice. "We must have . . . men who understand and can deal with industry's intricate structure and operation," he declared. But Senator Harry S. Truman, a Missouri Democrat, saw things differently. As chairman of the Senate Special Committee to Investigate the National Defense Program—soon to be known as the Truman Committee—he argued that it would be inviting corruption to accept representatives of companies with such a large stake in the defense program.

"I have had considerable experience in letting public contracts," Truman told the Senate, "and I have never yet found a contractor who, if not watched, would not leave the Government holding the bag."[3] Over the next three and a half years, Truman uncovered abundant evidence of excess profits, fraud, corruption, waste, extravagance, and mismanagement. The profits realized by some shipbuilders were so huge, one executive said, "If it hadn't been for taxes we couldn't have handled our profits without a steam shovel." And Edwin H. Sutherland, who studied the wartime behavior of seventy large corporations, found virtually all of them guilty of at least one "war crime."[4]

Two of the biggest scandals uncovered by the Truman Committee involved firms that held some of the largest contracts awarded during the war: the Curtiss-Wright Corporation and the Carnegie-Illinois Steel Corporation, principal subsidiary of United States Steel. In January 1943, the committee received complaints that the Curtiss-Wright plant in Lockland, Ohio, was turning out defective aircraft engines. "These engines were causing the deaths of some of our student pilots," Truman later declared.[5]

Following an investigation it was determined that even though the plant had been producing engines for almost two years, not a single one had been able to pass a required 150-hour quality test. Inspectors who protested against being pressured into approving defective engines were branded troublemakers and fired or transferred. Only after the Truman Committee brought these conditions to the attention of the public did the Air Force make its own inquiry, which confirmed the committee's finding of "gross negligence."[6]

Faulty inspection procedures and faked tests also figured in the Carnegie Steel case. The committee discovered that the steel plate to be used in construction of navy and merchant vessels did not meet specifications for tensile strength but had been passed by inspectors anyway. Top management tried to blame everything on lower-echelon workers, which prompted one committee member to observe: "How incredible its seems that subordinates . . . would risk their entire future without the hope of reward."[7]

Truman's determination to prevent profiteers from lining their pockets at the expense of the public paid off for both the nation—and for himself. It is estimated that upward of fifteen billion dollars was saved by the committee's efforts, plus the deterrent effect on the activities of shady contractors and influence peddlers. "The relatively few cases of graft and corruption discovered after the war supports the conclusion that the Committee forced higher standards on contractors and contracting officers than would have been the case its absence," states one authority.[8]

And the favorable publicity generated by the committee's activities made the Missourian an unexpected compromise candidate for the Democratic vice-presidential nomination in 1944. "Oh, shit!" the dazed Truman exclaimed in surprise when told he had been tapped by Roosevelt as his running mate.[9]

The Harding scandals were the last hurrah of old-fashioned thievery on the national level. In the wake of the New Deal, World War II, and the Cold War, big-time corruption became the domain of big business and industry. In the seventy years since the Ohio Gang tried to pry the dome off the Capitol, corruption became more sophisticated, more subtle. Of course, some politicians and bureaucrats are still obtuse enough to be caught dipping in the till—especially during the reign of Ronald Reagan—but such cases are far less common than they used to be. Governmental corruption is now more likely to be concerned with stealing elections as in Watergate or skullduggery on an international scale as in the Iran-Contra affair.

The Cold War gave birth to a permanent war economy, creating giant industries whose sole function was to produce goods and services of value only to the government. Other industries—including the railroads, airlines, shipping companies, and aircraft manufacturers—also demanded government subsidies. It became common practice for ailing industries to rattle the tin cup for government subsidies and loan guarantees to bail them out of troubles resulting from the stupidities of their own managers. If the government doesn't save us, they wail, it will mean the end of free enterprise—a concept gone, in fact, the way of the bustle and the buggy whip.

Bid-rigging, conflict of interest, looting financial institutions, influence peddling, and—in the case of defense contractors—huge cost overruns for defective equipment have become the accepted mode of ripping off the American taxpayer. Such institutionalized deceit is often protected by secret slush funds that run into the millions of dollars which are doled out through political action committees (PACs) to complaisant candidates in both parties and to officials to win contracts. As a result, a

network of politicians on the take, generals for hire, and consultants in corruption occupies an important place in American
government and business.

Franklin Roosevelt's death on April 12, 1945, thrust a shocked
Harry Truman into the White House—and into public view.
Some Americans had a shadowy recollection that the new president had had something to do with a Senate committee that had
rooted crooks out of the defense program, but to most he seemed
a reincarnation of the feckless Warren Harding. Superficial sim-
ilarities between Harding and Truman abounded. Both men
were products of the Middle West, were poorly educated, and
had come up through corrupt political organizations. Both liked
nothing so much as a friendly round of bourbon and ribald
stories with the cronies. And both had become president only
because they were acceptable to all factions of their parties, in
other words the lowest political denominator. Yet a vast chasm
separated Truman from Harding. Truman had a basic integrity
and a boundless capacity to expand his limited horizons.

The problems confronting the new president would have given
pause to a man even better prepared for the office than Truman.
He had not only to lead the country through the closing days of
World War II but to guide it around the pitfalls of the transition
to peace. But with a flinty determination, Truman faced up to
every problem and three of his achievements—the establishment
of the Marshall Plan, the organization of the Atlantic alliance,
and the Korean intervention—set the course for American policy
for four decades.

On the domestic side, Truman fared less well. The Fair Deal,
his attempt to complete the unfinished business of the New Deal,
was snagged in an unsympathetic Congress. Truman also turned
out to be too tolerant of his friends. Like Harding, he surrounded himself with cronies from Missouri and old World War I
buddies whose indiscretions helped to create what Republicans
happily called the "mess in Washington." When they were tripped
up, Truman's instincts were to defend them and check up later.
As president, he faithfully followed the precept he had learned in

Missouri politics: Loyalty was the most important virtue. Instead of getting rid of those who embarrassed him and didn't have the wit or grace to get out from underfoot, Truman instinctively leaped to the jugular of those who challenged the integrity of his men. "My people are honorable—all of them are!" he snapped.

Thus the Truman era was a field day for assorted fixers, five-percenters, and influence peddlers who battened onto the government. Smooth, shrewd, and unscrupulous, they offered their services as guides to the bureaucratic maze and the richness which lay at the end of it. A swollen federal budget, the millions of dollars' worth of surplus property waiting for disposal, the existence of cheap government credit, opportunities in such expanding programs as housing, and above all, the marvelous intricacies of the tax system with its welter of loopholes and special exemptions for the knowing, provided limitless opportunities for fast-buck operators.[10]

They were aided and abetted in their operations by the low ethical standards of some of the men Truman brought with him to the White House. I. F. Stone, the radical journalist, painted a vivid portrait of them:

> The composite impression was of big-bellied, good-natured guys who knew a lot of dirty jokes, spent as little time in their offices as possible, saw Washington as a chance to make useful "contacts," and were anxious to get what they could for themselves out of the experience. They were not unusually corrupt or especially wicked . . . they were just trying to get along. The Truman era was the era of the moocher.[11]

They included such men as General Harry Vaughn, Truman's military aide; Edwin W. Pauley, a special assistant to the secretary of the army; and Donald S. Dawson, a ranking White House assistant. All were old friends from either Missouri or his years in the Senate. Like the men themselves, the scandals in which they were involved were small-time stuff, but they allowed the Republicans to foster an impression of an administration as honeycombed with graft as those of Harding and Grant.

Pauley, a California oil man and onetime treasurer of the Democratic National Committee, was among the first to be tripped up.

With the end of the war and a worldwide shortage of grain, speculators were bidding up commodity prices and Pauley (who may or may not have had access to information from the Department of Agriculture) profited to the tune of $932,703 from grain speculation over a three-year period. Dr. Walter Graham, the president's personal physician, engaged in similar speculations on a less extravagant basis. In all, a House committee reported, 823 federal employees netted anywhere from ten to twenty million dollars in similar operations during 1947 and 1948.[12]

Gregarious, jovial Harry Vaughn caused Truman the most trouble. Vaughn had worked for Truman as a senatorial assistant and, after service in the army during World War II, was elevated by the new president to military aide and brigadier general, much to the consternation of the military establishment. In his new post, Vaughn pretty much operated as he had before the war, carrying on the "reference function" which is a large part of the real work of Congress and its staff. This consists of doing favors for fat cats with enough clout to merit such help. The problem was that Vaughn was no longer operating from a back room in the Senate Office Building but in the exalted atmosphere of the White House.[13]

Word quickly spread that General Vaughn was a good man to know—a telephone call from him to a government agency would expedite a loan or allocation of surplus property. Old friends renewed acquaintances, including John Maragon, a weasly former Kansas City bootblack who had parlayed a brassy audacity into a lucrative career as a five-percenter. Vaughn used his influence to help several of Maragon's clients win special preferences from various government agencies. In exchange for his help, one of Maragon's clients gave the general seven deep freezers, scarce items immediately after the war, to be distributed as he saw fit. Vaughn kept one and gave the rest to the White House, Truman's home in Independence, and several colleagues in the administration. Later, these freezers were transformed into the symbol of the corruption said to pervade the Truman administration.[14]

Vaughn continued to lend a hand to Maragon as well as to other influence peddlers and was finally tripped up when a New England furniture manufacturer complained to the pro-

Republican New York *Herald-Tribune* that he had been shaken down by a five-percenter who assured him that he had direct access to the presidential military aide. When a Senate committee began looking into the charges, Truman angrily refused to let Vaughn testify, but later changed his mind when it was looked upon as tacit admission of guilt. For two days, a squirming Vaughn was grilled about his relationship to the five-percenters and their various deals. In the end Maragon was found guilty of perjury and the committee stated it had no doubt that Vaughn had made his operations and those of others possible.

Truman neither asked for his old friend's resignation nor criticized him privately. When Vaughn volunteered to resign, he recalled that the president "got up and walked over and put his arm around my shoulder. He said, 'Harry, they're just trying to use you to embarrass me. You go out there and tell 'em to go to hell. We came in together and God damn it, we're going out together!' "[15] Even Vaughn's critics were forced to recognize he received nothing for his activities except the freezers, a box of cigars, and occasional meals and drinks. He had dispensed influence worth hundreds of thousands of dollars to the fixers who swarmed about him merely to be regarded as a fellow to be reckoned with in Washington.

In rapid succession scandal also struck the Truman-era Reconstruction Finance Corporation, the Department of Justice, and the Internal Revenue Service, where sixty-one employees were caught in cases involving the bribery of income tax agents. The RFC, created during the depths of the Depression to provide low-interest loans to harried businessmen, had been allowed to linger on long after the original reason for its establishment disappeared. As was to be expected when a government agency is turned loose with vast sums at its disposal and supervision is lax, a school of sharks ripped at it. Investigators found that a significant number of the loans had been made in clear defiance of sound business practices and the agency treated the suggestions of Donald Dawson, the president's chief patronage advisor, as virtual commands.[16]

Once again, Truman made the same hotheaded mistake he had made in the Vaughn affair by refusing to allow Dawson to face his accusers. Witness after witness linked him to the strange doings at the RFC. Records indicated that Dawson and William E. Boyle, the chairman of the Democratic National Committee, had, over a fifteen-month period, made scores of calls regarding loans to just one of the RFC directors. By the time Truman permitted Dawson to testify, no one believed his denials of exercising undue influence on the agency.

One of the more interesting characters flushed out by the inquiry was E. Merl Young, a Dawson protégé and "expediter" of RFC loans. Young's story was a true Horatio Alger tale—Washington style. Beginning as a $1,080-a-year government messenger in 1940, he worked himself up to a position as an RFC loan examiner. After he had approved loans to several firms, he left the agency and was placed on their payrolls. Next, he teamed up with a Washington lawyer named Joseph Rosenbaum, who specialized in representing applicants for loans before the RFC. In return for his efforts on behalf of Rosenbaum's clients, the attorney showered him with hundreds of thousands of dollars in fees and expensive gifts, including an $8,500 royal pastel mink coat for Young's wife, a White House secretary.*

Under questioning, Dawson denied he was responsible for Merl Young's rapid rise in Washington, but Senator J. William Fulbright, an Arkansas Democrat, exasperated by the aide's evasions, finally exploded: "If his influence or if his power to obtain salaries did not run to his association and close friendship with you, I cannot tell where it did run to." As for Young, he denied everything, claiming among other things that he had paid for the infamous mink coat. These protestations got him jailed for perjury. Truman brushed aside all the charges against Dawson, who in fact later claimed to be the last member of the Truman staff to leave the White House. "I watched the inauguration ceremony on television in the President's office," Dawson later told an interviewer. "When Eisenhower raised his hand and took the oath of office, I got up and walked out the door."[17]

---

* Rosenbaum obtained the coat at a discount and the firm which sold it to him put in for an RFC loan.

The Republican formula for victory in 1952 was "K_1C_2": Korea, Communism and Corruption. Of these, Dwight D. Eisenhower's vow to end the Democratic "mess in Washington" most stirred the multitude. All the talk of mink coats, deep freezers, and influence peddling had plunged the nation into one of its periodic binges of self-righteous indignation. Full play was allowed the thesis, always perversely attractive to Americans, that the country was teetering on the brink of moral collapse. Suddenly, graft in government became the root of all evil. Point-shaving by college basketball teams, mass cheating among West Point cadets, skyrocketing divorce rates, and mounting crime were all the fault of the hapless fellow in the White House. Preparing to run for the Senate, Mike DiSalle, Ohio's Democratic governor, was asked if he thought corruption would be an issue in the campaign. "I guess so," was the shrugged reply. "But I don't know who is going to take the affirmative."[18]

The American people have always been pushovers for political crusades—as long as only a minimum of personal sacrifice is demanded—and in Eisenhower they had a leader who was a past master of such pseudo-religious flimflam. In the early part of the 1940s he led the great crusade in Europe that destroyed Nazism; in the latter part of the decade, he was chief of North Atlantic Treaty Organization forces, which stood guard against the advance of communism. Thus an important part of Eisenhower's intellectual baggage was a tendency to drape military and political realities with overheated rhetoric. Now he prepared to lead another crusade, this one to drive the "crooks and cronies" from Washington.

Along with his vice-presidential running mate, Richard M. Nixon, the wolfishly ambitious junior senator from California, Eisenhower mounted a bitter attack against Democratic corruption. "When we are through, the experts in shady and shoddy government operations will be on the way back to the shadowy haunts in the shadowy sub-cellars of American politics from which they came," he told a cheering audience in Iowa. Nixon chimed in with the charge that "this administration is going to go down in history as a scandal-a-day administration."

Republicans were still chortling over this one-two punch

against the Democrats when the New York *Post* reported with lip-smacking relish that in 1950 a "millionaire's club" had secretly provided Nixon with a $16,000 fund to augment his senatorial salary. Dana C. Smith, the Pasadena attorney who had set up the fund, explained that seventy-six bankers, real estate speculators, and oil company executives had chipped in an average of $250 each to help Nixon become a national spokesman for conservatism and integrity in government. None of the money was for Nixon's personal use; everything had been spent on stationery, printing, travel, and the like.[19]

Early reactions to the *Post* story were predictable. The delighted Democrats declared that in view of Eisenhower's own emphasis on high morality in government, Nixon should be dropped from the ticket forthwith. The Republicans charged that the whole thing was a leftist conspiracy, but insiders were furious at Nixon for having led them into this trap. The atmosphere of integrity which surrounded Eisenhower was a far too valuable property to be jeopardized by even the remotest link to anyone who was politically tainted. Demands poured in for Nixon's resignation. Even more ominous was the silence from Eisenhower.

Unalloyed gloom settled over Nixon and his staff. There was a flood of editorials (including one from the leading pro-Eisenhower journal, the New York *Herald-Tribune*) urging him to withdraw. In Portland, Oregon, hecklers greeted him with signs reading: "Shh! Anyone who mentions $16,000 is a Communist" and "No Mink Coats for Nixon—Just Cold Cash." Nixon's closest advisors agreed that the only way he could salvage his candidacy was to bare his soul—and finances—on a nationwide radio and television hookup.

Fifty-five million Americans may have watched or listened on the evening of September 23, 1952, as Nixon struggled to preserve his political career. None of the money contributed to the fund had gone into his own pocket, he began. "Every penny of it was used to pay for political expenses that I did not think should be charged to the taxpayers." There were jabs at Adlai Stevenson, the Democratic presidential candidate, who (it had just been disclosed) had a special fund to pay extra money to underpaid top-rank state employees when he was governor of Illinois, and at Senator John J. Sparkman of Alabama, his running mate, who had put his wife on the Senate payroll.

"I don't happen to be a rich man," a tearful Nixon continued. "I worked my way through college. . . . We live rather modestly . . . Pat [Mrs. Nixon] doesn't have a mink coat . . . but she does have a respectable Republican cloth coat. . . . One thing I should tell you . . . we did get something—a gift—after the election. . . . It was a little cocker spaniel dog . . . black and white spotted. And our little girl—Tricia, the six-year-old—named it Checkers. And you know, the kids love that dog and I just want to say this right now, that regardless of what they say about it, we are going to keep it."

A last master stroke followed. "I know you wonder whether or not I am going to stay on the Republican ticket or resign. Let me say this: I don't believe I ought to quit because I am not a quitter. . . . But the decision, my friends, is not mine. . . . Wire or write the Republican National Committee whether you think I should get off; and whatever their decision is I will abide by it." By this slick maneuver, Nixon had outflanked Eisenhower and his liberal Eastern-establishment advisors who wanted him off the ticket and put it in the hands of the National Committee, whose Old Guard members were as conservative as he was.

Eisenhower, his wife, and several key aides watched Nixon's performance on a television set in the manager's office at the Cleveland Public Auditorium where the candidate was to speak later that evening. Intermittently, the general jabbed with a pencil at a small pad while Mrs. Eisenhower dabbed at her eyes with a handkerchief. When it was over, a mob of thirteen thousand of the party faithful who had seen the speech on television stamped their feet and yelled "We want Dick! We want Dick!" Eisenhower immediately sent Nixon a telegram congratulating him on his performance, but reserving a final decision until a meeting the next night in Wheeling, West Virginia.

The Republican National Committee was swamped by a blizzard of telephone calls and telegrams praising Nixon's courage and demanding that he remain on the ticket. The *Herald-Tribune* now claimed that Nixon had "cleared the air" while the Denver *Post* said he had "talked his way into the hearts of millions." *Variety*, the show-business bible, called the Checkers speech a successful soap opera. The next evening a more weighty voice delivered its verdict. As soon as Nixon's plane landed at a hilltop airfield near Wheeling, a lone figure darted out of a waiting crowd and climbed aboard the craft. Flashing his famous high-octane grin, Eisenhower put an arm around the surprised Nixon and enthusiastically declared: "You're my boy!"

In view of Eisenhower's commitment to morality in government it was expected that the general would establish the most exacting standards of conduct for the members of his administration. But under Eisenhower, *conflict of interest* became a household word. He failed not only to establish such standards, states David A. Frier, who has made the most thorough study of the subject, "but failed to even set the proper tone for an ethically strong adminis-tration by providing it with a personal example of impeccable behavior."[20]

Eisenhower's overwhelming victory over Stevenson represented not only a victory of party but also the return to power in Wash-ington of the businessman after twenty years of Democratic con-trol. Conservative by instinct and training, the general admired men who had amassed fortunes in business and industry. To a man who had never done it, there was something mystical about having met a payroll. He staffed his administration with business-men, but this was not the main cause conflict of interest was so frequent during his regime. Conflict of interest is as old as gov-ernment itself, and is not solely the burden of any one party. Eisenhower's appointees ran afoul of statutes against it because they reflected the moral imperatives of the corporate world which had nurtured them. They had a curious inability to discriminate between the welfare of businesses from which they came and that of the government.

There was Charlie Wilson who thought "What's good for Gen-eral Motors is good for the country"; Harold E. Talbott, who used the office of secretary of the air force to drum up business for his management consulting firm;* and Peter A. Strobel, the Commissioner of Buildings, who pressured the army into settling a claim held by his engineering company. There was the glacial Sherman Adams, Eisenhower's resident hatchet man, whose vicuña coat joined the Truman regime's deep freezers in our political folklore. And there was the Dixon–Yates utility contract, assailed as the biggest "giveaway" since Teapot Dome.

Ask almost anyone today to identify Dixon and Yates and you will probably receive either a blank stare or a wobbly guess that they were a comedy team popular in 1950s. Yet, as Eisenhower's first term reached midpoint, the names of these two Southern utility executives dominated the headlines and the ensuing scandal rocked the administration to its roots. Ostensibly, the affair stemmed from a dispute as to who would furnish additional electric power needed by the city of Memphis—the public-owned Tennessee Valley Authority or a private power company.[21]

TVA had been created by the New Deal as a combined navigation, flood control, and power project to revitalize the Tennessee Valley, and it was an unqualified success. But the growing prosperity of the area created a demand for more power, not only from the expanding cities and farm communities but also from the Atomic Energy Commission. TVA's decision to build steam-generating plants to supplement the water power which turned its first generators brought it into conflict with the private power industry and the business-oriented Eisenhower administration, which decreed that it should not be allowed to expand its existing capacities.

Thus, when Memphis officials asked that a new TVA steam-generating plant be constructed to provide additional power for their city, the administration rejected the proposal. Under the terms of a substitute plan, a private company organized by Edgar A. Dixon, president of Mid-South Utilities, and Eugene A. Yates,

* Talbott, who headed off a congressional investigation by resigning, did not slip out of Washington in the dark of night, however. He was awarded the Medal of Freedom as a flight of jet fighters dipped their wings in salute, 1,800 troops marched by, and the Air Force Band tootled away on "So Long, It's Been Good to Know You." It was almost enough to make a man want to be caught with his hand in the till.

board chairman of the Southern Company, was organized to produce power to be sold to the Atomic Energy Commission, but delivered to the TVA at a point near Memphis. TVA would then buy the power from the AEC and deliver it to the city.

The Dixon–Yates contract was violently opposed by TVA and public-power supporters who regarded it as the first step in the emasculation of the TVA. They claimed it was excessively costly to the government and was a "giveaway" to the private utilities. A bitter battle ensued, but the affair would have been too complicated for most Americans had not Stephen Mitchell, the chairman of the Democratic National Committee, charged that the president had engaged in questionable conduct in approving the contract. Mitchell broadly hinted that Eisenhower had given his approval because Bobby Jones, a famous golfer and presidential golfing partner, was a director in one of the firms involved in the Dixon–Yates combine.*

An angry Eisenhower brushed off these charges with the promise to make public the full facts concerning the contract negotiations. A week later, the Bureau of the Budget released what it said was a complete chronology of the transaction, which seemed to silence all but the most vociferous critics. But Senator Lister Hill, an Alabama Democrat and an original sponsor of TVA, made public a startling disclosure on February 18, 1955, after examining the documents. He said Adolphe H. Wenzell, a vice-president of First Boston Corporation, the investment banking firm which arranged for the financing of the Dixon–Yates combine, had also served as an unpaid consultant to the Budget Bureau on the contract and was instrumental in its approval. Wenzell's dual role in the negotiations had been purposely suppressed, Hill charged.

This disclosure revitalized the opposition to Dixon–Yates. Charges of blatant conflict of interest on Wenzell's part were accompanied by demands for cancellation of the contract— especially after Wenzell told a congressional committee that administration officials had been fully informed of First Boston's

---

* Eisenhower's passion for golf was so strong that this joke was popular in Washington: A foursome out on the course at the Burning Tree Club was approached one day by a Secret Service agent, who asked, "May the President play through? War has been declared."

ties to Dixon–Yates. Eisenhower remained adamant in his decision to press ahead with the contract but undermined his own case by revealing a lack of knowledge about it. The president's bumbling led Arthur Krock of the *New York Times*, an administration supporter, to observe that it was guilty of "a series of indefensible blunders, including an effort to cover up errors which . . . it should have been obvious would be exposed. . . . As Napoleon cynically remarked, a blunder is worse than a crime."

In the end, the entire unhappy affair was finally closed out when Memphis authorities (who had been opposed to Dixon–Yates all along) announced that the city would build a generating plant to meet its own needs. Somewhat disingenuously, the White House claimed that inasmuch as TVA had been prevented from expanding its operations, their basic position had been vindicated. Harry Truman, still smarting from Eisenhower's attacks on him, took a different view. "The trail of double dealing and deceit in this affair leads right to the White House—and straight up to that desk in the West Wing where I used to sit," he declared during the 1956 presidential campaign. Nevertheless, public confidence in Eisenhower, who had become a father figure to millions of Americans, was unshaken and he was re-elected to a second term by an even greater margin than four years before.

An old Russian proverb—there is usually one for every situation—states that when the wind blows those at the top of the tree have farthest to fall. In Dwight Eisenhower's Washington, no one was higher in the tree than Sherman Adams.[22] Taciturn and hardworking, Adams, a former governor of New Hampshire, was one of Eisenhower's earliest supporters for the presidency, and was his most powerful and influential aide. He handled tasks the president found either boring or distasteful, particularly politics, patronage, and domestic affairs.* Adams was so influential that

---

* Curiously, another former New Hampshire governor, John Sununu, was called upon to perform the same task for George Bush and got into trouble for his use of government aircraft for private affairs. Like Adams, Sununu was also fired after he offended Republican congressional members and was given the final shove by someone else than the President—in this case Bush's son.

he was regarded as the second most important person in the government. His influence was such that Eisenhower refused to approve policy papers that were not initialed "S.A. O.K." Adams aroused the ire of politicians because a significant part of his job was to say no to favor-seekers. He became the "abominable no man" while the president was loved by all.

Adams projected such an image of Yankee rectitude and incorruptability that little stock was first placed in charges that surfaced before the House Legislative Oversight Committee in June 1958, that he had used his influence to assist Bernard Goldfine, a New England textile manufacturer, in resolving his difficulties with the Securities and Exchange Commission and the Federal Trade Commission. In turn, Goldfine was said to have given him a $700 vicuña coat and a $2,400 Oriental rug and had picked up the tab for some $2,000 in hotel bills.

Instead of denying everything as expected, Adams admitted having accepted Goldfine's largess and making telephone inquiries about the cases pending against his friend, but then claimed he had done nothing improper. Here, at last, was a scandal the press and public could get its teeth into. It did not involve a complex utilities contract or the transgressions of comparatively unknown subcabinet-level officials, as in most of the conflict-of-interest cases that had surfaced in the Eisenhower administration. Adams's vicuña quickly became as famous as Harry Vaughn's deep freezers and Merl Young's mink.

Paradoxically, the Republicans were as eager to get rid of Adams as the Democrats. As the guardian of the Oval Office door and Eisenhower's chief hatchet man, he had made many enemies among the party faithful. Republican leaders were also worried that the affair would cost them votes in the midterm congressional elections. The final decision on Adams's future lay, however, with the president, who had his own problems with gifts from friends and admirers. Eisenhower had accepted presents ultimately valued at hundreds of thousands of dollars, including a herd of blooded cattle for his farm at Gettysburg.

"A gift is not necessarily a bribe," Eisenhower told a packed news conference in an attempt to show faith in his aide. "One is evil, the other is a tangible expression of friendship." The circumstances surrounding such gifts were vital in determining their propriety. "Among these circumstances," said the president, "are the character and the reputation of the individual, the record of his subsequent actions, and evidence of intent or lack of intent to exert undue influence." With this bit of philosophizing out of the way, he turned to a defense of Adams. "I personally like Governor Adams. I admire his abilities. I respect him because of his personal and official integrity. I need him."

Eisenhower's plaintive "I need him" had little effect on the Democrats and the Republican Old Guard, particularly after Senator Fred Payne of Maine, the recipient of a $3,500 interest-free loan from the ubiquitous Goldfine, was defeated for renomination. The president caved in to the demands for Adams's head. As was his usual practice when faced with a distasteful task, he dodged it and sent Vice-President Nixon to ask Adams for his resignation. Not long afterward, he tried to lessen the blow by inviting Adams back to the White House and presenting him with a large sterling silver punch bowl in honor of his "Tireless Service to the Public" and "Brilliant Performance of Every Duty."

The Eisenhower years came to an end with what may well be the second stolen presidential election in American history. Unlike the Hayes–Tilden contest in 1876, the evidence of chicanery in 1960 remains tantalizingly inconclusive. The basic facts are simple enough, however. John F. Kennedy defeated Richard Nixon by the smallest margin in American history—34,221,463 to 34,108,582 votes—or just 112,881 votes. With the presidency turning on only .1 percent of the ballots, it was only natural that the bloodhounds would fan out in such ballot-box finagling. And they found it.

Earl Mazo, a reporter for the New York *Herald-Tribune* and later Nixon's admiring biographer, began digging into the returns in notoriously corrupt Cook County, Illinois, and in Texas, the home of Senator Lyndon B. Johnson, the Democratic vice-presidential candidate.[23] He found evidence of rampant fraud and skullduggery in favor of the Democratic candidates in both baliwicks. Without the votes of Illinois and Texas, Kennedy would have been defeated and Nixon elected president. In eleven states a shift of less than 1 percent of the vote would have switched their electoral votes from the Democratic column to the Republican.

In Chicago, Mazo said, Mayor Richard J. Daley's machine employed "virtually every time-proven big-city trick, from voting tombstones and floaters to spoiling Republican ballots and tallying the 'votes' of those who had once lived on streets evacuated for superhighways." Daley's men did their work so well that the Democrats came out of Chicago with a big enough majority to enable the Kennedy–Johnson ticket to carry Illinois by only 8,858 votes out of 4,757,409 cast. The Republicans made an informal check of only 669 precincts in Cook County and came up with a net gain of 4,539 votes for Nixon. The Mafia controlled the important West Side wards and Sam Giancana, a don who shared the favors of party girl named Judith Exner with Kennedy, often bragged to her, "Listen honey, if it wasn't for me your boyfriend wouldn't even be in the White House."[24]*

And in Texas where Johnson had won the name "Landslide Lyndon" by winning an election by 87 votes in 1948, Mazo said "the election shenanigans ranged from ballot-box stuffing and jamming the Republican column on voting machines to misreading ballots cast for Republicans and double counting those for Democrats." The results in one precinct of Angelina County were typical. Only 86 people cast ballots, yet the official tally was 148 for Kennedy–Johnson to 24 for Nixon–Lodge. The Democratic ticket carried Texas by 46,257 of the 2,311,084 counted. There were also reports of irregularities by the Republicans in some states.

Soon after Mazo's first reports began appearing in the *Herald-Tribune*, he received a call from Nixon asking him to drop by for a chat. Mazo assumed that Nixon, who had received additional information regarding alleged electoral frauds, was planning to demand a federal investigation. Instead, he was in for a shock. Nixon asked him to discontinue the investigation for the sake of

---

* FBI wiretaps also revealed large Mafia donations to the Kennedy campaign during the pivotal Democratic primary race in West Virginia, which Kennedy had to win to show that a Catholic could carry an overwhelmingly Protestant state. Thomas Reeves, *A Question of Character: A Life of John Kennedy* (New York: 1991), p. 166.

national unity. "No one steals the presidency of the United States," he declared.

This was by far Richard Nixon's finest hour.

"We have over two million employees," said John F. Kennedy, shrugging off corruption charges during his administration. "You've got a good many people that take advantage or attempt to influence them to seek private gain. . . . Some succumb. Most do not." Kennedy spoke in 1962, as Camelot was being shaken by the disclosure of the shady operations of Billy Sol Estes, a Texas wheeler-dealer who built an empire on nonexistent ammonia-storage tanks and friendly contacts with the Department of Agriculture. No matter what his own personal indiscretions with women may have been, Kennedy took quick action to nip rumors that high-ranking officials were involved, and his administration emerged from the episode without serious blemish.

There was also the case of Navy Secretary Fred Korth, who used official stationery to drum up business for his Fort Worth bank and invited favored customers to cruise on the navy yacht. He was quickly shunted into oblivion with little ceremony. But foreshadowing the future, the "Irish Mafia" that surrounded Kennedy also opted for police-state methods against those who incurred their ire. Although Kennedy projected an image of idealism, his men wiretapped foes and dragooned the Internal Revenue Service into auditing their income tax returns.

Lyndon Johnson, who came to the White House following Kennedy's assassination in 1963, had a snake-oil salesman's manner that made many Americans automatically pat their wallets for reassurance. He was bedeviled by his past sponsorship of Bobby Baker, who parlayed the relationship into a multimillion-dollar fortune—and a jail term. Questions were also raised about how Johnson became one of the richest men ever to occupy the White House after a career spent entirely in public office. Estimated by *Life* magazine at some $14 million, the Johnson fortune purportedly owed its growth to the wise investment of Mrs. Johnson's comparatively modest inheritance in several remarkably lucrative broadcasting properties. It did not pass unnoticed, however, that the Federal Communications Commission issued several rulings of immense importance to the Johnson interests at a time when Johnson's clout in Washington was growing by Texas-sized leaps and bounds.

Nevertheless, in spite of such periodic tremors, corruption appeared to have subsided as an issue in American public life by the 1970s. Scandals of the magnitude of the Credit Mobilier and Teapot Dome seemed like relics of long-buried societies. To most Americans, corruption had become a phenomenon that plagued the "soft" states of Asia, Africa, and Latin America rather than their own society.

And then came Watergate.

XVII

"I Am Not a Crook!"

How MANY PEOPLE now recall that one of Richard M. Nixon's first jobs was as a barker for a wheel of chance at the Slippery Gulch Rodeo in Prescott, Arizona? The youthful Nixon ran a legal wheel where prizes of hams and sides of bacon were the "come-on" for backroom poker and crap games. This seems altogether fitting because for more than forty years Nixon has been the consummate pitchman of American politics. Throughout his remarkable career, he has favored such oratorical sleight-of-hand as "I'm glad you asked that question" and "Now, what I am going to do is unprecedented in the history of American politics."[1]

Undoubtedly Nixon's most artful piece of political legerdemain was resurrecting himself from the political grave following his defeat by John Kennedy in 1960, a humiliating loss of the California governorship, and a disastrous "last press conference" two years later. In 1968, he came back from the shadows to win the presidency from the Democrats, bitterly divided by the Vietnam war and various social issues. Not even such artful political conspirators as Machiavelli or Abraham Lincoln could have more ably plotted his return to the national limelight.

To a people who desperately wished to put aside the searing divisions of the 1960s, Nixon offered leadership. He promised an end to the unwinnable war in Vietnam; to provide law and order after a period of instability, race riots, and assassinations; and to reunite a bitterly divided nation. "The next President must . . . calm [America's] angers, ease its terrible frictions and bring its people together again in peace and mutual respect," he declared.

Somewhere early in his political career, Nixon had acquired the derisive nickname "Tricky Dick." He never entirely lived it down, but as he climbed from senator to vice-president and finally to the White House, he gained a new measure of respect. By 1968, people were claiming to see a new Nixon, a man who had changed, who had risen from the ashes of defeat, who had tempered his harsher positions, who had become less strident, less accusatory than the ambitious young politician of previous incarnations.[2]

Few men came to the White House better prepared than Nixon. He was intelligent, tenacious, and self-disciplined; he had a capacity for hard work and a grasp of the complexity of domestic and world affairs. Moreover, he had demonstrated a political adroitness that earned the grudging respect of even his most unrelenting enemies. Nixon was unable to deliver on his promises during his first term, but by 1972, the war was winding down and the cities were comparatively peaceful. Most hopeful of all was the prospect of real peace throughout the world. His initiatives toward China and the Soviet Union were universally acclaimed and he appeared certain of re-election by a landslide. And then he tossed it all away.

In the narrowest sense, Nixon's presidency foundered on the bungled "third-rate burglary" of the offices of the Democratic National Committee in the Watergate office building, but in reality he was a victim of his own character. When the American people were finally ready to trust him, he was incapable of trusting America and its institutions. As the Greek philosopher Heraclitus observed many centuries ago, "A man's character is his fate."

In spite of all his successes, Nixon regarded himself as an outsider and disguised a visceral resentment toward those he felt had slighted him in a Uriah Heapish humility. He saw plots and conspiracies everywhere: in the press, in the wealthy Eastern establishment that dominated the Republican party, and in the top levels of the Washington bureaucracy—especially in the Central Intelligence Agency, which he believed had helped Kennedy in 1960. But he was not destroyed by these outside forces; it was all of his own doing. Nixon's ambitions, his insecurities, his aloofness, his resentments, his inability to inspire popular confidence, his penchant for secrecy—these were the things that forced him from the presidency.

Out of these failings grew the "Enemies List," the use of the CIA, the FBI, the IRS, and the White House "plumbers" to harass and strike at opponents and critics; intimidation of the press; "dirty tricks"; and the invocation of national security and the police state to cloak criminal action. In August 1971, John Dean 3d, the White House counsel, circulated a memo to the staff with the president's approval that set the tone. "How can we maximize the fact of our incumbency in dealing with persons known to be active in their opposition to our Administration?" he asked. "Stated a bit more bluntly—how can we use the available federal machinery to screw our political enemies?"[3]

Obsessed by the steady leakage of administration policy initiatives to the press, Nixon and his national security adviser, Henry A. Kissinger, ordered wiretaps on the telephones of National Security Council staffers, White House aides, and journalists under the guise of protecting national security. The publication in 1971 by the *New York Times* of the Pentagon Papers, a highly classified history of the American involvement in Vietnam, was the last straw. John Ehrlichman, a presidential assistant, organized a special investigative unit—the "plumbers"—to plug the leaks. On the recommendation of Charles Colson, G. Gordon Liddy and E. Howard Hunt were hired to supervise the operation.

If a computer search had been made for the two most absurdly dangerous men in Washington, it would have come up with Liddy and Hunt. Both had a history of flamboyance and trouble. Hunt, a onetime CIA officer and pseudonymous writer of paperback

thrillers, had a reputation for off-the-wall "cowboy" operations.*
Liddy was a former Bureau of Narcotics official whose major
claim to fame was that he had devised Operation Intercept, a
program designed to halt the flow of drugs from Mexico that had
succeeded only in angering thousands of returning American
tourists by creating mile-long tie-ups at border crossing points.

Liddy and Hunt brought on board James W. McCord, Jr., a
onetime CIA security man, and four Cuban exiles known to
Hunt from the Bay of Pigs operation. The first task of these
"plumbers" was the burglary of the office of the Los Angeles
psychiatrist treating Daniel Ellsberg, the former NSC staffer
charged with leaking the Pentagon Papers, with the hope of
finding information that would discredit him. Under White
House pressure, the CIA provided them with spy paraphernalia
and later on a psychiatric profile of Ellsberg.

Liddy also masterminded the disappearance of Dita Beard, a
lobbyist for International Telephone & Telegraph. A memo written by Beard fell into the hands of columnist Jack Anderson and
revealed an offer by the company to finance the 1972 Republican
convention in San Diego to the tune of $400,000 in exchange for
a favorable Justice Department ruling on its plan to absorb a large
insurance company. The money had been paid and Attorney
General John Mitchell gave the green light to the merger. With
the press and congressional investigators clamoring to talk to
Beard, Liddy whisked her away to a private hospital in Denver,
which conveniently reported she was too sick to be interviewed.
As a result of the heat generated by the Beard memo, the convention was eventually held in Miami.

In the meantime, the "dirty tricks" division of the Committee
to Re-Elect the President (CREEP) was also at work sabotaging

---

* While a successful secret agent is supposed to have a passion for anonymity, Hunt is said
to have arrived in Mexico City to take up his duties in a highly conspicuous yellow Cadillac
convertible, and during the Bay of Pigs fiasco he got drunk and openly displayed his CIA
credentials. He had retired from the CIA and was working at a routine public relations job
when hired by the White House.

Typical of Hunt's literary output is *The Coven* in which Jake Gault, the hero, confronts a
senator's wife: "Mind-blowing hot pants concealed her delta as she flexed a knee and one
long and lovely leg . . . stretching back her arms, she resembled Athena in full flight. And
just as braless. . . ."

and wreaking havoc in the campaigns of the various candidates for the Democratic presidential nomination. Some of their actions were silly, such as sending two hundred unordered pizzas to Senator Edmund Muskie's Washington headquarters or placing stink bombs in his Tampa office. Other tactics were vicious. Letters were sent smearing Senator Henry Jackson as a closet homosexual, and press leaks accused Hubert Humphrey of consorting with call girls. Forged documents were also created to implicate the Kennedy administration in the murder in 1963 of South Vietnamese President Ngo Dinh Diem.

Planning for the Watergate operation began in January 1972.[4] Liddy, who along with Hunt had been transferred to the staff of CREEP, unveiled a program—to be called Gemstone—to spy on radical and antiwar leaders and to disrupt their activities that included bugging, mugging and kidnapping. The price tag was a cool million dollars. John Mitchell, who was soon to take over CREEP, rejected it and told Liddy to come up with something more "realistic" and at the end of March a $250,000 proposal was approved. Checks totaling $89,000 in illegal corporate contributions to the campaign were laundered through a Mexican bank, and earmarked for the project. Another $25,000 check, directly from CREEP funds, was also added.

George McGovern, now the front-runner for the Democratic nomination, was Gemstone's first target but the attempt to bug his headquarters failed. The team next turned its attention to the office of Lawrence F. O'Brien, the Democratic National Chairman.* Two decades after the event, the unanswered questions of Watergate are who ordered the bugging of the DNC and why. In fact, Nixon's basic defense over the years has been that *he* knew nothing of it and could not understand *why* anyone would want to

---

* Larry O'Brien was not the first Democratic politician named O'Brien whose office was burgled by the Republicans. In 1930, Herbert Hoover ordered the Office of Naval Intelligence to break into the New York City office of another O'Brien to search for documents said to contain derogatory information about the president. ONI operatives broke into the office, only to find it empty. When O'Brien was finally located, he was placed under surveillance. The agents determined the he was a minor figure unlikely to have had access to important documents and the project was called off. Nathan Miller, *Spying for America: The Hidden History of American Intelligence* (New York: 1989), pp. 216–217.

do such a damn-fool thing. Nixon and his supporters have hinted that it was the work of the CIA or the Joint Chiefs of Staff, who were said to be eager to undercut the architect of détente with China and the Soviet Union.

Yet Nixon had been angry at O'Brien since the 1960 campaign, which he had managed for Kennedy. By 1972 he was obsessed with O'Brien and the fear that he might have evidence concerning large secret contributions made by Howard Hughes to Nixon's campaigns over the years or about a questionable loan to his feckless brother Don. O'Brien had also been sniping at the coincidence of the favorable antitrust settlement for ITT and its willingness to subsidize the GOP convention. No one ever assumed responsibility for actually ordering the break-in or was convicted of it, although several men went to jail for participating in it or taking part in the cover-up. Nevertheless, the evidence indicates the orders came from John Mitchell in response to unrelenting pressure from Nixon to discover what Larry O'Brien knew.

After two botched attempts, the burglars got into the DNC offices on May 27, 1972, and McCord placed taps on O'Brien's phone and that of an assistant. The bug on O'Brien's phone failed to work and Mitchell was dissatisfied with the information presented him. Liddy was ordered to get better intelligence and on the night of June 17, McCord and the four Cubans returned to the Watergate. Shortly after 1:00 A.M. the following day, a security guard spotted a garage door taped open and called the police, who placed the burglars under arrest at gunpoint. They were caught wearing rubber gloves and with bugging equipment and $3,200 in consecutively numbered hundred-dollar bills on them. Hunt and Liddy, who were monitoring the break-in from nearby, fled in a wild panic.

The president was at his vacation home at Key Biscayne in Florida when he learned of the arrests the following day. "It sounded preposterous" and he dismissed it as "some sort of prank," he later wrote in his memoirs. "It has to be some of the crazies" over at CREEP, he told H. R. Haldeman, his chief of staff, and instructed him to "get it as confused as possible." "Bizarre business," Nixon scribbled on a memo prepared for the guidance of his press secretary. "There's no involvement whatever by W H personnel."[5]

And so the cover-up began.

For the next 784 days, the American people were enmeshed in Watergate. Watergate even created a whole new vocabulary— *stonewalling* and *twisting slowly, slowly in the wind; limited hang-out* and *expletive deleted*. The basic pattern of lies, deceit, and deception was quickly put in place. Worried that the trail might lead to John Mitchell and the White House aides who had organized the "Plumbers" unit, Nixon involved himself in the cover-up from the beginning. He looked for a way to channel hush money to the burglars to ensure their silence and attempted to obstruct an FBI investigation. Nixon was concerned that the FBI might stumble upon the trail of secret funds that had been laundered in Mexico and funneled to the burglars by CREEP. At a meeting with Haldeman and Ehrlichman on June 23, the president decided to use the CIA to get the FBI to call off its Mexican inquiry.

No one seems to have discussed the possibility that the president might admit that some of his people had, in mistaken zeal, tried to bug the DNC, apologize, and then get on with the presidential campaign. Undoubtedly Nixon thought he could not come clean—even if he wanted to—because the break-in was merely the tip of the iceberg. Even the most cursory inquiry into the affair would lead to the exposure of what Mitchell was to call "White House horrors"—all the other crimes committed by the "plumbers" and CREEP's "dirty tricks" division. To admit one illegal activity would lead to the discovery of all.

That afternoon, Richard Helms, the director of Central Intelligence, and his deputy, General Vernon Walters, were summoned by Haldeman to the White House. Walters, who had built a military career on a facility for languages—he spoke eleven with some degree of fluency (and, it was said, talked too much in all of them)—had been a Nixon favorite since 1959 when he had braved a stone-throwing anti-Yankee mob in Caracas with the then vice-president. Haldeman told them that the president wanted them to tell L. Patrick Gray, the New England lawyer recently named acting head of the FBI after the death of long-time chief, J. Edgar Hoover, to drop the Mexican side of the inquiry. If the FBI pressed too hard, they were to say, legitimate CIA operations abroad would be jeopardized.

Helms replied, in effect, that he knew of no such operation but Haldeman insisted that Walters discuss the matter with Gray. Over the next several days, Walters and Gray sparred with each other over the Mexican connection, with the FBI chief all but imploring Walters to ask him to restrict the investigation in the interests of national security. Finally, on July 6, Walters firmly told Gray that the investigation constituted no threat to ongoing CIA operations in Mexico. The CIA also flatly rejected a White House proposal that it put up the bail and pay the legal and family expenses of the burglars.[6]

Nixon, in an attempt to deal with the public reaction to the burglary, directed John Dean to launch an inquiry into the affair. Dean's real role was to keep the lid on until at least the presidential election in November was over. Meantime, as a result of leaks, two young reporters for the Washington *Post*, Bob Woodward and Carl Bernstein, dredged up enough material to keep the Watergate story on the front page, but it had little impact outside Washington.[7]* A Gallup poll reported that 48 percent of the American people had never heard of the break-in.

Woodward and Bernstein focused on the money trail between the burglars and CREEP. In actuality, the real story lay in the Oval Office, where Nixon was orchestrating the cover-up and obstructing justice. He had involved the FBI and CIA and top White House aides in it; he had authorized the payment of hush money to the burglars and approved the destruction of incriminating documents.

---

* Woodward and Bernstein claimed the information came from a source they called Deep Throat. Although they have declined to identify Deep Throat, there is speculation that he was John Dean, or Fred Fielding, Dean's assistant, or Alexander Haig, who followed Haldeman as Nixon's chief of staff, among others. Others doubt that a single Deep Throat existed, but was a composite of sources. It is not unknown for a reporter who wishes to keep control of a story to tell his editors that he has sources who will speak *only* to him.

McGovern was unable to ignite voter outrage over Watergate and it had no effect upon the outcome of the election. On November 7, 1972, the president and his running mate, Spiro T. Agnew, were re-elected by a landslide. He won 60.7 percent of the total vote and carried every state except Massachusetts. But Nixon's satisfaction was tempered by the fact that the Democrats maintained control of Congress—and with it the power to instigate investigations and to issue subpoenas and swear witnesses.

Within a few months after the election, the cover-up began to unravel. The key figure was Chief Judge John J. Sirica of the U.S. District Court in Washington. Known as "Maximum John" because of his insistence on handing out stiff sentences to those convicted in his court, he also had an aversion to being lied to under oath. Liddy's soldier-of-fortune decision to be the fall guy by assuming full responsibility for the break-in, plus the stonewalling of Hunt, McCord, and the Cubans angered him. Once they pleaded guilty, Sirica made it plain that he intended to impose heavy sentences on them in an effort to ferret out the truth. At the same time, the Senate established a Watergate investigating committee to be headed by Senator Sam Ervin, a crusty North Carolina Democrat and onetime judge.

Buckling under Sirica's heavy-handed judicial blackmail, McCord wrote the judge a letter, which was read out in open court on March 23, 1973. It alleged there had been "political pressures" on the defendants to plead guilty, that perjury had been committed and that figures more exalted than Liddy were involved. With the notable exception of McCord (whose sentence was postponed), the burglars got stiff terms: Liddy six to twenty years; Hunt a "provisional" thirty-five years; and the Cubans a similarly "provisional" forty years each. "You must understand that I hold out no promises or hopes of any kind," Sirica told them. "But I do say that should you decide to speak freely I would have to weigh that factor in appraising what sentence will finally be imposed in each case."

McCord was immediately interviewed by the Senate Watergate

investigators and implicated John Dean and Jeb Magruder, Mitchell's deputy at CREEP, in the cover-up. A wave of fear swept through the White House, and it was everyone for himself. With varying degrees of speed, Nixon aides scurried about and obtained lawyers, went to the prosecutors, testified before the grand jury, were interviewed by Senate investigators, and leaked to the press. Like a striptease, the various layers of the cover-up were peeled away from the White House.

On April 30, in an effort to save himself, Nixon began throwing aides and friends overboard: Haldeman, Ehrlichman, and Dean were fired; Attorney General Richard Kleindienst and Pat Gray resigned. But Watergate, like Topsy, just grew and grew. By mid-1973, there were at least six separate investigations into its various aspects. A Washington grand jury indicted Haldeman, Ehrlichman, Mitchell, Dean, Magruder, and others on Watergate-related charges. Another jury, in New York, was looking into ties between former Commerce Secretary and CREEP treasurer Maurice H. Stans and fugitive financier Robert Vesco. The new attorney general, Elliot Richardson, had appointed a special Watergate prosecutor, Boston lawyer Archibald Cox, to conduct an investigation. And on May 17, 1973, the Senate Watergate Committee began its hearings.

Over the next thirty-seven days the ornate Old Senate Caucus Room, the same chamber where the Teapot Dome drama had been acted out nearly a half-century before, was the scene of a morality play. The American people were transfixed by the unfolding of a combination mystery story, soap opera, and psychodrama. If Richard Nixon was the unseen villain of the piece, Sam Ervin was the hero. He portrayed himself as a simple country lawyer but had graduated from Harvard Law School with honors. Ervin's slow drawl, white hair, quivering jowls, eyebrows that seemed permanently atwitch, and his eloquence in defense of the Constitution and individual rights made him into a cult figure. "Sam," said one observer, "is the only man who can read the transcript of a telephone conversation and make it sound like the King James version of the New Testament."

The hearings began with the small fry—the ex-policemen, the secretaries, the diligent but lowly members of CREEP—and built up to the star performers. John Dean finally appeared on June 25, and over the next four days accused the president of the United States of grave crimes. Hunched over the witness table with his mouth only inches from the microphone, Dean outlined the progress of the cover-up in startling detail. The White House countered by accusing him of him being its mastermind. Ehrlichman set the tone for the White House rebuttal by saying anything that was done was "well within both the constitutional duty and obligation of the President."

The exchange was fascinating, but the central questions of Watergate—What did the President know and when did he know it?—seemed unlikely to be resolved. Dean had incriminated Nixon, but there was no one to support his testimony. And then, on July 16, Alexander Butterfield, who was in charge of White House internal security, revealed the existence of an Oval Office taping system. For the last two years, he said, every word spoken there had been taken down by the voice-operated system, making it possible to check the authenticity of Dean's charges.*

Both the committee and special prosecutor demanded the tapes, but Nixon battled to keep them in his possession on grounds of national security and executive privilege. As the wagons were circled in the White House, the case went to the courts, with the final outcome destined for the Supreme Court. In the meantime, while Nixon was proclaiming "I am not a crook!", the nation was diverted by the decline and fall of Spiro Agnew, the paragon of law and order.

Throughout the Watergate hearings, Agnew had kept a low profile, playing a lot of golf and serving as host to various visiting dignitaries. Obviously, he hoped to keep his distance from the White House scandals and emerge as an untarnished candidate

---

* Nixon was hardly the first to install a secret tape machine in the White House. Both Franklin Roosevelt and John F. Kennedy used such devices; Herbert Hoover had a secretary listen in on telephone conversations and take shorthand notes. Roosevelt was one of those "bugged" in this fashion while he was president-elect.

for the Republican presidential nomination in 1976. Or if lightning struck, he would be Nixon's constitutionally ordained successor if Watergate forced the president out of office. These
possibilities must have been pleasing to a man smarting over the
undisguised contempt with which he was regarded by Nixon and
his aides. The president often joked that Agnew was his insurance policy against being assassinated.

Agnew's fantasies were rudely shattered in August 1973 by the
news that federal prosecutors were investigating him for having
taken bribes and kickbacks from highway contractors while he
was county executive of Baltimore County in Maryland from
1962 to 1967 and governor of Maryland from 1967 to 1969. Such
rumors had been circulating for years but were unproved. Some
of the payments were said to have been made even after Agnew
became vice-president. He was also suspected of accepting a
bribe in exchange for a high-level appointment in the General
Service Agency and payments to augment his salary.

Agnew blustered his innocence, calling the charges "damned
lies." But in October he quickly caved in under the threat of
indictment, or impeachment, or both, and resigned after cop-
ping a plea on tax-evasion charges. He paid a $10,000 fine and
was placed on three years' probation; Maryland authorities demanded repayment of $250,000 he was alleged to have received
as kickbacks. Gerald Ford, the veteran Republican leader in the
House, was named to succeed him as vice-president.[8]

The sleazy Agnew sideshow did not deflect interest from the
main ring for long, however. Nixon's bold attempt to head off the
demands of Archibald Cox for the tapes by firing him and Attorney General Richardson in a "Saturday Night Massacre" created
a firestorm of protest. These dismissals convinced many doubters
that Nixon really had something to hide. House Democratic
leaders ordered an inquiry into the possibility of impeaching the
president, and a new special prosecutor, Leon Jaworski, a Texas
lawyer, was named.

The net was closing inexorably about Nixon. Several top
aides—Haldeman, Ehrlichman, Mitchell, Kleindienst, and
Charles Colson among others—were convicted of or pleaded
guilty to various crimes. Nixon himself was named in a secret

Watergate grand jury report as an "unindicted co-conspirator." On July 24, 1974, the Supreme Court rejected the president's arguments of executive privilege and ruled 8 to 0 that he must turn over the tapes to Jaworski. Three days later, the House Judiciary Committee voted articles of impeachment. "Richard M. Nixon has acted," the committee intoned, "in a manner contrary to his trust as President and subversive of constitutional government, to the great prejudice of the cause of law and justice and to the manifest injury of the people of the United States."

Under duress, on August 5, 1974, Nixon released the tape of the June 23, 1972, meeting—known as "the smoking gun—in which he had instructed Haldeman and Ehrlichman to use the CIA to block the FBI investigation.* By taping himself, Nixon had recorded the drama of his own unworthiness for the presidency. Americans heard their leader talking as if he was a Mafia don organizing the rackets in Brooklyn. "I don't give a shit what happens," Nixon declared at one point. "I want you all to stonewall it, let them plead Fifth Amendment; cover up or anything else if it'll save it, save the plan."

Following these thunderbolts, all the Republicans who had voted against impeachment announced that they would change their votes when the matter came before the full House. Such Republican stalwarts as Senator Barry Goldwater of Arizona told Nixon he stood no chance of acquittal. Faced with impeachment, Nixon went on national television on the evening of August 8, 1974. But this time there was to be no "Checkers" speech, no last-minute rabbit from the hat, and he announced his resignation as of noon the following day. True to character, though, he tried sleight of hand. He was resigning not because of the impeachment threat but because he no longer had "a strong enough political base" in Congress to maintain himself in office.

As Nixon flew off to a California exile, his wife Pat seemed to sum it all up. "It's so sad," she said as the helicopter began to rise

* "I should have destroyed [the tapes]," Nixon told a television interviewer several years later. "There were several reasons why they were not burned. First, when the taping system was disclosed . . . I was in the hospital with pneumonia, and I just couldn't make tough decisions like that. Second, I had bad advice, from well-intentioned lawyers who had . . . the cockeyed notion that I would be destroying evidence."

from the White House grounds. "It's so sad." In the East Room of the White House, Gerald Ford attempted to exorcise the baleful spirit of his predecessor from American public life. "Our long nightmare is over," he proclaimed.

For a month, President Ford was bathed in public good will—mainly because he was *not* Richard Nixon. But on September 8, 1974, he signed a proclamation granting America's most notorious "non-indicted co-conspirator" a "full, free and absolute pardon" for any crimes he "committed or may have committed" during his presidency. It was time, said Ford, to end this "American tragedy" and move on. But the pardon was not accompanied by an act of contrition by Nixon and produced Ford's own firestorm. There were charges of a "corrupt bargain" between Nixon and Ford in which it was alleged that Ford had agreed to pardon Nixon if he were ousted from the presidency in exchange for being appointed vice-president. Barring the discovery of an Oval Office tape to that effect, however, such charges are likely to remain in the area of conjecture. Nevertheless, the anger stirred by the pardon helped cost Ford election to the presidency on his own in 1976.

Nixon had escaped criminal punishment for Watergate, but at least twenty-five of his aides and associates went to jail for terms of up to slightly over four years, with Liddy doing the longest stretch. In the years since, some have become rich writing Watergate books or on the lecture circuit; several found God. Nixon himself has refused to be exorcised. Although his enemies thought he had been buried at the crossroads with a stake through his heart, he rose once again to regain stature as an elder statesman and commentator on world affairs. It has been estimated that he has made three million dollars from books and television appearances since becoming the only American president ever to be forced to resign from office. Who says crime doesn't pay?

*   *   *

Watergate cracked the crust of public complacency that had scabbed over the issue of corruption in the United States. Yet it was unlike everything that had gone before. Compared with Watergate, Teapot Dome and its concomitant crudities was routine. Most important, the traditional motives of political skullduggery were absent in Watergate. Upward of $60 million was harvested by CREEP by techniques that ranged from auctioning off ambassadorships to shaking down contractors. Yet, except for Nixon's questionable tax returns and other sleazy attempts to enrich himself, there was no evidence that anyone tried to steal anything—except the 1972 presidential election—which, ironically, was already safely in the bag.

Watergate was about power, not money. Loyalty to the president rather than personal enrichment was the lodestar of the men involved in corrupting the electoral process. Unhampered by constitutional limitations and untroubled by moral constraints, they believed what was good for Richard Nixon was good for the United States. John Ehrlichman summed it up when he said: "The President is the government."

Watergate was no sudden aberration, however. The ground had been plowed and planted long before. The affair was the logical consequences of what Arthur Schlesinger has dubbed the "imperial presidency." Since the era of Franklin Roosevelt, he contends, the presidency has assumed control over the making of foreign policy at the expense of Congress, the judiciary, the press, and public opinion, which had previously exercised some restraints on the successive occupants of the White House. Presidents assumed an air of infallibility in the making of war and peace and, not unexpectedly, it was carried over into the domestic sector. What Nixon did was to carry the imperial presidency to its ultimate end: a revolutionary challenge to the separation of powers.

In the wake of Watergate, there was the usual demand for reform. Congress joined with Jimmy Carter, Ford's Democratic successor in the White House—who campaigned on a platform of "I'll never lie to you"—to declare a new era of post-Watergate morality. Ethical standards, guidelines, restraints on power, new laws and regulations flowed from the legislative mills. Senior government officials, members of Congress, and political candidates are required to file reams of paper about their income, honoraria, property, and debts. An Office of Government Ethics was created to police missteps by executive-branch employees. To prevent a repetition of Nixon's dismissal of Archibald Cox, special prosecutors can no longer be fired by presidential order.

Politicians also piously railed against the excesses of campaign funding and spending. Walter Mondale, Carter's vice-president, said the Watergate hearings had demonstrated that "Government and government decisions [were] up for sale to the highest bidder." Public funding of elections was suggested as a solution and Congress conceded such support for presidential elections. But Republican and Democratic incumbents, determined to keep potential opponents from gaining financial parity, successfully blocked public funding for congressional elections.

But there was a catch. The reforms laid the foundation for the next round of corruption. In the old days, such powerful figures as Senate Majority Leader Lyndon Johnson could collect cash in envelopes and then dole it out to colleagues. Now that's illegal, but the so-called special interests have had little difficulty in evading these laws. CREEP-style shakedowns have been replaced by political action committees (PACs). While PACs are limited to a contribution of $5,000 per candidate, subsidiary PACs were created to circumvent the law. An interest group, such as the American Medical Association, can by law establish one PAC per candidate, but its state and local affiliates could duplicate this support around the nation. And loopholes still enabled "fat cats" to give extravagantly by using family and friends as conduits for individual contributions. In 1988, Michael Dukakis received contributions of more than $100,000 each from 130 supporters; George Bush got 267 such donations.

XVIII

"It's Morning in America!"

YOU'VE REALLY GOT to hand it to Ronald Reagan. While preaching against waste, fraud, and abuse of government power, he presided for eight years over an administration that combined the old-fashioned graft of the Grant and Harding eras with an undisguised grab for power that would have done credit to Richard Nixon. Yet, when he left the White House as the first president since Dwight Eisenhower to serve out two terms, he had a higher public approval rating than any modern American Chief Executive. Had he chosen to run again and were it permitted by the Constitution, he would have easily been re-elected.[1]*

Under Reagan's somnolent eye, as many as 225 of his appointees faced allegations of ethical or criminal wrongdoing. Some went to jail, others were forced to resign, and some were cleared—well, almost. Thievery and manipulation occurred on a grand scale and the amount of loot took a quantum leap compared to previous corruption. Rip-offs at the Department of Housing and Urban Development will come to four to eight billion dollars. Bailing out the bankrupt savings and loan companies will cost the taxpayers perhaps as much as five hundred billion—half a *trillion* dollars.

* The Republicans, in revenge against Franklin Roosevelt, sponsored Article Twenty-two, which limits a president to two terms.

341

Not every case was so serious, but the record is replete with conflict of interest, perjury, wiretapping, outrageous expenses charged to the government, misfeasance in enforcing the law, questionable loans, trading on White House connections and tax irregularities as well as ordinary stealing. Once he was out of office, Reagan sold his celebrity to the Japanese for two million dollars. And the Iran-Contra affair, in which the president out-did Nixon and by neatly finessing the blame onto his aides, rivaled Watergate in its disdain for constitutional procedures. Reagan's reaction was similar to that of the piano player in the house of prostitution who maintained he didn't know what was going on upstairs.

Boyishly optimistic even in his seventh decade, he had a knack for reflecting and giving voice to the aspirations of ordinary Americans. Unlike his predecessor Jimmy Carter, who saw the presidency as an impossible job and scolded the people for the sin of "malaise," he had a compelling, almost mythic, vision of America. "To me our country is a living, breathing presence, unimpressed by what others say is impossible, proud of its own success, generous ... always impatient to provide a better life for its people in a framework of a basic fairness," Reagan said in announcing his candidacy for the presidency in 1980.

Paradoxically, while he had come to Washington as an enemy of what he called "govment," Reagan demonstrated that the presidency could function after a series of failed presidencies. Lyndon Johnson had fallen victim to Vietnam and Nixon to Watergate. Gerald Ford tried to heal the scars of Watergate in his two years as caretaker president but was unable to reverse the decline of public confidence in government and in 1976 he was beaten by Jimmy Carter, a former navy officer, peanut farmer, and one-term governor of Georgia.

Curiously enough, Americans regard the presidency as the only job in the country in which experience is not required, and Carter made a virtue of his political inexperience. Exuding moral certitude, he ran as much against the Washington political establishment as against Ford. Carter came to the capital to clean up government scandal, but scandal erupted under his very nose. Although his campaign slogan was "Why Not the Best?," he was surrounded by third-raters and his administration was beset by small-time corruption that ran into the new Ethics in Government law and kept a series of special investigators busy.

Bert Lance, his former campaign manager, was forced to resign as director of the Office of Management and Budget after being indicted on thirty-three charges resulting from his shady banking practices in Georgia. Lance was exonerated—sort of. Fourteen counts were dismissed by a judge and a jury found him innocent of six charges; the remaining charges were dropped after Lance signed a consent agreement not to violate the banking laws in the future.[2] In a sign of the times, two other key aides, Hamilton Jordan and Tim Kraft, were investigated on allegations of having sniffed cocaine, but no charges were ever brought. These were hardly charges that would have been pursued in pre-Watergate days.

Undoubtedly the most serious damage done to Carter's reputation was by his alcoholic brother Billy. Billy Carter was not the first presidential brother to get in trouble: Orville Grant was involved in the selling of Indian post traderships; Sam Houston Johnson kited checks; Don Nixon was mixed up with Howard Hughes. At first, the nation was amused by Billy Carter's redneck capers, but the smiles died when it was learned he had accepted $220,000 to lobby for Libya's terrorist-sponsoring leader, Muammar Qaddafi, and had failed to register as a foreign agent.[3]

These minor scandals had little to do with Carter's loss of the presidency, however. Though most Americans saw him as a man of intelligence and integrity, he was unable to project an image of leadership, especially in his handling of the Iran hostage crisis. For the first time since Herbert Hoover in 1932, the voters rejected an elected incumbent president and put their future in the hands of a onetime movie actor, pitchman for right-wing causes, and governor of California. "It's morning in America!" Reagan proclaimed in triumph.

Ronald Wilson Reagan —as a good Democrat his father named him after Woodrow Wilson—lived in a fantasy world created in Hollywood and over the years make-believe blossomed into reality. Often as president, he referred to some event he had seen in a movie as if it were fact. He was a salesman whose main customer was himself. He denied the reality of a boyhood blighted by an alcoholic and frequently unemployed father and created the myth that he had lived a Huck Finn existence. He was like the cartoon character Mr. Magoo—who, nearly blind but always optimistic, loudly describes the happy things occurring about him while the reality is one of perils and disasters. Soon, the pretense became the reality because Reagan found it was easy to believe in what he wanted to believe.[4]

One of Reagan's major fantasies was that the United States had achieved greatness through the efforts of individual heroes who overcame the forces of nature on their own. But, as Lou Cannon notes in his perceptive biography, he never seemed to notice that the frontier had been pushed ever westward and the transcontinental railroad built with the backing of the federal government. He admired Franklin Roosevelt, voted four times for him, and was grateful for the assistance the New Deal had given his parents in the darkest days of the Depression. Roosevelt, though, like the old pioneers, was among his individual heroes, not part of the government.

Reagan's disdain of government was at the heart of the corruption that plagued his administration. An administration's ethical climate is set by the man at the top. Reagan's low esteem for government, his belief that it was naturally corrupt, led to his never insisting that his aides follow the highest standards. In 1976, when he made his first try at the Republican presidential nomination, his supporters published a book of quotations listing the candidate's position on 155 issues. Ethics in government was not one of them. Four years later, his campaign staff issued a list of Reagan's positions on seventy issues and, once again, government ethics was not among them. Nor did he mention the subject in his memoirs.[5]

If Reagan had believed in government, he might have issued edicts insisting that his appointees follow Grover Cleveland's dictum that "public office is a public trust." But he came to Washington with the intention of dismantling the government. Moreover, he was far removed from the day-to-day operations of his administration.* While he set general policy—to win the Cold War against the "evil empire" and to "get the government off the backs of the people"—he was uninterested in the details of governance. And he understood neither the new ethical environment prevailing in the wake of Watergate, nor the increased capacity in the government and the press to detect violations.

The lavish Reagan inaugural in 1981 set the tone for what was to come. The most expensive in history—just as the election campaign itself was the most costly ever—it brought an aura of opulence to the White House. Obviously, this was not to be merely an administration of the rich, but one of and for those rich who were unashamed to flaunt their wealth. The 1980s became a time of greed and plunder, with scandals tainting everything from Wall Street to the clergy. Looking on were the president's men, many from Southern California, where they had seen vast amounts of money made quickly in the entertainment and defense industries. They transferred the easy virtue of this world to Washington and proceeded to use their time there to line their own pockets.

Not long after Reagan assumed office, he invited a group of big-city mayors to a White House reception. Ritually shaking hands with those present, he addressed one man, Samuel R. Pierce, Jr., as "Mr. Mayor." Much to the embarrassment of all, he was told Pierce was the president's own secretary of housing and urban development. Reagan's failure to recognize Pierce was typical of Reagan's attitude toward the agency. He never visited it during his entire eight years in office and had little interest in its operation, although it doled out billions of dollars in government funds and was widely viewed as a sinkhole of mismanagement and corruption.[6]

Pierce, known as "Silent Sam" because of the low profile he kept, was a New York labor lawyer who was completely out of his depth as an administrator. Bored with the job, he stayed on only

* Representative Lee Hamilton, an Indiana Democrat, reports that during one White House briefing on the MX missile, Reagan interrupted to recount "the plot from *War Game*, the movie. This was his only contribution."

because he hoped eventually to be appointed to the Supreme Court. He was in his office only from 10:00 A.M. to 4:00 P.M. each day and spent much of his time watching soap operas on television. Like President Reagan, Pierce delegated most of his power to assistants. He seemed happiest when taking foreign and domestic junkets at the expense of the taxpayers, making at least five jaunts to the Soviet Union.

Corruption has bedeviled HUD since its creation in 1965. During the succeeding years, hundreds of real estate speculators and lenders have been convicted of mortgage fraud. In both Democratic and Republican administrations there were numerous cases of HUD money that was earmarked to help the poor being used to finance country clubs, swimming pools, golf courses, and luxury apartments. Members of Congress also used HUD as their own personal piggy bank to funnel government money to campaign contributors. "During much of the 1980s, HUD was enveloped by influence peddling, favoritism, abuse, greed, fraud, embezzlement and theft," the House Government Operations Committee concluded unanimously after a protracted investigation. "In many housing programs, objective criteria gave way to political preference and cronyism, and favoritism supplanted fairness."[7]

Top officials took dozens of trips to luxury resorts and sent the bill to real estate operators and builders with whom they did business. Other senior officials attempted to sell several housing projects without competitive bidding to a Reagan campaign lawyer. An assistant secretary was forced to resign after it was disclosed that he had HUD staffers work on his book (*Privatizing the Public Sector*) on government time. The undersecretary resigned after it was learned he had earned $145,000 moonlighting for a group selling books and tapes on how to make money in real estate. The head of the San Francisco office resigned after agreeing to repay $6,800 in travel expenses, including a Republican fundraiser at Disneyland.[8] One staffer, nicknamed Robin HUD, stole $5.5 million and, following a "higher law," gave most of it to the poor.

The evidence indicated that as Pierce yawned in boredom the Moderate Rehabilitation program, designed to encourage low-income housing, was looted. At the direction of Deborah Gore Dean, his executive assistant, these grants were handed out to friends who had left HUD to rake in big money as consultants or to Republican bigwigs. The agency's inspector general, Paul Adams, whose warnings were ignored by Pierce, reported that more than $5.7 million in consulting fees were paid to just twenty recipients. The White House used HUD "as a dumping ground for the dregs," said one official. "We just had a lot of slimy people."

James Watt, who had offended almost everyone as Reagan's interior secretary, garnered $300,000 in public funds to arrange loans for three projects. John Mitchell, Nixon's former attorney general, was paid $75,000 by a Miami developer to lobby at HUD while he was a close companion of Deborah Dean's mother. Carla Hill, HUD secretary under Gerald Ford, lobbied Pierce to lift a ban against a firm that subsequently defaulted on loans at a likely loss to HUD of more than $300 million. Hill, who was appointed U.S. trade representative in the Bush administration, contended that this was legitimate legal work rather than influence peddling.

Three years after Reagan had flown off into the California sunset, everybody was still promising reform and the HUD investigation was still proceeding at a snail's pace. In the meantime, "Silent Sam" Pierce achieved the dubious honor of being the first current or former cabinet official to take the Fifth Amendment before a congressional investigating committee since Albert B. Fall of Teapot Dome fame.

"All in all, I think we've hit the jackpot."

So said President Reagan on October 15, 1982, as he signed into law the Garn–St. Germain Act, part of his program of getting government off the backs of business. The nation's savings and loans were freed from restrictive federal regulation and given permission to expand beyond their traditional role of making home loans. Now they could use federally insured deposits to buy and develop all sorts of properties. The new law proved a jackpot—but not for most Americans, who will pick up the tab for Reagan's misadventure in deregulation. It was a bonanza for the high-rollers, the get-rich-quick-artists, the swindlers, and the crooks who saw a gilt-edged chance to strike it rich.[9]

Ivan F. Boesky, the Wall Street manipulator, acquired a small "thrift" in upstate New York; then Vice-President Bush's son Neil became a director of Silverado Banking in Denver; Andrew F. Cuomo, the son of Governor Mario Cuomo of New York, tried to purchase one in Delray Beach, Florida; Ricky Strauss, son of Robert Strauss, former chairman of the Democratic National Committee, became a director of a Dallas institution. And in Irvine, California, Charles H. Keating, Jr., bought the old-line Lincoln Savings and Loan. The foxes were moving in on the chicken house.

Reagan understood little about the S&L business. His idea of a savings and loan president was George Bailey, the idealistic hero of Frank Capra's 1946 movie *It's a Wonderful Life*. Until the coming of deregulation, the savings and loan business was a financial backwater. S&Ls loaned money to individuals to buy homes. Period. They did not make loans for office buildings or shopping centers or high-flying oil-drilling ventures. In the 1970s, this staid existence was upset by the double-digit inflation resulting from the Vietnam war and the flight of depositors to higher-yield money market funds while the thrifts were left with portfolios of low-interest home mortgages. Congress was faced with the alternative of either shrinking the industry or deregulating and allowing it to become more aggressive.

Under heavy S&L industry lobbying, Congress made three key decisions that helped bring about the fiasco: S&Ls were allowed to pay much higher interest rates; to generate the additional funds to pay higher interest rates they were permitted to invest in anything they wished; depositors were allowed to open an unlimited number of accounts, each insured up to $100,000. Supervision was limited and accounting rules were relaxed by Richard Pratt, the head of the Federal Home Loan Bank Board, the regulatory agency overseeing the thrifts, which allowed troubled S&Ls to conceal their insolvency. Pratt later left for a high-paying job on Wall Street.

Soon, some S&Ls were offering up to 13 percent interest along with federal insurance and they were awash in cash. The thrift industry was turned into a huge casino where only the taxpayers could lose. Money poured out of the S&Ls into speculative investments in real estate, condominiums, oil and gas ventures, and high-interest "junk" bonds. Pin-striped pillars of the leading legal and accounting firms cloaked these schemes in respectability. Living like royalty, the insiders bought luxurious estates, planes, and yachts with the deposits. One Florida S&L operator purchased $13 million worth of art and took it home for "safekeeping." Another high-roller bought a two-million-dollar California beach house and took his wife on a "gastronomique fantastique" tour of European restaurants and defended it as a scouting trip for investments. "You think it's easy eating in three-star restaurants twice a day, six days a week?" he protested.[10]

The ink was hardly dry on the Garn–St. Germain Act when federal regulators noticed something was amiss. When Edwin Gray, Pratt's successor, complained about these freewheeling operations, he was branded a "re-regulator"—one of the ultimate insults in the Reagan administration. The gross misuse of other people's savings was allowed to persist because Reagan administration policymakers and key members of Congress looked the other way or accepted millions in campaign contributions from greedy S&L kingpins. As Treasury secretary, Donald Regan, a onetime Wall Street bond salesman, pushed ideological deregulation, no matter what; James Baker 3d, as a top Reagan aide and Regan's successor, dragged his feet for years as the cost of a bailout mounted. David Stockman, the Reaganite ideologue who ran the Office of Management and Budget, blocked the hiring of badly needed S&L examiners. The Justice Department, headed by Reagan crony Edwin Meese 3d, was also extraordinarily lax in its response to criminality.

The entire rickety structure was finally brought down by the shakeout of the real estate and financial markets in the late 1980s. Fraud was discovered in over 60 percent of the failed thrifts. When depositors sought their money they learned that it had been invested in worthless buildings and land, junk bonds, or had been stolen outright. The taxpayers are now stuck with bailing out these federally insured accounts at astronomical cost. The failure to confront the S&L crisis early on—a bailout in 1984 would have cost $40 billion—allowed a serious problem to metastasize into the worst financial scandal in American history. Reports of mob influence and Central Intelligence Agency money laundering operations circulated and the taxpayer was the guarantor of deposits resulting from drug trafficking.

Yet, most Americans failed to appreciate the magnitude of the scandal, perhaps because it had not touched them personally or the sums of money being bandied about were too large to be readily comprehended. And then Charles Keating appeared on the scene to give the S&L scandal a human face.

Keating is a onetime Olympic swimmer, an Ohio banker, and businessman who was charged in 1979 by the Securities and Exchange Commission with fraud in making millions of dollars in insider loans. Without confirming or denying the allegations, he signed a consent order not to violate securities laws. In 1981, he was tapped by Reagan as envoy to the Bahamas, but publicity about the SEC case resulted in the scrapping of the nomination. Three years later, he bought Lincoln Savings, a California S&L, for $51 million, and began using its billion dollars in federally insured assets to finance development projects all over the country, including a $50 million loan to his old friend, John Connally, the Texas wheeler-dealer and secretary of Treasury in Nixon's cabinet.* Under Keating, Lincoln engaged in every kind of business except lending on home mortgages, according to a Public Broadcasting System exposé.†

Keating funneled millions into the projects of his Phoenix-based American Continental Corporation, putting $200 million of Lincoln's money into Estrella, a planned community for 200,000 people to be built in the Arizona desert. Another $300 million was swallowed by the Phoenician Hotel, a 130-acre luxury resort near Scottsdale, Arizona. Even Keating was later quoted as

* Keating served as manager of Connally's short-lived campaign for the Republican presidential nomination in 1979.

† The program, written, produced, and reported by Marion Goldin, was shown on *Frontline* on May 1, 1990.

saying it was "the kind of mausoleum idiots built." He put most of his family on the payroll, and his son Charlie, whose only previous experience was as a busboy, received total compensation of $1.1 million annually. In all, federal examiners estimated that the Keating family took out $34 million in salaries, bonuses, and stock sales. Keating, a long-time fighter against pornography, also made large donations to his antipornography organization, Citizens for Decency Through Law. Federal authorities charge that depositors' money was used to fund the contributions.

To maintain this life-style and his mushrooming business, Keating needed ever-increasing amounts of money for American Continental. In an effort to reduce scrutiny by regulators he floated a multimillion issue of junk bonds in its name, but the bonds were sold in Lincoln's offices. Purchasers, mostly elderly retirees, were attracted with offerings of high interest and the lack of insurance was glossed over. In all, about $250 million of these bonds were sold. Not until American Continental went bankrupt did they learn they had traded in their life's savings for worthless paper.

In the meantime, federal regulators had grown alarmed by Keating's operations and Ed Gray of the Federal Home Loan Bank Board began a push to limit the amount of an S&L's direct investment in real estate to 10 percent of its assets. Keating, who had half a billion dollars more in direct investments than the regulation allowed, went into high gear in a lobby against this effort. He hired Alan Greenspan, chairman of the Council of Economic Advisers under Ford and later to chairman of the Federal Reserve Board, to produce a study claiming that such investments were not jeopardizing industry stability. Greenspan also wrote the San Francisco office of the FHLB seeking an exemption for Lincoln. He was paid $40,000 by a law firm representing Keating. One of the nation's leading accounting firms, Arthur Young, chimed in with a report diagnosing Lincoln as sound and charging government harassment.* Ed Gray reported that Arthur Liman, the attorney for Michael Milken, the jailed

---

* The man who wrote this report later went to work for Keating at a salary of $954,000 a year.

junk-bond king, and for Keating, threatened to sue the FHLB on Keatings's behalf.

When this heavy artillery failed to bring about a change in the regulation, Keating tried other methods. First he offered Gray a job with his firm; when Gray refused, he tried to pack the board with one of his own business associates. And when that didn't get Lincoln exempted from the regulation, he turned to the politicians. Keating had always been a generous contributor to the campaigns of lawmakers of both parties and now increased his largess. No one knows how much he has contributed, but Keating himself is said to have claimed he spent eleven million dollars in his attempt to get rid of Gray.[11]

He gave a total of $1.4 million to five senators who had oversight over the FHLB—Dennis DeConcini and John McCain, Arizona's Democratic and Republican senators; John Glenn, a onetime astronaut and Ohio Democrat; Donald W. Riegle, Jr., a Michigan Democrat; and Alan Cranston, a California Democrat. Acting in concert, they called in the regulators in April 1987 and put pressure upon them in Keating's behalf. It was an impressive show of political clout and it delayed government action against Lincoln, a postponement that may have cost the taxpayers millions more in bailout funds.

When asked if his contributions had influenced the Keating Five—as they became known—Keating was refreshingly frank: "I certainly hope so," he declared. The senators denied any wrongdoing and claimed that part of their job is to assist constituents, whether it is helping with Mrs. McGillicuddy's Social Security check or Charlie Keating's difficulties with the regulators. But as William Black, one of the regulators, noted: "There were lots of constituents that needed protecting, but the one constituent who put more than a million bucks in contributions to the five senators is the only one that got protection. All the others got the shaft."[12]

In Washington, Ed Gray had been replaced as head of the FHLB by M. Danny Wall, who, as a Senate staffer, had written the original deregulation bill. At Wall's order, oversight of Lincoln was removed from the San Francisco office, which was complaining about Keating's activities, to Washington, and nothing was done for two years. Finally, in April 1989, Washington acknowledged that Lincoln was unsound and the federal government took it away from Keating. In all, the total loss to the taxpayers was estimated at $2.5 billion.

The Keating Five was investigated by a special counsel appointed by the Senate Ethics Committee who recommended a full-scale inquiry of Cranston, DeConcini and Riegle.* Cranston was formally rebuked by the Senate but the others escaped punishment. The bondholders filed suit against Keating; the Justice Department, the SEC, the Federal Elections Committee, and the courts are all looking into allegations of fraud and illegal loans. Years will be required to untangle the mess. And Charles Keating? Despite being convicted of security fraud in the sale of the junk bonds, he flatly denies any wrongdoing and has sued to regain control of Lincoln.

Almost every level of the Reagan regime—from the cabinet downward—was shot through with corruption. Ed Meese, the bumbling White House counsel and later attorney general, was twice investigated by special prosecutors and got off with "not proven" verdicts. "He left his shirttail hanging out at such length that it was easy for those who wished him ill to try to pull him down," said one aide.[13] Michael Deaver, Reagan's "minder," was charged with influence peddling and convicted of perjury. The Environmental Protection Agency under Anne Burford was rocked by charges of political favoritism and mismanagement. Rita Lavelle, head of EPA's waste management program, was convicted of lying to Congress and obstructing a congressional investigation. Paul Thayer, the number-two man in the Defense Department, resigned the day before the SEC charged him with passing insider information along to friends, from which they made three million dollars. Thayer pled guilty to obstruction of justice and went to jail for nineteen months. Pentagon procurement programs were found to be shot through with fraud and bribery.

And so it went . . . on and on.

---

* Ferdnand St. Germain, the Rhode Island Democrat who co-sponsored the S&L deregulation bill, lost his bid for re-election when it was disclosed he was using the credit card of the U.S. League of Savings Institutions for his personal entertainment.

Reagan drifted lazily over this morass of corruption like a hot-air balloon in Macy's Thanksgiving Day parade. Like Harry Truman, he dismissed attacks on the integrity of his administration as "phony" and an attempt to strike at him through his subordinates. "I have a feeling that there's a certain amount of politics involved in all this and I have a feeling that I'm really the target they would like to get at, and they are doing it by going after these other people," he told Lou Cannon.[14]

Periodically, congressional Democrats attacked the "sleaze factor" in the Reagan administration, but they were hardly credible critics. Back in 1980, five Democratic members of the House and a Republican were caught in an FBI sting operation called AB-SCAM in which they were videotaped while accepting bribes from an Arab "sheik." Michael "Ozzie" Meyers of Pennsylvania boasted: "Bullshit walks; money talks." John Jenrette of South Carolina told an undercover FBI agent "I've got larceny in my blood." Richard Kelly, a Florida Republican, was taped stuffing $25,000 in cash into his pockets and asking "Does it show?"[15]

In 1989, Texas Democrat Jim Wright became the first Speaker of the House ever to resign amid allegations of misconduct. He was charged with sixty-nine violations of House rules, including the use of the sales of a book of his speeches as the means to evade House limitations on outside income. Wright had earned $55,000 in "royalties"—at the unheard-of rate of 55 percent—on the book that was published by a longtime friend. The friend's printing company happened to have been paid $265,000 for services to the Speaker's campaign committee the previous year. Wright had also pressured federal regulators on behalf of the operators of some troubled Texas S&Ls and accepted $145,000 in gifts from a Fort Worth businessman with an interest in legislation before the House.

Wright's resignation was followed by that of Representative Tony Coehlo of California, the Democratic whip, after his involvement in a $100,000 junk-bond deal raised ethical questions. Two years before, Coehlo observed, it wouldn't have caused a raised eyebrow. Ironically, he had been one of the principal exponents of using the sleaze theme against Reagan.

Thomas Foley, the Washington Democrat who succeeded

Wright as Speaker, had a mandate to clean up the House's act. But public perception of Congress was further damaged by disclosures that in the dark of night, its members had voted to increase their pay, had kited checks on the House bank and welshed on thousands of dollars in outstanding bills at the House restaurant. In the wake of these miniscandals, demands were being made for an end to the job security enjoyed by members of Congress. Limitations on the number of terms lawmakers can serve in the hope of bringing new blood to Capitol Hill may well be the result of the lawmakers' own perverse inability to at least present an appearance of ethical behavior. After all, the Founding Fathers had no intention of creating a corps of permanent jobholders.

Perhaps the most bizarre—and most important—case of governmental corruption in the Reagan years was the Iran-Contra affair.[16] Like Watergate, it was more about the exercise of power than old-fashioned theft. Iran-Contra revealed the existence of a shadow government operating within the White House that conducted a campaign of lying, deceit, and duplicity that led to the breakdown of the orderly processes of government. In the bicentennial year of the Constitution, the nation caught a glimpse of a secret government that in action and words expressed disdain for constitutional values and processes. Iran-Contra blighted the closing months of Ronald Reagan's presidency—and, had any other president been involved, might have resulted in impeachment.

The affair was an outgrowth of Reagan's policy of assisting anticommunist "freedom fighters" wherever they might appear. In Nicaragua, secret aid was funneled to the anti-Sandinista Contras under the direction of William Casey, the head of the CIA. Casey had a history of shady dealings. As a businessman, he had been involved in several scrapes that raised questions about the propriety, if not the legality, of some of his dealings. As Reagan's campaign manager in 1980, he figured in a flap over the means by which the Reagan campaign obtained a copy of the briefing book used to prepare Jimmy Carter for a televised debate between the two candidates. In 1983, he was investigated for trading of stocks in companies doing business with his agency.

Casey launched a secret war against the Sandinistas, supplying arms, money, and training to the Contras through a network of covert operatives with experience in the Caribbean and Southeast Asia. These tactics were designed to deceive congressional opponents, who worried about the dangers of being dragged unwittingly into another quagmire like Vietnam, this time in Central America. Saudi Arabia, Israel, South Africa, and Brunei were solicited for funds and equipment for the Contras. The CIA mined a Nicaraguan port and directed the firing of oil-storage depots in violation of international law.

Increasingly uncomfortable with the open-ended nature of Casey's not-so-secret war, Congress rebelled and in October 1984 approved the first of a series of laws, known collectively as the Boland amendment, that specifically barred the CIA, the Defense Department, "or any agency or entity of the United States involved in intelligence activity" from using its funds to support the Contras. Anyone who thought these restrictions would force Reagan to close down the secret war in Central America obviously had not reckoned with the depth of his commitment to the Contras. "The President repeatedly made it clear in public and private that he did not intend to break faith with the Contras," Robert McFarlane, the head of the National Security Council, later told congressional investigators.

While Reagan lobbied Congress and the public for restoration of military assistance to the Contras—insinuating that those who opposed such aid were soft on communism—Casey prepared a cover for the CIA. Although the agency was required by law to report its activities to Congress, the National Security Council operated without oversight from any outside authority. Accordingly, active direction of the anti-Sandinista campaign was turned over to the NSC.

Marine Lieut. Col. Oliver L. North, an NSC staffer, became Casey's surrogate. Casey designed the policy; North carried it out. Boyish, intense, and patriotic, North, like the president, was obsessed with the Contras. Working with Casey, he presided over a network of conservative fundraisers and ex-intelligence and military operatives that reached from the jungles of Central America to the discreet world of numbered Swiss bank accounts. Later, the Presidential Review Board headed by ex-Senator John Tower of Texas faulted Casey for failing to press for organizational responsibility for the struggle to be transferred to the CIA, but this was exactly what Casey was trying to avoid. In fact, he needed an activist NSC to circumvent the congressional restrictions on the CIA's own operations. Had Oliver North not existed, he would have had to invent him.

The fiction of outside financing of the Contras collapsed early in November 1986 in Lebanon, halfway across the world from the Nicaraguan jungles. A Beirut magazine with links to the Iranian radicals who had taken over the country disclosed that McFarlane, who had left the NSC the previous year, had made a secret visit to Teheran in May 1986. In an effort to obtain the release of several Americans held captive in Lebanon by terrorists, the United States had supplied Iran with military hardware. Reagan—who had repeatedly declared he would never negotiate with terrorists and had condemned Iran as a member of an "international Murder, Inc."—was alleged to have authorized the mission.

Reagan flatly denied these claims, but two days before Thanksgiving, Attorney General Meese revealed that arms had indeed been shipped to Iran to establish ties with Iranian "moderates" and to obtain the release of the hostages. He also disclosed that upwards of $30 million in profits from the sale was missing and had probably had been siphoned off to the Nicaraguan rebels. Meese asserted that only Vice-Admiral John M. Poindexter, McFarlane's successor, and Colonel North had been involved in the secret plan to divert funds to the Contras and the president knew nothing about it. Poindexter resigned from the NSC and North was fired.

The Iran-Contra affair quickly mushroomed into Washington's biggest scandal since Watergate and undermined confidence in Reagan. Questions were raised about his truthfulness and competence, especially after he claimed to be unable to remember important details and insisted, appearances to the contrary, that he hadn't traded arms for hostages. For most

Americans, the key issue was neither the shipment of arms to Iran nor the diversion of funds to the Contras in violation of the Boland amendment. Rather, it was the administration's deceitfulness in lying to its own people. The secret exchange of arms for hostages made a cynical mockery of Reagan's highly publicized policy of refusing to deal with terrorists. Washington's efforts to counter terrorism was left in shreds and the president was exposed to ridicule.

Reagan's supporters contended that the scandal originated with a pair of overzealous staff members who thought they were doing what the president wanted. In effect, Reagan was a befuddled bystander and the episode was merely part of an ongoing struggle between the White House and the Congress for control of American foreign policy. But testimony before a House–Senate investigating committee revealed that the president was deeply involved in the affair.

Over the next eight months, the nation watched breathlessly as a lurid tale of covert operations, "shredding parties," secret Swiss bank accounts, and shady international arms dealings unfolded in the newspapers and on the television screens. Casey and North were the centerpieces of the melodrama. Investigations by a House–Senate committee revealed that North had established a private network to supply the Nicaraguan guerrillas, Contras were under Casey's guidance, and Casey had urged—and directed—the trading of arms for hostages and the use of the siphoned-off funds to supply the Contras.

Three Americans were eventually released by the terrorists, but another three were kidnapped—leaving Iran with more than 2,000 TOW antitank missiles and other weaponry while the extremists held the same number of captives they had had in the first place. Unprepared for the bazaar mentality of the Iranians, American officials had been utterly bamboozled. "Our guys got taken to the cleaners," observed Secretary of State George Shultz. The picture that emerged was one of greed, duplicity, and incompetence—and of American policy out of control.

In the end, the investigators found no "smoking gun" that linked Reagan to the diversion of funds to the Contras in violation of the Boland amendment, although North's testimony before the congressional inquiry had seemed to draw the net about him. "I never carried out a single act, not one, in which I did not have the authority of my superiors," he declared. But Poindexter, who exhibited a surprisingly weak memory in other matters, took the president off the hook. He had authorized the diversions himself, the admiral said, because he thought that was what Reagan wanted. Reagan claimed to have been vindicated although many Americans simply did not believe this version of events.

Brushing up against a self-imposed deadline and wishing to avoid another constitutional confrontation with a president so soon after Watergate, the committee left the numerous unanswered questions to be resolved by the special prosecutor. Casey died of a brain tumor, making him a convenient scapegoat, but nearly a dozen people involved in the affair either pleaded guilty or were convicted of various charges. North was convicted of lying to Congress, but on appeal his conviction was reversed on technical grounds. Poindexter also escaped punishment for similar reasons.

Whatever the final outcome of the Iran-Contra affair, several points are clear. Reagan condoned the creation of a private network outside the government to carry out a secret foreign policy. Ranking officials repeatedly lied to Congress and the American people about the extent of the administration's efforts on behalf of the Contras. Deals were cut with disreputable middlemen to trade arms for hostages, and the United States had been forced to go begging to its allies for alms. Reagan's supporters defended the initiative with the argument that the means may have been badly flawed, but the release of the hostages and survival of the Nicaraguan resistance justified everything. The president's only fault, they maintained, was to bend an imperfectly worded law to secretly execute a policy too sophisticated to be grasped by the American people. But that blames democracy for the shortcomings of its leaders.

The wish for incorruptible government is a stubborn ideal, dating back perhaps to the beginning of the Chinese civil service some two thousand years ago. Despite wave after wave of corruption and greed, it abides. But it also faces an equally stubborn reality as politicians, businessmen, and bureaucrats forego no opportunity to pick the public pocket. In the 1990s, corruption has taken on an international flavor with the agonizingly slow unveiling of the activities of the Bank of Credit and Commerce International (BCCI). Its customers include the CIA, international drug traffickers, Arab terrorists, and the Mafia and it had no trouble in buying friends in the upper reaches of American politics—particularly Democrats.

In the final analysis, corruption abides like death and taxes. Robert Penn Warren put it best in *All the King's Men* when he had his fictional political boss, Willie Stark, order a hatchet man to dig up some dirt on a supposedly unblemished political enemy: "There is always something," Willie declared. "Man is conceived in sin and born in corruption and passeth from the stink of the didie to the stench of the shroud. There is always something."

Notes

CHAPTER I

1. *Records of the Virginia Company*, Susan M. Kingsbury, ed. (Washington: 1933), Vol. III, pp. 71, 92.
2. Joel Hurstfield, *Freedom, Corruption and Government in Elizabethan England* (London: 1973), pp. 137–160; G. E. Aylmer, *A Short History of England in the 17th Century* (New York: 1963), pp. 33–34, 38–41.
3. William B. Schurz, *The Manila Galleon* (New York: 1939), pp. 305–313.
4. The most readily available accounts of the early days of the Virginia colony are George F. Willison, *Behold Virginia: The Fifth Crown* (New York: 1951), and Herbert L. Osgood, *The American Colonies in the Seventeenth Century* (Gloucester, Mass.: 1951), Vol. I.
5. "Nova Britannia" in *Tracts and Other Papers Relating Principally to the Origins, Settlement and Progress of the Colonies in North America*, collected by Peter Force (Washington: 1836), Vol. I.
6. For Argall's background, see the entries in the *Dictionary of National Biography*, the *Dictionary of American Biography*, and Willison, *op. cit.*, *passim*.
7. J. A. Doyle, *English Colonies in America* (New York: 1882), pp. 206–207.
8. For an account of Argall's rule see Willison, *op. cit.*, pp. 179–186.
9. Virginia Records, Vol. I, pp. 350–351.
10. William Stith, *The History of the First Discovery and Settlement of Virginia*, originally published in 1747 (New York: 1969), p. 149. For an account of Argall's rule see pp. 145–156.

11. Wesley F. Craven, *Dissolution of the Virginia Company* (Gloucester, Mass.: 1964), pp. 1–23, Chapter V.
12. For the history of the Massachusetts Bay Colony see James T. Adams, *The Founding of New England* (Boston: 1921).
13. *Ibid.*, pp. 161–162, and John Winthrop, *Winthrop's Journal*, John K. Hosmer, ed. (New York: 1908), Vol. I, pp. 143–144.
14. For a brief account of New Netherland see John E. Promfret, *Founding the American Colonies* (New York: 1970), Chapter XII.
15. *The Memorial History of the City of New York*, James G. Wilson, ed. (New York: 1892), Vol. I, pp. 193–196.
16. Kieft's administration is covered in *ibid.*, Chapter VII, and more briefly in M. R. Werner, *It Happened in New York* (New York: 1957), pp. 25–29.

CHAPTER II

1. For background on Fletcher, see *The Memorial History of New York City*, Vol. I, pp. 489–490.
2. The most complete account of the Leisler affair and its aftermath is Jerome R. Reich, *Leisler's Rebellion* (Chicago: 1953).
3. Samuel Eliot Morison, *The Oxford History of the American People* (New York: 1972), Vol. I, p. 174.
4. Hugh F. Rankin, *The Golden Age of Piracy* (Williamsburg, Va.: 1969), pp. 54–59.
5. For the Madagascar trade see Patrick Pringle, *Jolly Roger: The Story of the Great Age of Piracy* (New York: 1953), pp. 130–138, and James G. Lydon, *Pirates, Privateers and Profits* (Upper Saddle River, N.J.: 1970), Chapter II.
6. *Documents Relative to the Colonial History of the State of New York*, E. B. O'Callagahn, ed. (Albany, N.Y.: 1854), Vol. IV, p. 447.
7. *Ibid.*, p. 446.
8. *Ibid.*, p. 421.
9. *Ibid.*, pp. 327, 384, 463, 528.
10. *Memorial History*, Vol. I, p. 512.
11. For an account of Bellomont's administration see *ibid.*, Vol. II, Chapter I.
12. *Colonial Documents*, pp. 443–451.
13. *Ibid.*, pp. 673–674, and Gustavus Myers, *History of the Great American Fortunes* (New York: 1936), pp. 41–42.

14. Fletcher's answer to the charges against him is in *Colonial Documents*, pp. 443–451, and Lydon, *op. cit.*, p. 59.
15. The most complete account of Lord Cornbury's rule is in *Memorial History*, Vol. II, Chapter II.
16. For the Carolina pirates see Shirley C. Hughson, *The Carolina Pirates and Colonial Commerce 1670–1740* (Baltimore: 1894).
17. For Blackbeard see Pringle, *op. cit.*, and Rankin, *op. cit.*
18. *The Colonial Records of North Carolina*, William L. Saunders, ed. (Raleigh, N.C.: 1866), Vol. II.

CHAPTER III

1. For a portrait of the American colonies on the eve of the Revolution see Lawrence H. Gipson, *The Coming of the Revolution* (New York: 1954), Chapter II.
2. John C. Miller, *Origins of the American Revolution* (Boston: 1943), pp. 83–86.
3. Gipson, *op. cit.*, pp. 28–33; David Loth, *Public Plunder* (New York: 1938), p. 53.
4. Bernard Bailyn, *The Ideological Origins of the American Revolution* (Cambridge, Mass.: 1967).
5. John Adams, *Dairy of John Adams*, L. H. Butterfield, ed. (Cambridge, Mass.: 1961), Vol. I, p. 238.
6. Clarence W. Alvord, *The Mississippi Valley in British Politics* (Cleveland: 1917), Vol. I, pp. 283–284.
7. A. M. Sakolski, *The Great American Land Bubble* (New York: 1936), p. 13.
8. *Ibid.*, pp. 22–25; Loth, *op. cit.*, pp. 50–51.
9. James T. Flexner, *George Washington: The Forge of Experience 1732–1775* (Boston: 1965), p. 293.
10. Bernhard Knollenberg, *George Washington: The Virginia Period 1732–1775* (Durham, N.C.: 1964).
11. Herbert B. Adams, *Washington's Interest in Western Lands*, Johns Hopkins University Studies in Historical and Political Science (Baltimore: 1885), Vol. III.
12. Flexner, *op. cit.*, p. 303.
13. For Vandalia I have followed the accounts in Robert Sobel, *The Money Manias* (New York: 1973), Chapter I; Thomas P. Abernathy,

Western Lands and the American Revolution (New York: 1937), Chapters II and III; and Loth, *op. cit.*, pp. 58–64.

CHAPTER IV

1. Thomas Jones, *History of New York During the Revolutionary War* (New York: 1879), Vol. I, p. lii.
2. John C. Miller, *Triumph of Freedom* (Boston: 1948), pp. 471–472.
3. George Washington, *Writings of Washington*, John C. Fitzpatrick, ed. (Washington: 1931), Vol. IV, p. 124.
4. *Ibid.*, Vol. XIII, pp. 312–313, 383.
5. Quoted in Robert A. East, *Business Enterprise in the American Revolutionary Era* (New York: 1938), p. 180.
6. E. James Ferguson, *The Power of the Purse* (Chapel Hill, N.C.: 1961), p. 76.
7. For assessments of Morris see *ibid.*, Chapter V; East, *op. cit.*, Chapter VI; and Clarence L. Ver Steeg, *Robert Morris, Revolutionary Financier* (Philadelphia: 1954).
8. Bingham's activities are covered in Robert C. Alberts, *The Golden Voyage: The Life and Times of William Bingham* (Boston: 1969).
9. Nathan Miller, *Sea of Glory: The Continental Navy Fights for Independence 1775–1783* (New York: 1974), pp. 55–57, 203–204, 212–214.
10. Theodore Thayer, *Nathanael Greene: Strategist of the American Revolution* (New York: 1960), pp. 228–236.
11. Willard M. Wallace, *Appeal to Arms* (Boston: 1951), p. 169.
12. Alexander Hamilton, *The Works of Alexander Hamilton*, Henry Cabot Lodge, ed. (New York: 1904), Vol. I, pp. 199–209.

CHAPTER V

1. Constitutional Convention, June 22, 1787. Quoted in *The Mind of Alexander Hamilton*, Saul K. Padover, ed. (New York: 1958), p. 430.
2. John C. Miller, *Alexander Hamilton: Portrait in Paradox* (New York: 1959), p. xi.
3. Jonathan Daniels, *Ordeal of Ambition* (New York: 1970), p. 26.
4. John D. Hicks, *The Federal Union* (Boston: 1937), p. 198.
5. Quoted in Charles A. Beard, *An Economic Interpretation of the Constitution* (New York: 1935), p. xiv.
6. *Annals of Congress*, 1st Congress, 1st Session (Washington: 1834), p. 221.

7. William Maclay, *The Journal of William Maclay* (New York: 1927), pp. 28–29.

8. *Ibid.*, p. 173.

9. Quoted in Nathan Schachner, *Alexander Hamilton* (New York: 1961), p. 238.

10. Report on the Public Credit, Hamilton, *Works*, Vol. II, pp. 229, 283.

11. Maclay, *op. cit.*, pp. 173–174.

12. Schachner, *op. cit.*, pp. 249–250.

13. Maclay, *op. cit.*, pp. 183–184.

14. For Duer's career see Nathan Schachner, *The Founding Fathers* (New York: 1954), pp. 85–87, and the *Dictionary of American Biography*.

15. Beard, *op. cit.*, pp. vi, 14–15.

16. Maclay, *op. cit.*, p. 230.

17. *Ibid.*, p. 204.

18. *Ibid.*, p. 228.

19. *Ibid.*, pp. 231–232.

20. Fisher Ames, *Works*, Seth Ames, ed. (Boston: 1854), Vol. I, p. 80.

21. *The Papers of Thomas Jefferson*, Julian P. Boyd, ed. (Princeton: 1965), Vol. XVII, pp. 205–208.

22. Miller, *op. cit.*, p. 250.

23. Frank Monaghan, *John Jay* (New York: 1935), p. 323.

24. Washington, *op. cit.*, Vol. XXXIV, p. 410.

CHAPTER VI

1. Quoted in William L. Mackenzie, *Life and Times of Martin Van Buren* (Boston: 1846), p. 209.

2. Marquis James, *The Life of Andrew Jackson* (Indianapolis: 1938), pp. 489–495.

3. On this point see James L. Bugg, *Andrew Jackson: Democratic Myth or Reality* (New York: 1963).

4. Leonard White, *The Federalists* (New York: 1948), p. 259.

5. For fuller accounts of Jefferson and the patronage see Malone, *op. cit.*, Chapter V, and Merrill D. Peterson, *Thomas Jefferson and the New Nation* (New York: 1970), pp. 666–681.

6. Loth, *op. cit.*, p. 100.

7. Reginald Horsman, *The War of 1812* (New York: 1969), pp. 120–121.

8. James, *op. cit.*, p. 240.

9. Paul V. Van Riper, *History of the United States Civil Service* (Evanston, Ill.: 1958), p. 33.

10. Myers, *op. cit.*, pp. 72–73, 206.
11. For Astor's career in the fur business see Kenneth W. Porter, *John Jacob Astor, Business Man* (Cambridge: 1931), Vol. II, and John Upton Terrell, *Furs by Astor* (New York: 1963).
12. George Thayer, *Who Shakes the Money Tree?* (New York: 1973), p. 28.
13. For the early history of Tammany, see M. R. Werner, *Tammany Hall* (New York: 1928), Chapters I and II.
14. See Charles A. Wiltse, *John C. Calhoun: Nationalist* (Indianapolis: 1944), pp. 344–346, and *Congressional Globe.*
15. Carl R. Fish, *The Civil Service and the Patronage* (New York: 1905), p. 128.
16. Denis T. Lynch, *Epoch and a Man: Martin Van Buren and His Time* (Port Washington, N.Y.: 1971), pp. 324–325, 328.
17. Fish, *op. cit.*, pp. 125–127.
18. Alexis de Tocqueville, *Democracy in America* (London: 1862), Vol. I, pp. 228, 238, 281.
19. Martin Van Buren, *The Autobiography of Martin Van Buren*, John C. Fitzpatrick, ed. (New York: 1973), Vol. I, pp. 264–269.

CHAPTER VII

1. Glyndon G. Van Deuson, *Thurlow Weed: Wizard of the Lobby* (Boston: 1947), p. 212.
2. Werner, *op. cit.*, pp. 71, 85.
3. Gerald W. Johnson, *America's Silver Age* (New York: 1939), p. 110.
4. Claude M. Fuess, *Daniel Webster* (New York: 1968), p. 378.
5. Bray Hammond, *Banks and Politics in America* (Princeton: 1957), p. 601.
6. Fawn Brodie, *No Man Knows My History* (New York: 1966), pp. 194–198.
7. For the history of the B.U.S., see Hammond, *op. cit.*
8. Myers, *op. cit.*, p. 78.
9. George Rogers Taylor, *The Transportation Revolution 1815–1860* (New York: 1968), p. 98.
10. Stewart H. Holbrook, *The Story of American Railroads* (New York: 1947), pp. 36–37.
11. Taylor, *op. cit.*, p. 92.
12. *Ibid.*, p. 101.
13. Myers, *op. cit.*, pp. 544–545.
14. Richard O'Connor, *Iron Rails and Broken Men* (New York: 1973), p. 18.

15. Quoted in F. A. Cleveland and F. W. Powell, *Railroad Promotion and Capitalization in the United States* (New York: 1909), p. 199.

16. Myers, *op. cit.*, pp. 454–456.

17. Philip S. Klein, *President James Buchanan* (University Park, Pa., 1969), p. 339, and Roy F. Nichols, *The Destruction of American Democracy* (New York: 1948), pp. 188–189.

18. Myers, *op. cit.*, Chapter XIII.

CHAPTER VIII

1. George Templeton Strong, *Diary of George Templeton Strong*, Allan Nevins, ed. (New York: 1952), Vol. III, p. 148.

2. Colonel Regis de Trobriand, quoted in *The Blue and the Gray*, Henry S. Commager, ed. (Indianapolis: 1950), p. 725.

3. *Report of Select House Committee on Government Contracts*, Report No. 2, 37th Congress, 2nd Session (Washington: 1862), p. x.

4. Carl Sandburg, *Abraham Lincoln: The War Years* (New York: 1939), Vol. I, pp. 339–400.

5. Fish, *op. cit.*, pp. 169–172.

6. Quoted in W. A. Swanburg, *Jim Fisk: The Career of an Improbable Rascal* (New York: 1959), p. 17.

7. *Official Records of the Union and Confederate Armies* (Washington: 1899), Series III, Vol. II, pp. 188–189.

8. Fred A. Shannon, *The Organization and Administration of the Union Army 1861–1865* (Cleveland: 1928), p. 71.

9. *Official Records, loc. cit.*, p. 193.

10. Erwin S. Bradley, *Simon Cameron* (Philadelphia: 1966), pp. 176–177.

11. *Congressional Globe*, February 7, 1862, p. 711.

12. *Report of the Select House Committee*, p. ii.

13. *Congressional Globe*, February 7, 1862, p. 712.

14. *Report of the Select House Committee*, pp. iii–iv.

15. Myers, *op. cit.*, pp. 278–298.

16. *Report of the Select House Committee*, pp. xiv–xxxiii, lii–liii.

17. Allan Nevins, *The War for the Union* (New York: 1959), Vol. I, pp. 343–344; Shannon, *op. cit.*, p. 112.

18. *Report of the Select House Committee*, p. 2.

19. Shannon, *op. cit.*, p. 69.

20. *Official Records*, pp. 193–194.

21. My account of the Hall Carbine controversy is based upon

R. Gordon Wasson, *The Hall Carbine Affair* (Danbury, Conn.: 1971), and *Report of the Select House Committee*, pp. lxiv–lxxli.

22. Bradley, *op. cit.*, pp. 201–205.
23. This section is based primarily on James Ford Rhodes, *History of the United States* (New York: 1904), Vol. V, pp. 274–313.
24. *Congressional Globe*, June 9, 1864, p. 2823.

CHAPTER IX

1. See H. Wayne Morgan, ed., *The Gilded Age: A Reappraisal* (Syracuse: 1968).
2. Leonard White, *The Republican Era* (New York: 1958), pp. 8–9.
3. Allan Nevins, *The Emergence of Modern America* (New York: 1927), pp. 181–182.
4. Allan Nevins, *Hamilton Fish: The Inner History of the Grant Administration* (New York: 1936), pp. 131–134.
5. Henry Adams, *The Education of Henry Adams* (New York: 1931), pp. 260–262.
6. Quoted in Stewart H. Holbrook, *The Age of Moguls* (New York: 1953), pp. 34–35.
7. Quoted in Swanberg, *op. cit.*, p. 26.
8. The account of the "Erie War" is based upon Swanberg, *op. cit.*, Chapters 3–9, and Myers, *op. cit.*, Chapter X.
9. The story of the gold conspiracy is based upon *The Gold Panic Investigation*, House Report No. 31, 41st Congress, 2nd Session (Washington: 1870), and Swanberg, *op. cit.*, Chapters 13–16.
10. *Gold Panic Investigation*, p. 253.
11. *Ibid.*, p. 152.
12. *Ibid.*, p. 9.
13. *Ibid.*, p. 232.
14. *Ibid.*, pp. 251–253.
15. *Ibid.*, p. 11.
16. *Ibid.*, p. 157.
17. *Ibid.*, p. 142.
18. From an unidentified news clipping inserted in the record, *ibid.*, pp. 37–38.
19. *Ibid.*, p. 38.
20. Quoted in Swanberg, *op. cit.*, p. 154.
21. Adams, *op. cit.*, p. 271.

CHAPTER X

1. Myers, *op. cit.*, pp. 439–441.
2. The basic documents for the Credit Mobilier Scandal are the *Report of the Select House Committee on the Credit Mobilier Investigation*, Report No. 77, 42nd Congress, 3rd Session (Washington: 1873) and *Report of the Select House Committee on the Credit Mobilier Investigation* (No. 2), Report No. 78, 42nd Congress, 3rd Session (Washington: 1873).
3. House Report No. 78, p. xiv. A later estimate has reduced the total plunder to about $16.5 million. Robert W. Fogel, *The Union Pacific: A Case in Premature Enterprise* (Baltimore: 1960), p. 72.
4. A graphic account of the building of the Union Pacific is contained in G. C. Quiett, *They Built the West* (New York: 1934).
5. Oscar Lewis, *The Big Four* (New York: 1938), p. 23.
6. Peter Lyon, *To Hell in a Day Coach* (Philadelphia: 1968), pp. 32–33.
7. Myers, *op. cit.*, p. 522.
8. House Report No. 78, p. 514.
9. Quoted in Frederick H. Gillett, *George Frisbie Hoar* (Boston: 1934), p. 68.
10. The Grant scandals are discussed in detail in Nevins, *Fish, op. cit.*; William B. Hesseltine, *Ulysses S. Grant, Politician* (New York: 1935); and James Ford Rhodes, *History of the United States* (New York: 1929), Vol. VII.
11. For Boss Shepherd and his era, see Constance McLaughlin Green, *Washington: Village and Capital, 1800–1878* (Princeton: 1962), Chapter XIV.
12. The first complete account of Bristow's attack on the Whiskey Ring is H. V. Boynton, "The Whiskey Ring," *North American Review* (October 1876). See also Nevins, *Fish, op. cit.*

CHAPTER XI

1. *New York Times*, June 14, 1974.
2. *New York Times*, August 2, 1871.
3. Alexander B. Callow, Jr., *The Tweed Ring* (New York: 1966), p. 201.
4. *New York Times*, August 2, 1871.
5. *New York Times*, July 22, 1871.
6. Callow, *op. cit.*, pp. 204–205.
7. *New York Times*, August 2, 1871; Werner, *op. cit.*, p. 160.

8. Callow, *op. cit.*, p. 6.
9. Werner, *op. cit.*, pp. 134–137.
10. *Ibid.*, p. 194.
11. For Tweed's biography, see Denis T. Lynch, *"Boss" Tweed* (New York: 1927); Callow, *op. cit.*; and Werner, *op. cit.*
12. Lynch, *op. cit.*, p. 50.
13. Werner, *op. cit.*, pp. 112–124; Callow, *op. cit.*, Chapter 3.
14. Albert Bigelow Paine, *Thomas Nast* (Gloucester, Mass.: 1967), p. 143.
15. Callow, *op. cit.*, pp. 166–167; Werner, *op. cit.*, p. 161.
16. Werner, *op. cit.*, p. 172.
17. *Ibid.*, pp. 162–165.
18. Werner, *op. cit.*, pp. 206–207.
19. Callow, *op. cit.*, pp. 241–243.
20. Lynch, *op. cit.*, p. 362.
21. Paine, *op. cit.*, p. 170.
22. *Ibid.*, p. 179.
23. *Ibid.*, pp. 181–182.
24. Callow, *op. cit.*, Chapter 17.
25. Lynch, *op. cit.*, p. 418.

CHAPTER XII

1. James Bryce, *The American Commonwealth* (New York: 1888), Vol. II, p. 164, and Henry Adams, "The Session," *The North American Review* (April 1869), p. 617.
2. Quoted in Robert V. Bruce, *1877: The Year of Violence* (Chicago: 1970), p. 12.
3. Richard F. Hofstadter, *The American Political Tradition and the Men Who Made It* (New York: 1949), p. 168.
4. David J. Rothman, *Politics and Power* (Cambridge: Mass.: 1966), pp. 194–195, and John A. Garraty, *The New Commonwealth* (New York: 1968), p. 231.
5. Quoted in Matthew Josephson, *The Robber Barons* (New York: 1934), p. 352.
6. For Blaine's career see Hofstadter, *op. cit.*, pp. 171–174, and Charles Edward Russell, *Blaine of Maine* (New York: 1931).
7. Quoted in Ray Ginger, *Age of Excess* (New York: 1965), p. 99.
8. Quoted in Hofstadter, *op. cit.*, p. 174.
9. For the Arkansas railroad affair see Russell, *op. cit.*, Chapter XVI, and Rhodes, *op. cit.*, Vol. VII, pp. 258–271.

10. Harry Bernard, *Rutherford B. Hayes and His America* (Indianapolis: 1954), p. 301.
11. *Ibid.*, p. 313.
12. *Ibid.*, pp. 318–319.
13. C. Vann Woodward, *Reunion and Reaction* (Boston: 1967), p. 18.
14. *Ibid.*
15. Bernard, *op. cit.*, p. 332.
16. Woodward, *op. cit.*, pp. 68–74.
17. *Ibid.*, p. 98.
18. *Ibid.*, pp. 159–165.
19. C. Vann Woodward, *Origins of the New South 1877–1913* (Baton Rouge: 1966), pp. 56–74.

CHAPTER XIII

1. William L. Riordan, *Plunkitt of Tammany Hall* (New York: 1948), pp. 43–44.
2. *Ibid.*, pp. 39–40.
3. For Croker's career, see Werner, *op. cit.*, Chapter VI.
4. Thomas C. Cochran and William Miller, *The Age of Enterprise* (New York: 1961), pp. 154–160, and Matthew Josephson, *The Politicos* (New York: 1938), pp. 425–426.
5. John G. Sproat, *The Best Men: Liberal Reformers in the Gilded Age* (New York: 1968), p. 257.
6. Josephson, *op. cit.*, pp. 125–126, and *The Nation*, July 1, 1880.
7. Quoted in Cochran, *op. cit.*, p. 160.
8. David M. Jordan, *Roscoe Conkling of New York* (Ithaca, N.Y.: 1971), p. 415.
9. Thayer, *op. cit.*, p. 38.
10. For the Star Route frauds, see J. Martin Klotche, "The Star Route Cases," *The Mississippi Valley Historical Review*, December 1935, and *Responses of the Presidents to Charges of Misconduct* (New York: 1974), pp. 148–159.
11. Josephson, *op. cit.*, Chapter XII.
12. *Ibid.*, pp. 429–433.
13. William Allen White, *Masks in a Pageant* (New York: 1928), p. 79.
14. David Graham Phillips, *The Treason of the Senate* (Chicago: 1964), p. 59.
15. Josephson, *op. cit.*, pp. 450–452.
16. On this point see Gabriel Kolko, *Railroads and Regulation* (Princeton, N.J.: 1965).

17. Cochran, *op. cit.*, pp. 170–172.
18. For biographies of Hanna see Herbert Croly, *Marcus Alonzo Hanna* (New York: 1912), and Thomas Beer, *Hanna* (New York: 1929). A fresh assessment of Hanna is badly needed.
19. White, *op. cit.*, pp. 154–155.
20. Harold U. Faulkner, *Politics, Reform and Expansion* (New York: 1959), pp. 203–204.
21. Lincoln Steffens, *The Autobiography of Lincoln Steffens* (New York: 1931), p. 606.

CHAPTER XIV

1. William L. Manchester, *Disturber of the Peace* (New York: 1950), pp. 116–117, and Henry L. Mencken, *A Carnival of Buncombe*, Malcolm Moos, ed. (Baltimore: 1956), p. 32.
2. Alice Roosevelt Longworth, *Crowded Hours* (New York: 1933), p. 324.
3. Frederick Lewis Allen, *Only Yesterday* (New York: 1931), p. 125.
4. H. F. Alderfer, quoted in Samuel Hopkins Adams, *Incredible Era* (New York: 1964), pp. 188–189.
5. Mark Sullivan, *Our Times* (New York: 1972), Vol. VI, pp. 16–19.
6. Andrew Sinclair, *The Available Man* (New York: 1965), pp. 41–42, and M. R. Werner and John Starr, *Teapot Dome* (New York: 1959), p. 10.
7. Sullivan, *op. cit.*, p. 29.
8. Francis Russell, *The Shadow of Blooming Grove* (New York: 1968), p. 331.
9. William E. Leuchtenberg, *The Perils of Prosperity* (Chicago: 1958), p. 86.
10. Sullivan, *op. cit.*, pp. 138–144.
11. Adams, *op. cit.*, pp. 234–236.
12. Longworth, *op. cit.*, p. 324.
13. Sinclair, *op. cit.*, p. 298.
14. John D. Hicks, *Republican Ascendency* (New York: 1960), pp. 30–31, 53, 62–63.
15. My account of the oil lease cases is based on Adams, *op. cit.*; Werner and Starr, *op. cit.*; Burl Noggle, *Teapot Dome: Oil and Politics in the 1920's* (New York: 1965); and Sullivan, *op. cit.*
16. For a detailed account of Slattery's activities, see Noggle, *op. cit.*
17. Arthur M. Schlesinger, Jr., *The Crisis of the Old Order* (New York: 1959), p. 55.

CHAPTER XV

1. Charlie Forbes's peccadilloes are covered in Russell, *op. cit.*, pp. 554–558; Adams, *op. cit.*, Chapter XXII; and Sullivan, *op. cit.*, pp. 229–241.
2. Adams, *op. cit.*, pp. 296–297.
3. *Ibid.*, pp. 511–512; Adams, *op. cit.*, pp. 323–324.
4. Sullivan, *op. cit.*, pp. 232–237; Werner and Starr, *op. cit.*, pp. 95–100.
5. White, *op. cit.*, p. 432.
6. Schlesinger, *op. cit.*, p. 53.
7. Sullivan, *op. cit.*, pp. 277–285.
8. Werner and Starr, *op. cit.*, pp. 119–127; Sullivan, *op. cit.*, pp. 304–318.
9. Sullivan, *op. cit.*, p. 323.
10. *Ibid.*, pp. 335–337, and Werner and Starr, *op. cit.*, pp. 145–146.
11. Sullivan, *op. cit.*, p. 329.
12. *Ibid.*, pp. 352–357, and Adams, *op. cit.*, pp. 412–421.
13. Werner and Starr, *op. cit.*, Chapter VII.
14. *Ibid.*, pp. 194–208, and Noggle, *op. cit.*, pp. 182–184.
15. Werner and Starr, *op. cit.*, pp. 210–222.
16. *Ibid.*, Chapter IX.
17. *Ibid.*, pp. 260–265.
18. *Ibid.*, pp. 281–289.
19. Adams, *op. cit.*, pp. 433–434.

CHAPTER XVI

1. *The Public Papers and Addresses of Franklin D. Roosevelt*, ed. by Samuel Rosenman (New York: 1938), Vol. V, p. 424, and *Responses of the Presidents*, p. 259.
2. Arthur M. Schlesinger, Jr., *The Coming of the New Deal* (New York: 1958), pp. 16–20; William E. Leuchtenberg, *Franklin D. Roosevelt and the New Deal* (New York: 1963), pp. 338–339; and Richard D. Hofstadter, *The Age of Reform* (New York: 1960), p. 310.
3. Quoted in Donald H. Riddle, *The Truman Committee* (New Brunswick, N.J.: 1964), p. 66.
4. Harry S. Truman, *Memoirs* (New York: 1955), Vol. I, pp. 178–179, and Edwin H. Sutherland, *White Collar Crime* (New York: 1949), p. 175.

5. Trumen, *op. cit.*, p. 184.

6. U.S. Senate, 77th Congress, 1st Session, Special Committee Investigating the National Defense Program, Report 10, Part 10 (Washington: 1943), pp. 16–25, and Truman, *op. cit.*, p. 184.

7. U.S. Senate, 77th Congress, 1st Session, Special Committee Investigating the National Defense Program, Report 10, Part 7 (Washington: 1943), pp. 1–6, and Riddle, *op. cit.*, pp. 148–149.

8. Riddle, *op. cit.*, pp. 154–155.

9. Donovan, Robert J., *Conflict and Crisis* (New York: 1977), p. xiii.

10. Jules Abels, *The Truman Scandals* (Chicago: 1956), p. 1.

11. Quoted in Patrick Anderson, *The President's Men* (New York: 1968), p. 90.

12. Blair Bolles, *How to Get Rich in Washington* (New York: 1952), pp. 41–42; *Responses of the Presidents*, pp. 277–278; and Abels, *op. cit.*, pp. 39–40.

13. George A. Graham, *Morality in American Politics* (New York: 1952), p. 167.

14. This account of Harry Vaughn's affairs is based on *Responses of the Presidents*, pp. 278–280; Anderson, *op. cit.*, pp. 98–105; Abels, *op. cit.*, pp. 44–52, and Cabell Phillips, *The Truman Presidency* (New York: 1966), pp. 404–406.

15. Anderson, *op. cit.*, p. 105.

16. For the RFC scandal see Abels, *op. cit.*, pp. 15–21; Bolles, *op. cit.*, pp. 127–151; Anderson, *op. cit.*, pp. 107–110; *Responses of the Presidents*, pp. 280–283; Congressional Quarterly Service, *Congress and the Nation 1945–1964* (Washington: 1965), pp. 1700, 1709–1710; and U.S. Senate, Committee on Banking and Currency, *Favoritism and Influence*, Interim Report, Feb. 5, 1951 (Washington: 1951).

17. Anderson, *op. cit.*, p. 110.

18. William Lee Miller, *Piety Along the Potomac* (Boston: 1964), pp. 30–31, and David A. Frier, *Conflict of Interest in the Eisenhower Administration* (Baltimore: 1970), p. 7.

19. This account of the Nixon fund affair is based on the sympathetic version in Earl Mazo and Stephen Hess, *Nixon: A Political Portrait* (London: 1969), Chapters 7 and 8.

20. Frier, *op. cit.*, pp. 9–10.

21. Aaron Wildavsky, *Dixon Yates: A Study in Power Politics* (New Haven: 1962) is the most complete account of this affair. I have also consulted the shorter account in Frier, *op. cit.*, Chapter 5.

22. For the Adams case I have relied on Anderson, *op. cit.*, pp. 149–167;

Frier, *op. cit.*, Chapters 2 and 14, and Sherman Adams, *First Hand Report: The Story of the Eisenhower Administration* (New York: 1961).
23. For a summary of Mazo's findings see Mazo and Hess, *op. cit.*, pp. 242–249.
24. Quoted in Thomas C. Reeves, *A Question of Character: A Life of John F. Kennedy* (New York: 1991), p. 214.

CHAPTER XVII

1. Philip Potter, "Nixon: Political Pitchman," in *Candidates 1960*, ed. by Eric Sevareid (New York: 1959), pp. 69–70.
2. For Nixon's resurrection see Stephen E. Ambrose, *Nixon: The Triumph of a Politician* (New York: 1989), Chapters 3–7.
3. Quoted in London Sunday *Times* Team, *Watergate* (New York: 1973), p. 79.
4. For the Watergate operation see *Ibid.*, J. Anthony Lukas, *Nightmare: The Underside of the Nixon Years* (New York: 1976), and Stanley L. Kutler, *The Wars of Watergate* (New York: 1990).
5. Quoted in Ambrose, *op. cit.*, p. 560.
6. For the CIA and Watergate see Thomas Powers, *The Man Who Kept the Secrets* (New York: 1979), pp. 330–345.
7. For Woodward and Bernstein's account see *All the President's Men* (New York: 1975).
8. Agnew's decline and fall is covered in Aaron Latham, "Closing in on Agnew," *New York*, November 26, 1973.

CHAPTER XVIII

1. The basic sources for Reagan's life and times are Gary Wills, *Reagan's America* (Garden City, N.Y.: 1987), and Lou Cannon, *President Reagan: The Role of a Lifetime* (New York: 1991).
2. See *U.S. News & World Report*, February 4, 1980.
3. See *Time*, August 4, 1980.
4. Wills, *op. cit.*, p. 161.
5. Cannon, *op. cit.*, p. 794.
6. For the HUD scandals see *Newsweek*, August 7, 1989; *National Journal*, September 16, 1989; Washington *Post*, June 18, 1989.
7. Cannon, *op. cit.*, p. 796.
8. Washington *Post* Magazine, September 22, 1991.
9. For the S&L scandals see Stephen Pizzo, Mary Fricker, and Paul

Muolo, *Inside Job: The Looting of America's Savings & Loans* (New York: 1991); James R. Adams, *The Big Fix: Inside the S&L Scandal* (New York: 1991); *Newsweek*, May 21, 1990; "Other People's Money," *Frontline*, May 1, 1990; *New York Times*, November 9, 1989.

10. *Newsweek*, May 21, 1990.
11. New York *Times*, November 8, 1989.
12. *Frontline*, May 1, 1990.
13. Cannon, *op. cit.*, p. 795.
14. *Ibid.*, p. 800.
15. For ABSCAM see *Congressional Quarterly's Guide to Congress*, 3d ed. (Washington: 1982).
16. For Iran-Contra see Nathan Miller, *Spying for America: The Hidden History of U.S. Intelligence* (New York: 1989).

Bibliography

Abels, Jules. *The Truman Scandals* (Chicago: 1956).

Abernathy, Thomas P. *Western Lands and the American Revolution* (New York: 1937).

Adams, Henry. *The Education of Henry Adams* (New York: 1931).

_____. "The Session," *The North American Review* (April 1869).

Adams, Herbert B. *Washington's Interest in Western Lands*, Johns Hopkins University Studies in Historical and Political Science (Baltimore: 1885), Vol. III.

Adams, James R. *The Big Fix: Inside the S&L Scandal* (New York: 1991).

Adams, James T. *The Founding of New England* (Boston: 1921).

Adams, John. *Diary of John Adams*, L. H. Butterfield, ed. (Boston: 1961), Vol. I.

Adams, Samuel Hopkins. *Incredible Era* (New York: 1964).

Adams, Sherman. *First Hand Report: The Story of the Eisenhower Administration* (New York: 1961).

Alberts, Robert C. *The Golden Voyage: The Life and Times of William Bingham* (Boston: 1969).

Allen, Frederick Lewis. *The Great Pierpont Morgan* (New York: 1949).

_____. *Only Yesterday* (New York: 1931).

Alvord, Clarence W. *The Mississippi Valley in British Politics* (Cleveland: 1917), 2 vols.

Ambler, Charles H. *George Washington and the West* (New York: 1971).

Ambrose, Stephen E. *Nixon: The Triumph of a Politician* (New York: 1989).

Ames, Fisher. *Works*, Seth Ames, ed. (Boston: 1854), Vol. I.

Anderson, Patrick. *The President's Men* (New York: 1968).

Aylmer, G. E. *A Short History of Seventeenth-Century England* (New York: 1963).

Bailyn, Bernard. *The Ideological Origins of the American Revolution* (Cambridge, Mass.: 1967).

Beard, Charles A. *An Economic Interpretation of the Constitution* (New York: 1962).

Beer, Thomas. *Hanna* (New York: 1929).

Bernard, Harry. *Rutherford B. Hayes and His America* (Indianapolis: 1954).

Boardman, Fon W. *America and the Gilded Age* (New York: 1972).

Bolles, Albert S. *The Financial History of the United States* (New York: 1896).

Bolles, Blair. *How to Get Rich in Washington* (New York: 1952).

Bonomi, Patricia U. *A Fractious People: Politics and Society in Colonial New York* (New York: 1971).

Bowers, Claude M. *Party Battles of the Jackson Period* (New York: 1922).

Boynton, H. V. "The Whiskey Ring," *The North American Review* (October 1876).

Bradley, Erwin S. *Simon Cameron* (Philadelphia: 1966).

Brodie, Fawn, *No Man Knows My History* (New York: 1966).

Bruce, Philip A. *Economic History of Virginia in the Seventeenth Century* (New York: 1895), 2 vols.

Bruce, Robert V. *1877: The Year of Violence* (Chicago: 1970).

Bryce, James. *The American Commonwealth* (New York: 1888), 2 vols.

Bugg, James L. *Andrew Jackson: Democratic Myth or Reality* (New York: 1963).

Callow, Alexander B., Jr. *The Tweed Ring* (New York: 1966).

Cannon, Lou. *President Reagan: The Role of a Lifetime* (New York: 1991).

Carman, Harry. *Lincoln and the Patronage* (New York: 1943).

Chambers, William N. *Old Bullion Benton* (Boston: 1956).

Channing, Edward. *A History of the United States 1761–1789* (New York: 1930).

Chappell, Absalom H. *Miscellanies of Georgia* (Columbus, Ga.: reprinted 1928).

Cleveland, F. A. and F. W. Powell. *Railroad Promotion and Capitalization in the United States* (New York: 1909).

Cochran, Thomas C., and William Miller. *The Age of Enterprise* (New York: 1961).

Commager, Henry J. (ed.). *The Blue and the Grey* (Indianapolis: 1950).

Congressional Quarterly Service. *Congress and the Nation 1945–1964* (Washington: 1965).

_____. *Congressional Quarterly's Guide to Congress*, 3d ed. (Washington: 1982).

Cosmas, Graham A. *An Army for Empire* (Columbia, Mo.: 1971).

Coulter, E. Merle. *Georgia: A Short History* (Chapel Hill, N.C.: 1960).

Craven, Wesley F. *Dissolution of the Virginia Company* (Gloucester, Mass.: 1964).

_____. *The Southern Colonies in the Seventeenth Century* (Baton Rouge: 1949).

Croly, Herbert. *Marcus Alonzo Hanna* (New York: 1912).

Daniels, Jonathan. *Ordeal of Power* (New York: 1970).

Donovan, Robert J. *Conflict and Crisis* (New York: 1977).

Doyle, J. A. *English Colonies in America* (New York: 1882).

East, Robert A. *Business Enterprise in the American Revolutionary Era* (New York: 1938).

Faulkner, Harold U. *Politics, Reform and Expansion* (New York: 1959).

Ferguson, E. James. *The Power of the Purse* (Chapel Hill, N.C.: 1961).

Fish, Carl R. *The Civil Service and the Patronage* (New York: 1905).

Flexner, James T. *George Washington: The Forge of Experience 1772–1775* (Boston: 1965).

Flynn, John T. *Graft in Business* (New York: 1931).

Fogel, Robert W. *The Union Pacific: A Case in Premature Enterprise* (Baltimore: 1960).

Force, Peter (ed.). *Tracts and Other Papers Relating Principally to the Origins, Settlement and Progress of the Colonies in North America* (Washington: 1836), Vol. I.

Franklin, Benjamin. *The Writings of Benjamin Franklin*, Albert H. Smyth, ed. (New York: 1906), Vol. VI.

Freeman, Douglas S. *George Washington: A Biography* (New York: 1951), Vols. II and III.

_____. *Lee*, abridged by Richard Harwell (New York: 1961).

Frier, David A. *Conflict of Interest in the Eisenhower Administration* (Baltimore: 1970).

Frontline. "Other People's Money," broadcast on PBS, May 1, 1990.

Fuess, Claude M. *Daniel Webster* (New York: 1966).

Garraty, John A. *The New Commonwealth* (New York: 1968).

Gates, Paul W. *The Illinois Central Railroad and Its Colonization Policies* (Cambridge, Mass.: 1934).

Gillett, Frederick H. *George Frisbie Hoar* (Boston: 1934).

Ginger, Ray. *Age of Excess* (New York: 1965).

Gipson, Lawrence H. *The Coming of the Revolution 1763–1775* (New York: 1954).

Goldman, Eric. *The Crucial Decade—and After* (New York: 1960).

————. *Rendezvous with Destiny* (New York: 1956).

Graham, George A. *Morality in American Politics* (New York: 1952).

Green, Constance McLaughlin. *Washington: Village and Capital, 1800–1878* (Princeton: 1962).

Hamilton, Alexander. *The Works of Alexander Hamilton*, Henry Cabot Lodge, ed. (New York: 1904), Vols. I and II.

Hammond, Bray. *Banks and Politics in America* (New York: 1966).

Haney, Louis H. *A Congressional History of the Railways of the United States* (Madison, Wis.: 1908).

Haskins, Charles H. "The Yazoo Land Companies," *Papers of the American Historical Association* (October 1891).

Heidenheimer, Arnold. *Political Corruption* (New York: 1970).

Hesseltine, William B. *Ulysses S. Grant, Politician* (New York: 1935).

Hicks, John D. *The Federal Union* (Boston: 1937).

————. *Republican Ascendency* (New York: 1960).

Hofstader, Richard. *The Age of Reform* (New York: 1960).

————. *The American Political Tradition and the Men Who Made It* (New York: 1949).

Holbrook, Stewart. *The Age of Moguls* (New York: 1953).

————. *The Story of American Railroads* (New York: 1947).

Hoogenboom, Ari. *Outlawing the Spoils* (Urbana, Ill.: 1961).

Horsman, Reginald. *The War of 1812* (New York: 1969).

Hughson, Shirley C. *The Carolina Pirates and Colonial Commerce 1670–1740* (Baltimore: 1894).

Hurstfield, Joel. *Freedom, Corruption and Government in Elizabethan England* (London: 1973).

James, Marquis. *The Life of Andrew Jackson* (Indianapolis: 1938).

Jefferson, Thomas. *The Papers of Thomas Jefferson*, Julian P. Boyd, ed. (Princeton: 1965), Vol. XVII.

Johannsen, Robert W. *Stephen A. Douglas* (New York: 1973).

Johnson, Gerald W. *America's Silver Age* (New York: 1939).

Jones, Thomas. *History of New York During the Revolutionary War* (New York: 1879), 2 vols.

Jordan, David M. *Roscoe Conkling of New York* (Ithaca, N.Y.: 1971).

Josephson, Matthew. *The Politicos* (New York: 1938).

————. *The President Makers* (New York: 1964).

————. *The Robber Barons* (New York: 1934).

Kaufman, Richard F. *The War Profiteers* (Indianapolis: 1970).

Kingsbury, Susan M. (ed.). *Records of the Virginia Company* (Washington: 1906–1935), 4 vols.

Kirkpatrick, Franklin P. *The Image of the Federal Service* (Washington: 1964).

Klein, Philip S. *President James Buchanan* (University Park, Pa.: 1969).

Klotche, J. Martin. "The Star Route Cases," *The Mississippi Valley Historical Review* (December 1935).

Knollenberg, Bernhard. *George Washington: The Virginia Period 1732– 1775* (Durham, N.C.: 1964).

Kolko, Gabriel. *Railroads and Regulation* (Princeton, N.J.: 1965).

Kutler, Stanley L. *The Wars of Watergate* (New York: 1990).

Latham, Aaron. "Closing in on Agnew," *New York*, November 26, 1973.

Leuchtenberg, William E. *Franklin D. Roosevelt and the New Deal* (New York: 1963).

_____. *The Perils of Prosperity* (Chicago: 1958).

Lewis, Oscar. *The Big Four* (New York: 1938).

Lewis, Paul. *The Grand Incendiary: A Biography of Samuel Adams* (New York: 1973).

London Sunday *Times* Team. *Watergate* (New York: 1973).

Longworth, Alice Roosevelt. *Crowded Hours* (New York: 1938).

Loth, David. *Public Plunder* (New York: 1938).

Lukas, J. Anthony. *Nightmare: The Underside of the Nixon Years* (New York: 1976).

Lydon, James G. *Pirates, Privateers and Profits* (Upper Saddle River, N.J.: 1970).

Lynch, Denis T. *"Boss" Tweed* (New York: 1927).

_____. *Epoch and a Man: Martin Van Buren and His Time* (Port Washington, N.Y.: 1971).

_____. *The Wild Seventies* (New York: 1941).

Lyon, Peter. *To Hell in a Day Coach* (Philadelphia: 1968).

MacKenzie, William L. *Life and Times of Martin Van Buren* (Boston: 1846).

Maclay, William. *The Journal of William Maclay* (New York: 1927).

McDonald, Forrest. *We the People* (Chicago: 1958).

Magrath, Peter. *Yazoo* (Providence: 1966).

Malone, Dumas. *Jefferson the President, First Term* (Boston: 1970).

Manchester, William L. *Disturber of the Peace* (New York: 1950).

Mazo, Earl, and Stephen Hess. *Nixon: A Political Portrait* (London: 1969).

Mencken, Henry L. *A Carnival of Buncombe*, Malcolm Moos, ed. (Baltimore: 1956).

_____. *Notes on Democracy* (New York: 1926).

Miller, John C. *Alexander Hamilton: Portrait in Paradox* (New York: 1959).

_____. *Origins of the American Revolution* (Boston: 1943).

————. *Triumph of Freedom* (Boston: 1948).

Miller, Nathan. *Sea of Glory: The Continental Navy Fights for Independence 1775–1783* (New York: 1974).

————. *Spying for America: The Hidden History of U.S. Intelligence* (New York: 1989).

Miller, William Lee. *Piety Along the Potomac* (Boston: 1964).

Monaghan, Frank. *John Jay* (New York: 1935).

Morgan, H. Wayne (ed.). *The Gilded Age: A Reappraisal* (Syracuse: 1968).

Morison, Samuel Eliot. *The Oxford History of the American People* (New York: 1972).

Myers, Gustavus. *History of the Great American Fortunes* (New York: 1936).

Namier, Lewis. *England in the Age of the American Revolution* (London: 1961).

Nevins, Allan. *The Emergence of Modern America* (New York: 1927).

————. *Frémont* (New York: 1939).

————. *Hamilton Fish: The Inner History of the Administration* (New York: 1936).

————. *John D. Rockefeller* (New York: 1940), Vol. II.

————. *The War for the Union* (New York: 1959), Vol. I.

Nichols, Roy F. *The Destruction of American Democracy* (New York: 1948).

Noggle, Burl. *Teapot Dome: Oil and Politics in the 1920's* (New York: 1965).

O'Callaghan, E. B. (ed.). *Documents Relative to the Colonial History of the State of New York* (Albany: 1854), Vol. IV.

O'Connor, Richard. *Iron Rails and Broken Men* (New York: 1973).

Official Records of the Union and Confederate Armies (Washington: 1899), Series III, Vol. II.

Osgood, Herbert L. *The American Colonies in the Seventeenth Century* (Gloucester, Mass.: 1951), 3 vols.

Padover, Saul (ed.). *The Mind of Alexander Hamilton* (New York: 1958).

Paine, Albert Bigelow. *Thomas Nast* (Gloucester: 1957).

Parmet, Herbert S. *Eisenhower and the American Crusades* (New York: 1972).

Peterson, Merrill O. *Thomas Jefferson and The New Nation* (New York: 1970).

Phillips, Cabell. *The Truman Presidency* (New York: 1966).

Phillips, David Graham. *The Treason of the Senate* (Chicago: 1964).

Pomfret, John E. *Founding of the American Colonies* (New York: 1970).

Porter, Kenneth W. *John Jacob Astor, Businessman* (Cambridge, Mass.: 1931), 2 vols.

Potter, Philip. "Nixon: Political Pitchman" in Eric Severeid, ed., *Candidates 1960* (New York: 1959).

Powers, Thomas. *The Man Who Kept the Secrets* (New York: 1979).

Pringle, Patrick. *Jolly Roger: The Story of the Great Age of Piracy* (New York: 1953).

Quiett, G. C. *They Built the West* (New York: 1934).

Rankin, Hugh F. *The Golden Age of Piracy* (Williamsburg, Va.: 1969).

Reeves, Thomas. *A Question of Character: A Life of John F. Kennedy* (New York: 1991).

Reich, Jerome R. *Leisler's Rebellion* (Chicago: 1953).

Responses of the Presidents to Charges of Misconduct, C. Vann Woodward, ed. (New York: 1974).

Rhodes, James Ford. *History of the United States from the Compromise of 1850* (New York: 1910–1919), 7 vols.

Riddle, Donald H. *The Truman Committee* (New Brunswick, N.J.: 1964).

Riordan, William. *Plunkitt of Tammany Hall* (New York: 1948).

Roosevelt, Franklin. *The Public Papers and Addresses of Franklin D. Roosevelt*, ed. by Samuel Rosenman (New York: 1938), Vol. V.

Rothman, David J. *Politics and Power* (Cambridge, Mass.: 1966).

Runcie, John D. "The Problem of Anglo-American Politics in Bellemont's New York," *William and Mary Quarterly* (April 1969).

Russell, Bertrand. *Freedom versus Organization* (New York: 1962).

Russell, Charles Edward. *Blaine of Maine* (New York: 1931).

Russell, Francis. *The Shadow of Blooming Grove* (New York: 1968).

Sandburg, Carl. *Abraham Lincoln, The War Years* (New York: 1939), 4 vols.

Sakolski, A. M. *The Great American Land Bubble* (New York: 1932).

Saunders, William L. (ed.). *The Colonial Records of North Carolina* (Raleigh: 1886), Vol. I.

Schachner, Nathan. *Alexander Hamilton* (New York: 1961).

———. *The Founding Fathers* (New York: 1954).

Schlesinger, Arthur M. Jr. *The Coming of the New Deal* (New York: 1958).

———. *The Crisis of the Old Order* (New York: 1959).

———. *The Imperial Presidency* (Boston: 1973).

Schurz, William L. *The Manila Galleon* (New York: 1939).

Seldes, George. *The Great Quotations* (New York: 1963).

Seligman, Ben B. *The Potentates* (New York: 1971).

Shannon, Fred A. *The Farmer's Last Frontier* (New York: 1945).

———. *The Organization and Administration of the Union Army* (Cleveland: 1928), 2 vols.

Sinclair, Andrew. *The Available Man* (New York: 1965).

Smith, Frank E. *The Yazoo River* (New York: 1954).

Smith, William. *The History of the Late Province of New York* (New York: 1830), 2 vols.

Sobel, Robert. *The Money Manias* (New York: 1973).

Sproat, John G. *The Best Men: Liberal Reformers in the Gilded Age* (New York: 1968).

Stannard, Mary N. *The Story of Virginia's First Century* (Philadelphia: 1928).

Steinberg, Alfred. *The Bosses* (New York: 1972).

Steffens, Lincoln. *The Autobiography of Lincoln Steffens* (New York: 1931).

Stith, William. *The History of the First Discovery and Settlement of Virginia* (Original edition: 1747; New York: 1969).

Strong, George Templeton. *Diary of George Templeton Strong*, Allan Nevins, ed. (New York: 1952), Vol. III.

Sullivan, Mark. *Our Times* (New York: 1972), Vol. VI.

Sutherland, Edwin H. *White Collar Crime* (New York: 1961).

Swanberg, W. A. *Citizen Hearst* (New York: 1961).

———. *Jim Fisk: The Career of an Improbable Rascal* (New York: 1959).

Taylor, George Rogers. *The Transportation Revolution 1815–1860* (New York: 1947).

Terrell, John U. *Furs by Astor* (New York: 1963).

Thayer, George. *Who Shakes the Money Tree?* (New York: 1973).

Thayer, Theodore. *Nathanael Greene: Strategist of the Revolution* (New York: 1960).

de Tocqueville, Alexis. *Democracy in America* (London: 1862), 2 vols.

Truman, Harry S. *Memoirs* (New York: 1955), Vol. I.

Twain, Mark, and Charles Dudley Warren. *The Gilded Age* (New York: 1964).

U. S. Congress. *America State Papers*, Public Lands (Washington: 1832), Vol. I.

U. S. House of Representatives. *Reports of the Select Committee on Government Contracts*, 37th Congress, 2nd Session (Washington, 1862).

———. *The Gold Panic Investigation*, House Report No. 31, 41st Congress, 2nd Session (Washington: 1870).

———. *Report of the Select House Committee on the Credit Mobilier Investigation*, Report No. 27, 42nd Congress, 3rd Session (Washington: 1873).

———. *Report of the Select House Committee on the Credit Mobilier Investigation* (No. 2), Report No. 78, 42nd Congress, 3rd Session (Washington: 1873).

U. S. Senate. *Profiteering*, Senate Document No. 428, 65th Congress, 2nd Session (Washington: 1918).

———. *Report of the Special Committee on Investigation of the Munitions Industry*, 74th Congress, 2nd Session, 5 Vols.

_____. *Special Committee Investigating the National Defense Program*, 77th Congress, 1st Session, Reports 7 and 10, Part 10 (Washington: 1943).

_____. Committee on Banking and Currency. *Favoritism and Influence*, Interim Report, Feb. 5, 1951 (Washington: 1951).

Van Buren, Martin. *The Autobiography of Martin Van Buren*, John C. Fitzpatrick (ed.) (New York: 1973), 2 vols.

Van Doren, Carl. *Benjamin Franklin* (New York: 1938).

Van Dusen, Henry. *Thurlow Weed: Wizard of the Lobby* (Boston: 1947).

Van Riper, Paul V. *History of the United States Civil Service* (Evanston, Ill.: 1958).

Ver Steeg, Clarence L. *Robert Morris, Revolutionary Financier* (Philadelphia: 1954).

Wallace, Willard M. *Appeal to Arms* (Boston: 1951).

Washington, George. *The Writings of George Washington*, John C. Fitzpatrick (ed.) (Washington: 1931–1940), Vols. IV, XIII, XXXIV.

Wasson, R. G. *The Hall Carbine Affair* (Danbury, Conn.: 1971).

Werner, M. R. *It Happened in New York* (New York: 1957).

_____. *Tammany Hall* (New York: 1928).

_____, and John Starr. *Teapot Dome* (New York: 1959).

White, Leonard. *The Federalists* (New York: 1948).

_____. *The Republican Era* (New York: 1958).

White, William A. *Masks in a Pageant* (New York: 1928).

Wildavsky, Aaron. *Dixon Yates: A Study in Power Politics* (New Haven: 1962).

Williamson, Harold F., and Arnold R. Daum. *The American Petroleum Industry* (Evanston, Ill.: 1959).

Willison, George F. *Behold Virginia! The Fifth Crown* (New York: 1952).

Wills, Garry. *Reagan's America* (Garden City, N.Y.: 1987).

Wilson, James G. (ed.). *The Memorial History of the City of New York* (New York: 1892), 4 vols.

Wiltse, Charles A. *John C. Calhoun: Nationalist* (Indianapolis: 1944).

Winthrop, John. *Winthrop's Journal*, John K. Hosner, ed. (New York: 1908), Vol. I.

Woodward, Bob, and Carl Bernstein. *All the President's Men* (New York: 1974).

Woodward, C. Vann. *Origins of the New South 1877–1913* (Baton Rouge: 1966).

_____. *Reunion and Reaction* (Boston: 1967).

Young, Eleanor M. *Forgotten Patriot: Robert Morris* (New York: 1950).

Index

About the Author

Nathan Miller, a former correspondent for the *Baltimore Sun* and former Senate staffer, is the author of numerous books—including *Spying for America* and (with John Loftus) *The Belarus Secret*, both available from Paragon House. His latest book, a biography of Theodore Roosevelt, will be published in 1992. He lives in Washington, D.C.